MODERN
AMERICAN
HISTORY ★ A
Garland
Series

Edited by
FRANK FREIDEL
Harvard University

CONTOURS OF PUBLIC POLICY, 1939–1945

Richard N. Chapman

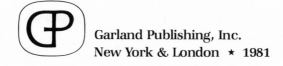
Garland Publishing, Inc.
New York & London ★ 1981

Library of Congress Cataloging in Publication Data

Chapman, Richard N., 1945–
　　Contours of public policy, 1939–1945.

　　(Modern American history)
　　Originally presented as the author's thesis (Ph.D.)—Yale.
　　Bibliography: p.
　　Includes index.
　　1. United States—Politics and government—1933–1945.
I. Title.　II. Series.
JK261.C48 1981　　　973.917　　　80-8460
ISBN 0-8240-4851-2　　　　　　　AACR2

All volumes in this series are printed on acid-free,
250-year-life paper.
Printed in the United States of America

For My Wife

MARILYN

CONTOURS OF PUBLIC POLICY, 1939-1945

Preface, August 1980

This study of Congressional politics and public policy during World War II--completed in 1976 and submitted as a doctoral dissertation to the Graduate School of Yale University--is primarily concerned with the question: "What happened to the New Deal during the Second World War?" Did the New Deal end, as Barton J. Bernstein insisted, "not because of the conservative opposition, but because it ran out of ideas"? That notion, when tested, proved erroneous. The "conservative opposition," embodied in a powerful anti-reform coalition in Congress, halted the New Deal in 1939, strove to reverse its policies during World War II, and sought to prevent a revival of reform after the war was over.

A secondary theme of this study is the institutional rivalry between Congress and the Presidency. That institutional conflict deserves further comment here because events in the 1970s have provoked much scholarly and popular debate about the nature of the Presidency and its proper relationship to Congress in the American constitutional system. The debate seems to have moved through two distinct phases: During the early 1970s, alarm was voiced about the overweening power and pretensions of an "imperial Presidency." Now the fear is that the executive is too weak, rather than too strong. In the latter view, "Presidential leadership" is needed to energize and make the Federal government effective, irrespective of the purposes pursued.

Those who urge "Presidential leadership" as a remedy for what ails American government will find little comfort in the pages that follow. Both the partisans and detractors of Franklin D. Roosevelt have acknowledged his considerable talents as a persuader and political leader. And yet--as this study demonstrates-- between 1939 and 1945, Roosevelt had meager success in winning Congressional approval of his domestic policy prescriptions. To be sure, during World War II FDR subordinated those prescriptions to the more exigent necessities of preparedness, foreign policy, and war, but even so, there is little reason to believe that he would have been more successful in the postwar era, had he lived. Such speculation aside, on those occasions when Roosevelt displayed unequivocal leadership on the home front during World War II, Congress frequently defied the President, sometimes jeopardizing measures he deemed vital to successful prosecution of the war. That Congressional resistance arose, in part, from institutional rivalry between the executive and legislative branches. By 1943, if not before, Congress was pitted against the President, and the mingling of partisan, ideological, sectional, interest group, and institutional conflicts proved too potent a combination even for Roosevelt to overcome.

And so a review of the relationship of Congress and the President during the Second World War yields only sobering implications. The dissolution of political parties into quarreling factions--a development also described in this study--has frequently deprived Presidents of the means to influence Congress. One is tempted to suggest that a President who accepts Congressional intransigence will be labeled an "inadequate leader," while one who seeks to circumvent or override that intransigence seems equally sure to be branded an "imperial President" (just as FDR was occasionally condemned as a would-be dictator during both the New Deal and World War II periods).

Given the state of the union, recent pleas for "Presidential leadership" are understandable and predictable. Yet Presidential leadership, however desirable in and of itself, seems unlikely to overcome fundamental institutional problems in the American system of government. Until those problems are resolved, Presidential leadership alone may be unavailing. As FDR himself once said, in what would have been at least a partially accurate comment about his wartime experience on the home front: "It's a terrible thing to look over your shoulder when you are trying to lead--and to find no one there."

****

The present version of this work varies slightly from the original dissertation. Some modest revisions have been made, especially in chapter one. The major change is that the roll-call tables reproduced as appendices to the dissertation are not included here because of their great length. For those readers who might wish to consult the tables in the original dissertation, the references to them remain in the footnotes.

Many persons assisted in the preparation of this study. I owe special thanks to John L. McCarthy who introduced me to Guttman scaling analysis and generously permitted the use of computer programs that he had developed. Wayne Moyer helped complete the research on Congressional voting patterns. Michael Sherry and Allan Winkler provided essential advice and encouragement. John Morton Blum was both a patient editor and an expert teacher who helped me avoid many errors of fact and interpretation.

I also wish to acknowledge the receipt of a small grant from the Wells College Advisory Committee, which facilitated supplementary research on this topic during the summer of 1977.

Finally, the greatest debt is to my wife, Marilyn, whose steadfast loyalty enabled me to see the project through to the end.

Richard N. Chapman
Wells College
Aurora, New York

TABLE OF CONTENTS

INTRODUCTION

Fascination with the drama of American military and diplomatic participation in World War II has obscured developments on the home front. As one historian has written, "Domestic politics during World War II has been little investigated and its importance underestimated: until it is studied in detail, our understanding of the New Deal will not be complete."[1] This work, a narrative and analysis of Congressional politics and public policy during the Second World War, endeavors to fill the gap in existing scholarship on domestic affairs between 1939 and 1945.

Most accounts of the New Deal end in 1938. Some authors suggest that President Franklin D. Roosevelt deliberately abandoned domestic reform after that time in order to prepare for war.[2] Others attribute the demise of the New Deal to recrudescent conservatism in Congress.[3] Revisionists critical of liberal reform insist that the New Deal collapsed because of its own deficiencies.[4] Few scholars have studied the debates over public policy that followed the struggles of the New Deal years.

Yet controversy over domestic policy did not cease with the outbreak of war in Europe or with the Japanese air raid on Pearl Harbor. Guttman scaling analysis of Senate and House roll call votes between 1939 and 1945 indicated that political conflict

---

[1]John A. Salmond, "Postscript to the New Deal: The Defeat of the Nomination of Aubrey W. Williams as Rural Electrification Administrator in 1945," Journal of American History LXI (September 1974), p. 435.

[2]See Charles A. Beard and George H. E. Smith, The Old Deal and the New (New York, 1940), pp. 244-283; Broadus Mitchell, Depression Decade: From New Era Through New Deal, 1929-1941 (New York, 1947), p. 369; and Nicholas Halasz, Roosevelt Through Foreign Eyes (Princeton, 1961), p. 96. See also Raymond Moley, Rexford G. Tugwell, and Ernest K. Lindley, "Symposium: Early Days of the New Deal," in Morton J. Frisch and Martin Diamond, eds., The Thirties: A Reconsideration in the Light of the American Political Tradition (De Kalb, Ill., 1968), p. 140.

[3]See, for example, William E. Leuchtenburg, Franklin D. Roosevelt and the New Deal (New York, 1963), pp. 252-274.

[4]Barton J. Bernstein, "The New Deal: The Conservative Achievements of Liberal Reform," in Barton J. Bernstein, ed., Towards A New Past (New York, 1969), pp. 263-288.

over reform persisted and intensified during those years.[5] Legislative roll call analysis revealed the existence of a powerful
Congressional opposition composed of Republicans and "renegade
Democrats," nominal members of the President's party who consistently voted against his legislative program. Beginning in 1939
and with increasing frequency thereafter, Republicans and renegade Democrats, as Guttman scaling analysis again revealed, were
occasionally assisted by a faction of "orthodox Democrats," those
who had gone along with the Administration in the past but who
were no longer reliable Presidential supporters.

Guttman scaling also identified the kinds of issues that
provoked conflict between the Administration and its adversaries.
The large questions that dominated Congressional deliberations
during the war included the survival of New Deal agencies and
policies, the role of reform in wartime, and the content of the
government's postwar program. Given those concerns, it seemed
evident that Congressional decisions during World War II helped
determine both the substance of and the possibilities for postwar
public policy.

No satisfactory study has been made of Congress between
1939 and 1945. Roland A. Young's Congressional Politics in the
Second World War provides a useful introduction but fails to
focus on the struggle between the Roosevelt Administration and
the Congressional opposition. That struggle is the theme of this
dissertation. What effect did the Congressional opposition have,
during World War II, on the New Deal legacy? Were the factions
that controlled Congressional decision-making able to use that
power to shape the contours of postwar public policy? Those are
the chief questions considered here.

_____

[5]Guttman scaling analysis is a useful tool for deciphering
legislative politics. By comparing votes of each legislator to
the votes of all other legislators on a set of roll calls, patterns of legislative responses are identified and isolated.
Guttman scaling analysis arranges roll calls that make such a
pattern into a scale reflecting the level of support or opposition
that each roll call received from the body of legislators. The
first item on a scale is usually a roll call on which a few legislators voted against the majority of their colleagues. As each
item in the scale is added, the small number in the original
voting bloc are joined by other legislators on each roll call.
It becomes possible to determine the composition of contending
forces on any scalable roll call by examining the opposing voting
blocs divided on the scale by that roll call. For a fuller explanation of Guttman scaling procedure, see Lee F. Anderson, Meredith W. Watts, Jr. and Allen R. Wilcox, Legislative Roll-Call
Analysis (Evanston, Ill., 1966), pp. 89-121; and John L. McCarthy,
"Reconstruction Legislation and Voting Alignments" (Ph.D. dissertation, Yale University, 1970), chapter one and appendix.

The present work is not an inclusive account of domestic politics during World War II. Such an undertaking would be a forbidding task. Rather my study concentrates on a series of significant, representative episodes, all of which were part of the wartime "battle of Washington," the continuing dispute between reformers and their adversaries about the purposes of Federal policy and the nature of the good society. A different set of episodes might have yielded slightly different conclusions, but my premise has been that the incidents treated here illustrate the pattern of Congressional politics between 1939 and 1945.

CHAPTER 1

THE CONGRESSIONAL OPPOSITION AND THE NEW DEAL

On March 4, 1939, the United States Congress celebrated its
150th anniversary. With the world on the edge of war, the or-
ganizers of the anniversary ceremonies wanted to emphasize "the
contrast between our own kind of free government and the despo-
tism that threatened to envelop all Europe." So it was that a
special joint session of Congress heard the President, the
Chief Justice of the Supreme Court, and its own legislative leaders describe the past glories, present adversities, and uncertain future of democratic institutions.[1]

President Franklin D. Roosevelt, who had just returned from
reviewing naval maneuvers with the Atlantic fleet, was under-
standably preoccupied with foreign threats to the democratic way
of life. In his remarks to Congress, the President affirmed the
vitality of American democracy and issued a warning to its enemies:

> Today . . . the United States will give no encourage-
> ment to the belief that our processes are outworn, or
> that we will approvingly watch the return of forms of
> government which for 2,000 years have proved their
> tyranny and instability alike.[2]

Aimed at European ears, those words portended American involvement in the war yet to come.[3]

Others were thinking on that day not of future international perils, but of the internal controversies of the past.
March 4, 1939, marked not only the 150th anniversary of Congress.
It was also the sixth anniversary of the Roosevelt Administration. During the previous six years, the New Deal had provoked
continual political strife. Supreme Court Chief Justice Charles

---

[1]Quotation from Representative Sol Bloom, The Autobiography
of Sol Bloom (New York, 1948), pp. 223-224. For descriptions
of the anniversary ceremonies, see the New York Times, March 5,
1939, pp. 1, 43, 45-46; Washington Post, March 5, 1939, pp. 1,
15; Time, March 13, 1939, pp. 14-15; and Congressional Digest
18 (1939), pp. 101-102.

[2]Samuel I. Rosenman, ed., The Public Papers and Addresses
of Franklin D. Roosevelt, vol. 8: 1939, War and Neutrality
(New York, 1941), p. 151.

[3]Joseph P. Lash, Roosevelt and Churchill, 1939-1941 (New
York, 1976), p. 63.

1

Evans Hughes, who personified judicial opposition to the President, stirred memories of that strife, especially the "court-packing" episode of 1937.[4] In his commemorative address to Congress, the Chief Justice pointedly praised Constitutional safeguards, checks and balances, separation of powers, and judicial restraint of "gusts of passion and prejudice which in misguided zeal would destroy the basic interests of democracy." Only if the government pursued a "wise conservatism," he declared, would the American system be preserved.[5] Such words seemed to encourage resistance to the New Deal.

Resistance to the President's program had already stiffened. For the first time since taking office, Roosevelt faced a substantial Republican minority. On January 4, 1939, when the President presented his annual message to Congress, his adversaries gave him what _Time_ called a "thorough-going razz."[6] The reception on March 4 was polite, but outward appearances clothed lasting antagonisms.

Republicans who had long protested against a rubber-stamp Congress considered the 150th anniversary celebration a timely reaffirmation of Congressional independence. House minority leader Joseph W. Martin (R., Mass.) praised the resurgence of the legislative branch. "There have been occasions," he said in a radio address on March 4, "when forgetful of the lessons of man's experience, majorities in Congress have abandoned independence and willingly become subservient to the Chief Executive. On such occasions our country and the cause of liberty and freedom have suffered." Martin joined Senate minority leader Charles McNary (R., Ore.) in predicting that the period of "subservience" was at an end.[7]

Republicans could afford optimism. By 1939, the Democratic Party had split into quarreling factions. Dissident Democrats frequently combined with Republicans to oppose the Administration.[8] Only two years earlier, it had seemed inconceivable that

---

[4]Stephen T. Early to William Hassett, February 28, 1939, President's Official File 419, FDR papers, FDR Library. See also _Washington Post_, March 5, 1939, p. 15.

[5]Quotations from _Congressional Digest_ 18 (1939), p. 116.

[6]_Time_, January 16, 1939, pp. 11-12.

[7]Quotation from _New York Times_, March 5, 1939, p. 43. See also _Washington Post_, March 5, 1939, p. 4.

[8]The best study of the rise of Congressional opposition is James T. Patterson, _Congressional Conservatism and the New Deal_ (Lexington, Ky., 1967), pp. 82-249. For the sources of Democratic dissension, see also Bascom N. Timmons, _Garner of Texas_ (New York, 1948), pp. 214-227.

the President would encounter serious resistance from Congress. After Roosevelt's great triumph in the 1936 Presidential election, wrote Federal Reserve Chairman Marriner Eccles, New Dealers

> felt we could at last write the full ticket of things we thought would best serve the needs of the country. Let the President merely write his "O.K." across the head of that ticket and it would be just a matter of time before the new Congress passed what was wanted.[9]

Despite that expectation, and huge Democratic majorities, the 75th Congress (1937-1938) obstructed parts of the Administration's program.[10]

As the first session of the 75th Congress began, "renegade Democrats," those who had always viewed the New Deal with suspicion, planned their attack. Senator Josiah W. Bailey (D., N.C.) urged "formation of a conservative bloc" led not by the tiny Republican minority but by the conservative "Democrats in the Senate--Glass, George, Adams, Burke, Moore, King, Gerry, perhaps Smith, and surely myself, and some others of whom I have hopes." They would "put forward the conservative policies and create the background for the contest in 1940."[11]

While those self-styled conservatives plotted among themselves, other Congressional Democrats counseled Presidential moderation. Vice President John Nance Garner had long been worried that the President might get "too far off the main beaten highway."[12] When the President's 1936 campaign occasionally took on overtones of a crusade against wealth, the Vice President became alarmed. He feared the intoxication of victory might lead Roosevelt on. After the election, Garner

---

[9]Marriner S. Eccles, Beckoning Frontiers: Public and Personal Recollections (New York, 1951), p. 266.

[10]Patterson, Congressional Conservatism, pp. 85-187; William E. Leuchtenburg, Franklin D. Roosevelt and the New Deal (New York, 1963), pp. 231-251.

[11]Quotations from Patterson, Congressional Conservatism, p. 83; and John Robert Moore, Senator Josiah William Bailey of North Carolina (Durham, N.C., 1968), p. 127. "Renegade Democrats" were those members of the President's party who voted regularly with Republicans in opposition to the Administration. Senator Robert F. Wagner (D., N.Y.) labeled them "Republicans in disguise." See Robert F. Wagner, speech, November 5, 1944, Box 591-BB-123, Wagner papers, Georgetown University Library.

[12]Garner to Jesse H. Jones, August 28, 1934, box 10, Jones papers, Library of Congress.

urged restraint. He advised the President to concentrate on revising experimental legislation: "We are not putting out a fire, now," he said. Garner also told Roosevelt to reduce expenditures and balance the budget. The Vice President faithfully reflected the views of "orthodox Democrats" like Senators Pat Harrison (D., Miss.) and James F. Byrnes (D., S.C.), who also thought the national emergency was over.[13]

Orthodox Democrats outlined a program of budgetary retrenchment and policy review, but the President had other ideas. In April 1936 Roosevelt had hinted to Secretary of the Treasury Henry Morgenthau, Jr., "Next year . . . I'm really going to be radical. . . . I am going to recommend a lot of radical legislation." Morgenthau cautioned, "You are going to be very careful about money spending," and Roosevelt answered, "Yes, I am." "Well, then," the Secretary of the Treasury concluded, "I don't care how radical you are in other matters." The President was sensitive to the demand for economy, but neither he, nor his closest advisers, nor New Dealers in Congress were ready to abandon reform.[14]

In quick succession, several events during the first session of the 75th Congress (January-August 1937) threw the Democratic Party into turmoil. Roosevelt's refusal to act against sit-down strikes organized by the Congress of Industrial Organizations enraged Garner and upset Byrnes. Like most of their colleagues, they saw the strikes and the CIO as a threat to private property. Then the President unveiled his court-reorganization plan. Despite herculean efforts by Senate majority leader Joseph Robinson (D., Ark.) and the nominal support of Harrison and Byrnes, Congress defeated the President's plan. The court fight made feelings raw, as did Presidential interference in the race to succeed Robinson, who died suddenly on July 14, 1937. With Roosevelt's assistance, New Dealer Alben Barkley (D., Ky.) won by a single vote over Harrison, the candidate of the orthodox Democrats. Shortly thereafter, Harrison

---

[13]Quotations from Timmons, _Garner of Texas_, pp. 212, 230. See also _New York Times_, November 21, 1936, p. 8, December 18, 1936, p. 1, December 24, 1936, p. 2; Harold Ickes, _The Secret Diary of Harold Ickes_, vol. II: _The Inside Struggle, 1936-1939_ (New York, 1954), pp. 37, 63; Arthur Krock, _Memoirs: Sixty Years on the Firing Line_ (New York, 1968), pp. 181-182; Patterson, _Congressional Conservatism_, pp. 128-134; and Paul K. Conkin, _The New Deal_ (New York, 1967), pp. 101-102. "Orthodox Democrats" were moderate party supporters who had gone along with most of the New Deal without evincing much enthusiasm for it.

[14]John M. Blum, _From the Morgenthau Diaries_, vol. I: _Years of Crisis, 1928-1938_ (Boston, 1959), p. 267. See also J. Joseph Huthmacher, _Senator Robert F. Wagner and the Rise of Urban Liberalism_ (New York, 1968), p. 220.

led opposition to the President's minimum wage and maximum hours bill. He was unable to prevent Senate passage of that legislation, but in the House, Rules Committee Chairman John O'Connor (D., N.Y.) collaborated with two other Democratic renegades, Eugene E. Cox (D., Ga.) and Howard W. Smith (D., Va.) to block action.[15] By the end of its first session, the 75th Congress was not totally out of Roosevelt's control, but the President and the orthodox Democrats had moved apart.[16]

Encouraged by that development, Senator Bailey and his fellow renegades stepped up their attacks on the President. In December 1937, Bailey drafted a "conservative manifesto," a statement of principles around which anti-New Deal Democrats and Republicans could rally. As Harold Ickes wrote in his diary, "the war is on fiercer than ever between the reactionaries and liberals within the Democratic party."[17]

In 1938, Roosevelt and his opponents fought over reorganization of the executive branch. Renegade Democrats and Republicans, cooperating closely, charged that the Administration's proposed executive reorganization plan would permanently diminish the role of Congress and grant the President "all the

---

[15]"Voting Record of Howard Smith," folder 66, box 706-LA-719, Wagner papers, Georgetown University Library. See also Timmons, Garner of Texas, pp. 214-224; Patterson, Congressional Conservatism, pp. 84-124, 134-138, 146-148, 179-184; Frances Perkins, The Roosevelt I Knew (New York, 1946), pp. 319-324; Tom Connally, My Name is Tom Connally (New York, 1954), pp. 184-192; Henry F. Ashurst, A Many Colored Toga: The Diary of Henry Fountain Ashurst (Tuscon, Ariz., 1962), pp. 368, 374-375; James F. Byrnes, All in One Lifetime (New York, 1958), pp. 98-100; Alben W. Barkley, That Reminds Me (Garden City, N.Y., 1954), pp. 154-156; Joseph W. Martin, Jr., My First Fifty Years in Politics (New York, 1960), p. 73; Ickes, Diary II, p. 182; Booth Mooney, Roosevelt and Rayburn (Philadelphia, 1971), pp. 99-101; James M. Burns, Congress on Trial: The Legislative Process and the Administrative State (New York, 1949), pp. 72-74; and Lawrence H. Chamberlain, The President, Congress, and Legislation (New York, 1946), p. 180.

[16]Patterson, Congressional Conservatism, pp. 159-163, 184-187; Timmons, Garner of Texas, pp. 228-229; New York Times, August 20, 1937, p. 16. See also John M. Allswang, The New Deal and American Politics (New York, 1978), pp. 113-121.

[17]Quotations from Moore, Bailey, p. 144; and Ickes, Diary II, p. 288. For accounts of the "conservative manifesto," see Moore, Bailey, pp. 144-159; and Patterson, Congressional Conservatism, pp. 200-210.

powers of a dictator," as Senator Bailey declared. Roosevelt ridiculed such accusations, but his reorganization bill, after passing the Senate, provoked the "bitterest fight that has occurred in the House of Representatives in the last fifty years," according to one observer. The President appeared to be genuinely surprised when the House, on April 8, narrowly defeated the measure. That startling result, arising from serious Democratic disunity, led renegade Democrats to hope that the New Deal might at last be brought to a standstill.[18]

Roosevelt, stung by his defeat on executive reorganization and increasingly resentful of anti-New Deal "copperheads," attempted to purge dissident Democrats from the party.[19] In the 1938 Democratic primaries, the President intervened directly against Senators Walter F. George (D., Ga.), "Cotton Ed" Smith (D., S.C.), Millard Tydings (D., Md.), and Representative John O'Connor (D., N.Y.), and indirectly against other Democratic renegades. The "purge" offended many influential members of the President's party. Senator Byrnes recalled that he tried to dissuade Roosevelt from the "folly" of trying "to control the legislative branch of the government." The President refused to listen, so Byrnes "left no doubt in his mind that I would do everything in my power to help my friends who were marked to fall under the ax."[20]

Vice President Garner was equally opposed to the purge. The men singled out for punishment constituted "a group of prominent Democrats" who had "wintered and summered" together since 1913.[21] The altkampfer of Garner's party, they had

---

[18] Richard Polenberg, Reorganizing Roosevelt's Government: The Controversy Over Executive Reorganization, 1936-1939 (Cambridge, Mass., 1966), pp. 125, 160-175. See also Samuel I. Rosenman, memorandum, April 8, 1938, box 5, Rosenman papers, FDR Library; and Patterson, Congressional Conservatism, p. 233.

[19] Samuel I. Rosenman, ed., The Public Papers and Addresses of Franklin D. Roosevelt, vol. 7: 1938, The Continuing Struggle for Liberalism (New York, 1941), p. 395. See also Polenberg, Reorganizing Roosevelt's Government, p. 183; and Allswang, New Deal and American Politics, pp. 121-126.

[20] Quotations from Byrnes, All in One Lifetime, pp. 100-104. For reactions to the purge, see James A. Farley, Jim Farley's Story (New York, 1948), pp. 120-122, 145-146; Jesse H. Jones, Fifty Billion Dollars: My Thirteen Years with the RFC (New York, 1951), p. 91; Bernard M. Baruch, The Public Years (New York, 1960), pp. 258-259; Mooney, Roosevelt and Rayburn, pp. 104-108.

[21] Paraphrase of a reminiscence by Joseph Tumulty, quoted in Otis L. Graham, Encore for Reform (New York, 1967), p. 28.

suffered through lean years of Republican domination. "I have
marched and fought for causes with some of these men," the Vice
President declared. "The places they hold represent their life
achievements, their struggles, their ambitions, their service
to party and country." Roosevelt "may have reason to be provoked at them," but he was wrong in trying to defeat them.[22]

Further, the Vice President had heard reports that "the
left-wingers had decided that the party was not big enough for
both them and the conservatives." The purge looked like a deliberate effort to "dismantle the old-line Democratic Party and
set up a 'liberal' party." Garner wanted to preserve the traditional two-party system, where Democrats and Republicans faced
each other in formal opposition without true hostility. The
traditional system acted as a damper on radical change, thereby
serving the interests of those with a stake in the existing social order. Garner emphasized that a party must have "all sorts
of views, and through a reconciliation and adjustment of those
views, you get harmony and a program. . . . A Party has got to
strike a balance." If "left-wingers" succeeded in purging the
conservatives, they would divide the country into "two political
camps," a reactionary party representing wealth and a radical
party representing discontent. Political conflict over the distribution of wealth would intensify and the built-in "balance"
inhibiting radical change would be gone. Garner believed that
Democrats who wanted to remain, in Roosevelt's sarcastic phrase,
"a Democratic Tweedledum to a Republican Tweedledee," had to
stay in the party and counteract the influence of the "extreme
liberals" around the President.[23]

Orthodox Democrats were therefore relieved when the purge
failed. Every renegade opposed by Roosevelt gained renomination except O'Connor. That setback in the primaries was only a
prelude. In the November 1938 elections, Republicans scored
astonishing gains. Their strength in the House surged from 89
to 169. They added eight seats in the Senate. Only during the
wartime election of 1942 did the Democratic Party under Roosevelt take a worse beating, though on both occasions the Democrats retained nominal control of both houses of Congress.[24]

---

[22]Quotations from Timmons, Garner of Texas, pp. 232-234.
See also Farley, Jim Farley's Story, pp. 137-138.

[23]Quotations from Timmons, Garner of Texas, pp. 230, 236;
and Rosenman, Public Papers and Addresses of FDR 8: 1939,
p. 63. The phrase "formal opposition without true hostility"
is borrowed from Hans Rogger and Eugen Weber, eds., The European Right (Berkeley, Calif., 1966), p. 117. See also Byrnes,
All in One Lifetime, pp. 104-105; and Seymour M. Lipset, Political Man (Garden City, N.Y., 1960), pp. 31, 40.

[24]Charles M. Price and Joseph Boskin, "The Roosevelt
'Purge': A Reappraisal," Journal of Politics 28 (1966),

Economic conditions undoubtedly influenced the outcome of the 1938 elections. Whatever his other problems, Roosevelt had at least been able to claim credit for returning prosperity. Then, late in 1937, a severe recession occurred. The slump damaged the President's prestige and exposed the New Deal to sharp criticism.[25] "Roosevelt's recession" helped the Republican Party out of its grave. After four years of lop-sided Democratic majorities in Congress, the tide had turned. Republicans would present a more formidable opposition than in the past. Renegade Democrats, infuriated by the purge, would assail almost anything that came from the White House. Together, those Democrats and the Republicans formed a bipartisan opposition that threatened the Administration's domestic objectives.[26]

The President did not seem overly concerned. A reporter asked, "Will you not encounter coalition opposition" in the new Congress? Roosevelt replied simply, "No, I don't think so." On November 14, 1938, he wrote Josephus Daniels: "Frankly I think we will have less trouble with the next Congress than with the last."[27]

To make that prediction come true, the President needed the cooperation of the orthodox Democrats, who now held the balance of power between the bipartisan opposition and the Administration's supporters. Obtaining that cooperation, Roosevelt soon found, would not be easy. Garner, Byrnes, Harrison, and other party chieftains interpreted Democratic losses in the November elections as a sign of popular dissatisfaction with the New Deal. In effect, they construed the election as "a victory for the

---

pp. 660-670; Charles O. Jones, The Minority Party in Congress (Boston, 1970), p. 17; Patterson, Congressional Conservatism, pp. 261-290; Farley, Jim Farley's Story, pp. 137-150; Martin, My First Fifty Years, p. 81.

[25]Wesley C. Clark, Economic Aspects of a President's Popularity (Philadelphia, 1943), pp. 11-40; Hadley Cantril, ed., Public Opinion 1935-1946 (Princeton, N.J., 1951), p. 756; James M. Burns, The Lion and the Fox (New York, 1956), p. 338; Patterson, Congressional Conservatism, pp. 188-189; Conkin, The New Deal, pp. 96-97; Leuchtenburg, FDR and the New Deal, p. 271.

[26]Patterson, Congressional Conservatism, pp. 288-291; Farley, Jim Farley's Story, p. 137; Martin, My First Fifty Years, p. 82; Mooney, Roosevelt and Rayburn, pp. 108-111; Elliott Roosevelt, ed., F.D.R.--His Personal Letters, 1928-1945, vol. 2, 1938-1945 (New York, 1950), p. 827.

[27]Franklin D. Roosevelt, Complete Presidential Press Conferences of Franklin D. Roosevelt, vols. 11-12, 1938 (New York, 1972), pp. 12:222-223; Carroll Kilpatrick, ed., Roosevelt and Daniels (Chapel Hill, N.C., 1952), p. 178.

right." They were convinced the Democrats risked defeat in 1940 if the Administration failed to heed the electoral mandate.[28]

In their post-election dealings with the President, the orthodox Democrats pressed him to follow a more moderate course. During a tense interview on December 17, 1938, Garner told Roosevelt that concessions had to be made to the new spirit of independence in Congress. He asked the Chief Executive not to appoint "radical lame ducks to high executive offices." Finally, Garner warned that "with nearly a hundred Democrats removed from the Congressional ranks, conditions were ripe for a coalition" with the Republicans. The Democrats still had a "large majority in Congress, but . . . not a New Deal majority." Therefore, to restore party unity, Roosevelt should make drastic cuts in Federal spending and abandon the New Deal. If he refused to do so, Garner declared, the orthodox Democrats would join Republicans and renegades in opposition to the Administration.[29]

The Keynesian Reformers

As earlier, orthodox Democrats were urging a turn to the right to bring the President and the traditional Democratic Party back together again. Other elements meanwhile were pushing Roosevelt to continue the New Deal. Among those who favored continued reform were the young Keynesians of the Roosevelt Administration. Many of these self-conscious pioneers of the fiscal revolution in the United States, who were "bootlegging" John Maynard Keynes' "heretical views," belonged to an advisory group organized under the auspices of the National Resources Committee, the chief economic planning agency of the Federal government.[30] The membership of that group included Thomas C. Blaisdell, director of the monopoly study for the Securities and Exchange Commission; Lauchlin B. Currie, assistant director, Division of

[28]Quotation from Timmons, Garner of Texas, p. 240. See also Farley, Jim Farley's Story, pp. 146-148, 153-154; and Congressional Digest 18 (1939), p. 2.

[29]Quotations from Timmons, Garner of Texas, pp. 238-240. Acting Budget Director Daniel Bell described Roosevelt's reaction to the conversation with Garner in his Memorandum of Conference with the President, December 19, 1938, Fiscal and Monetary Advisory Board 38.3, Records of the Bureau of the Budget, Record group 51, National Archives. See also Ickes, Diary II, pp. 530-531; Farley, Jim Farley's Story, p. 158; Patterson, Congressional Conservatism, pp. 291-292; and Washington Post, December 16, 1938, p. 17, December 18, 1938, section III, p. 6.

[30] Quotation from Lauchlin B. Currie, statement in connection with "The Keynesian Revolution and Its Pioneers," American Economic Review LXII (May 1972), p. 139.

Research and Statistics, Federal Reserve Board; Charles W. Eliot, executive officer of the National Resources Committee; Mordecai Ezekiel and Louis Bean, economic advisers to the Secretary of Agriculture; Leon Henderson, executive secretary of the Temporary National Economic Committee; Isador Lubin, Commissioner of Labor Statistics, Department of Labor; Gardiner C. Means, director of the Industrial Section of the National Resources Committee; and Harry D. White, economist for the Treasury Department.[31]

The Keynesians associated with the National Resources Committee did not always concur on the nuances of economic policy, but they agreed that the Administration had to seek full recovery through permanent, planned compensatory fiscal policy. The temporary pump-priming of the early New Deal had failed to restore the economy to health, they believed, because the system needed sustained Federal deficits to compensate for the downward swing of the business cycle and the consequent dearth of private investment. The NRC economists proposed deficit-financed public works as a form of public investment to supplement private investment. Further, they urged redistribution of income through progressive taxation and government spending on relief, public assistance, and social security programs. The increase in mass purchasing power resulting from a redistribution of wealth would, they argued, enlarge aggregate demand for goods and services and thereby expand production and employment.[32]

Striving for "system and order committed to an articulate and articulated doctrine of welfare capitalism," the economists

---

[31]For the functions of this advisory group, called the Industrial Committee, see "Vote of the Advisory Committee," May 9, 1937, files of Thomas C. Blaisdell, box 6, Industrial Committee, Records of NRPB, Record Group 187, National Archives. See also John M. Blum, From the Morgenthau Diaries, vol. II: Years of Urgency, 1938-1941 (Boston, 1965), p. 14; and Currie, statement, p. 141.

[32]See the discussion by the National Resources Committee Keynesians in the Morgenthau Diary, vol. 147, pp. 204-238; see also the testimony of Alvin H. Hansen and Lauchlin B. Currie, U.S., Congress, Temporary National Economic Committee, Investigation of Concentration of Economic Power, Hearings before the Temporary National Economic Committee, part 9, Savings and Investment, 76th Congress, 1st Session, 1939, pp. 3495-3559, 3837-3854; and Louis H. Bean, "Eighty Billion Dollars--When?" The Agricultural Situation 23 (May 1939), pp. 11-15. For background, see Roy Blough, The Federal Taxing Process (New York, 1952), pp. 240-242; Robert LeKachman, The Age of Keynes (New York, 1966), pp. 78-111, 123-137; Herbert Stein, The Fiscal Revolution in America (Chicago, 1969), pp. 131-168; and Blum, Years of Urgency, pp. 14-15.

of the National Resources Committee offered an organizing vision
for the New Deal.[33] Since its inception in 1933, Roosevelt's
program had been a series of improvisations plagued by contradic-
tions and confusions. Federal intervention on behalf of powerful private interests frequently clashed with efforts to eliminate inequities in the American political economy and to assist
the "lower third" of society.[34] The New Deal always seemed in
pursuit of two irreconcilable goals, reform and recovery, but
that apparent contradiction could be resolved, the NRC economists felt sure, through a combination of public planning and
Keynesian fiscal policy. "This administration," they declared,

> is committed to a wide social program, which includes
> social security, parity of farm prices and farm in-
> come, better housing, work for the unemployed, and
> minimum wages and maximum hours for the employed; all
> pointed toward higher living standards and juster dis-
> tribution of the gains of civilization. Validation
> of this series of commitments depends upon wider dis-
> tribution of an immensely enlarged national income.[35]

Properly applied, the Keynesians contended, compensatory fiscal
policy would achieve both prosperity and reform.

Inside the Roosevelt Administration, two major obstacles
hindered the application of compensatory fiscal policy. The
first was Secretary of the Treasury Henry Morgenthau, Jr., an
unrelenting foe of deficit finance. The second impediment was
the President's own vacillation. Circumstances had pushed
Roosevelt toward a new conception of Federal fiscal policy,
but the President, who had not yet fully grasped the content of
Keynesian theory, continued to wish for fiscal orthodoxy. Vexed
by contradictory advice and political pressures, Roosevelt
might return to balanced budgets. That had happened in 1937,

---

[33]Quotation from Barry D. Karl, Charles E. Merriam and
the Study of Politics (Chicago, 1974), p. 248. See also Richard
V. Gilbert and others, An Economic Program for American Democ-
racy (New York, 1938), pp. vi-ix, 41-91; David Cushman Coyle,
Roads to a New America (Boston, 1938), pp. 147-352; and Alan
Sweezy, "The Keynesians and Government Policy, 1933-1939,"
American Economic Review LXII (May 1972), pp. 116-124.

[34]LeKachman, Age of Keynes, pp. 113-122, 143; Otis L.
Graham, Jr., Toward A Planned Society: From Roosevelt to Nixon
(New York, 1976), pp. 21-27, 49, 64-67.

[35]Industrial Committee, "Emerging Industrio-Governmental
Problems," November 9, 1937, minutes of Industrial Committee
meeting of November 30, 1937, 106.5, Records of NRPB, Record
Group 187, National Archives.

with dreadful results.[36]

Keynesian economists blamed the recession of 1937-38 on the
President's decision to balance the budget in 1937. The senior
government official who held that view was Marriner Eccles,
Chairman of the Board of Governors of the Federal Reserve System. According to Eccles, in 1936 the government spent substantial sums on the recovery and relief programs, and also paid a
soldiers' bonus of $1.7 billion. The cash deficit of the Trea-
sury increased to $4 billion, "representing the government's net
contribution to consumer disposable income." With recovery
under way, businessmen, orthodox Congressional Democrats, and advisers like Secretary of the Treasury Morgenthau urged the
President to cut Federal spending. Roosevelt, whose own economic ideas were conventional, did so. Also in 1937, the new
Social Security Act went into effect, and $2 billion of social
security taxes were collected from people with a high propensity
to consume. The Treasury actually ended up with a cash surplus
for the first nine months of 1937. As Eccles pointed out, "the
government in 1937 was reducing consumer disposable income by
almost $4 billion." The return to a balanced budget, he con-
tended, plunged the country into a steep recession.[37]

By the end of 1937, the Administration needed a new recovery program. Yet the Secretary of the Treasury still clung
stubbornly to a traditional approach. According to Morgenthau,
private enterprise would take up the slack caused by reduced
Federal expenditures, if an atmosphere of business confidence
could be created. Deficit spending frightened businessmen, the
Secretary believed, because they feared inflation and higher
taxes as results of an unbalanced budget. It was time, Morgenthau firmly maintained, to "see whether business could achieve
recovery and full employment."[38]

The Secretary's views were endorsed by bankers and industrialists both within and without the government. The Business

[36]LeKachman, Age of Keynes, pp. 123, 137-139; Stein, Fiscal
Revolution, pp. 91-102; Blum, Years of Crisis, pp. 380-386;
Blough, Federal Taxing Process, pp. 241-242. See also Samuel
I. Rosenman, memorandum, April 13, 1938, box 5, Rosenman papers,
FDR Library.

[37]Quotations from Eccles, Beckoning Frontiers, pp. 294-295.
See also Lauchlin B. Currie, "Causes of the Recession," April 1,
1938, box 29, Lubin papers, FDR Library; Kenneth D. Roose, "The
Recession of 1937-38," Journal of Political Economy LVI (1948),
pp. 239-248; Currie, statement, American Economic Review, p. 140;
LeKachman, Age of Keynes, p. 124; and Alvin H. Hansen, Full Recovery or Stagnation? (New York, 1938), pp. 7-8, 274.

[38]Quotation from Blum, Years of Crisis, p. 388. For business fears of deficit spending, see Stein, Fiscal Revolution,
pp. 74-90.

Advisory Council of the Department of Commerce urged the President to follow a "policy of cooperation" with business. The industrialists and financiers who served on that Council blamed the recession on such New Deal reforms as the undistributed profits tax, the capital gains tax, and stock market regulation, which had allegedly driven risk capital into hiding and penalized free enterprise. To halt the recession, so they argued, the government must encourage private business by creating a better climate for economic activity. The Business Advisory Council recommended an end to statements critical of the business community; encouragement of enterprise through balanced budgets, tax reductions, and a moratorium on further reform; an end to anti-trust litigation; and revision of the Wagner Act to inhibit the growth of "radical" labor movements.[39]

Roosevelt accordingly faced a choice between budget balancers and business appeasers on the one hand, and deficit spenders on the other. His decision in favor of the spenders came as no surprise to his closest advisers. Morgenthau ruefully admitted, "I never had a chance." The President regarded the recession as proof the business community hated him and the New Deal. He told his Secretary of the Treasury that capital had gone on strike, that "business was deliberately causing the depression in order to hold a pistol to his head and force a retreat from reform."[40] If Roosevelt accepted the orthodox prescription for recovery, balanced budgets and business appeasement, he would defer to the groups that had most venomously criticized him. Compensatory spending offered recovery without sacrifice of the New Deal or admission of past error. In April 1938, the President sent Congress a multi-billion dollar spending program to combat the recession.[41]

The shift back to deficit-financed public works in the spring of 1938 looked like an acceptance of Keynesian economics. But

---

[39] Robert E. Wood to Daniel C. Roper, January 3, 1938, Daniel C. Roper to Marvin H. McIntyre, January 5, 1938, Robert H. Jackson to President, January 17, 1938, Business Advisory Council, "Statement of Policy for Amendments to the National Labor Relations Act," January 20, 1938, James Roosevelt to President, February 21, 1938, W. A. Harriman to President, April 20, 1938, President's Official File 3-Q, FDR papers, FDR Library.

[40] Quotations from Morgenthau Diary, vol. 147, pp. 234-235, FDR Library; and Blum, Years of Crisis, p. 390. See also Roosevelt, FDR.--His Personal Letters 2: 1938-1945, pp. 740-741.

[41] Rosenman, Public Papers and Addresses of FDR 7: 1938, pp. 221-235; Patterson, Congressional Conservatism, p. 234; Blum, Years of Crisis, pp. 417-426.

no one knew how lasting Roosevelt's commitment really was. Secretary Morgenthau, untouched by the "new economics," encouraged
the President's longing for balanced budgets. The business community remained surly. And the elections of 1938 emboldened
Republicans and Democrats who equated compensatory spending with
fiscal insanity.[42]

To avoid a repetition of the uncertainties of 1937-38, when
the Administration had shifted toward budget-balancing and then
back toward deficit spending, the National Resources Committee
Keynesians recommended creation of a Fiscal and Monetary Advisory Board that would "report directly to the President and . . .
advise him on fiscal and monetary policy."[43] Frederic A. Delano,
Roosevelt's uncle and head of NRC, and a cautious proponent of
countercyclical fiscal policy, explained:

> The duties of the Board would be to provide the Ad-
> ministration with a continuous review and formulation
> of policy for the Federal fiscal and monetary program
> in its relation to the trends of business activity and
> national income. It would obtain current information
> as to the amount and character of public expenditures,
> the sources of government income, the volume of pri-
> vate investment and savings, and the additions to buying
> power resulting from public spending. On the basis of
> this information the Board would formulate current fis-
> cal policies, serve the President in an advisory capac-
> ity in determining when to recommend that public ex-
> penditures should be expanded and when contracted in
> order to promote sustained business activity. . . .

As Delano's memorandum revealed, the National Resources Committee wanted the new board to become the President's council
of economic advisers, a development that in the Keynesian view
would make the Federal government a more purposeful and profi-
cient manager of the national economy.[44]

---

[42]LeKachman, Age of Keynes, p. 125.

[43]Quotation from Delano to President, August 12, 1938,
President's Official File 3484, FDR papers, FDR Library. See
also Morgenthau Diary, vol. 145, p. 84 and vol. 150, pp. 308-
309, FDR Library; Delano to President, June 6, 1938, President's
Official File 3484, FDR papers, FDR Library; John Miller, "A
Fiscal Advisory Board," July 21, 1938, files of Thomas C. Blaisdell, box 5, Records of NRPB, Record Group 187, National Archives; and minutes of Industrial Committee meeting of March 15,
1938, 106.5, Records of NRPB, Record Group 187, National Archives.

[44]Quotation from Delano to President, August 12, 1938, Central Office Correspondence 104.1, Records of NRPB, Record Group

The Keynesians thought there was little chance Roosevelt would approve their proposal unless they could first gain the acquiescence of the Secretary of the Treasury. Morgenthau looked on fiscal policy as the exclusive province of the Treasury and the Bureau of the Budget and resented any intrusion into his domain.[45] Still, he did not feel he could gracefully refuse the request from the National Resources Committee. He even saw some good coming of it. If "the economists who work down the line . . . think they've got something to help, why, fine." Instead of going "up on the Hill" and talking "against our program . . . maybe they will talk it over here. I don't know; I doubt that, but maybe they will."[46]

On October 10, 1938, Morgenthau asked the President to authorize establishment of an advisory committee. Roosevelt agreed to do so, but he refused to make the fiscal group a permanent agency. Instead, in a typical metaphor, he told Morgenthau that the compensatory spenders could have a "free pass to the ball games for this season." The President decided that the membership of the Fiscal and Monetary Advisory Board would consist of Eccles for the Federal Reserve Board, Delano for the National Resources Committee, Daniel Bell for the Bureau of the Budget, and the Secretary of the Treasury. Their responsibility, said Morgenthau, was to oversee "the spending program for '39-'40, on the eve of the election."[47]

Marriner Eccles and the National Resources Committee Keynesians thought the new Fiscal and Monetary Advisory Board should provide the President with a steady stream of economic advice based on Keynesian principles and thereby neutralize the Secretary of the Treasury's antagonism to deficit spending. During a discussion with Morgenthau on October 11, 1938, Eccles said the group should devote itself to the timing of "Government compensatory spending to replace private spending." Morgenthau disagreed. He wanted the new board to bring the budget as close to balance as possible. Treasury technicians projected two $4 billion deficits in a row, Morgenthau complained, and

---

187, National Archives. See also Morgenthau Diary, vol. 144, pp. 221-231, FDR Library; and minutes of Industrial Committee meeting of October 6, 1938, 106.5, Records of NRPB, Record Group 187, National Archives.

[45] Thomas C. Blaisdell to Frederic A. Delano, July 13, 1938, and July 14, 1938, files of Thomas C. Blaisdell, box 5, Records of NRPB, Record Group 187, National Archives; Morgenthau Diary, vol. 145, pp. 84-87, FDR Library.

[46] Morgenthau Diary, vol. 145, p. 87, FDR Library.

[47] Morgenthau Diary, vol. 145, pp. 87, 252-253, vol. 146, p. 29, FDR Library.

being a conservative fellow, this four billion dollar
deficit on top of another four billion dollar deficit
naturally scares me, and I think it would scare any
business man, because we're going into the unexplored
realm. Maybe we can do it; I don't know.[48]

The Treasury Secretary, realizing that the Keynesians would
try to use the Fiscal and Monetary Advisory Board to overwhelm
his resistance to deficits, responded by stressing the vulnerability of the government's credit position. At a dinner conference with the National Resources Committee economists on
October 23, 1938, he put forward his case. "Some people," Morgenthau declared, "would like to see [the government] . . . continue to spend a lot of money, and without increasing the taxes.
And that sleight of hand is getting more and more difficult."
The Secretary insisted that the government must "get the deficit
smaller" by cutting expenditures, raising taxes, or increasing
national income so that existing tax rates would bring in larger revenues. To promote a higher national income, Morgenthau,
as earlier, favored "peace for the business man." Seeing the
expectation of profit as an important energizing force in the
economy, he wanted to allay business fears of New Deal policies
and encourage private investment.[49]

The NRC economists agreed, in the words of Charles Eliot,
"that the goal of a higher national income is the right approach." But they did not agree on the means to achieve that
goal. The deficits that frightened Morgenthau held no terror
for the Keynesians. They doubted that "peace for the businessman" would, by itself, bring recovery, for businessmen might not
make new capital investments until consumption absorbed existing
industrial capacity. To achieve a higher national income, the
Keynesians suggested an expansion of deficit-financed public
works in order to supplement private investment; increased relief expenditures as a contribution to net consumer disposable
income; and "giving larger incomes to the lower third" by
"taking more away from the top group through taxes."[50]

Since they could agree only on the self-evident necessity
for a higher national income, Morgenthau and the National Resources Committee appeared to be at an impasse. But then the
Secretary advanced another proposition. Certain activities of
the government were largely self-liquidating. Government

---

[48]Quotations from Morgenthau Diary, vol. 145, pp. 252-253
and vol. 146, p. 338, FDR Library.

[49]Quotations from Morgenthau Diary, vol. 147, pp. 204, 221-
222, FDR Library. See also Blum, Years of Urgency, p. 13.

[50]Quotations from Morgenthau Diary, vol. 147, pp. 220,
225-227, FDR Library.

agencies made loans for housing, rural electrification, business financing, rural rehabilitation, public works, and other purposes. Borrowers repaid the loans and the money was recovered. Morgenthau suggested a vast expansion of self-liquidating loans as a way to bolster the economy without burdening the budget. He asked, "Can we produce one, two, three, or four billion dollars worth of projects which could be financed outside the budget?"[51]

At last Morgenthau had found common ground with the National Resources Committee Keynesians. Lauchlin Currie reacted enthusiastically:

> While economically there is no particular reason why you shouldn't increase the national debt year after year after year, actually, politically, feasibly . . . we can't go on expecting to run a deficit year after year; the community is not going to stand for it. Eventually, we're just going to have to work out some other way of handling this thing.[52]

The "other way of handling this thing" was self-liquidating projects. The Keynesians were willing to recede to this position because loans for self-liquidating projects, though not charged against the official budget, would have much the same effect as a formal deficit.

NRC economists understood the implications of the conference with the Secretary of the Treasury. At their next meeting on October 27, 1938, the Keynesians "agreed that further work would be required with respect to a list of projects which might be financed outside the budget." Lauchlin Currie advocated development of government corporations that would operate on the basis of self-liquidating loans. Mordecai Ezekiel was more specific, listing the Rural Electrification Administration, rural rehabilitation loans, farm tenancy loans, a Federal Railway Equipment Corporation, and a Toll Road Authority as elements of a Keynesian program that would raise national income without adding to the bookkeeping deficit. Impressed by his presentation, Ezekiel's colleagues asked him to prepare studies of self-liquidating projects for the use of the Fiscal and Monetary Advisory Board.[53]

---

[51]Morgenthau Diary, vol. 147, p. 231, FDR Library. On self-liquidating loans made by the Reconstruction Finance Corporation, see Jones, Fifty Billion Dollars, pp. 163-172.

[52]Morgenthau Diary, vol. 147, p. 236, FDR Library.

[53]Quotation from minutes of Industrial Committee meeting of October 27, 1938, 106.5, Records of NRPB, Record Group 187, National Archives. See also Mordecai Ezekiel, "Project Outline,"

While the Keynesians reviewed plans for self-liquidating projects, they also tried to educate Morgenthau about compensatory fiscal policy. On December 5, 1938, the National Resources Committee taught a seminar in the new economics for the Secretary of the Treasury. Morgenthau remained unpersuaded by what he disdainfully called "this stuff." A Washington Star editorial cartoon captured the situation: Marriner Eccles was shown conducting a New Deal band to the tune of "Merrily we must spend our way, spend our way, spend our way." In the background, Morgenthau was playing a big bass horn, and coming out of that was "Deficit keeps a growin' big, growin' big, growin' big."[54]

Disagreement within the Fiscal and Monetary Advisory Board mirrored the debate taking place outside the Administration. Fiscal conservatives were demanding a recovery policy based on balanced budgets and government favors for business. On December 10, 1938, Senator Harry F. Byrd (D., Va.), one of the leading Democratic renegades, assailed Roosevelt's spending program as "crackpot" and a "tragic failure." Byrd heaped special abuse on Marriner Eccles because of his role as an outspoken advocate of continued deficit finances.[55]

Eccles regarded Byrd as an unsophisticated thinker who relied on "popular aphorisms" and cracker barrel sophistry. The Federal Reserve Chairman took Byrd seriously only because his invective was an extreme expression of views held "inside the Administration by such highly placed figures as Vice President John Garner, Secretary Cordell Hull, Jesse Jones, Senators James Byrnes and Pat Harrison." On December 23, Eccles fired a broadside at Byrd. The cutbacks in spending proposed by the Senator would sink the economy, Eccles said. Furthermore, Byrd didn't care about deficits; he just wanted to liquidate the New Deal. All Americans, Eccles declared, "whether rich or poor," had "a right to a decent place to live . . . to security in old age and to protection against temporary unemployment . . . a right to adequate medical attention and to equal educational opportunities. . . ." He told Byrd, "The government expenditures which you condemn have in large part been the means of

---

October 27, 1938, minutes of Industrial Committee meeting of October 27, 1938, 106.5, Records of NRPB, Record Group 187, National Archives.

[54]Morgenthau Diary, vol. 147, pp. 384-386, vol. 154, pp. 282-302, vol. 155, pp. 7, 24, vol. 157, p. 93, FDR Library. For Washington Star cartoon, "The Sour Note," by C. K. Berryman, see illustration number 8, following p. 280 in Blum, Years of Crisis.

[55]New York Times, December 11, 1938, section I, p. 36. See also Eccles, Beckoning Frontiers, p. 312.

translating these basic rights into realities. I am convinced
that your program is . . . a program of retrogression and not
of progress. . . ."[56]

As the debate between Eccles and Byrd illustrated, the
issue was joined much as it had been in the winter of 1937-38
and, in lesser measure, in 1933-34. Twice before the cry had
gone up that "recovery must precede reform," and twice before
Roosevelt had rejected that plea. For the third time, Republicans, renegade and orthodox Democrats, businessmen and some
officials within the Administration argued, "You can't have recovery and reform, too."[57] Compensatory spenders, on the other
hand, denied "that the old regime must be restored to power" in
order to attain recovery. Through Keynesian reform, they asserted, the Administration could have prosperity and the New
Deal, too.[58]

At the center of the contending forces, Roosevelt looked
one way and moved another. At first, he appeared to yield to
those who were urging balanced budgets and business appeasement.
The President's annual message, delivered January 4, 1939, contained conciliatory phrases intended to pacify his Congressional
critics. "We have now passed the period of internal conflict in
the launching of our program of social reform," Roosevelt told
Congress. His Administration would "invigorate the processes
of recovery in order to preserve our reforms." Those phrases
seemed to signal an end to the New Deal.[59]

Yet the President had not abandoned his goals. Calling his
program of social and economic reform "basic" to future progress,
he reminded Congress that all Americans had a right to an equitable "share of material success and of human dignity." He spoke

---

[56]Eccles, Beckoning Frontiers, pp. 312-316.

[57]Quotations from Arthur J. Altmeyer, The Formative Years
of Social Security (Madison, Wis., 1966), p. 9; and Jonathan
Daniels, Frontier on the Potomac (New York, 1946), p. 159. See
also Morgenthau Diary, vol. 155, p. 171, FDR Library; and
Blough, Federal Taxing Process, pp. 243-244.

[58]Quotation from Industrial Committee, "Emerging Industrio-
Governmental Problems," November 9, 1937, minutes of Industrial
Committee meeting of November 30, 1937, 106.5, Records of NRPB,
Record Group 187, National Archives. See also Gilbert and
others, An Economic Program for American Democracy, pp. vi-ix,
41-87.

[59]Rosenman, Public Papers and Addresses of FDR 8: 1939,
p. 7; Barton J. Bernstein, "The New Deal: The Conservative
Achievements of Liberal Reform," in Barton J. Bernstein, ed.,
Towards A New Past (New York, 1969), p. 277.

of "better provision for our older people under our social security legislation," and of providing better care for the medi-
cally needy. Most important, he refused to reduce government
spending. Roosevelt offered placating words, but he did not
announce the end of reform.[60]

The President revealed his real intentions at the Jackson
Day dinner on January 7, 1939. He called for all true Democrats
to rally to the New Deal. Only by remaining a liberal party, he
told his audience, could the Democrats retain the confidence of
the people. "Nominal Democrats who . . . are convinced that our
party should be a conservative party" should join the Republicans. To most of his listeners, Roosevelt still sounded aggressive.[61]

As always, the President wished to keep his options open,
but he was determined to push on as far as he could, with or
without the cooperation of Democratic dissidents. His attitude,
described as "damned Dutch stubbornness" by Vice President
Garner, forced the orthodox Democrats closer to overt resistance.
Garner, thoroughly disgusted, concluded that further cooperation
with Roosevelt was impossible. According to his biographer,
"Garner was . . . convinced that the President wanted no peace
with the party moderates and conservatives and had no intention
of considering their viewpoint in legislative matters." More
strongly than ever, the Vice President felt "Roosevelt isn't
leading the whole party, only the left-wing faction."[62]

Members of that "left-wing faction" were elated by Roosevelt's qualified support for their position. The annual budget
message, submitted to Congress on January 5, 1939, made it
clear that the President would not repeat the mistake of 1937.
He admitted the economic necessity of Federal deficits. "I believe I am expressing the thought of the most far-sighted students of our economic system in saying that it would be unwise
either to curtail expenditures sharply or to impose dramatic
new taxes at this stage of recovery." Deficits were justified,
Roosevelt went on, because they triggered rather than retarded
business activity.[63]

---

[60]Rosenman, Public Papers and Addresses of FDR 8: 1939,
pp. 5-6, 9-10.

[61]Quotation from Rosenman, Public Papers and Addresses of
FDR 8: 1939, p. 63. See also Timmons, Garner of Texas, p. 242;
and Patterson, Congressional Conservatism, p. 293.

[62]Quotations from Timmons, Garner of Texas, pp. 237, 240;
and Farley, Jim Farley's Story, p. 163. See also Morgenthau
Diary, vol. 165, p. 48, FDR Library.

[63]Quotations from Rosenman, Public Papers and Addresses of
FDR 8: 1939, pp. 46-47. See also Stein, Fiscal Revolution, pp.
124-125; Time, January 16, 1939, p. 13; and Newsweek, January 9,
1939, p. 52.

Such views were far removed from the 1932 Presidential campaign, when Roosevelt had castigated Hoover for reckless spending. And yet it was not evident that the President had wholeheartedly accepted compensatory fiscal policy as a permanent strategy of economic growth. He expressed hope that a higher national income would eventually eliminate Federal deficits, and favored "moderate" tax increases to offset an enlarged national defense program. He also recommended that Congress pass legislation to separate self-liquidating loans from non-recoverable expenditures, a bookkeeping change that would make the deficit seem smaller.[64]

Disregarding those ambiguities in Roosevelt's position, Marriner Eccles and the National Resources Committee Keynesians interpreted the budget message as a triumph for the principles of compensatory fiscal policy. On January 11, Eccles congratulated the President and then went on to warn him that "this position is being and will continue to be attacked by reactionary Republicans as well as Democrats, by large financial interests, and by the press generally which reflects their views." To counteract the assault on compensatory fiscal policy, Eccles suggested that Roosevelt instruct the cabinet, particularly the Secretary of the Treasury, to "participate in a program of presenting your case to the country."[65] Roosevelt evidently followed Eccles' advice, for he asked all cabinet officers to support "the position taken in my annual message to the Congress as well as in the budget message--a policy generally known as the 'compensatory fiscal policy.'" He specifically requested that the Secretary of the Treasury explain "the soundness of the case" for deficit spending.[66]

Lending Instead of Spending

The President's request left Morgenthau frustrated. As long as Roosevelt believed that a reduction in expenditures would cause a renewed recession, then Morgenthau had lost his struggle to balance the budget. Therefore the Secretary changed tactics. Instead of trying to cut the deficit down, Morgenthau fought to keep spending from going up. He also continued to press for a rapprochement with the business community. Here Roosevelt was, for the moment, more encouraging. On February 17, shortly before

---

[64]Rosenman, Public Papers and Addresses of FDR 8: 1939, pp. 36-37, 46-47; Blum, Years of Urgency, p. 16; Stein, Fiscal Revolution, pp. 118, 120-121.

[65]Eccles to President, January 11, 1939, President's Official File 962, FDR papers, FDR Library.

[66]President to Cabinet, January 21, 1939, President's Official File 962, FDR papers, FDR Library. See also Currie, statement, American Economic Review LXII (May 1972), p. 141.

leaving for maneuvers with the Atlantic fleet, the President
finally made the "talk of peace to business" that Morgenthau had
long been urging. Roosevelt declared that no new taxes were
forthcoming and that business had every reason to be bullish
about the future.[67]

That statement pleased Morgenthau, who told the press on
February 23 that he was glad the President was trying to conciliate the business community, for "Businessmen ought to feel that
the Administration wants them to make money." The following day,
Secretary of Commerce Harry Hopkins--considered the chief
apostle of the New Deal--called for reconciliation between business and the Administration. The government's objective, Hopkins
said, was "to create an environment in which private capital will
be encouraged to invest." Over the next two weeks, Morgenthau,
Under Secretary of the Treasury John W. Hanes, Senate Finance
Committee Chairman Pat Harrison (D., Miss.), and House Ways and
Means Committee Chairman Robert Doughton (D., N.C.) echoed
Hopkins' sentiments. Newspaper columnists interpreted the appeasement talk as proof of a new pro-business posture.[68]

Roosevelt, however, would not venture beyond rhetoric.
When he returned from the naval training exercise, he ridiculed
proposed tax cuts and other peace-offerings to business. At a
White House luncheon on March 6, the President reminded Morgenthau that the Administration hoped to avoid concessions to industrial and financial interests. Two days later the Secretary
once again pleaded for a program of tax adjustments for business. "Recovery in 1940," Morgenthau said, "would enhance our
chance greatly of having the next President a liberal President."
Roosevelt agreed that a boom would help elect a liberal, but
refused to coax prosperity from a grudging business community.[69]

After flirting briefly with business appeasement, the President reaffirmed his commitment to compensatory fiscal policy, the

_____

[67]Quotation from Morgenthau Diary, vol. 147, p. 204, FDR
Library. See also Morgenthau Diary, vol. 160, p. 1. FDR Library;
and Blum, Years of Urgency, p. 17.

[68]Quotations from Blum, Years of Urgency, p. 18; and New
York Times, February 25, 1939, p. 1. See also New York Times,
February 24, 1939, pp. 1, 8, February 25, 1939, pp. 1, 3, February 26, 1939, section IV, p. 3, February 28, 1939, p. 2, March 3,
1939, p. 1, and March 4, 1939, p. 1.

[69]Quotation from Blum, Years of Urgency, p. 20. See also
Morgenthau Diary, vol. 168, p. 29, vol. 169, p. 217, FDR Library;
New York Times, March 22, 1939, p. 1; and Beatrice B. Berle and
Travis B. Jacobs, Navigating the Rapids, 1918-1971: From the
Papers of Adolf A. Berle (New York, 1973), pp. 199-200.

position he had taken, though not unreservedly, in his budget message. With the deficit forecast at $3.3 billion for the fiscal year beginning July 1, 1939, Roosevelt probably ruled out large additional increments in direct Federal spending as a way to promote further recovery. Practical and political difficulties stood in the way of that course of action. The projected deficit for fiscal 1940 would bring the gross public debt to over $44 billion, close to the statutory limit of $45 billion. Although the Administration could request an increase in that limit, Congress might not go along. The Senate Finance Committee, chaired by Harrison and loaded, as Morgenthau put it, with "every 'purgee' that wasn't purged," would try to block any effort to increase the debt ceiling. Roosevelt therefore faced a dilemma. For the good of the nation, as well as for selfish political reasons, the Administration needed a fuller measure of economic recovery. Congressional reluctance to raise the debt ceiling made substantial increases in deficit spending problematical. Moreover, the President, still sensitive to attacks on his fiscal policy, wanted to keep the Federal deficit from growing too big. As for business appeasement, Roosevelt had clearly rejected that policy. So a new lending program, outside the budget, was the only remaining option.[70]

On April 20, 1939, as the economy continued to show signs of weakness, the members of the Fiscal and Monetary Advisory Board agreed that the outlook was discouraging. The deficit for fiscal 1940 might keep the economy from collapsing, but with recovery proceeding more sluggishly than analysts earlier had hoped, that deficit now seemed inadequate to bring about additional gains in production and employment. Even if Congress adopted the President's 1940 budget in its entirety--an outcome that was by no means sure--expenditures were scheduled to decline gradually after January 1, 1940. The situation, supporters of countercyclical public finance were convinced, required a larger government stimulus.[71]

Two leading Administration Keynesians decided to press for remedial action. In a memorandum submitted to National Resources Committee economists on May 13, Mordecai Ezekiel and Louis Bean blamed "rumors of war and dangers of war abroad" for intensifying

---

[70] Quotation from Morgenthau Diary, vol. 147, p. 236, FDR Library. See also Stein, Fiscal Revolution, pp. 120-121; LeKachman, Age of Keynes, p. 137; Harold D. Smith, Memorandum of Conference with the President, December 22, 1939, Smith papers, FDR Library; Morgenthau Diary, vol. 165, p. 166, FDR Library; and John M. Carmody to Lester B. Reed, July 22, 1939, Reader File, vol. 1, FWA, Carmody papers, FDR Library.

[71] Thomas C. Blaisdell to Frederic A. Delano, April 22, 1939, Files of Thomas C. Blaisdell, box 5, Records of NRPB, Record Group 187, National Archives.

business uncertainty and crippling economic recovery in the
United States. European upheavals coupled with American domestic maladjustments, they contended, threatened a repeat of the
1937-38 recession, unless the Administration moved quickly and
resolutely. Bean and Ezekiel advised that

> a new vigorous program . . . be initiated now, so
> that it can get through Congress in time to become
> effective in late 1939 and early 1940. Such a pro-
> gram must be sufficiently vigorous to provide a posi-
> tive business expansion here regardless of the uncer-
> tainties created by the maneuverings abroad. It must
> show the dictator that democracies too can act to
> provide jobs and welfare for their people.[72]

After linking new recovery efforts to the challenge of
European dictatorship, Bean and Ezekiel recommended establishment of a "Federal (Fiscal) Agency to finance self-liquidating
projects outside the budget." They also proposed "Passage of a
bill providing for a broad program of road and highway projects,
on a self-liquidating scale," passage of the necessary legislation "to provide for an immediate start on re-equipping the
railroads," and "similar self-liquidating investments in the
fields of farm tenant purchase, low cost housing, utility
equipment, etc." Such a recovery plan would "make it possible
to guarantee an expansion in demand and business activity over
the next couple of years," they concluded.[73]

Bean, Ezekiel, and the rest of the National Resources Committee Keynesians believed that the time for action had arrived.
The President was coming to the same conclusion. He directed
Thomas G. Corcoran, an unofficial adviser and envoy, to confer
about new recovery proposals with NRC chairman Frederic A.
Delano and Harold D. Smith, the recently-appointed budget director and a committed advocate of macroeconomic planning. On
May 12, Corcoran told Smith and Delano "that the President proposed to send a message to Congress on or about May 25 and wished
advice concerning what should be included from the Fiscal and
Monetary Advisory Board and the Budget."[74]

---

[72]Louis H. Bean to Robert W. Hartley, May 13, 1939, and Mordecai Ezekiel and Louis H. Bean, "Confidential Memorandum on Internal Progress vs. European Unsettlement," Industrial Committee
106.5, Records of NRPB, Record Group 187, National Archives.

[73]Mordecai Ezekiel and Louis H. Bean, "Confidential Memor-
andum on Internal Progress vs. European Unsettlement," Industrial
Committee 106.5, Records of NRPB, Record Group 187, National
Archives.

[74]Charles W. Eliot, Memorandum for the Files, May 23, 1939,
Fiscal and Monetary Advisory Board 766, Records of NRPB, Record
Group 187, National Archives. See also Harold D. Smith, Daily

Three days later, the National Resources Committee Keynesians discussed Roosevelt's request for new recovery proposals. The President, Delano assured the economists, recognized the danger of another recession and wanted a program of preventive action. Since the economic outlook was so gloomy, Leon Henderson replied, the National Resources Committee should be bold, should state "not merely what things they think politically feasible, but what should be done." Harry White, more attuned to "political realities," thought that the NRC should propose a lending program, "outside the budget," along the lines of the Bean-Ezekiel memorandum. White's cautious approach prevailed, and the group designated Lauchlin Currie to combine earlier studies of self-liquidating projects and present a statement for further consideration.[75]

On May 20, the Keynesians met again with Delano and with two other National Resources Committee members, Beardsley Ruml and Charles E. Merriam. Drawing heavily on the work of Bean and Ezekiel, Currie recommended loans for public works, rural rehabilitation projects, railroad equipment, toll roads, small businesses, and export trade. That list failed to satisfy everyone. Charles Eliot, executive officer of NRC, suggested that old age pensions, a national health plan, and Federal aid to education be included. Ruml thought the Administration's fiscal policy overly timid and dismissed Currie's lending program as a collection of half-measures instead of a decisive attack on the problem. Perhaps Currie would have agreed that only huge government deficits would produce full economic recovery, but he and most of the other Keynesians were more interested in a practical plan than Congress might accept than a visionary program that would be rejected out of hand.[76]

On May 23, the National Resources Committee Keynesians presented their recommendations to the Fiscal and Monetary Advisory Board. "It is almost the unanimous opinion among Administration officials and technicians," they noted, "that there is little if any prospect for marked recovery during the next two years."

Memoranda, May 12, 1939, Smith papers, FDR Library. For the importance of the new budget director, see Rexford G. Tugwell, The Enlargement of the Presidency (Garden City, N.Y., 1960), p. 402 n.

[75] Notes Taken by John Miller, May 15, 1939, Fiscal and Monetary Advisory Board 766, Records of NRPB, Record Group 187, National Archives.

[76] Charles W. Eliot, Memorandum for the Files, May 23, 1939, Fiscal and Monetary Advisory Board 766, Records of NRPB, Record Group 187, National Archives.

There is a further political factor, namely, there
will probably develop a strong tendency on the part
of certain groups to forego the prospects of immediate profits or plant expansion until after the
election.[77]

The Keynesians' fear that private business would let the
economy collapse in order to defeat the New Deal was not entirely without foundation. During the first week of May, the
United States Chamber of Commerce, holding its annual convention
in Washington, listened to speeches roasting Roosevelt and his
policies. Senator Byrd told the assembled businessmen that the
present government in Washington was the "most wasteful and
autocratic bureaucracy that this or any other country has ever
been inflicted with," and called for the dismantling of the New
Deal.[78] George H. Davis, retiring President of the Chamber of
Commerce, demanded that business be liberated from the strait-
jacket of New Deal policies. The 26-point program adopted by
the convention reeked with hostility toward the Administration.[79]

The torrent of criticism from organized industry and finance reinforced the New Dealers' belief that "Big Business is
in a sitdown strike to wreck the New Deal."[80] To frustrate
that intention, the Keynesians argued, a new recovery plan was
essential. In their May 23 statement to the Fiscal and Monetary Advisory Board, the NRC economists recommended

a program of immediate action designed to ensure a
substantially increased national income in 1940 and
to protect us against a sharp downturn in business

---

[77]Quotation from Statement for the Fiscal and Monetary Advisory Board, May 23, 1939, Fiscal and Monetary Board 38.3,
Records of the Bureau of the Budget, Record Group 51, National
Archives. See also Charles W. Eliot, Memorandum for the Files,
May 23, 1939, Fiscal and Monetary Advisory Board 766, Records
of NRPB, Record Group 187, National Archives; Morgenthau Diary,
vol. 191, p. 7, FDR Library; and Harold D. Smith, Daily Memoranda, May 22, 1939, Smith papers, FDR Library.

[78]New York Times, May 3, 1939, p. 1.

[79]New York Times, May 4, 1939, pp. 1, 4, May 5, 1939,
pp. 1, 6-7, May 7, 1939, section IV, p. 7. See also Adolf A.
Berle, Diary, May 16, 1939, box 210, Berle papers, FDR Library.

[80]New York Times, May 14, 1939, section IV, p. 3. See also
Leon Henderson to President, May 17, 1939, box 36, Henderson
papers, FDR Library.

during the next fifteen months. . . . Congress should not adjourn until an adequate program has been inaugurated.[81]

Having presented their case, the Keynesians hoped the Fiscal and Monetary Advisory Board would concur and transmit their proposals to the President. That possibility depended on the attitude of the Secretary of the Treasury. At the May 23 meeting, he refused to accept the National Resources Committee plan. Perhaps Morgenthau did not think the situation was "as bad as our group thinks," speculated Charles Eliot, or perhaps he did not believe the time was "propitious for action."[82]

In contrast to the Secretary of the Treasury, Marriner Eccles agreed with his fellow Keynesians that the economic situation was critical, but despaired of securing Congressional approval of a new recovery plan. "If Mr. Eccles is right" in saying that Congress favored "a conservative approach," Eliot commented acidly, "then . . . the time has come (as someone has jokingly suggested) for the President to resign and let Garner make a mess of it." Eliot still preferred "a long-range major program" but realized that an unenthusiastic Secretary of the Treasury, a cautious President, and a rebellious Congress would probably produce a "mustard plaster"--that is, "some amelioration of the situation pending the submission of a long-range major program in the fall or even as a 1940 platform."[83]

While the Keynesians worked to build a consensus on the Fiscal and Monetary Advisory Board, they launched an extensive publicity campaign to prepare Congress and the country for a new recovery plan. During the week of May 17, Administration insiders leaked reports of another spending-lending program to the press.[84] The Keynesians also used the Temporary National

---

[81]Statement for the Fiscal and Monetary Advisory Board, May 23, 1939, Fiscal and Monetary Advisory Board 38.3, Records of the Bureau of the Budget, Record Group 51, National Archives.

[82]Quotation from Charles W. Eliot, "Estimate of Situation," May 24, 1939, Fiscal and Monetary Advisory Board 766, Records of NRPB, Record Group 187, National Archives. See also Harold D. Smith, Daily Memoranda, May 23, 1939, Smith papers, FDR Library.

[83]Charles W. Eliot, "Estimate of Situation," May 24, 1939, Fiscal and Monetary Advisory Board 766, Records of NRPB, Record Group 187, National Archives.

[84]Charles W. Eliot, Memorandum for the Files, May 23, 1939, Fiscal and Monetary Advisory Board 766, Records of NRPB, Record Group 187, National Archives; Morgenthau Diary, vol. 192, p. 45, FDR Library.

Economic Committee as a sounding board for their proposals.
TNEC, a special Congressional commission charged with investigating the concentration of economic power in the United States,
was just starting hearings on the insufficiency of private investment. Leon Henderson, Economic Coordinator of TNEC, joined
Assistant Secretary of State Adolf A. Berle, Jr. in suggesting
that the Administration stage-manage the testimony before the
committee. The plan, Berle wrote the President, was to "ask
the committee . . . to recommend immediately . . . a Public
Works Finance Corporation" that would make loans for self-liquidating projects.[85]

Roosevelt endorsed Berle's strategy and gave the hearings a
send-off by writing a letter to Senator Joseph O'Mahoney (D.,
Wyo.), the chairman of TNEC. The President said, in part, "It
is our task to find and energetically adopt those specific measures which will bring together idle men, machines, and money."
Roosevelt's letter, with its hope that something concrete would
result from the hearings, had the desired effect of focusing
public attention on the testimony of Keynesian economists who
wanted to promote a new recovery program.[86]

Among those invited to explain countercyclical fiscal policy
to the TNEC was Alvin Hansen of Harvard, already the foremost
American disciple of Keynes. Lauchlin Currie also addressed the
commission, but perhaps the key witness before TNEC was Adolf
Berle, who self-importantly viewed himself as the New Deal's
roving economic troubleshooter. He began his testimony on
May 23 with the argument that "the private financial system as
at present constituted does not work." Because private capital
was paralyzed by fear, or was on strike against the New Deal, or
because investment opportunities simply did not exist, available
savings were not being channeled into productive enterprise and
business expansion. Therefore, said Berle, the Federal government had to supplement inadequate private investment with public
investment. He proposed doing so through a "Public Works Finance
Corporation" that "would make it possible for the . . . Agencies
of the United States Government to finance" self-liquidating
projects directly. Such projects, Berle predicted, would increase national income "by about two and a half times the amount
spent on heavy capital construction."[87]

---

[85] Berle to President, May 10, 1939, President's Official
File 3322, FDR papers, FDR Library; Henderson to E. M. Watson,
n.d., President's Official File 3322, FDR papers, FDR Library;
New York Times, May 14, 1939, section I, pp. 1, 3.

[86] President to O'Mahoney, May 16, 1939, President's Official
File 3322, FDR papers, FDR Library; New York Times, May 17, 1939,
p. 1.

[87] Quotations from U.S., Congress, Temporary National Economic Committee, Investigation of Concentration of Economic Power,

Had he stopped there, Berle's testimony might have been effective. But he went on, and appeared to suggest government nationalization of investment. He urged consideration of a bill "providing for capital credit banks, whose business it should be to provide capital for those enterprises which need it." As though that were not sufficiently controversial, Berle seemed to say that Federal lending and spending might cause "the government . . . gradually . . . to own most of the productive plants of the United States."[88] Those words proved politically damaging. In the months to come, the opposition used Berle's statements to attack Roosevelt's lending proposals as a blueprint for socialism. Almost from the moment of its inception, then, the Administration's new recovery program was given an undeserved aura of radicalism that made it vulnerable to Congressional critics.[89]

The day before Berle delivered his politically inept testimony, the President hinted broadly that the Administration might present a new economic program to Congress. In a speech to the American Retail Federation, Roosevelt ridiculed the negativism of his opponents and promised that his Administration would pursue all its major policies, particularly compensatory fiscal policy. From the President's remarks, many journalists concluded that he was seriously considering another spending-lending plan.[90]

Hearings before the Temporary National Economic Committee, part 9, Savings and Investment, 76th Congress, 1st Session, 1939, pp. 4066, 4068, 4078. See also Berle to President, August 16, 1938, President's Secretary's File 77, FDR papers, FDR Library; Leon Henderson to President, May 25, 1939, President's Official File 3322, FDR papers, FDR Library; and Berle and Jacobs, Navigating the Rapids, pp. 194-234.

[88] Quotations from U.S., Congress, Temporary National Economic Committee, Investigation of Concentration of Economic Power, Hearings before the Temporary National Economic Committee, part 9, Savings and Investment, 76th Congress, 1st Session, 1939, pp. 4069, 4078. See also Berle to President, March 24, 1938, President's Secretary's File 77, FDR papers, FDR Library; and New York Times, May 24, 1939, p. 10.

[89] Lawrence Sullivan, Bureaucracy Runs Amuck (Indianapolis, 1944), pp. 120-121; Morgenthau Diary, vol. 194, pp. 15-21, FDR Library.

[90] Rosenman, Public Papers and Addresses of FDR 8: 1939, pp. 341-352; Frederic A. Delano to President, May 22, 1939, and President to Frederic A. Delano, May 24, 1939, President's Personal File 72, FDR papers, FDR Library; Leon Henderson to William Hassett, May 15, 1939, box 36, Henderson papers, FDR Library; Morgenthau Diary, vol. 192, p. 45, FDR Library; New York Times, May 22, 1939, p. 1, May 23, 1939, p. 16, May 24, 1939, p. 10, May 28, 1939, section IV, p. 7.

With so many signs pointing in that direction, the opposition mounted a vigorous counterattack. Spokesmen for the business community, including Owen D. Young of General Electric, Alfred P. Sloan of General Motors, and Thomas M. Girdler of the American Iron and Steel Institute, blamed the New Deal for the nation's chronic unemployment.[91] Senators Harry F. Byrd (D., Va.) and Robert A. Taft (R., O.) joined businessmen in condemning the Administration. Taft called compensatory fiscal policy "one of the most dangerous fallacies ever adopted by any government." Byrd charged that the President had swallowed Keynesian economics "hook, line, and sinker." The Republican National Committee organized a "National Debt Week" observance to "arouse the American people to the dangers involved in a mounting national debt."[92]

Meanwhile, Roosevelt awaited specific recommendations from the Fiscal and Monetary Advisory Board. Because of the tension between Morgenthau and compensatory spenders like Eccles, that group had difficulty reaching agreement. Finally, on June 2, the Board produced a letter, addressed to the President, calling for immediate action to increase national income in 1940. Although the Secretary of the Treasury assented to the letter, he had not yet accepted the lending plan drawn up by the National Resources Committee Keynesians. He claimed still to be looking for "a good recovery program."[93]

Then on June 4, Morgenthau stunned Treasury aide Harry White by adopting the entire National Resources Committee plan. The Secretary told White that he did not want to engage in

---

[91] U.S., Congress, Temporary National Economic Committee, Investigation of Concentration of Economic Power, Hearings before the Temporary National Economic Committee, part 9, Savings and Investment, 76th Congress, 1st Session, 1939, pp. 3615-3616, 3628-3631, 3667-3668; New York Times, May 19, 1939, p. 12, May 21, 1939, section IV, pp. 2, 7, May 26, 1939, p. 1; Leonard P. Ayres, "Lending Our Way to Recovery," box 716, Spend-Lend (S. 2759, Barkley Act), Taft papers, Library of Congress.

[92] Quotations from Robert A. Taft, transcript of speech, May 23, 1939, box 1252, Taft papers, Library of Congress; and New York Times, May 21, 1939, p. 1, May 24, 1939, p. 11. See also Frank E. Gannett, transcript of speech, April 1, 1939, box 16, Gannett papers, Cornell University Library.

[93] Quotation from New York Times, May 23, 1939, p. 1. See also Harold D. Smith, Daily Memoranda, May 12, 1939, May 23, 1939, May 25, 1939, and June 2, 1939, Smith papers, FDR Library; Fiscal and Monetary Advisory Board to President, June 2, 1939, Fiscal and Monetary Advisory Board 766, Records of NRPB, Record Group 187, National Archives; and Frederic A. Delano to Charles W. Eliot, May 25, 1939, Fiscal and Monetary Advisory Board 766, Records of NRPB, Record Group 187, National Archives.

pointless disputation over "compensatory budget or pools of unused savings." He had a program in mind "that the President would attempt to have adopted by Congress as soon as possible."

> My program would, first, be planned to take care of the people in the lower one-third, and second, would at no place compete with private capital and, third, would be self-liquidating. I had in mind a slum clearance under U.S.H.A. [United States Housing Authority]: highways and bridges and tunnels.

White, heartened by the unexpected turn of events, remarked that "his friends would not believe" a program totalling "some $4,000,000,000."[94]

That evening Morgenthau telephoned Presidential secretary Marguerite ("Missy") LeHand to say, we have a "swell recovery program" that will "give us a prosperous year in 1940." Some of the suggestions required Congressional approval, so "Missy" should ask Roosevelt "not to close the door" on new legislation when he next spoke to the House and Senate leadership.[95]

Morgenthau's support for self-liquidating projects represented a partial triumph for Keynesian principles. Yet the Secretary of the Treasury was no Keynesian convert. Instead he worried that the pressures of an upcoming election year might produce a last-minute spate of Federal spending that would enlarge the deficit. Secretary of the Interior Harold Ickes would probably solicit additional funds for his Public Works Administration. Congressional advocates of deficit spending, led by Senator Claude Pepper (D., Fla.), would support increases in relief and public works appropriations, with or without Administration backing. And Marriner Eccles had drawn up his own spending program.[96]

With "the pulse of Washington the way it is now," said Morgenthau, the potential for at least a miniature spending spree still existed. The Secretary, mindful of what had occurred in 1938, told his staff on June 6: "rather than have a spending program sneak up on me in the dark, I thought I'd get out a recovery program of my own to give to the President." In order to preempt additional spending and larger deficit, he adopted

---

[94]Morgenthau Diary, vol. 194, pp. 1, 5, FDR Library; Blum, Years of Urgency, p. 38.

[95]Morgenthau Diary, vol. 194, pp. 1-2, FDR Library.

[96]Harold D. Smith, Daily Memoranda, June 5, 1939, Smith papers, FDR Library; Morgenthau Diary, vol. 195, pp. 139-263, FDR Library; New York Times, May 22, 1939, p. 1, May 30, 1939, p. 4.

the Keynesian-inspired lending plan, which--as Under Secretary
Hanes glumly admitted--was "the lesser of two evils."[97]

Once Morgenthau had made up his mind, events moved rapidly.
At a morning conference on June 6, the Fiscal and Monetary Advisory Board approved a memorandum for the President, proposing
"that a comprehensive program of action should be initiated at
once." A few hours later, Morgenthau, Eccles, and Smith presented their memorandum to Roosevelt "and he liked it enormously." The President told the Board "to have a Recovery Program ready for him to send to Congress not later than the 1st
of July and to surround it with all kinds of secrecy--no leaks."
Morgenthau proudly unveiled the lending plan, which came as no
surprise to Roosevelt who knew that the National Resources Committee had tried for two weeks to get Morgenthau's support for
such a program. The President reacted favorably: "he said,
'Let's try and make it a self-liquidating program entirely.'"
Morgenthau was euphoric:

> I am extremely happy because if [the program is] . . .
> self-liquidating [and] non-competitive [with private
> enterprise] why I can put my shoulder to it 100 per-
> cent. . . . this is the final culmination of what I
> have been working for. . . . [It won't be] old fash-
> ioned pump priming. . . . Give Senator Pepper my re-
> gards. (Laughter) And tell him the pump priming
> is dry.[98]

Roosevelt asked for a recovery program by July 1. The Fiscal and Monetary Advisory Board immediately began screening all
the self-liquidating projects suggested during the previous
eight months. During that selection process, the Board tried
to anticipate the reaction of Congress. Too many controversial
items thrown into one bill would diminish the chances for passage. The President therefore asked his advisers to concentrate on expanding existing programs rather than trying to get
something "revolutionary or new."[99]

---

[97]Quotations from Morgenthau Diary, vol. 194, pp. 88, 116,
FDR Library.

[98]Quotations from Morgenthau Diary, vol. 194, pp. 201, 238,
239, 241, FDR Library. See also Harold D. Smith, Memorandum of
Conference with the Fiscal and Monetary Advisory Board and the
President, June 6, 1939, Smith papers, FDR Library; Frederic A.
Delano to President, May 22, 1939, and President to Frederic A.
Delano, May 24, 1939, President's Personal File 72, FDR papers,
FDR Library.

[99]Morgenthau Diary, vol. 195, p. 137, FDR Library. See
also Blum, Years of Urgency, p. 39.

Two major projects failed to meet Roosevelt's criteria.
The first was a "Rural Telephone Administration" modeled after
the Rural Electrification Administration. "Rural telephone"
had never been tried before, and it might compete with private
telephone service. The Secretary of the Treasury, who insisted
on a program that would not disturb business confidence, vetoed
all projects competitive with private enterprise. The second
project jettisoned was "government acquisition, control, and
operation of bankrupt railroads." About that proposal, Morgenthau commented, "It's a good thing I've got a strong heart."
Eccles liked the idea of nationalizing certain railroads, but
he admitted that such a suggestion was "badly timed," and would
never win Congressional approval.[100]

Morgenthau, whose views encompassed both fiscal conservatism and humanitarian concern for the poor, now spoke for giving
"more substance to the New Deal principle of raising the standard
of living for the lower third of the nation." He favored an expansion of the rural rehabilitation projects administered by the
Farm Security Administration. Eccles complained that farm tenancy loans "may have real value as a social project" but they
were not the "type of investment" that would have as great a
multiplier effect as "some other expenditures." Morgenthau replied with a spirited defense:

What I'm trying to do here is . . . to bring to the
President's attention our pledge of the New Deal that
we're going to take care of the lower third. Now,
here is an enormous group [indigent farmers] we have
made a start on, and I'd like to see it continue.

The Secretary won the point. The New Deal, he felt, had barely
scratched the surface of poverty in the United States.[101]

On the morning of June 14, the Fiscal and Monetary Advisory
Board finished stitching together a "program to increase national income in 1940." The committee recommended more money
for farm tenancy loans, public housing, self-liquidating public
works, up to one billion dollars for toll roads, canals and
bridges, large sums for export loans, railroad equipment pur-
chases, and "rapid expansion of the Food Stamp Plan for distributing surplus commodities." Roosevelt accepted the entire

---

100
      Quotations from Morgenthau Diary, vol. 195, pp. 148,
210, 226, FDR Library. See also Harold D. Smith, Daily Memoranda, June 13, 1939, Smith papers, FDR Library.

101
      Quotations from Morgenthau Diary, vol. 195, pp. 189,
198-199, FDR Library.

package, the plan that Mordecai Ezekiel and Louis Bean had submitted one month before.[102]

In retrospect, the Keynesians had reason to be gratified by the success of their efforts. They had instigated the establishment of the Fiscal and Monetary Advisory Board, thus institutionalizing, temporarily at least, the principles of countercyclical public finance. In the budget message of 1939, the President had moved closer than ever before to the Keynesian position. By their persistent agitation within the fiscal advisory group, the NRC economists had elicited a new recovery program that represented a further reorientation of fiscal policy and, if enacted, would give employment to approximately one million persons.

The balance sheet showed negative entries as well. The split between Morgenthau and Eccles had hindered the effectiveness of the Fiscal and Monetary Advisory Board. Although the compromise lending plan recommended by the board was avowedly Keynesian, it was not large enough to be more than a "mustard plaster," in Charles Eliot's telling phrase. As a discouraged Marriner Eccles conceded, if the program "covers only a million people, it's pretty small in relationship to the gravity and the size of the problem we have presented."[103]

Yet the lending plan seemed the most that the Keynesians could extract from Morgenthau, the President, and the Congress. Substantial sums would go for social investments, such as better housing, rural electrification, relocation of poor farmers, and jobs for the unemployed. The program, in a limited and imperfect way, embodied the spirit of the New Deal and the principles of Keynesian reform.[104]

The Works Financing Act of 1939

Congress had gone through a long session, and most Congressmen yearned to escape the oppressive Washington summer, but Roosevelt sought action on the Administration's recovery plan before adjournment. The House of Representatives provided an opportunity to unveil the new program when on June 16 it passed

---

[102]Morgenthau Diary, vol. 195, pp. 260-263, 289-300, FDR Library; Harold D. Smith, memorandum of conference with the Fiscal and Monetary Advisory Board and the President, June 14, 1939, Smith papers, FDR Library; Blum, Years of Urgency, pp. 39-40.

[103]Morgenthau Diary, vol. 195, p. 241, FDR Library.

[104]See C. Benham Baldwin to Harry D. White, July 17, 1939, Correspondence, 1935-42, AD 140-01, box 107, Records of the Farm Security Administration, Record Group 96, National Archives.

the Work Relief and Public Works Appropriation Act of 1939, which transferred $125,000,000 from the work relief appropriation to the Public Works Administration. By allocating funds for PWA, the House hoped to continue the system of direct grants to states and localities for non-Federal public works.[105]

The President opposed continuation of PWA on that basis. Worried that national defense outlays might have to be increased in the near future, he had deliberately left PWA out of his fiscal 1940 budget. As recently as May 12, Roosevelt had told his new budget director, Harold D. Smith, that efforts by Secretary Ickes to make PWA permanent were "not in accord with his program."[106] The President had decided on loans instead of direct grants as a way of financing public works, and he feared that the well-known preference of states and municipalities for grants, "free money," would kill self-liquidating projects before they ever got under way.[107]

On June 19, the President arranged for Senator James F. Byrnes (D., S.C.), acting chairman of the Appropriations Committee, to write a letter requesting instructions on how to dispose of the House's Work Relief and Public Works Appropriation Act of 1939. In reply, Roosevelt intended to propose self-liquidating projects as an alternative to the $125,000,000 for PWA. Byrnes carried out his part of the strategy in a letter made public on June 21. Did the President believe the transfer of funds wise?, he asked.[108] "I am opposed to this provision," Roosevelt answered, because it would take money away from the work relief program and "165,000 men who are badly in need of work will have to be dropped from the . . . rolls."

> I believe there is a better way to accomplish the laudable purposes of this bill. . . . there are certain types of public improvements . . . which should be undertaken at times when there is need

[105]Congressional Record, 76th Congress, 1st Session, pp. 7282-7386; New York Times, June 13, 1939, p. 1, June 16, 1939, p. 2, June 17, 1939, p. 1.

[106]Quotation from Harold D. Smith, Memorandum of Conference with the President, May 12, 1939, Smith papers, FDR Library. See also Harold D. Smith, Memoranda of Conferences with the President, June 14, 1939 and June 30, 1939, Smith papers, FDR Library; Morgenthau Diary, vol. 195, pp. 310-313, FDR Library; John M. Carmody to James M. Mead, July 21, 1939, Reader File, vol. 1, FWA, Carmody papers, FDR Library; New York Times, June 14, 1939, p. 5; Rosenman, Public Papers and Addresses of FDR 8: 1939, pp. 70-74, 296.

[107]Morgenthau Diary, vol. 195, p. 218, FDR Library.

[108]Morgenthau Diary, vol. 197, pp. 296-301, FDR Library.

for a stimulus to employment. At such times the Federal Government should furnish funds for projects of
this kind at a low rate of interest, it being clearly
understood that the projects themselves shall be self-
liquidating and of such a nature as to furnish a maximum of employment per dollar of investment.

There seems no reason why there should not be
adopted as a permanent policy of the government the development and maintenance of a revolving fund fed from
the earnings of these government investments and used
to finance new projects at times when there is need of
extra stimulus to employment.

The President then outlined his 3.86 billion-dollar lending
program, broken down into seven categories: (1) non-Federal
public works, such as water works, sewage treatment plants,
bridges, hospitals, and other municipal projects; (2) self-
liquidating toll roads, including bridges, high-speed highways
and city by-passes; (3) railroad equipment purchase and leasing;
(4) rural electrification; (5) farm tenant loans for farm pur-
chases, rural rehabilitation, minor improvements and repairs;
(6) foreign loans for the purpose of promoting American trade;
(7) expansion of the public housing program.[109]

The letter served Roosevelt's purposes well. Not only had
he protected scarce work relief funds, he implied that Congress
was "busting the budget" by allocating money for PWA. In recom-
mending the substitution of his multi-billion dollar lending
plan for the modest public works appropriation, the President
assumed the guise of a fiscal conservative. Self-liquidating
projects, so Roosevelt argued, would hold down the deficit while
putting idle investment capital to productive use.[110]

The "revolving fund," an idea which Roosevelt had toyed
with since 1938, was the cleverest feature of his whole proposal.
If approved, the revolving fund would make permanent a number of
government operations whose existence had depended on yearly appropriations. The President, even as he tried to disarm his
critics, sought to place several New Deal programs beyond the
reach of Congress.[111]

Roosevelt promised to send his proposal to Capitol Hill just
as soon as appropriate legislation could be drafted. Initially,

---

[109] Rosenman, Public Papers and Addresses of FDR 8: 1939,
pp. 372-375.

[110] Rosenman, Public Papers and Addresses of FDR 8: 1939,
p. 372. See also Morgenthau Diary, vol. 155, pp. 238-288, FDR
Library.

[111] See Charles W. Eliot, Memorandum for the Advisory Com-
mittee, March 14, 1938, Fiscal and Monetary Advisory Board 766,
Records of NRPB, Record Group 187, National Archives; and Milo
Perkins to Aubrey Williams, n.d., box 3, Williams papers, FDR
Library.

Treasury Department lawyers drew up three separate pieces of
legislation: a Federal Revenue Finance Corporation Bill, a
Rural Security and Electrification Financing Corporation Bill,
and a United States Construction Corporation Bill. But Congressional leaders considered three separate bills, in addition to
the public housing measure already pending in Congress, too
cumbersome. They pleaded with the President to reduce the
legislation to the smallest possible dimensions. Complying with
that request, Treasury counsel Ed Foley combined the three bills
into a multi-purpose measure,the Self-Liquidating Projects Bill,
which would establish a United States Works and Finance Authority to sell government-guaranteed bonds and make loans for the
various self-liquidating enterprises.[112]

The intractable head of the Reconstruction Finance Corporation, Jesse H. Jones, vigorously opposed the finance authority provision. Jones was an anomaly among New Dealers. A
wealthy Houston businessman, with banking, real estate, and publishing interests, he had long been a force in Texas and national Democratic politics. In 1932, at the urging of John
Nance Garner and Pat Harrison, President Hoover appointed him
to the board of directors of the RFC. Roosevelt made Jones
chairman, and he transformed the corporation into a flexible
instrument of state capitalism. Under his direction, RFC extended billions of dollars in loans to banks, railroads, insurance companies, and industries. By 1939, Jones ruled a financial fiefdom. He expanded his already excellent business connections by placing loyal subordinates in business and law firms
all over the country.[113]

Influence with the business community was one source of
Jones' political strength. The other was his harmonious relationship with Congress. Jones assiduously cultivated good will
on Capitol Hill. He dispensed valuable favors, mainly in the
form of RFC loans to deserving constituents of senior Congressmen. Because he ran the RFC on a non-partisan basis, he maintained friendly relations with the Republicans. A skillful
lobbyist, Jones spent a great deal of time in Capitol cloakrooms
and became adept at manipulating House and Senate committees.

---

[112]Morgenthau Diary, vol. 197, pp. 13, 28-30, vol. 198,
pp. 285-287, vol. 201, p. 253-A, FDR Library; Harold D. Smith,
Memorandum of Conference with the President, June 23, 1939,
Smith papers, FDR Library; James H. Rowe to E. M. Watson, June
12, 1939, President's Official File 2694, FDR papers, FDR
Library.

[113]Bascom N. Timmons, Jesse H. Jones: The Man and the
Statesman (New York, 1956), pp. 36-37, 59, 64, 66-73, 78, 116-
117, 122; Jones, Fifty Billion Dollars, pp. 1-254, 512-513,
602-608; Arthur M. Schlesinger, Jr., The Coming of the New Deal
(Cambridge, Mass., 1965), pp. 425-426.

The attention he lavished on Congress paid off in prestige and power. Republicans, renegade and orthodox Democrats trusted him as they did no other administrator in the government.[114]

Though Jones worked for Roosevelt, on occasion the head of the RFC acted like a rebellious baron who presumed to negotiate as an equal with his nominal suzerain. As one observer noted, "Mr. Jones . . . in dealing with . . . [the] President developed forgetfulness as a fine art." Half of Roosevelt's orders, Jones simply ignored. To be sure, such insubordination had its uses-- Jones wisely turned down White House requests to furnish RFC loans to Roosevelt backers--but in matters of public policy it proved troublesome, especially since Jones never accepted the goals of the New Deal.[115]

The chairman of RFC, both an architect and beneficiary of the status quo, had little sympathy for the underdog, and he disapproved of the President's tax, labor, relief, and social security policies. His ideological allies were such enemies of the New Deal as Senators Walter F. George (D., Ga.) and Robert A. Taft (R., O.). Like them, he believed it was time for the government to curtail its involvement in the private economy. New Deal activists often complained that Jones sabotaged the Administration from within, by obstructing lending for recovery.[116]

Jones viewed with suspicion any effort to supplant his domination of RFC. When Roosevelt designated him to head the newly-created Federal Loan Agency, Jones declined to accept the job until permitted to retain supervision of RFC. He feared that the President was trying to "kick him upstairs." In the same manner, he interpreted the new recovery plan as an effort to take government lending away from his prudent management. He raised one objection after another until Roosevelt finally allowed him to alter the Self-Liquidating Projects Bill to his own liking.[117]

---

[114]Timmons, Jones, pp. 243-244, 258-259, 263-265; Jones, Fifty Billion Dollars, pp. 9, 28; John H. Crider, The Bureaucrat (Philadelphia, 1944), p. 245; Schlesinger, Coming of the New Deal, p. 431. See also materials in boxes 65-73, Jones papers, Library of Congress.

[115]Quotation from Daniels, Frontier on the Potomac, pp. 31-32. See also Graham, Toward A Planned Society, p. 48; and Richard F. Fenno, "President-Cabinet Relations: A Pattern and a Case Study," American Political Science Review LII (1958), pp. 388-405.

[116]Timmons, Jones, pp. 273-274; Kenneth Crawford, "Jones Believed Kicked Upstairs," New York Post, June 24, 1939, box 97, Carmody papers, FDR Library; Aubrey Williams, "The New Deal," n.d., p. 86, box 44, Williams papers, FDR Library.

[117]Timmons, Jones, pp. 274-275; Kenneth Crawford, "Jones Believed Kicked Upstairs," New York Post, June 24, 1939, box 97,

Jones insisted on joint Federal Loan Agency-Reconstruction Finance Corporation control of lending. Secretary Morgenthau, Harry White, and Ed Foley warned that giving control to Jones would emasculate the bill. In the end, the President acceded to Jones' demands in order to enhance the chances of the bill in Congress. On matters within Jones' competence, like government lending, he could sway some ten votes in the Senate and forty votes in the House. Those votes might be crucial to passage of the bill.[118]

Ignoring the protests of the Treasury Department, Jones and RFC counsel Claude Hamilton rewrote the Self-Liquidating Projects Bill. They excised the section establishing a U.S. Works and Finance Authority and gave RFC responsibility for financing the program. Jones claimed that his changes were made "only to help to get the bill through." He argued that Congress would never enact the program unless RFC handled the money. To soothe Morgenthau's hurt feelings, Jones promised, "the way we've got this thing . . . I believe it will go through with . . . very little trouble, Henry."[119]

In spite of Jones' assurances, the Administration was headed for a difficult struggle on Capitol Hill. During the previous five months, Congress had been relatively quiescent. Early in the session, however, the bipartisan opposition, joined by disgruntled orthodox Democrats, had cut the President's supplemental work relief request from $875,000,000 to $725,000,000. That defeat had little lasting significance, but it revealed Roosevelt's vulnerability, should the orthodox Democrats defect to the opposition.[120]

Carmody papers, FDR Library; Morgenthau Diary, vol. 201, pp. 288-298, vol. 202, p. 68, FDR Library; Thomas G. Corcoran to President, September 25, 1939, President's Secretary File 139, FDR papers, FDR Library; Adolf A. Berle, Diary, June 26, 1939, box 210, Berle papers, FDR Library; Jones, Fifty Billion Dollars, pp. 530-533; Blum, Years of Urgency, pp. 40-41.

[118]Morgenthau Diary, vol. 152, pp. 130-131, vol. 201, pp. 288-298, 300, 310, 338-341, 349-350, vol. 202, pp. 67-68, FDR Library; "Notes on RFC," box 98, Carmody papers, FDR Library; editorial, Washington News, July 11, 1939, box 262, Jones papers, Library of Congress; Schlesinger, Coming of the New Deal, p. 431.

[119]Quotations from Morgenthau Diary, vol. 202, pp. 12-14, FDR Library. See also Hamilton to Jones, July 6, 1939, box 198, Jones papers, Library of Congress; and Morgenthau Diary, vol. 201, pp. 289-290, vol. 202, pp. 66-20, 66-21, 66-22, 66-23, 66-24, FDR Library.

[120]Congressional Record, 76th Congress, 1st Session, pp. 288-343; Morgenthau Diary, vol. 152, pp. 146-155, FDR Library; Rosenman, Public Papers and Addresses of FDR 8: 1939, pp. 54-59; New York Times, January 15, 1939, p. 34; Byrnes, All in One

Since that setback in January, the Administration and the Congressional opposition had fought a series of skirmishes without decisive result. The President had nominated and obtained confirmation of several New Deal disciples, including Harry Hopkins as Secretary of Commerce, Frank Murphy as Attorney General, Felix Frankfurter and William O. Douglas as Supreme Court Justices, and James P. Pope as TVA director. The only nomination to fail was that of Thomas R. Amlie to a position on the Interstate Commerce Commission. Amlie, a former Progressive Party Congressman from Wisconsin, held left-of-center views unacceptable to a majority of Senators. When it became obvious that orthodox Democrats would join Republicans and renegades in opposition to Amlie, Roosevelt withdrew the nomination.[121]

The President's outstanding legislative victory occurred in March, with the passage of the Executive Reorganization Act. In the Senate, the Harrison-Byrnes faction of orthodox Democrats provided the margin of victory over the opposition. Likewise, the orthodox Democrats in the House voted with their party and enabled the Administration to prevail.[122]

On the other hand, Roosevelt lost another battle over relief funds when the House reduced a second supplemental request from $150,000,000 to $100,000,000. That cut resulted from a rift between urban and rural Democrats. In the past, the two blocs had log-rolled relief funds and farm subsidy payments through the House but now they were quarreling over appropriations. In the Senate, New Deal forces led by Senator Claude Pepper (D., Fla.) attempted to restore the $50,000,000 to the relief appropriation. But the Byrnes-Harrison faction again defected to the bipartisan opposition of Republicans and

---

Lifetime, p. 87; Patterson, Congressional Conservatism, pp.294-298. For Senate roll call vote on the supplemental work relief appropriation, see Appendix II, Guttman scaling table 4, item 8; and Congressional Record, 76th Congress, 1st Session, p. 887.

[121]Joseph P. Harris, The Advice and Consent of the Senate (Berkeley, Calif., 1953), pp. 133-134, 139-145; Patterson, Congressional Conservatism, p. 299; New York Times, March 2, 1939, p. 2. For Senate roll call votes on confirmations, see Appendix II, Guttman scaling table 1, item 9 and Guttman scaling table 2, item 20; and Congressional Record, 76th Congress, 1st Session, pp. 429, 629, 3788.

[122]Patterson, Congressional Conservatism, pp. 299-302. For Congressional roll call votes on executive reorganization, see Appendix I, Guttman scaling table 1, items 19, 67, 75 and Appendix II, Guttman scaling table 1, items 20, 26; and Congressional Record, 76th Congress, 1st Session, pp. 2502-2505, 3050-3051, 3092-3093, 3104-3105.

renegade Democrats, and the Senate sustained the House action.[123]

Orthodox Democrats also played a central role in eliminating the undistributed profits tax. The President regarded the measure as a symbol of his commitment to more equitable taxation. Senate Finance Committee Chairman Harrison took a different view. Echoing the criticism of the business community, Harrison argued that the tax was an irritant and deterrent to private enterprise and ought to be discarded. In May, after weeks of executive-legislative wrangling, Roosevelt grudgingly allowed Harrison and House Ways and Means Chairman Doughton to have their way.[124]

As the tax dispute illustrated, the division over recovery methods remained deep. The Administration, unwilling to rely on the business community, still emphasized compensatory lending and spending. Republicans, renegade and orthodox Democrats favored business appeasement and fiscal conservatism. The Self-Liquidating Projects Bill was caught in that crossfire of conflicting purposes.[125]

The new recovery plan, Roosevelt realized, would encounter obstinate resistance from hostile Congressional factions. Republicans and renegade Democrats attacked the scheme in vitriolic terms. Senator Taft described it as "dangerous" and "immoral," while Representative John Taber (R., N.Y.) said that the President's proposal was "a subterfuge to break down the Budget Act and to evade the statutory limitation on the public debt." It was "nothing but another gigantic spending plan, pure and simple. . . ."[126] More ominous was the attitude of the orthodox Democrats. At a meeting of Roosevelt and Congressional leaders on June 23, Senator Harrison could scarcely conceal his distaste for the program. Vice President Garner thought "This bill in some particulars is the worst that has come up here." Senator

---

[123] Patterson, Congressional Conservatism, pp. 302-305. For Senate roll call vote on the second supplemental work relief appropriation, see Appendix II, Guttman scaling table 3, item 9; and Congressional Record, 76th Congress, 1st Session, p. 4109.

[124] New York Times, May 13, 1939, p. 1, May 16, 1939, p. 1; Blum, Years of Urgency, pp. 21-30.

[125] Leon Henderson to President, June 23, 1939, President's Secretary's File 150, FDR papers, FDR Library.

[126] Robert A. Taft, speech notes, n.d., box 717, Spend-Lend 1939, Taft papers, Library of Congress; John Taber, "Comment on the Latest Roosevelt Spending Program," June 23, 1939, box 63, Taber papers, Cornell University Library.

Byrnes reluctantly supported the plan, but he ducked responsibility for managing the bill on the Senate floor.[127]

Further difficulties arose during the two weeks of negotiations with Jesse Jones over the final shape of the Self-Liquidating Projects Bill. The delay allowed Congressional resistance to solidify. On July 10, Representative Lindsay Warren (D., N.C.), a usually dependable orthodox Democrat, announced his opposition to the program. Senator Robert F. Wagner (D., N.Y.), the loyal New Dealer whose Banking and Currency Committee would hold hearings on the bill, warned that Congressional tempers were short and prospects for success not good.[128]

Off to a shaky start, the Self-Liquidating Projects Bill needed the Administration's unequivocal support. Jesse Jones, the "big man" on Capitol Hill, had pledged full cooperation. Morgenthau, however, did not trust him and advised the President to demand obedience from his Loan Administrator. Roosevelt did so, and Jones promised to lobby for the bill, to "shuffle around" on the hill, as he put it.[129]

Nevertheless, the Loan Administrator lacked enthusiasm for the President's plan. Although he had been permitted to modify the bill, Jones still considered the proposed legislation unnecessary, unwise, and an implicit criticism of his past performance as head of RFC. Soon there were disturbing indications that Jones was quietly undermining the Self-Liquidating Projects Bill.[130] On July 13, Jones, Morgenthau, and John Carmody, director of the new Federal Works Agency, held a private session to prepare for press conferences and Congressional testimony on the lending measure. At this meeting, Jones betrayed his real feelings and disparaged the program. Carmody, a fervent New Dealer who was more honest than tactful, accused Jones of

---

[127] Quotation from Timmons, _Garner of Texas_, pp. 243-245. See also Morgenthau Diary, vol. 198, pp. 285-287, FDR Library; and Harold D. Smith, Memorandum of Conference with the President, June 23, 1939, Smith papers, FDR Library.

[128] Morgenthau Diary, vol. 202, pp. 150-152, FDR Library; _New York Times_, July 11, 1939, p. 1, July 12, 1939, p. 2, July 13, 1939, p. 1; Patterson, _Congressional Conservatism_, pp. 318-319.

[129] Morgenthau Diary, vol. 202, pp. 58-59, 144-161, vol. 203, pp. 32-38, FDR Library.

[130] Morgenthau Diary, vol. 203, pp. 34, 38, FDR Library; Blum, _Years of Urgency_, p. 40; Stein, _Fiscal Revolution_, p. 121.

disloyalty to the President, of reactionary leanings, and of calculated duplicity.[131]

The following day, Jones showed that Carmody's charges were not unwarranted. In his testimony before the Senate Banking and Currency Committee, Jones damaged the bill's chances for passage. Ed Foley, the Treasury's legislative liaison, reported:

> . . . Jesse Jones' testimony . . . hurt the bill materially and it is now definitely in trouble. While Jones stated he was in sympathy with the general objectives of the bill, it was obvious from his manner and intonation that he was critical of many of its features. While the record will not disclose hostile statements on Mr. Jones' part, nevertheless his attitude toward the bill was deprecatory.[132]

Jones, a master of the art of saying one thing and meaning another, had communicated his feelings without being openly critical. As Foley said,

> every newspaperman in the room knew that Jones was opposed to the legislation. . . . every man on the Committee knows when Jones is in favor of anything and every man on the Committee knows when Jones is against something, by his attitude; he's down there all the time, it's Jones' Committee.

Jones had wiped out the positive effect of three previous witnesses. A reporter for the New York Times summed up the impact of his testimony: "Somebody's got to come down and bail this out or it will never pass."[133]

At the same time, the President's proposal was under assault from a different direction. Those Congressmen interested in a pork-barrel public works program considered the lending plan undesirable. They had an ally in Harold Ickes, the truculent head of the Public Works Administration, who thought the

---

[131]Drew Pearson, "Merry-Go-Round," July 14, 1939, box 19, Jones papers, Library of Congress; Morgenthau Diary, vol. 203, pp. 143-144, FDR Library.

[132]Morgenthau Diary, vol. 203, pp. 101-102, FDR Library. For Jones' testimony, see U.S., Congress, Senate, Committee on Banking and Currency, Works Financing Act of 1939, Hearings before the Committee on Banking and Currency, 76th Congress, 1st Session, 1939, pp. 87-109.

[133]Morgenthau Diary, vol. 203, pp. 242-245, FDR Library. See also James M. Mead to President, July 22, 1939, and E. M. Watson to Jones, July 26, 1939, President's Official File 3732, FDR papers, FDR Library.

lending bill was "cockeyed." Ickes, and other New Dealers who shared his opinion, privately belittled the self-liquidating projects measure as a dubious hybrid, "splending," and wished instead for another PWA appropriation.[134]

Marriner Eccles and Lauchlin Currie also looked favorably on a new PWA appropriation, which they viewed as a supplement to the lending bill. Congress, however, would be unlikely to approve both the lending program and a new PWA appropriation. On July 14, Representative Joseph Starnes (D., Ala.), an orthodox Democrat who led the pork barrel forces in the House, introduced a bill appropriating $350,000,000 for PWA. The Starnes Bill undercut the President's plan. It attracted Democrats who could see little political advantage in self-liquidating projects, but who "hoped to capitalize in the next election on direct federal grants for public works."[135]

At this juncture, the fate of the Self-Liquidating Projects Bill, assailed by Jones and the Congressional opposition from the right, by Ickes and other spenders from the left, and by Starnes' pork-hungry Congressmen, appeared highly uncertain. To make matters worse, the Administration found it difficult to arouse public support for the plan. According to public opinion polls, a majority of the American people favored an end to deficit spending and lending. The press and the business lobbies, almost uniformly hostile to the President's proposal, applauded the public's attitude.[136]

---

[134]Harold D. Smith, Memorandum of Conference with the President, June 16, 1939, Smith papers, FDR Library; Morgenthau Diary, vol. 204, pp. 117-118, FDR Library; Robert W. Hartley to H. H. Waite, July 21, 1939, Central Office Correspondence 146, Records of NRPB, Record Group 187, National Archives; John Carmody to James M. Mead, July 21, 1939, Reader File, vol. 1, FWA, Carmody papers, FDR Library; Boyd Fisher to John Carmody, August 7, 1939, box 56, Carmody papers, FDR Library; Ickes, Diary II, pp. 657-658; Berle and Jacobs, Navigating the Rapids, p. 235; New York Times, June 27, 1939, p. 6.

[135]Quotation from Blum, Years of Urgency, p. 40. See also Currie to President, July 17, 1939, President's Official File 3719, FDR papers, FDR Library; Morgenthau Diary, vol. 204, p. 150, FDR Library; New York Times, July 15, 1939, p. 16.

[136]New York Times, July 16, 1939, p. 9, July 24, 1939, p. 2, July 31, 1939, p. 2; John C. Gebhart, "Spending-Lending--Theory and Practice," July 31, 1939, box 716, Spend-Lend, 1938-40, Taft papers, Library of Congress; Committee of Utility Executives, "Use of 'Self-Liquidating' Funds to Subsidize Government Competition with Private Enterprise," July 17, 1939, box 717, Spend-Lend-For the Floor (1939), Taft papers, Library of Congress; Morgenthau Diary, vol. 197, pp. 153, 155, FDR Library; Stein, Fiscal Revolution, pp. 117-118.

Congress, meanwhile, approached open rebellion against the President. On July 20, the opposition in the House of Representatives passed a resolution authorizing a hostile investigation of the National Labor Relations Board, an action that underscored the President's diminished influence on Capitol Hill.[137] That same day, Senate majority leader Alben Barkley removed the phrase "self-liquidating projects" from the title of the measure, which now became the Works Financing Bill of 1939. That change was intended to quiet Senator Taft and others who charged that many of the projects contemplated under the program were not truly self-liquidating. The substitute also omitted the provision for a revolving fund, the most controversial part of the bill because it would have by-passed the appropriations process. Further, the revised version of the bill deleted a section on railroad equipment that would have allowed the government to determine designs and specifications. The railroads, seeing another step toward eventual nationalization, had objected to that provision.[138]

By rewriting the bill, Barkley disarmed some of the criticism in the Banking and Currency Committee and ensured that the measure would be favorably reported to the Senate. As Taft admitted on July 20, Barkley had removed about half of the "outrageous things" in the President's program.[139] Opposition members of the Banking and Currency Committee still pressed for reductions in all authorizations called for in the program. Senators Barkley and Wagner conceded a $250,000,000 cut in the toll highways and bridges section.[140]

Aided by the President and the Treasury Department, Administration leaders deflected other efforts to eviscerate the measure.[141] On July 22, the Banking and Currency Committee reported

---

[137]New York Times, July 20, 1939, pp. 1-2, July 21, 1939, pp. 1-2, July 22, 1939, p. 6; Patterson, Congressional Conservatism, pp. 316-318. For House roll call votes on the NLRB investigation, see Appendix I, Guttman scaling table 2, items 9, 11; and Congressional Record, 76th Congress, 1st Session, pp. 9592-9593.

[138]See copies of S. 2759, Self-Liquidating Projects Bill of 1939, and S. 2864, Works Financing Act of 1939, box 717, Spend-Lend, 1938-1940, Taft papers, Library of Congress. See also Morgenthau Diary, vol. 203, p. 33, vol. 204, pp. 198-215, FDR Library; New York Times, July 20, 1939, pp. 1-2, July 21, 1939, p. 18; Timmons, Garner of Texas, p. 244; and Stein, Fiscal Revolution, p. 122.

[139]New York Times, July 21, 1939, p. 2.

[140]New York Times, July 22, 1939, p. 1.

[141]Morgenthau Diary, vol. 204, pp. 185-187, 198-215, FDR Library; New York Times, July 23, 1939, p. 1.

the Works Financing Bill to the Senate. Wagner, justifiably proud that he had steered the bill through, told Secretary Morgenthau, "I don't think you could have gotten it out of every committee. . . . Finances would [not] have reported it for you. . . . At least Pat Harrison didn't think so."[142]

On July 25, the Senate began consideration of the Works Financing Bill. Barkley warned his colleagues that Congress would not be permitted to adjourn until it had decided the issue "one way or the other." The opposition could not talk the bill to death, but would have to go on record and take full responsibility. Evidently, that was the strategy the President wanted his legislative leaders to follow.[143]

The opposition accepted the challenge. When Barkley opened debate, he encountered fierce criticism. After a stubborn defense of Roosevelt, the New Deal and the Works Financing Bill, Barkley left the field to the Democratic renegades and the Republicans. For two days, they castigated the Administration's fiscal policy.[144]

Senator Byrd covered the main points in the opposition's indictment. The Works Financing Bill, he charged, was a clever New Deal trick to circumvent the statutory national debt limit. Citing Jesse Jones' testimony before the Banking and Currency Committee, he asserted, "there is going to be a large loss from the government lending corporations," and "those losses will have to be transferred to the direct debt." Therefore, Byrd declared, "this scheme is nothing more than a spending scheme masquerading as a lending scheme.[145]

Byrd then attacked compensatory fiscal policy, "the experiment of spending ourselves into prosperity on borrowed money." It was a policy, said Byrd, that would end in national disaster. Senator Taft agreed. "Lending is exactly as bad as spending," he said, because it would have the same effect in destroying business confidence. Only the hope of profits could bring

[142] Morgenthau Diary, vol. 205, p. 205, FDR Library. See also Huthmacher, Wagner, pp. 257-258.

[143] Congressional Record, 76th Congress, 1st Session, pp. 9930-9938; New York Times, July 26, 1939, pp. 1-2. See also Rosenman, Public Papers and Addresses of FDR 8: 1939, pp. 402-403.

[144] Congressional Record, 76th Congress, 1st Session, pp. 10010-10032, 10037-10084, 10138-10159.

[145] Congressional Record, 76th Congress, 1st Session, pp. 9934, 10038.

recovery, and there could be no expectation of profit as long as the government pursued unsound policies.[146]

The Works Financing Bill would exacerbate the nation's economic problems, Taft alleged, because it would subsidize competition with private banks, utilities, railroads, and commercial farmers. Business and agriculture faced the problem of excessive supply for shrunken markets. Rural electrification, the farm tenancy program, road construction and government banking would, so he argued, create more surplus capacity while actually reducing the private sector's share of the market.[147]

Shifting to another theme, opposition leaders questioned the need for the Works Financing Bill. Economic conditions did not require such a program, Senator Warren Barbour (R., N.J.) asserted. Therefore, "political considerations" must "have inspired the measure." The Works Financing Bill, he charged, was a gigantic Presidential pork barrel for 1940, "a bill to slip another ace into the deck of the New Deal. . . . We all know that the President is motivated by the approach of the 1940 election."[148]

Other opposition spokesmen complained that Roosevelt was once again treating Congress like a rubber stamp. Senator John Townsend (R., Del.) reminded his colleagues, "for seven consecutive sessions the Congress has been told what is must legislation--what must pass before it may adjourn." Senator Millard Tydings (D., Md.) urged Congress to protect its Constitutional authority against encroachment by the Chief Executive. The Works Financing Bill, he said, "involves indirect appropriations and takes away from the appropriations committee the power to act." It would establish a "double budget and double debt system which are most dangerous."[149]

---

[146]Congressional Record, 76th Congress, 1st Session, pp. 10038, 10042, 10071.

[147]Congressional Record, 76th Congress, 1st Session, p. 10023. See also "The Farm Tenant Provisions of H.R. 7120," "The Rural Electrification Administration and the Self-Liquidating Projects Act of 1939," and "S. 2759 and H.R. 7120, Introduced in Congress to Provide for Financing and Constructing Self-Liquidating Projects, and for Other Purposes," box 716, Spend-Lend, 1938-40, Taft papers, Library of Congress; and Robert A. Taft, transcript of speech, July 14, 1939, box 1252, Taft papers, Library of Congress.

[148]Congressional Record, 76th Congress, 1st Session, p. 10071; New York Times, July 11, 1939, p. 1. See also Timmons, Garner of Texas, p. 263.

[149]Quotations from Congressional Record, 76th Congress, 1st Session, pp. 10029, 10048; and Patterson, Congressional

The opposition, clinching its case, insisted that the bill was an all-out assault on capitalism. Senator Taft referred to Adolf Berle's statement before the TNEC on May 23 as proof that the Administration desired state socialism. The Works Financing Bill, Taft said, would result in government nationalization of investment. "There is no doubt in my mind that the continued extension of Government lending leads inevitably to a totalitarian state in which the Government directs the commerce and industry and agriculture." Senator George, in a passionate appeal, urged the Senate to block this plan:

> I am against the bill. I do not care if some of its purposes are good; I do not care if I personally favor some of its purposes; I stand eternally against the entire movement [toward state socialism]. I set my face now sternly against the whole trend. . . .[150]

That statement reflected the mood of many Congressmen, Democrats as well as Republicans. The opposition, which neither understood nor accepted compensatory fiscal policy, doubted the feasibility of the Keynesian "hybrid society" toward which the New Deal seemed to be moving. The choice, in their view, was either to allow private capitalism to achieve recovery or to succumb to socialism.[151]

Speaking on behalf of the Administration, Senator Pepper rejected that reasoning. The limited purposes of the Works Financing Bill, he said, were to make further direct spending for public works unnecessary and, by raising national income, eventually to balance the budget. "I thought the lending bill was intended by the Administration to get away from the appropriation of Federal money and to let private enterprise, which would be the beneficiaries of these loans, try to bring back prosperity in a legitimate and usual way." What objection, Pepper wondered, could the opposition have to such a policy?[152]

Conservatism, p. 319. See also Harold W. Metz to Robert A. Taft, July 18, 1939, and "Memorandum on Constitutionality of Senate Bill 2864," box 716, Spend-Lend (S. 2759, Barkley Act), Taft papers, Library of Congress.

[150] Quotations from _Congressional Record_, 76th Congress, 1st Session, pp. 10064, 10158.

[151] _Congressional Record_, 76th Congress, 1st Session, p. 10070. See also Hansen, _Full Recovery or Stagnation?_, p. 8; Stein, _Fiscal Revolution_, pp. 89-90, 122-123; and Harrison Boyd Summers and Robert E. Summers, eds., _Planned Economy_ (New York, 1940), pp. 64-65.

[152] _Congressional Record_, 76th Congress, 1st Session, p. 10041.

One objection opposition spokesmen preferred not to state
openly. They, no less than Roosevelt and the New Dealers, were
thinking of the 1940 election. As Edmund E. Lincoln, a conservative economist for E. I. DuPont de Nemours & Co., advised
Senator Taft, "only the continuance of heavy government spending
can keep the radical political faction in power." Obstruction
of the President's program, he believed, offered the best chance
of defeating the New Deal in 1940.[153]

The first important vote on the Works Financing Bill came
on July 27 when Senator Byrd submitted an amendment to eliminate
from the bill the $500,000,000 authorization for public roads
construction. Some orthodox Democrats, like Senator Pat McCarran (D., Nev.), objected to toll roads. Others, like Senator
Alva Adams (D., Colo.), wanted to reduce the program to the
smallest possible dimensions. Twelve orthodox Democrats joined
the Republicans and the Democratic renegades, but on this vote,
Administration supporters defeated the amendment, 38 to 40.
Their victory was shortlived, for on the following day, Senator
Frederick Van Nuys (D., Ind.) moved to reconsider the vote re-
jecting the Byrd amendment. The motion carried, and the opposition, strengthened by additional Republican votes, eliminated the public roads provision, 42 to 38.[154]

Next the opposition attacked the $500,000,000 authoriza-
tion for railroad equipment loans. Senator Burton K. Wheeler
(D., Mont.) argued that this part of the bill was unnecessary,
because the RFC could already lend to the railroads. "The
Reconstruction Finance Corporation now has the money," he said,
"and it can make loans . . . for the purpose of buying new
equipment." Wheeler convinced ten orthodox Democrats and
three usually reliable New Deal senators, Homer T. Bone (D.,
Wash.), George W. Norris (Ind., Neb.) and Harry S Truman (D.,
Mo.). They assisted the opposition in removing the railroad
equipment provision by a vote of 45 to 32.[155]

---

[153] Edmund E. Lincoln, "Federal Spending, Industrial Production, and Wholesale Prices," box 717, Spend-Lend--For the
Floor (1939), Taft papers, Library of Congress; E. A. Rumely
to Frank E. Gannett, June 24, 1939, box 12, Gannett papers,
Cornell University Library; Patterson, Congressional Conservatism, p. 320.

[154] Congressional Record, 76th Congress, 1st Session, pp.
10179, 10297. See also "Proposed Amendments to S. 2864," n.d.,
box 717, Spend-Lend, 1938-, Taft papers, Library of Congress;
and New York Times, July 29, 1939, pp. 1, 3. For Senate roll
call votes on Byrd amendment, see Appendix II, Guttman scaling
table 1, items 22, 28, 29.

[155] Congressional Record, 76th Congress, 1st Session, p.
10336. For Senate roll call vote on Wheeler amendment, see
Congressional Record, 76th Congress, 1st Session, p. 10349.

Moving on, members of the opposition demanded passage of
an amendment expressly prohibiting government lending for projects competitive with private enterprise. Senator John Danaher
(R., Conn.) submitted a proviso so restrictive that it would
have made the program impossible to administer. Loyal Democrats fought off that attempt to emasculate the bill, but then
acquiesced in a more moderate amendment offered by Senator
Joseph O'Mahoney (D., Wyo.).[156]

On July 31, the President's adversaries made their last
significant effort to destroy the Works Financing Bill. Senator
Edward R. Burke (D., Neb.), one of the Democratic renegades, offered an amendment requiring specific Congressional approval of
every loan made under the bill. As Senator Barkley observed,
"if the amendment of the Senator from Nebraska should be adopted
. . . we might as well strike out all after the enacting clause."
The faction of orthodox Democrats joined Administration loyalists to defeat the Burke amendment.[157]

That outcome foreshadowed passage of the bill. The orthodox Democrats, satisfied with cuts and restrictions written
into the measure, no longer disapproved. Consequently, the
maximum strength mustered by Republicans and renegade Democrats
fell short of the number needed to defeat the Administration.
On July 31, the Senate passed the Works Financing Bill, 52 to
38.[158]

The bill that emerged from the Senate differed materially
from the one Barkley had introduced. That measure called for
$2.8 billion in loans, already a lesser sum than the $3.06
billion the President had proposed when he announced the program
on June 21. (The remainder of Roosevelt's original $3.86 bil-
lion lending plan was contained in an $800,000,000 housing bill
that had already passed the Senate.) By voting with Republicans and renegade Democrats on public roads and railroad equipment loans, the orthodox Democrats had deleted those sections
and reduced the total loan authorization to slightly more than
$1.6 billion. The orthodox Democrats left intact the public
works, farm security, and rural electrification provisions,
made a few other minor changes, and added $90,000,000 intended

---

[156]Congressional Record, 76th Congress, 1st Session,
p. 10435.

[157]Congressional Record, 76th Congress, 1st Session,
p. 10497. For Senate roll call vote on the Burke amendment,
see Appendix II, Guttman scaling table 1, item 14; and Congressional Record, 76th Congress, 1st Session, p. 10500.

[158]Congressional Record, 76th Congress, 1st Session,
p. 10512. For Senate roll call vote on passage of the Works
Financing Bill of 1939, see Appendix II, Guttman scaling
table 1, item 12.

for reclamation projects in the western United States. In effect, they transformed the bill into a public works and farm
program, which they were willing to support.[159]

Administration leaders considered Senate alterations de-
bilitating but hoped the entire recovery package might yet be
saved. They were counting on the House version of the bill,
which had suffered cuts in committee but had not been mutilated
as in the Senate. Ed Foley, acting as the Treasury's legislative liaison, explained the Administration's strategy:

> I don't think that we're in bad shape in the House.
> [Banking Committee Chairman] Steagall says . . . he
> won't have any trouble on the floor with this bill.
> So if he passes the bill the way he's reported it out
> . . . I think we'll go with the bill to a friendly
> conference, because Byrnes and Wagner and Barkley
> will be the Senate conferees for the majority--maybe
> Adams, maybe the four of them--so we'll have three out
> of the four Democrats Administration supporters, and
> I think we'll be able to fix the bill up pretty much
> in conference, and it will be so near the end of the
> session and they'll be so tired and anxious to get
> away that they'll agree to anything the conferees
> bring back. I don't think there will be a fight on
> the conference report.[160]

The success of Foley's strategy depended on winning House
approval of the lending bill. That, in spite of Representative
Steagall's optimism, looked unlikely. The House Democratic
steering committee had already warned of a "tide of opposition
to the measure." Other Administration supporters predicted
solid Republican resistance and reported that a large number of
Democrats showed "signs of being deflected" from support of the
President. Many members of the House, while not openly critical, could generate little enthusiasm for Roosevelt's program.
In their eyes, it lacked glamour, and they did not consider it
worth a protracted struggle. They wanted to dispose of the bill
quickly and go home.[161]

---

[159] New York Times, August 1, 1939, pp. 1, 10; Congressional
Record, 76th Congress, 1st Session, p. 11022; Patterson, Congressional Conservatism, p. 321.

[160] Morgenthau Diary, vol. 205, pp. 275-276, FDR Library.

[161] Quotations from Morgenthau Diary, vol. 204, p. 182, FDR
Library; and Nathan Straus to President, n.d., President's Official File 2694, FDR papers, FDR Library. See also James H.
Rowe to President, July 31, 1939, President's Official File
2694, FDR papers, FDR Library; Morgenthau Diary, vol. 203, pp.
20-21, FDR Library; and Patterson, Congressional Conservatism,
p. 319.

Some House Democrats still hoped to substitute a PWA appropriation for the lending bill. On July 25, spokesmen for pork barrel forces in the House urged Morgenthau to support the Starnes Bill, "a $350,000,000 PWA appropriation to be used on a 30 percent grant basis." Representatives Starnes (D., Ala.), Beam (D., Ill.) and Ford (D., Calif.) emphasized the election-year advantage of PWA grants. The political situation in their communities, they said, "would be bad if no PWA appropriation were forthcoming." Starnes claimed the House would pass the public works appropriation "in a minute if the President would approve it." On the other hand, "self-liquidating projects were not popular," and Starnes was "not sure that the votes could be found in the House to pass the Self-Liquidating Bill."[162]

Ignoring that threat, Morgenthau refused to support another PWA appropriation that would enlarge the deficit. Clinging to the self-liquidating formula, he subsequently announced at a press conference, "We are against [the Starnes public works bill]. . . . we are for the self-liquidating bill." Morgenthau's statement antagonized Starnes and other PWA advocates and further aggravated Democratic dissension in the House.[163]

Faced with an imminent collapse of party discipline, the House leadership redoubled efforts to rally Democratic members behind the Administration. On July 26, the Democratic steering committee discussed ways to overcome opposition to the lending bill. On July 28, the House Democratic caucus adopted a resolution pledging "continued support of and devotion to the great social and economic program" of the President.[164] That gesture, designed to inspire a united Democratic front, accomplished nothing. Democratic renegades continued to work closely with Republicans. By the end of July, the House had drifted almost completely out of control.[165]

In a last-minute effort to avert defeat, Administration leaders made deals with uncommitted Congressmen and exerted pressure on the recalcitrant. They associated the $1.95

---

[162]Morgenthau Diary, vol. 205, pp. 47-48, 51-52, FDR Library.

[163]New York Times, July 25, 1939, p. 1. See also Stephen T. Early to Harvey M. Smith, October 6, 1939, President's Official File 3744, FDR papers, FDR Library; and Adolf A. Berle, Diary, August 7, 1939, box 210, Berle papers, FDR Library.

[164]New York Times, July 29, 1939, pp. 1-2.

[165]New York Times, July 30, 1939, pp. 1, 3, July 31, 1939, p. 1, August 1, 1939, p. 1. See also Lauchlin Currie to President, July 31, 1939, President's Secretary's File 95, FDR papers, FDR Library.

billion lending bill with the $800 million housing bill already passed by the Senate and pending in the House. They hoped to gather maximum support for both measures by linking them together.[166]

On August 1, majority leader Sam Rayburn (D., Tex.) made a desperate appeal to his fellow Democrats, but the House defeated a motion to consider the lending bill, 167 to 193. Two days later, a similar motion to consider the housing bill also went down, 169 to 191. On lending, 47 dissident Democrats joined 146 Republicans. Sixty-three other Democrats, more than enough to have changed the result, did not vote at all. On housing, 54 Democrats joined 137 Republicans, and again large numbers of Democrats failed to vote.[167]

The Administration had suffered two humiliating defeats. Some of the Democrats who voted to consider the lending and housing measures would have opposed the bills themselves. If the House had voted directly on lending and housing legislation, the outcome would probably have been even more one-sided. Many Administration officials had not expected the bills to fail, which made the setbacks even more shocking. Jesse Jones had repeatedly assured Roosevelt and Morgenthau that the lending program would go through. Since Jones was now conveniently vacationing on the West Coast, he did not have to explain why he erred so badly in his forecasts.[168]

* * * * * * *

The voting alignments on lending and housing legislation revealed the pattern of opposition that had been forming in the House of Representatives throughout the session. GOP members and some 20 Democratic renegades comprised the core of the bipartisan opposition. The orthodox Democrats had either joined

---

[166] E. M. Watson to President, August 1, 1939, President's Secretary's File 150, FDR papers, FDR Library; Morgenthau Diary, vol. 206, pp. 2-15, 14-15, FDR Library; James H. Rowe to E. M. Watson, President's Official File 2694, FDR papers, FDR Library; Lauchlin Currie to President, July 31, 1939, President's Secretary's File 95, FDR papers, FDR Library.

[167] Congressional Record, 76th Congress, 1st Session, pp. 10716-10717, 10957-10958; New York Times, August 2, 1939, pp. 1-2, August 4, 1939, pp. 1, 4; Patterson, Congressional Conservatism, pp. 321-322; Huthmacher, Wagner, p. 358.

[168] Jones to Morgenthau, July 22, 1939, box 20, Jones papers, Library of Congress; Jones to President, July 23, 1939, box 135, pp. 247-248, vol. 205, pp. 206-208; FDR Library. See also Berle and Jacobs, Navigating the Rapids, pp. 234-235.

the opposition or abstained in large numbers. Their defection
deprived the Administration of the votes it needed to pass
Roosevelt's recovery program.

According to conventional interpretations, the bipartisan
alliance that killed the lending and housing measures was a
Southern Democratic-Republican coalition. That view has some
validity. About half of the Democratic renegades in the House
and 5 of the 12 renegades in the Senate were Southerners. Moreover, Southern Democrats like Byrd, Bailey, Cox, and Smith were
outspoken enemies of the Administration.[169]

Yet it is an oversimplification to describe the Congressional opposition as a Southern Democratic-Republican coalition.
That anticipates a development which did not fully materialize
until the 78th Congress (1943-1944). Southerners rarely voted
as a monolithic bloc but were divided like Congressmen from
other sections. In the House, 21 Southerners voted against the
Administration on lending, but 61 supported the President.
Again, on housing, more Southerners backed the Administration
than opposed it. Southern Congressmen provided more support
for the Administration than did members from midwestern or
eastern states.[170]

In seeking to understand the role of the Southern Democrats, it is useful to view the South as having two parties.

---

[169]The most consistent Democratic opponents of the Roose-
velt Administration were, in the Senate, Josiah W. Bailey (D.,
N.C.), William J. Bulow (D., S.D.), Edward R. Burke (D., Neb.),
Harry F. Byrd (D., Va.), Bennett Clark (D., Mo.), Walter F.
George (D., Ga.), Peter G. Gerry (D., R.I.), Carter Glass (D.,
Va.), Rush D. Holt (D., W.Va.), William H. King (D., Utah),
Ellison D. Smith (D., S.C.), and Millard E. Tydings (D., Md.),
and, in the House, Robert G. Allen (D., Pa.), C. Arthur Ander-
son (D., Mo.), William A. Ashbrook (D., O.), Thomas G. Burch
(D., Va.) Harry B. Coffee (D., Neb.), Eugene E. Cox (D., Ga.),
Patrick H. Drewry (D., Va.), Alfred J. Elliott (D., Calif.),
Charles I. Faddis (D., Pa.), Richard M. Kleberg (D., Tex.),
Charles F. McLaughlin (D., Neb.), Andrew J. May (D., Ky.), Hugh
Peterson (D., Ga.), William R. Poage (D., Tex.), A. Willis
Robertson (D., Va.), Dave E. Satterfield (D., Va.), Howard W.
Smith (D., Va.), Charles L. South (D., Tex.), and Clifton A.
Woodrum (D., Va.). The foregoing list, derived from Guttman
scaling tables in Appendices I and II, should be compared with
the lists compiled by Patterson in Congressional Conservatism,
pp. 340-343, 348-349.

[170]Patterson, Congressional Conservatism, p. 323. For House
roll call votes on lending and housing bills, see Appendix I,
Guttman scaling table 1, item 8 and Guttman scaling table 2,
item 14; and Congressional Record, 76th Congress, 1st Session,
pp. 10717, 10958.

One party, the renegades, functioned as an adjunct to the Republicans. The other party was, like the rest of the Democrats, split into orthodox and New Deal factions. In general, the orthodox Southern Democrats were prestigious senior Congressmen from predominantly rural districts who had no desire to abandon the Democratic Party. But after 1938, they no longer felt bound to support the President on controversial New Deal issues.[171]

That pattern applied to the whole Congress. The Republicans and renegade Democrats objected to virtually everything that Roosevelt recommended. Administration supporters lacked the votes to maintain control. The faction of orthodox Democrats, fairly well-defined in the Senate, more amorphous in the House, was a swing group. On disruptive New Deal issues--relief, labor policy, progressive taxation, public power, compensatory lending and spending--a varying number of orthodox Democrats joined the bipartisan opposition. On non-New Deal issues--confirmations, monetary powers, executive reorganization, national defense--the orthodox Democrats sided, even if reluctantly, with the President.[172]

---

[171]Patterson, Congressional Conservatism, pp. 335-337.

[172]The faction of orthodox Democrats, moderate party supporters, included, in the Senate, Alva B. Adams (D., Colo.), Charles O. Andrews (D., Fla.), John H. Bankhead (D., Ala.), James F. Byrnes (D., S.C.), Tom T. Connally (D., Tex.), A. Victor Donahey (D., O.), Guy M. Gillette (D., Ia.), Clyde L. Herring (D., Ia.), Edwin C. Johnson (D., Colo.), Scott W. Lucas (D., Ill.), Patrick A. McCarran (D., Nev.), Kenneth D. McKellar (D., Tenn.), John E. Miller (D., Ark.), Joseph O'Mahoney (D., Wyo.), John H. Overton (D., La.), Key Pittman (D., Nev.), George L. Radcliffe (D., Md.), Robert R. Reynolds (D., N.C.), Richard B. Russell (D., Ga.), Morris Sheppard (D., Tex.), Tom Stewart (D., Tenn.), Frederick Van Nuys (D., Ind.), David I. Walsh (D., Mass.), and Burton K. Wheeler (D., Mont.), and, in the House, C. Jasper Bell (D., Mo.), Schuyler O. Bland (D., Va.), John W. Boehne (D., Ind.), Joseph W. Byrns (D., Tenn.), J. Bayard Clark (D., N.C.), Ross A. Collins (D., Miss.), John M. Costello (D., Calif.), Colgate W. Darden (D., Va.), Wesley E. Disney (D., Okla.), Robert L. Doughton (D., N.C.), Wall Doxey (D., Miss.), Andrew Edmiston (D., W. Va.), Aaron L. Ford (D., Miss.), Clyde L. Garrett (D., Tex.), Vincent F. Harrington (D., Ia.), Luther A. Johnson (D., Tex.), Wade H. Kitchens (D., Ark.), Lawrence Lewis (D., Colo.), Louis Ludlow (D., Ind.), Dan R. McGeehee (D., Miss.), Guy L. Moser (D., Pa.), Jack Nichols (D., Okla.), Emmet O'Neal (D., Ky), Nat Patton (D., Tex.), Herron Pearson (D., Tenn.), Walter M. Pierce (D., Ore.), James G. Polk (D., O.), John E. Rankin (D., Miss.), Elmer J. Ryan (D., Minn.), Harry R. Sheppard (D., Calif), Joseph Starnes (D., Ala.), Henry B. Steagall (D., Ala.), Hatton W. Sumners (D., Tex.), Malcolm C. Tarver (D., Ga.), Edward T. Taylor (D., Colo.), Francis E. Walter (D., Pa.), Lindsay C. Warren (D., N.C.), and William M. Whittington (D., Miss.). See Guttman scaling tables in Appendices I and II, and Patterson, Congressional Conservatism, pp. 340-343, 348-349.

The Republican-renegade Democratic opposition, assisted by orthodox Democrats on crucial votes, exercised a veto over further extensions of the New Deal. The argument that the New Deal "ran out of fuel not because of the conservative opposition, but because it ran out of ideas" is a misinterpretation.[173] The Keynesian reformers of the Roosevelt Administration wanted to redeem the commitment to the lower third of society. Ironically, by the time they had pushed a cautious President closer to their position than ever before, the Administration lacked the votes it needed to act on their ideas. The political environment had changed, and the agenda of reform no longer commanded sufficient support.

The fate of the lending and housing bills proved that the Democrats lacked sufficient party cohesion to proceed any further. From its inception, the lending program had been tailored to suit the mood of an unmanageable Congress. The plan was so limited in scope and purpose that some of the Keynesians had been unhappy with it. Jesse Jones had diluted the program and Congress had further modified it. Still, in spite of every effort by the Administration, the opposition had defeated the lending and housing measures.[174] The conclusion was inescapable. If New Dealers could not get the lending and housing bills through, then they could not get much of anything through.

New Dealers found this situation galling. On August 5, Claude Pepper denounced the President's adversaries in an acrimonious Senate speech:

> I am unwilling to let this session of the Congress
> end without lifting my voice to decry the unrighteous
> partnership of those who have been willing to scuttle
> the American government and the American people . . .
> because they hate Roosevelt and what Roosevelt stands
> for.[175]

Senator Burke, interpreting those remarks as an attack on himself and his fellow Democratic renegades, interrupted and moved that the Senate rule Pepper out of order. Most Senators wanted to hear what he had to say, and while Burke indignantly retreated to a cloakroom, Pepper continued:

> I accuse this premeditated alliance of crucifying the
> lending program, which they knew would have given
> jobs to the unemployed and profit to the businesses of
> the country without a burden to the Nation's taxpayers,

---

[173]Bernstein, "The New Deal: The Conservative Achievements of Liberal Reform," p. 277.

[174]Stein, Fiscal Revolution, pp. 118, 122.

[175]Congressional Record, 76th Congress, 1st Session, p. 11165.

because they hated Roosevelt and . . . they wanted him
to fail . . . so that . . . they might . . . give the
Government of this Nation back to those who have always been the champions of special privilege. . . .[176]

Pepper's outburst expressed what many New Dealers said privately. In their view, the renegade Democrats and the Republicans hoped to defeat the New Deal in 1940 by frustrating the
Administration's efforts to foster recovery. Then they would
liquidate the achievements of the past decade.[177]

Senator Sheridan Downey (D., Calif.), trying to calm the
anger aroused by Pepper's tirade, pleaded for restraint on
both sides:

My own views have been expressed here at length upon
the expanding public debt and the lending program of
the United States Government. . . . We should all
struggle among ourselves to express our own ideas,
but it is my hope . . . we can move forward with
tolerance and fair understanding.

To that plea for moderation, Senator Bailey responded by char-
acterizing Pepper's remarks as "cowardly and mendacious."[178]

Opposition leaders like Bailey were in a triumphant and
unforgiving mood. They interpreted the defeat of the lending
program as a decisive turning point. "It is my opinion," a
Republican said, "that this vote marked the end of an era. . . .
it was the first definite clear-cut repudiation by Congress
of the theory that we can spend ourselves into prosperity."[179]

Several months after the defeat of the lending program,
Representative William Ditter (R., Pa.), who described himself
as an "old dealer," delivered a retrospective analysis of the
Administration's compensatory fiscal policy, which he defined
as "the attempt to reduce unemployment by providing the lower
income groups with 'purchasing power' derived from a mounting

---

[176] *Congressional Record*, 76th Congress, 1st Session,
p. 11166.

[177] Joseph Guffey to President, July 29, 1939, President's
Secretary's File 187, FDR papers, FDR Library.

[178] Quotations from *Congressional Record*, 76th Congress,
1st Session, pp. 11167-11168.

[179] Patterson, *Congressional Conservatism*, pp. 321-322.
See also Senator Styles Bridges to Frank E. Gannett, January 22,
1940, box 7, Gannett papers, Cornell University Library.

Federal debt."[180]   First, Ditter said,

> we had certain emergency expenditures. . . . A little
> later we began to hear about the necessity for priming
> the pump. . . . Then we were told. . . . that deficits
> were normal and perhaps even desirable. Finally, we
> were given a brand new label for the Government's
> spend-lend program. Its New Deal sponsors dubbed it
> "the theory of social investment."

> This . . . was the stage setting for the President's
> so-called lend-spend bill. . . . a step toward outright
> socialism. But . . . this House refused to even con-
> sider it, thanks to the solid Republican vote and the
> votes of independent Democrats. . . .

Despite that victory, Ditter warned, the "attempt to graft upon
our American system" the "discredited spending of the British
economist John Maynard Keynes" still continued. The work of
the Congressional opposition was not yet finished, Ditter announced, for it had to dismantle completely the New Deal. "Our
traditional economic system," he said, "can no more exist half
free and half socialized than this nation could have existed
half free and half slave. . . . we must rid ourselves of the
[New Deal's] false philosophy. . . ."[181]

The President, for his part, had been outwardly calm
about the defeat of the lending and housing bills. Privately,
he was furious. Roosevelt had hoped the lending program would
offer positive economic and political benefits. Blaming Jesse
Jones for "killing the Lending Bill," the President told Morgenthau that Jones "is in the dog house." But Jones, increasingly important as a liaison with business and Capitol Hill,
soon wheedled himself back into Roosevelt's good graces.[182]

For a time, Roosevelt considered reprisals against the
Congressmen who had blocked the lending and housing bills. He

---

[180]Quotations from Ditter to John Carmody, June 29, 1942,
box 53, Carmody papers, FDR Library; and Congressional Record,
76th Congress, 3rd Session, p. 6519.

[181]Congressional Record, 76th Congress, 3rd Session,
pp. 6519-6521.

[182]Quotations from Blum, Years of Urgency, p. 41. See also
Jones to Harry Hopkins, September 4, 1939, box 13, Jones papers,
Library of Congress; Jesse H. Jones, "Memorandum of Conversa-
tion with the President," September 1, 1939, Federal Loan Agency
File, Jones papers, Library of Congress; Aubrey Williams, "The
New Deal," n.d., p. 87, box 44, Williams papers, FDR Library;
and Farley, Jim Farley's Story, pp. 169-170.

evidently planned to cut off United States Housing Authority
loans to districts whose Congressmen had opposed the Administration. The President also instructed Budget Director Harold
Smith to "recommend more vetoes." Smith interpreted that as
"a reflex on his part . . . [because] Congress just defeated
the lending measure." The "boss is getting a little tempera-
mental," Smith decided. He "needs a vacation."[183]

On August 7, Roosevelt began that needed vacation. World
events soon cooled his wrath against Congress. In the months
ahead, the President would grow increasingly preoccupied with
the European war and would subordinate domestic concerns to
international goals. The New Deal, as a consequence, became
steadily more vulnerable to the reinvigorated Congressional
opposition.

---

[183]Quotations from Harold D. Smith, Memorandum of Conference with the President, August 2, 1939, Smith papers, FDR Library. See also President to Nathan Straus, August 4, 1939,
and August 25, 1939, President's Official File 2694, FDR papers,
FDR Library; and "Vote Taken in the House of Representatives,
August 1, 1939," President's Official File 3744, FDR papers,
FDR Library.

CHAPTER 2

DEFENSE AND DOMESTIC POLICY

With the outbreak of war in Europe, the President adjusted
his position on domestic affairs. He devoted more of his attention to foreign policy and military preparedness, and in the
interest of national unity, de-emphasized the New Deal. That
as yet undeclared transition from "Dr. New Deal" to "Dr. Win-
the-War" placed the Roosevelt Administration and its supporters
on the defensive. The Congressional opposition, sensing the
shift in political momentum, launched determined attacks on the
reforms of the 1930s.[1]

Reordering Priorities

On August 24, the day after the signing of the Nazi-Soviet
non-aggression pact, Roosevelt returned to Washington from his
holiday at Hyde Park. He instructed Budget Director Harold D.
Smith to defer a number of matters "until we knew the answer as
to whether or not there was to be a European war."[2] Given that
answer by the German offensive against Poland, the President
pledged in a radio broadcast on September 3 that the government would direct every effort toward keeping the country out
of the conflict. Roosevelt asked that partisanship and selfishness be adjourned and that "national unity be the thought
that underlies all others."[3]

In calling for unity, the President placed himself in an
anomalous position. His Administration represented a reform
movement that had divided the nation and the Congress. The
"reactionary revolt" in July and August had demonstrated the
President's diminished influence on Capitol Hill.[4] Now

---

[1]For Roosevelt's growing preoccupation with defense and
foreign policy after September 1939, see James M. Burns, The
Lion and the Fox (New York, 1956), pp. 383, 417; Robert A. Divine, The Illusion of Neutrality (Chicago, 1962), p. 230;
Elliott Roosevelt, ed., F.D.R.--His Personal Letters, 1928-
1945 vol. 2: 1938-1945 (New York, 1950), p. 847; and Nicholas
Halasz, Roosevelt Through Foreign Eyes (Princeton, 1961), p. 96.

[2]Harold D. Smith, Memorandum of Conference with the President, August 24, 1939, Smith papers, FDR Library.

[3]Samuel I. Rosenman, ed., The Public Papers and Addresses
of Franklin D. Roosevelt, vol. 8: 1939, War and Neutrality
(New York, 1941), p. 463.

[4]Quotation from Assistant Attorney General Norman Littel to
Mrs. John R. Boettiger, July 21, 1939, President's Secretary's
File 74, FDR papers, FDR Library.

Roosevelt proposed to call the Congress which had just defied him back into session to amend the Neutrality Act. Hostility toward the New Deal might doom the effort to free the President's hands in foreign policy.[5]

Events earlier that summer had already signaled the danger. In July, Administration supporters had endeavored to revise the Neutrality Act to speed the flow of American-made munitions to England and France. The effort foundered on July 11 when the Senate Foreign Relations Committee voted 12 to 11 to postpone consideration of neutrality legislation until the next session of Congress. Senators Walter F. George (D., Ga.) and Guy M. Gillette (D., Ia.), two of the President's purge targets in 1938, joined the isolationists to thwart Roosevelt. The failure of neutrality revision, agreed both Arther Krock of the New York Times and Freda Kirchwey of the Nation, resulted from Congressional distrust of the President and "general opposition to the New Deal."[6]

The setback in the Foreign Relations Committee suggested that Roosevelt would have to choose between the New Deal, whose star had waned, and his international objectives. Convinced that the security of the nation was imperiled, the President accelerated his movement toward "a new phase of his political career." He set out to rally a majority of the Congress and the public behind his defense and foreign policies.[7]

Beginning in mid-August, Roosevelt quietly indicated his willingness to come to terms with the opposition. He first adjusted his position on government spending. On August 5, the President had written Bernard Baruch,

> The defeat of the lending bill and the housing bill
> is bad because it creates a sudden and severe break

---

[5]The decision to call Congress into special session can be traced in Roosevelt, F.D.R.--His Personal Letters 2: 1938-1945, pp. 918-919; Franklin D. Roosevelt, Complete Presidential Press Conferences of Franklin D. Roosevelt, vols. 13-14: 1939 (New York, 1972), pp. 14:133-134, 139-140, 148-149; Rosenman, Public Papers and Addresses of FDR 8: 1939, p. 510. See also Divine, Illusion, pp. 266, 283-284 and Congressional Digest 18 (1939), pp. 225-226.

[6]For the abortive effort to revise the Neutrality Act, see the New York Times, July 9, 1939, p. 1, July 10, 1939, pp. 1-2, July 12, 1939, p. 1; Rosenman, Public Papers and Addresses of FDR 8: 1939, p. 381; Roosevelt, Complete Presidential Press Conferences 13-14: 1939, p. 14:34; Divine, Illusion, pp. 266-281; and Francis O. Wilcox, "The Neutrality Fight in Congress," American Political Science Review XXXIII (1939), pp. 811-825. Quotation from Divine, Illusion, p. 284.

[7]Divine, Illusion, pp. 230-231.

from government spending to practically no government
spending. . . . and, incidentally, I fear that there
will be a check to the present definite up-turn by
next Spring.[8]

Only two days later, Roosevelt asked the heads of executive departments, independent establishments, and other government agencies to institute every possible administrative and
operating economy. The "stiffer attitude" toward spending was
part of the President's general reordering of priorities in the
fall of 1939. On October 16, Roosevelt told Budget Director
Smith that he wanted "the Departments held at the present level
and below if possible" in the budget for fiscal 1941. Roosevelt "wanted all new works projects trimmed out," Smith reported. It was "his hunch that business conditions would continue to improve" and that public works "could be curtailed in
periods of advancing prosperity. He kiddingly told us," Smith
added, "that 'you spenders won't like this program.'" Agency
chiefs protested, but Roosevelt insisted on reductions in
budgetary estimates.[9]

Advocates of compensatory fiscal policy, particularly those
associated with the National Resources Planning Board, continued
to urge more deficit spending and lending. But the imperfect
vehicle for their views, the Fiscal and Monetary Advisory Board,
had lapsed into disuse. In the area of fiscal policy, Roosevelt receded toward the orthodox position of Senators Pat Harrison (D., Miss.), Walter F. George (D., Ga.), and others who
advised a "leveling off" of the Federal budget. By emphasizing
economy, the President could meet, at least partially, the demands of the fiscal conservatives. He could also leave room in
the budget for future increases in defense spending.[10]

---

[8]President to Baruch, August 5, 1939, President's Secretary's File 95, FDR papers, FDR Library.

[9]Quotations from Harold D. Smith, Memorandum of Conference
with the President, October 16, 1939, Smith papers, FDR Library.
See also Harold D. Smith, Memoranda of Conferences with the
President, August 7, 1939, and November 30, 1939, Smith papers,
FDR Library; New York Times, August 10, 1939, p. 1; Washington
Post, August 10, 1939, p. 1; Burns, Lion and the Fox, p. 416;
and Rosenman, Public Papers and Addresses of FDR 8: 1939,
p. 421.

[10]New York Times, September 15, 1939, p. 21; Arthur E. Burns
to John Carmody, September 30, 1939, box 96, Carmody papers, FDR
Library; Louis H. Bean, "The Prospect for Economic and Social
Progress in the United States," box 38, Bean papers, FDR Library;
Lauchlin Currie to President, November 3, 1939, President's Sec-
retary's File 95, FDR papers, FDR Library; Thomas C. Blaisdell,
"National Policy Toward Investment," December 8, 1939, National

Concurrent with the adjustment of his stand on fiscal policy, Roosevelt soft-pedaled other New Deal programs that had generated domestic dissension. For example, he placed Federal power policy "on ice . . . at least until the neutrality issue was settled." That decision to "go slow" on controversial policies hardened in October and November. On November 27, well after the successful conclusion of the neutrality fight, the President indicated that his Administration would not "undertake any new activities, even if laudable ones." Two weeks later, Roosevelt rejected the submission of an expanded health program and new health legislation to the upcoming session of Congress. In the midst of a world crisis Roosevelt valued national defense and foreign policy more highly than continuation of the New Deal, a continuation that Congressional attitudes made unlikely anyway.[11]

Cuts in Federal spending and subordination of the New Deal were means to an end, the appeasement of the orthodox and renegade Democrats. Amendment of the neutrality law depended on a rapprochement with those Congressional factions. Fortunately for Roosevelt, some of the most rabidly anti-New Deal Democrats, such as Senators Josiah W. Bailey (D., N.C.), Edward R. Burke (D., Neb.), Harry F. Byrd (D., Va.), and Carter Glass (D., Va.), were potential supporters of an interventionist foreign policy.[12]

Roosevelt was especially eager to subdue old feuds with Senators Gillette and George, who had immobilized the Senate Foreign Relations Committee in July. On September 3, Gillette wired the President and promised his support for repeal of the arms embargo. In his reply, Roosevelt thanked Gillette and remarked, significantly, "I am limiting the heads of the Executive Branch to more action and less words. I know you will understand."

Resources Planning Board, 9th Meeting, Central Office Correspondence, Records of NRPB, Record Group 187, National Archives; Harold D. Smith, Daily Memoranda, December 13, 1939, Smith papers, FDR Library, Lauchlin Currie to President, December 14, 1939, President's Secretary's File 116, FDR papers, FDR Library. Quotation from New York Times, August 27, 1939, p. 12. See also Morgenthau Diary, vol. 146, pp. 372-383, FDR Library.

[11]Quotations from Harold D. Smith, Memoranda of Conferences with the President, September 13, 1939, September 28, 1939, November 27, 1939, December 8, 1939, Smith papers, FDR Library. See also Roosevelt, F.D.R.--His Personal Letters 2: 1938-1945, p. 934; and Burns, Lion and the Fox, p. 396.

[12]Divine, Illusion, pp. 290-292; James T. Patterson, "Eating Humble Pie: A Note on Roosevelt, Congress and Neutrality Revision in 1939," Historian 31 (May 1969), pp. 407-414.

Senator George's intentions were more obscure. With the President's connivance, Bernard Baruch, Jesse Jones, and other emissaries called on George to lobby for his support. On September 18, Assistant Secretary of War Louis Johnson reported, "Senator George will vote to 'bring out immediately the Administration's neutrality bill.'" By the end of September, "conciliatory tactics" had won over a number of those who had consistently opposed Roosevelt on domestic policy.[13]

Detente with the dissident Democrats contributed to the successful outcome of the neutrality struggle. Senators James F. Byrnes (D., S.C.) and Tom T. Connally (D., Tex.), two prestigious orthodox Democrats, agreed to spearhead the drive for neutrality revision in the Senate. In the House, Administration leaders followed the President's advice and avoided controversies over such domestic issues as WPA, the wages and hours law, and an anti-lynching bill. Roosevelt also insisted that there be no third-term talk until the neutrality issue had been settled.[14]

On October 27, the Senate passed the repeal of the arms embargo, 63 to 20. Of the 12 Democratic renegades in the Senate, nine supported the Administration. The faction of orthodox Democrats also swung behind the President. A similar pattern developed in the House, which, early in November, passed the neutrality bill by a comfortable margin. In both House and Senate, the votes on neutrality revealed that the President had restored cohesion to his party and had re-established a working relationship with Congress.[15]

---

[13] Quotations from Divine, *Illusion*, pp. 292-293, 307; and Johnson to President, September 18, 1939, President's Secretary's File 187, FDR papers, FDR Library. Roosevelt's efforts to conciliate his adversaries are also described by Harold Ickes, *The Secret Diary of Harold Ickes*, vol. III: *The Lowering Clouds, 1939-1941* (New York, 1954), p. 27.

[14] Roosevelt, *F.D.R.--His Personal Letters* 2: 1938-1945, pp. 924-925, 941, 947; James F. Byrnes, *All In One Lifetime* (New York, 1958), p. 111; Tom Connally, *My Name is Tom Connally* (New York, 1954), p. 228; *New York Times*, September 22, 1939, p. 16; Ickes, *Diary* III, pp. 21-22, 27, 49; Josiah W. Bailey to President, October 4, 1939, President's Secretary's File 187, FDR papers, FDR Library; Robert F. Wagner to H. Landwer, October 12, 1939, box 502-LE-245, and Alben W. Barkley to Walter White, October 31, 1939, box 571-GF-333, Wagner papers, Georgetown University Library.

[15] Renegade Democrats who voted for repeal of the arms embargo were: Senators Bailey (D., N.C.), Burke (D., Neb.), Byrd (D., Va.), George (D., Ga.), Gerry (D., R.I.), King (D., Utah), Smith (D., S.C.), and Tydings (D., Md.). Renegades who opposed

The restoration of Democratic party unity, if only on foreign policy, was part of a larger campaign to promote national unity. On September 20, the President held a "National Unity Conference" attended by prominent Republicans, including Alfred M. Landon and Frank Knox (the 1936 Republican ticket) and minority leaders Charles McNary and Joseph Martin.[16] That meeting was designed to rally support for neutrality revision, but even after repeal of the arms embargo, the President sought to broaden his political base. He could not govern with support largely from New Dealers, only one faction of his party. He considered forming a coalition cabinet, an idea that he modified in June 1940, when he appointed Frank Knox and Henry Stimson, the leading Republican warhawks, to be Secretaries of Navy and War. He later named Jesse Jones, an orthodox Southern Democrat and the Administration's chief spokesman for big business, to be Secretary of Commerce.[17]

Roosevelt's gradual but perceptible movement away from the New Deal disturbed the Administration's reform-minded activists. They worried that the European war might accentuate reactionary trends in the United States and lead to the capture of the government by military and business interests. The immediate cause of their alarm was the establishment of the War Resources Board by the War and Navy Departments on August 9. Assistant Secretary of War Louis Johnson intended the new board to become the super-agency for managing the nation's defense program, much as

repeal were Senators Bulow (D., S.D.), Clark (D., Mo.), and Holt (D., W. Va.). Glass (D., Va.) did not vote but backed the President. For House and Senate roll calls on neutrality revision, see Congressional Record, 76th Congress, 2nd Session, pp. 1024, 1342-1345, 1356, 1389; and Appendix I, Guttman scaling table 1, items 31, 49, 58, 61. See also Divine, Illusion, pp. 325-331; and George C. S. Benson, "The Year in Congress" in William M. Schuyler, ed., The American Year Book, 1939 (New York, 1940), p. 26.

[16]New York Times, September 21, 1939, pp. 1, 16; Divine, Illusion, pp. 294-295; Byrnes, All In One Lifetime, p. 111.

[17]Editorial, Chicago Daily News, September 13, 1939, President's Official Files 3759, FDR papers, FDR Library; Harold D. Smith, Memoranda of Conferences with the President, November 13, 1939 and June 20, 1940, Smith papers, FDR Library; James M. Burns, Roosevelt: The Soldier of Freedom (New York, 1970), pp. 36-39; Harold Ickes, The Secret Diary of Harold Ickes, vol. II: The Inside Struggle, 1936-1939 (New York, 1954), p. 718 and Diary III, pp. 12, 15-16, 180-181, 204, 214-215, 314; Henry L. Stimson and McGeorge Bundy, On Active Service in Peace and War (New York, 1947), pp. 323-324; Bascom N. Timmons, Jesse H. Jones (New York, 1956), pp. 279-281; Byrnes, All In One Lifetime, p. 113; Roosevelt, F.D.R.--His Personal Letters 2: 1938-1945, pp. 975-977; George Fort Milton, The Use of Presidential Power, 1789-1943 (Boston, 1944), p. 293.

the War Industries Board had directed industrial mobilization during World War I.[18]

    That prospect the New Deal faction viewed with deep misgiving. At the urging of Assistant Secretary of War Johnson, the President had appointed to the board "a bunch of economic royalists," including Edward R. Stettinius, Jr., of U.S. Steel, Walter Gifford of A.T.T. and other businessmen deemed unfriendly to the Administration.[19] To New Dealers, the most obnoxious appointment was that of John Hancock, an investment banker associated with Lehman Brothers who had recently led a Wall Street assault on the Securities and Exchange Commission.[20] According to Secretary of the Interior Harold Ickes, Hancock and the other members of the War Resources Board were servants of the House of Morgan. Ickes feared that the new board would undo the reforms of the New Deal.

> We are in danger of repeating the terrible mistake
> that President Wilson committed at the time of the
> First World War. He had started out to give a
> really liberal Administration, but when war came
> everything was thrown to the big financial and
> other interests. There will be the same pressure
> at this time on the part of the big interests to
> take over and run the government.[21]

    Like Ickes, Tom Corcoran predicted that "in the event of war the War Resources Board will be running the Government." On September 4, Corcoran warned Budget Director Smith,

> with representatives of the War Department putting
> pins in a map in the President's office showing the

---

[18]Carlisle Bargeron, Confusion on the Potomac (New York, 1941), p. 17; New York Times, August 10, 1939, pp. 1-2; Washington Post, August 10, 1939, p. 1; Johnson to President, August 22, 1939, President's Official File 3759, FDR papers, FDR Library; Beatrice B. Berle and Travis B. Jacobs, Navigating the Rapids (New York, 1973), p. 238.

[19]Ickes, Diary II, pp. 716, 721. Quotation from Harold D. Smith, Daily Memoranda, September 4, 1939, Smith papers, FDR Library. See also Richard Polenberg, War and Society: The United States, 1941-1945 (Philadelphia, 1972), pp. 6-7 and Geoffrey Perrett, Days of Sadness, Years of Triumph (New York, 1973), p. 68.

[20]E. M. Watson to President, August 30, 1939, President's Official File 3759, FDR papers, FDR Library. See also Leon Henderson, diary, September 5, 1939, box 36, Henderson papers, FDR Library.

[21]Ickes, Diary II, p. 710.

progress of Germans in Poland . . . it would be more
difficult for civilians to see the President. This
. . . happened during the Wilson Administration and
many desirable programs were shoved aside.[22]

On September 12, Corcoran and Ickes held an informal strategy
session with Benjamin Cohen, Lauchlin Currie, Jerome Frank,
Robert Jackson, Isador Lubin, and Frank Murphy. They agreed
to monitor the activities of the War Resources Board and to
serve as a liberal junto that would resist the growing reactionary influences in the government.[23]

In the case of the War Resources Board, the apprehensions
of the New Deal faction were premature. Publicly, the President
endorsed the work of the board, perhaps because he recognized
its political utility during the neutrality struggle.[24] Privately, though, the President was incensed because Assistant
Secretary of War Johnson had activated the board without first
informing him or securing his consent. After examining the
organization charts for the War Resources Board, the President
exploded, "What do they think they are doing, setting up a
second government?" Roosevelt, Harold Smith reported, "does
not care to have the industrialists on this Board running the
Government." The President disposed of the irksome agency just
as soon as appearances would permit. Late in November, the
board submitted a final report and then disbanded.[25]

---

[22]Quotation from Harold D. Smith, Daily Memoranda, September 4, 1939, Smith papers, FDR Library.

[23]Ickes, Diary III, p. 5. See the accounts in John M.
Blum, From the Morgenthau Diaries, vol. II: Years of Urgency,
1938-1941 (Boston, 1965), p. 97 and David E. Lilienthal, The
Journals of David E. Lilienthal, vol. I: The TVA Years, 1939-
1945 (New York, 1964), p. 135.

[24]Polenberg, War and Society, pp. 6-7.

[25]Quotations from Harold D. Smith, Daily Memoranda, September 4, 1939 and September 7, 1939, Smith papers, FDR Library.
See also Harold D. Smith, Memorandum of Conference with the President, August 29, 1939 and Daily Memoranda, September 5, 1939,
Smith papers, FDR Library; Ickes, Diary II, p. 716; Roosevelt,
F.D.R.--His Personal Letters 2: 1938-1945, pp. 920-921; President to Clarence Cannon, September 5, 1939, President's Official
File 3759, FDR papers, FDR Library; Roosevelt, Complete Presidential Press Conferences 13-14: 1939, p. 14:193; and "Report
of the War Resources Board," President's Secretary's File 192,
FDR papers, FDR Library; Rosenman, Public Papers and Addresses
of FDR 8: 1939, pp. 586-587; Bureau of the Budget, War Records
Section, The United States at War: Development and Administration of the War Program by the Federal Government (Washington,
1946), p. 16.

New Dealers rejoiced and the opposition sulked.[26]   "The
expert services of business men are being sacrificed in Washington," editorialized the Milwaukee Sentinel, "and at a very critical time--to the demands of the bureaucratic cabal which has
dictated most of the important policies of the national administration for six years."

> The disbanding of the war resources board is a glaring
> case in point. . . . the majority of business men of
> this country . . . hold their COUNTRY FIRST when the
> call for preparedness comes.
>   But the Corcoran-Cohen "palace guards" decreed the
> "sacking" of the war resources board because some of
> its members didn't approve of the vagaries and vision-
> ary policies of the New Deal.[27]

But the Sentinel was ill informed. More important than the
"palace guards" in bringing about the downfall of the board was
Roosevelt's aversion to a super-agency which might become a
"second government."

Although the alarm of New Dealers about the War Resources
Board turned out to be unwarranted, their instincts about the
general situation were sound. An expanded defense program
would require coordination and cooperation among business, government, and the military. Industrialists, determined to end
their exclusion from the upper levels of government, would
have to be brought into the Administration.[28] Moreover, as
Corcoran had noted, the pressures of defense and diplomacy
would so distract the President that the New Deal faction would
have less access to him than before.

Rumors were already circulating that the Corcoran-Cohen
brains trust was "out the window." But the President had not
renounced unofficial advisers. Rather, as New York Times ana-
lyst Felix Belair suggested, the European war was a new emergency
forcing Roosevelt to rely on different personalities. "Social
and economic reforms have been all but forgotten," Belair wrote,
and the New Deal faction would gradually cease to be the key
idea group for the Administration. The President, Belair concluded, "feels the present is no time for new reform plans."[29]

---

[26]Cyrus Eaton to President, September 29, 1939, President's
Official File 3759, FDR papers, FDR Library.

[27]Editorial, Milwaukee Sentinel, n.d., President's Official File 3759, FDR papers, FDR Library.

[28]Perrett, Days of Sadness, p. 69.

[29]Quotations from New York Times, September 10, 1939, pp. 1,
50 and September 17, 1939, section IV, p. 7.

Whether out the window or not, the New Deal faction felt
insecure in the fall of 1939. The suspicion existed that the
President was selling out the New Deal.[30] Corcoran, who had
kept the "pieces together" for the Keynesians and the reformers,
was hurt by rumors that he had fallen from favor. The President was not taking him fully into his confidence and Corcoran
was "concerned because he does not know everything that is going
on." ". . . whereas Moley developed one kind of complex toward
the President," observed Budget Director Smith, "Corcoran quite
unconsciously may be developing another."[31] As Roosevelt
shifted to the right in his bid for party and national unity,
disillusionment of the "bright young men" of the New Deal grew.[32]

The President had decided that he could not wage war on
the home front while preparing the country to intervene in
Europe. He realized, as Adolf A. Berle, Jr., informed him on
January 3, 1940, that "some of the youngsters . . . are all for
taking on in this Congress a huge domestic program." Roosevelt
believed he had gone as far as he could "on domestic questions."
Someone else would have to "mop up" after him. When the emergency passed, and domestic concerns once again became preeminent, then the New Deal could be resuscitated. For the fore-
seeable future, defense had taken precedence over reform.[33]

The Politics of Preparedness

The neutrality struggle behind him, the President turned
to rearmament. In September 1939, General George C. Marshall,
Chief of Staff, had urged Roosevelt to expand the Army to its
authorized strength. The President, uncertain about the attitude of Congress, gave Marshall a portion of what he wanted.
He sought a modest increase in outlays for the Army and Navy,
while continuing to reduce other expenditures.[34] That trade-off

---

[30] Bargeron, _Confusion on the Potomac_, p. 20; Harold Ickes
to President, August 23, 1940, President's Secretary's File 73,
FDR papers, FDR Library.

[31] Quotations from Harold D. Smith, Daily Memoranda, September 4, 1939, Smith papers, FDR Library.

[32] Quotation from John Crider, _The Bureaucrat_ (Philadelphia,
1944), pp. 319-320. See also Ickes, _Diary III_, pp. 370-371,
390-391; and Ickes to President, August 23, 1940, President's
Secretary's File 73, FDR papers, FDR Library.

[33] Berle to President, January 3, 1940, President's Secretary's File 77, FDR papers, FDR Library; Ickes, _Diary III_,
p. 107; Halasz, _Roosevelt Through Foreign Eyes_, p. 96.

[34] Blum, _Years of Urgency_, p. 138. See also Blair Moody,
"The Politics of Domestic Strategy," in Ray F. Harvey and
others, _The Politics of This War_ (New York, 1943), pp. 27-28.

would prevent a rise in the annual deficit, a course recommended by such fiscal conservatives as Senators Pat Harrison (D., Miss.) and James F. Byrnes (D., S.C.), who thought rearmament should be financed out of cuts in non-military spending.[35]

Advocates of compensatory fiscal policy, particularly Marriner Eccles, disagreed with that approach. In a major speech on November 9, Eccles warned against precipitate cuts in non-military spending:

> We are hearing today proposals that the government should reduce some of the present expenditures, particularly for agricultural benefits and for work relief, in order that funds for an expanded armament program may be provided without an increased deficit or an increase in taxes.

A contraction in relief spending, said Eccles, would constitute a regressive tax on the lower third of society.

> In my opinion it would be unfair and unsound economically to pass increased armaments cost on to those of the low income groups who would profit the least out of foreign or domestic expenditure for armament, who are the least able to bear the costs and whose increased purchasing power is essential to our economic welfare.[36]

Eccles estimated, accurately as it turned out, that the underutilization of plant and labor was so great that the defense period would see a continuation of widespread unemployment. If reductions in non-military spending were unavoidable, then Eccles and other spenders believed those cuts should be made first in public works, which funneled a greater proportion of dollars into materials than into wages. Armaments spending, while socially less desirable, would replace public works as a form of government investment. Work relief expenditures should continue, said Eccles, for those funds would provide for the unemployed and, through the multiplier principle, further increase aggregate demand, consumption and production.[37]

Eccles believed the depressed American economy could easily absorb a larger deficit. But if Congress and the President wanted to keep the deficit from increasing, then taxes should be raised:

------

[35] New York Times, November 6, 1939, p. 4, November 22, 1939, p. 20.

[36] New York Times, November 10, 1939, p. 35.

[37] New York Times, November 10, 1939, p. 35, November 29, 1939, p. 11. See also Seymour E. Harris, The Economics of American Defense (New York, 1941), pp. 42-45, 173-177.

we should follow the unpopular but necessary course
of imposing additional taxation in order to meet the
added costs of our armament program and to reduce the
deficit without sacrificing the low income groups,
whose sustained and increasing purchasing power is
needed to sustain and increase production. Accordingly, additional taxation should be levied, not alone
upon war profits, but on those income groups now relatively undertaxed, among whom the greatest proportion
of savings that are unable to find profitable outlet
today are now accumulating. At the same time, I favor
increased domestic purchasing power by decreasing consumption taxes.[38]

Eccles proposed a fiscal policy that combined non-military and
armaments expenditures with a frankly redistributive tax program. The objective was to bring the industrial plant of the
United States up to full production and trigger economic growth
through the renewal of private investment that would follow
full production and accelerating demand.[39]

It was a bold proposal, a clear statement of late New Deal
economic policy, but one that attracted little support and invited heavy criticism. Eccles suggested an overhaul of the
regressive tax structure imposed by the Revenue Act of 1932
with its excises that bore heavily on consumption.[40] Critics
detected in his speech the leveling spirit of the 1935 "wealth
tax." As Felix Belair wrote, one of the reforms "definitely
projected but never attempted" by the New Deal "was the idea of
somehow breaking down the concentration of wealth in the nation." But, Belair went on, that was an idea whose time had
passed: "The unpopularity of such an attempt is now obvious."[41]

The unpopularity of Eccles' speech quickly became apparent.
Under Secretary of the Treasury John W. Hanes, who "was always

---

[38]New York Times, November 10, 1939, p. 35.

[39]Marriner Eccles, Beckoning Frontiers (New York, 1951),
pp. 331-332. For background, see Herbert Stein, The Fiscal Revolution in America (Chicago, 1969), pp. 147-168; Harris, Economics
of American Defense, pp. 129-188; and Donald W. Gilbert, "Taxation and Economic Stability," Quarterly Journal of Economics LVI
(1942), pp. 412-419.

[40]Randolph Paul, Taxation in the United States (Boston, 1954),
pp. 152-162, 241, 652, 671; Louis H. Kimmel, Federal Budget and
Fiscal Policy, 1798-1958 (Washington, 1959), pp. 148-151; Robert
A. Gordon, Economic Instability and Growth: The American Record
(New York, 1974), p. 55.

[41]Quotations from New York Times, September 17, 1939, Section IV, p. 7.

consistent . . . for business appeasement first, last, and all
the time," publicly repudiated Eccles.[42] "I don't think he
spoke for the Administration," Hanes told reporters. "I doubt
seriously if he spoke for Congress. I am certain he didn't
speak for the Treasury."[43]

Hanes was right. Eccles was out of step with the Treasury,
the President, and the Congress. Pat Harrison, Chairman of the
Senate Finance Committee, shuddered at the thought of a tax increase in an election year. More important, Harrison was philo-
sophically opposed to "soak-the-rich" taxation. He stuck to the
position that "other expenditures" would have to be curtailed
to make way for increased defense spending.[44]

The President, under partisan attack from Republicans and
under pressure from orthodox Democrats, recognized the political
necessity for reducing non-military expenditures in order to get
his modest armaments program approved by Congress. On November
15, Roosevelt told Budget Director Smith that he wanted to "cut
the deficit" as much as possible. During the following week,
the President reduced the budgets of the Department of Agriculture, Department of Commerce, and the independent agencies.
The cuts, Smith noted, "were quite severe." Roosevelt's goal,
according to newspaper reports, was to hold the deficit for
fiscal 1941 to $2,000,000,000 in spite of increases in national
defense appropriations.[45]

Late in December, Roosevelt permitted Marriner Eccles an
advance look at the annual budget message. In that message, the
President once again endorsed compensatory fiscal policy. But
he also called for reductions in practically every area of government operations except national defense.[46] Eccles protested

---

[42]Paul, Taxation, p. 255.

[43]Quotation from New York Times, November 17, 1939, p. 2.

[44]For Harrison's views and the political implications of
revenue policy, see Blum, Years of Urgency, pp. 16, 279-285;
New York Times, November 21, 1939, p. 1, November 22, 1939,
p. 1, January 5, 1940, p. 1; and Congressional Digest 19 (1940),
pp. 43-44.

[45]Quotations from Harold D. Smith, Memoranda of Conferences
with the President, November 15, 1939 and November 20, 1939,
Smith papers, FDR Library. See also New York Times, November 22,
1939, p. 1, November 23, 1939, p. 26, November 25, 1939, p. 1
and November 27, 1939, p. 1.

[46]Samuel I. Rosenman, ed., The Public Papers and Addresses
of Franklin D. Roosevelt, vol. 9: 1940 War and Aid to Democracies (New York, 1941), pp. 10-24.

that the cuts in relief spending portended hardship for the unemployed.

> I noted [Eccles wrote] that $500,000,000 had been cut
> from the previous year's relief appropriation; I felt
> this was a great mistake in view of the fact that there
> were still over eight million unemployed and that not
> more than three million of these had ever been cared
> for by the government even before relief appropriations
> were cut.

"You are absolutely right," the President replied.   "But with
the war in Europe likely to spread, we simply must get an increase in the military budget from last year's $1 billion, to
$1.5 billion the coming year."

> To do this [the President continued] with the total
> budget being what it is, the budget for relief is the
> only place from which I can transfer the additional
> funds that are needed for the military. Congress
> simply will not support an increase in the total
> budget so as to increase our military preparedness.
> There is no real pressure in the country for expendi-
> tures of that sort--but Congress will later support a
> further relief appropriation as pressures develop on
> all sides. In this roundabout way, I hope ultimately
> to take care of the unemployed. But even so, Marriner,
> despite the immediate decrease in relief appropria-
> tions, it is going to be extremely difficult to get
> Congress to pass the military budget.[47]

Roosevelt expected that the increased military estimates would
be held hostage by the opposition, perhaps abetted by isolationist progressives, unless he conceded reductions in non-defense
spending. In an election year, Republicans would be quick to
criticize any increase in the total budget as "Presidential
pork barrel," insurance for New Deal victory.

Spokesmen for the Congressional opposition had already
made such charges, both publicly and privately. Washington observer Carlisle Bargeron, in an account perhaps not altogether
apocryphal, described a meeting of opposition leaders in August
1939. Senators Robert A. Taft (R., O.), Harry F. Byrd (D.,
Va.), Arthur H. Vandenberg (R., Mich.) and others had gathered
to celebrate the defeat of the Administration's self-liquidating
projects and housing bills. In their view, spending was all
that was keeping Roosevelt and the "radical faction" in power,
and they believed Congress had dealt the New Deal a fatal blow.
But Byrd, the Cassandra of the fiscal conservatives, warned his
colleagues: "We are probably celebrating too soon. In a few

---

[47]Quotations from Eccles, Beckoning Frontiers, pp. 333-
334.

weeks they will be back up here with another spending program under the guise of National Defense."[48]

Senator Taft employed that argument in his campaign for the Republican Presidential nomination. The Senator discerned a direct connection between the defeat of the spending-lending plan in early August and submission of an expanded armaments program to the new session of Congress. Taft thought the New Dealers would rely on defense spending to perpetuate their regime. "Under the cloak of a preparedness program we are likely to find included every possible type of public works," he said on December 8. And again, on December 11, he predicted that the "business" of preparedness would be used to "cover up every expenditure which Congress has rejected."[49]

Taft's accusation, undoubtedly sincere, credited the President with greater guile than he deserved. Though Roosevelt had ample opportunity to do so, he was reluctant to use the defense program as a cloak for other purposes. On November 29, for example, Tom Corcoran, Ben Cohen, and Leland Olds, head of the Federal Power Commission, presented to Budget Director Smith a "national defense" power program, "which would make certain inter-connections, develop power on certain streams in the East . . . and build steam plants in certain locations. . . ." Smith was skeptical and "pointed out that the President had been inclined to trim off public works rather severely." Corcoran, Cohen and Olds "advanced this program as a national defense one," but neither Smith nor Roosevelt was convinced. As Smith confided to his diary, "the suggestion of building steam plants particularly was rather naive at this time, and would tend to stir up the whole power issue again."[50] If defense were used as a cover, a Congressional majority might delay or even attenuate military appropriations. Roosevelt's first priority was speedy ratification of the entire rearmament program, modest though it was. Once that was accomplished,

---

[48] Bargeron, Confusion on the Potomac, pp. 201-202. Senators Bailey and Glass expressed similar views. See Patterson, "Eating Humble Pie," pp. 407-408.

[49] Quotations from New York Times, December 9, 1939, p. 8 and December 12, 1939, p. 32. Taft's campaign for the Republican Presidential nomination can be followed in the New York Times, December 13, 1939, p. 1, December 14, 1939, p. 22, December 28, 1939, p. 14 and January 6, 1940, p. 1. See also James T. Patterson, Mr. Republican: A Biography of Robert A. Taft (Boston, 1972), pp. 205-217.

[50] Quotations from Harold D. Smith, Daily Memoranda, November 29, 1939, Smith papers, FDR Library. See also Roosevelt, Complete Presidential Press Conferences 13-14: 1939, pp. 14: 336-337; and Philip J. Fungiello, Toward a National Power Policy (Pittsburgh, 1973), chapter 9.

Congress could then decide whether to abide by the Administration's suggested limit on spending or to exceed the budget.[51]

Congress, with an eye on the upcoming election, snarled the President's strategy. Senator Taft and other opposition spokesmen continued to criticize the increase in defense outlays as another New Deal spending program to guarantee victory in 1940. Farm bloc and pork barrel forces disliked budgetary recommendations that slighted their pet projects and programs while boosting military spending. Isolationists perceived the beginnings of intervention in the European war. Those attitudes produced a Congressional insistence on careful review of the defense program.[52]

While the military appropriations bills hung fire in Senate and House subcommittees, the bipartisan opposition renewed its intermittent campaign to cut Federal spending below the President's budgetary estimates. Led by Representative Clifton Woodrum, a renegade Democrat, and Republicans John Taber and Joseph Martin, the opposition in the House of Representatives seized on the expansion of defense spending as a pretext to attack the fiscal policy and domestic programs of the New Deal. Opposition spokesmen claimed that the only way to avoid higher taxes or an increase in the national debt limit during an election year was to force reductions in the overall budget. On January 31, the House Appropriations Committee, acting at the behest of Representatives Woodrum and Taber, deleted $154,000,000 from the fiscal 1941 agricultural appropriation bill, an 18 percent decrease in the President's budgetary estimate. Two days later, the whole House, despite protests from Roosevelt and Secretary of Agriculture Henry A. Wallace, sustained the Appropriations Committee and passed a diminished farm bill of $722,000,000.[53]

---

[51]Eccles, Beckoning Frontiers, 333-334.

[52]Congressional unhappiness with the President's budget is reported in the New York Times, January 1, 1940, p. 1, January 2, 1940, p. 12, January 6, 1940, p. 1, January 7, 1940, section IV, p. 1 and February 24, 1940, p. 1. See also Harold D. Smith, Daily Memoranda, March 13, 1940, Smith papers, FDR Library; and Roosevelt, F.D.R.--His Personal Letters 2: 1938-1945, p. 1008.

[53]The efforts to reduce Federal spending can be traced in the New York Times, January 6, 1940, p. 6, January 12, 1940, p. 3, January 30, 1940, p. 1, February 1, 1940, p. 13, February 3, 1940, p. 1, February 4, 1940, p. 2, February 5, 1940, p. 1; Congressional Digest 19 (1940), pp. 1-4, 34-35; Floyd M. Riddick, "Third Session of the Seventy-sixth Congress," American Political Science Review XXXV (1941), pp. 285, 291; and Franklin D. Roosevelt, Complete Presidential Press Conferences of Franklin D. Roosevelt vols. 15-16: 1940 (New York, 1972), pp. 15: 112-113. For background, see Representative A. Willis

Opposition members in the House also engineered crippling cuts in appropriations for the National Labor Relations Board and the Wages and Hours Administration. Those agencies had powerful enemies on Capitol Hill because they implemented the pro-labor policy of the New Deal. As John L. Lewis, President of the Congress of Industrial Organizations, complained in a letter to House leaders Rayburn and Martin, the budget estimates for the two agencies were necessary and proposed cuts were "based primarily on the displeasure entertained for the legislation itself and not upon any fair estimate of the financial . . . needs of the agencies."[54] Lewis' protest was ignored, for in the House of Representatives, the bipartisan opposition had assumed command and seemed determined to force retrenchment. Like the defeat of the lending program the previous summer, the attack on the President's budget was made possible by the 1938 elections, which had cost House Democrats over 20 percent of their total strength and had decimated loyal New Dealers from the Midwest and Northeast.[55]

In contrast to the House, the Senate still remained sufficiently Democratic to overcome, on most occasions, the alliance between renegades and Republicans. With Roosevelt interceding on behalf of his budgetary recommendations, the Senate restored funds deleted from various appropriations bills by the House. In the case of the farm bill, for instance, the Senate added over $300,000,000 to the amount approved by the House.[56] The Senate also restored cuts made in the budgets of the National Labor Relations Board and the Wages and Hours Administration. The conference committee on the Labor-Federal Security appropriation bill accepted the Senate figure for the Wages and Hours

Robertson to President, December 21, 1939, President's Official File 185, FDR papers, FDR Library.

[54]Quotation from New York Times, March 26, 1940, p. 1. For Congressional attitudes toward NLRB and Wages and Hours Administration, see the New York Times, March 23, 1940, p. 1, March 27, 1940, p. 1, March 28, 1940, p. 1, March 29, 1940, p. 1; Time April 1, 1940, p. 14; Nation, 150 (April 6, 1940), pp. 433-434; Congressional Digest 19 (1940), pp. 67, 75-76, 98; and Harold D. Smith to President, March 26, 1940, President's Official File 119, FDR papers, FDR Library.

[55]On the effect of the 1938 elections, see the statement by Representative J. William Ditter in the New York Times, January 29, 1940, p. 7; Benson, "The Year in Congress," American Year Book, 1939, p. 17; James T. Patterson, Congressional Conservatism and the New Deal (Lexington, Ky., 1967), pp. 288-290.

[56]New York Times, February 7, 1940, p. 1, February 12, 1940, p. 30, February 19, 1940, p. 12, February 27, 1940, p. 1, February 28, 1940, p. 12, March 9, 1940, p. 1, March 10, 1940, section I, p. 9, March 20, 1940, p. 1, March 22, 1940, p. 10, March 23, 1940, p. 1; Riddick, "Third Session of the Seventy-sixth Congress," p. 292; Congressional Digest 19 (1940), p. 98.

Administration, but House conferees insisted on the NLRB cut in order to liquidate the Division of Economic Research, headed by David Saposs, a firm friend of union labor. Opposition members claimed that the Wagner Act did not specifically authorize the NLRB to conduct economic research and that the agency had exceeded the law in establishing such a division. The real target of the opposition's anger was Saposs, who had been vilified as a communist by some irresponsible detractors.[57]

The National Labor Relations Board ignored the interference by Congress and transferred the work of its Research Division to a newly-created Technical Division. Outraged by that maneuver, the House opposition inserted in another bill a proviso that "none of the appropriation 'Salaries, National Labor Relations Board, 1941' shall be obligated for the Division of Economic Research or for the Division of Technical Service." Because Saposs and his assistants accumulated and analyzed the data on which the Board based many of its decisions, the abolition of the division hampered the ability of the NLRB to function.[58]

The fate of the Technical Division of NLRB illustrated the manner in which Congressional powers were used to intervene in the application of policy by the executive branch. By reinterpreting the intent of reform legislation and by enforcing

---

[57]See Congressional Record, 76th Congress, 3rd Session, pp. 3454-3455. For David Saposs, see Herbert Harris, American Labor (New Haven, 1939), p. 394. The House-Senate dispute over NLRB is recounted in Arthur W. Macmahon, "Congressional Oversight of Administration: The Power of the Purse--II," Political Science Quarterly LVIII (1943), p. 391. See also David Saposs to Edward R. Burke, February 13, 1939, box 706-LA-719, David Saposs to Abe Murdock and Arthur D. Healey, April 17, 1940, box 709-LA-720, Wagner papers, Georgetown University Library.

[58]Newsweek, August 12, 1940, p. 35; New Republic 103 (November 4, 1940), pp. 621-622. Quotation from Riddick, "Third Session of the Seventy-sixth Congress," p. 292. See also Harry A. Millis and Emily Clark Brown, From the Wagner Act to Taft-Hartley (Chicago, 1950), pp. 51-52; and Roland Young, The American Congress (New York, 1958), pp. 218-219. Senator Robert F. Wagner, worried that the House amendment might nullify the National Labor Relations Act, tried to ensure that the NLRB could still discharge its responsibilities. When the appropriations bill came before the Senate, Wagner won acceptance for an amendment stating that no functions of the board under the National Labor Relations Act were repealed by the abolition of the Division of Economic Research and the Division of Technical Service. See Congressional Record, 76th Congress, 3rd Session, pp. 13091-13107; and J. Warren Madden, "The Functions of the NLRB Division of Economic Research," April 18, 1940, box 709-LA-720, Wagner papers, Georgetown University Library.

compliance with the altered interpretation, the opposition
sought to reverse policies ratified during the height of the
New Deal.[59] Throughout World War II, members of the opposition
conducted a guerilla war against reform by harassing programs
and personnel that they believed a majority of Congress no longer
supported.

Leaders of the opposition in the House grumbled because the
Senate, more responsive to Administration influence and to its
own spending blocs, restored most of the cuts made in the President's budget. Representative Taber berated the Senate for
undermining retrenchment, but the House itself, having made an
economy record, voted an increase of $67,450,000 to the appro-
priations of the National Youth Administration and the Civilian
Conservation Corps. Despite such generosity the opposition
seethed over the NYA. Representative Eugene E. Cox (D., Ga.),
the leader of the Democratic renegades, threatened an amendment
to the NYA appropriation that would forbid payment of any of the
funds to Aubrey Williams, head of the Youth Administration.
Cox charged that Williams "consorted with communists," an accusation seconded by Representative Hamilton Fish (R., N.Y.), who
said that Williams was "the most dangerous man in the government." Representative Malcolm Tarver (D., Ga.) soothed Cox and
dissuaded him from submitting his contemplated amendment, but
Williams, like David Saposs and other New Dealers, had become
a bete noire of the opposition.[60]

The Defense Program

The effort to weaken the New Deal through the appropriations process met with scant success in early 1940. Congress,
in an election year, had little enthusiasm for cutting domestic
expenditures. Any reductions in spending would likely be at
the expense of the War and Navy Departments. As Roosevelt had
foreseen, Congress dallied with the defense appropriations.
The House even reduced funds for the Army by about 10 percent.[61]

---

[59] Arthur W. Macmahon, "Congressional Oversight of Administration: The Power of the Purse--I," Political Science Quarterly LVIII (1943), pp. 161-163; Ernest S. Griffith, "The Changing Pattern of Public Policy Formation," American Political Science Review XXXVIII (1944), pp. 445, 455-457.

[60] New York Times, March 11, 1940, p. 1, March 22, 1940,
p. 10, March 26, 1940, pp. 1, 10, March 28, 1940, p. 1, March
29, 1940, p. 1, March 31, 1940, section IV, p. 3; Congressional
Record, 76th Congress, 3rd Session, pp. 3443-3451. See also
John Taber to Donald A. Cadzow, June 17, 1939, box 49, Taber
papers, Cornell University Library.

[61] Blum, Years of Urgency, p. 138; New York Times, April 1,
1940, p. 1.

Then came the hammer blows of the spring of 1940. In April, German naval units and assault troops conquered Denmark and Norway. Startled by rapid German advances, Congress began to move the military appropriations bills toward final passage.[62]   In May, Hitler's Wehrmacht struck France. As German armor crushed demoralized French formations, the President went before Congress to explain that the grave international situation demanded an increase in American military preparedness. Congress, persuaded more by German victories than by Roosevelt's oratory, responded with new and larger national defense appropriations. With France prostrate and the British Expeditionary Force reeling back across the channel, Congress, like the Administration and the country, was frightened. That fear triggered an outpouring of money for defense far in excess of any outlay ever before approved in peacetime. By October 15, the Congress, which began the year quarreling over a total budget of $8.4 billion, had appropriated more than $10 billion for preparedness.[63]

The large sums for rearmament began the process of converting American industry to munitions production. That development filled the opposition with mingled dread and hope. The defense program might be used as a shield for the reforms of the detested New Deal. But the emergency also offered an opportunity to regain full control over domestic policy. The Roosevelt Administration would need the collaboration or assent of opposition factions in Congress in order to pursue its foreign policy and preparedness goals.[64]

---

[62] On this point, see the explanation by Senator James F. Byrnes, Congressional Record, 76th Congress, 3rd Session, p. 8577.

[63] For descriptions of the German onslaught and American reaction, see Burns, Lion and the Fox, pp. 418-422; Blum, Years of Urgency, pp. 133, 159; Jerome Bruner, Mandate from the People (New York, 1944), p. 22; Gordon Wright, The Ordeal of Total War, 1939-1945 (New York, 1968), p. 167; and Perrett, Days of Sadness, p. 26. On Congressional appropriations, see Wilfred E. Binkley, President and Congress (New York, 1947), p. 263; Eccles, Beckoning Frontiers, p. 334; Riddick, "Third Session of the Seventy-sixth Congress," p. 291; George C. S. Benson, "The Year in Congress," in William M. Schuyler, ed., The American Year Book, 1940 (New York, 1941), pp. 31, 33-34; New York Times, October 25, 1940, p. 8; Rosenman, Public Papers and Addresses of FDR 9: 1940, pp. 198-205.

[64] Polenberg, War and Society, p. 8; Harris, Economics of American Defense, pp. 13-14; I. F. Stone, Business As Usual: The First Year of Defense (New York, 1941), pp. 13-17; Burnham Finney, Arsenal of Democracy: How Industry Builds Our Defense (New York, 1941), pp. 3-45; Jonathan Daniels, Frontier on the Potomac (New York, 1946), p. 159.

Opposition spokesmen made it clear that they would cooperate with the defense effort only on their own terms. Throughout
the spring and "spitfire summer" of 1940, they demanded concessions from the Administration. By its very existence, they argued, the New Deal imperiled the defense program. To buttress
their case, Republican leaders and business apologists pointed
to the reformist government of Premier Leon Blum as the cause
of France's military debacle. Repeatedly, they compared the
New Deal to the Front Populaire, a comparison that revealed the
intensity of their distrust of Roosevelt. Thomas E. Dewey,
Robert A. Taft, and Wendell Willkie, the three leading Republican
candidates for the Presidency, agreed that the New Deal was a
socialist-labor government hostile to the existing capitalist
economy. As Dewey said in a speech at Dallas on May 27,

> There has been a seven-year war here in our own coun-
> try. It has been a war by the Administration against
> business and against every vital and productive force
> of the nation. It has been a selfish war for power,
> waged against the men and the brains and the indus-
> trial plants we now need so urgently.

New Dealers, the opposition leaders argued, had preached class
warfare, prevented recovery, penalized business, fostered radical labor and subversive movements, and created a capricious
and autocratic bureaucracy. The New Deal, like "the Popular
Front that sapped the vitality of France and left her defense-
less," had so divided the nation and sabotaged its productive
capacity, that the defense program would inevitably fail under
the management of the Roosevelt Administration.[65]

If rearmament were to succeed, the policies of the New Deal
"must be reversed," said Senator Taft. The opposition prescribed
an interlocking six-point program to unify the nation behind the
defense program. "Evil" regulation of business by government
bureaucracy must be halted. Labor policy must be "equalized" in
favor of business, and appropriate provisions of the Wagner Act,

---

[65] For the Popular Front analogy and Republican charges
that the New Deal would hamper defense production, see Newsweek,
May 27, 1940, p. 37, June 3, 1940, pp. 30-32, June 24, 1940,
p. 32, August 26, 1940, p. 12, September 3, 1940, p. 11, October
21, 1940, p. 15; Time, February 12, 1940, p. 18, July 1, 1940,
p. 16; New York Times, February 4, 1940, p. 3, February 11, 1940,
pp. 1, 11; Wendell L. Willkie, "We the People," April 1940, box
47, Taber papers, Cornell University Library; Frank E. Gannett,
address, June 3, 1940, box 12, Gannett papers, Cornell University Library; New Republic 103 (September 2, 1940), pp. 330-331;
Joseph P. Lash, Eleanor and Franklin (New York, 1973), p. 810;
Joseph Barnes, Willkie (New York, 1952), p. 225; Ickes, Diary
III, p. 317. Quotations from Thomas E. Dewey, The Case Against
the New Deal (New York, 1940), pp. 124, 164.

Fair Labor Standards Act, and Walsh-Healey Act suspended in
order to assure an adequate and disciplined work force for industry. Wasteful non-military spending must be curtailed.
Demoralizing government competition with business must cease,
and industry must be encouraged with tax and amortization concessions, so as to restore confidence and the expectation of
profit. New Deal bureaucrats must be replaced with adminis-
trators sympathetic to the legitimate needs of American business. Lastly, the War Resources Board, or something like it,
must be revived, and the defense program managed by production
experts who could gain the necessary cooperation from private
enterprise. The alternative to those corrective measures would
be continued drift toward collectivism, as well as disunity and
fatal military weakness.[66]

The opposition's program for national defense was a re-
casting, in terms of the national emergency, of the familiar demands for business appeasement. Throughout the election campaign of 1940, Republican candidates called for a return to the
traditional American system that had laid the foundations of the
nation's material greatness, had won the First World War and
could, if necessary, win another. Even Willkie, who was prepared to accept much of the New Deal, argued that the reforms
of the 1930s had disabled the American economy. Preparedness,
therefore, was a two-front effort. To meet the foreign threat
it was necessary to eliminate the "bungling experimentation" of
the New Deal.[67]

Like their adversaries, New Dealers tried to use the national
emergency for their own purposes. They hoped the defense program
would inject new life into reform. Some had been disgruntled
when the President in May established the National Defense Advisory Commission and appointed as members prominent industrialists like Edward R. Stettinius, Jr., and William S. Knudsen.

---

[66]Quotation from New York Times, February 4, 1940, p. 3.
Details of the Republican program may be found in Robert A. Taft,
"New Dealism or Real Defense," Congressional Record, 76th Con-
gress, 3rd Session, pp. 4111A-4112A; Dewey, Case Against the New
Deal, pp. 131-165; Congressional Digest 19 (1940), pp. 161-162;
and Newsweek, May 27, 1940, pp. 35, 62, July 8, 1940, p. 14, Sep-
tember 30, 1940, p. 17; Republican National Committee, "A Pro-
gram for a Dynamic America," February 16, 1940, box 709-LA-720,
Wagner papers, Georgetown University Library; Lewis Corey, The
Unfinished Task: Economic Reconstruction for Democracy (New
York, 1942), pp. 32-36. See also Barnes, Willkie, pp. 216-217;
Patterson, Mr. Republican, pp. 235-236, 241; and Perrett, Days
of Sadness, p. 51.

[67]Newsweek, May 27, 1940, p. 37, June 3, 1940, p. 33, July
8, 1940, p. 50, September 16, 1940, p. 36; Barnes, Willkie, pp.
194-195; Perrett, Days of Sadness, pp. 72-73. Quotation from
Dewey, Case Against the New Deal, p. 128.

Reformers believed the President had caved in to pressure from
the press, the business community, and opposition spokesmen who
were clamoring for industrialists to run the defense program.
Nor were the New Dealers pleased by the appointments of Knox,
Stimson and Jones to the cabinet.[68] Further concern developed
over the President's neglect of the home front. On August 29,
for example, Representative Jerry Voorhis (D., Calif.) urged
the President not to ignore the domestic problems facing the
United States. In his reply on October 3, Roosevelt declared
that the grave international situation made it necessary to
consider only those problems of an immediate nature related to
national defense.[69]

But if some New Dealers feared the President was sacrificing the home front on the altar of his foreign policy, they
also recognized that without the defense program, the Administration would probably be trounced by an electorate still
smarting from the recession of 1937-38 and fatigued with Roosevelt and the New Deal.[70] As one sympathetic political observer
wrote, without the defense program,

> The bottom would drop out of the new prosperity;
> there would be a quick revival of interest in domes-
> tic problems; there would be intense dissatisfaction
> with the party in power and a surge of sentiment for
> throwing the rascals out. Restoration of peace in
> Europe would be an unmitigated political calamity to
> the Roosevelt Administration.[71]

---

[68] Harold D. Smith, Memorandum of Conference with the President, May 19, 1940 and Daily Memoranda, June 1, 1940, Smith
papers, FDR Library; Congressional Record, 76th Congress, 3rd
Session, p. 8694; Stone, Business As Usual, pp. 126, 159; Crider, Bureaucrat, pp. 319-320; Bargeron, Confusion on the Potomac, pp. 24-25; Perrett, Days of Sadness, pp. 69-70; Burns,
Lion and the Fox, p. 417; Milton, Use of Presidential Power,
pp. 292-293.

[69] Voorhis to President, August 29, 1940, President's Official File 3744, FDR papers, FDR Library. See also Roosevelt,
Complete Presidential Press Conferences 15-16: 1940, pp. 15:
452-521; Congressional Record, 76th Congress, 3rd Session, pp.
8241-8242; New York Times, February 12, 1940, p. 11. For the
liberal isolationist point of view, see Jerome N. Frank, Save
America First (New York, 1938), pp. 109-180.

[70] Bargeron, Confusion on the Potomac, pp. 22-23; Perrett,
Days of Sadness, p. 41.

[71] Kenneth G. Crawford, "War and the Election," Nation 150
(February 10, 1940), p. 162.

The unhappy New Deal activists were partially mollified by hints
that the industrialists were election-year window dressing and
that Knox and Stimson would be figureheads. The real show, it
was rumored, would be run by reformers like Tom Corcoran and
Leon Henderson.[72]

The President's choice of a Vice Presidential nominee also
heartened New Dealers. The delegates to the 1940 Democratic
convention wanted an orthodox party regular, like Speaker William Bankhead, Federal Loan Administrator Jesse H. Jones, or
Federal Security Administrator Paul V. McNutt. Roosevelt considered those men "reactionary" and refused to run with any of
them. Instead he selected Secretary of Agriculture Henry A.
Wallace as his running mate.[73]

Wallace, formerly a progressive Republican from Iowa, had
never been a member of the "inner circle" of the New Deal.
Yet he possessed qualities that made him acceptable to the New
Deal faction. Under the tutelage of compensatory spenders like
Mordecai Ezekiel and Louis Bean, Wallace had educated himself
about the new economics. He had also become something of a
liberal philosopher, for he did not consider the New Deal a
finished achievement and hoped to press on with the agenda of
reform. As Secretary of Agriculture, Wallace had helped build
the partnership between workers and farmers that constituted
an important source of New Deal political strength. Lately
the friendship between agriculture and labor had begun to cool,
but Wallace remained the favorite of left-wing groups like the
National Farmers Union and CIO that called for continued
farmer-labor collaboration.[74]

---

[72]Stone, Business As Usual, p. 259; Bargeron, Confusion
on the Potomac, pp. 24-25; Jonathan Daniels, White House Witness, 1942-1945 (Garden City, N.Y., 1975), pp. 47-48.

[73]Bernard F. Donahoe, Private Plans and Public Dangers:
The Story of FDR's Third Nomination (Notre Dame, Ind., 1965),
pp. 165-179. See also Timmons, Jones, pp. 277-279; James A.
Farley, Jim Farley's Story (New York, 1948), pp. 253-256, 289-
306; Burns, Lion and the Fox, pp. 429-430; Samuel I. Rosenman,
memorandum on events of July 10-19, 1940, box 5, Rosenman
papers, FDR Library.

[74]Donahoe, Private Plans and Public Dangers, p. 12; John
M. Blum, ed., The Price of Vision: The Diary of Henry A. Wal-
lace, 1942-1946 (Boston, 1973), pp. 15-16, 20-21, 32-33; Edward
L. and Frederick H. Schapsmeier, Prophet in Politics: Henry
A. Wallace and the War Years, 1940-1965 (Ames, Ia., 1970),
p. xiv; Christiana McF. Campbell, The Farm Bureau and the New
Deal (Urbana, Ill., 1962), pp. 169-174.

Roosevelt said he chose Wallace because they shared the same general ideas. His decision was probably influenced as well by the expectation that Wallace would attract the votes of midwestern farmers to the Democratic ticket. In any event, the nomination of Wallace helped conciliate those who worried that the President was betraying the New Deal in order to gain support for his defense and foreign policies. Most New Dealers eventually accepted the view of Harry Hopkins, who argued that the United States "must marshal [its] . . . complete economic strength for the task of defense." Rearmament would not mean a retreat "from our social and economic objectives" but, Hopkins concluded, would provide the means "to abolish poverty from the land." Temporarily reassured, New Dealers portrayed the choice in 1940 as liberal democracy and anti-fascism with Roosevelt, or reaction and appeasement with Willkie.[75]

In November, the President won handily, but only the war in Europe enabled him to overcome the third term issue, dissatisfaction with the New Deal, and Willkie's personal attractiveness as a candidate. A Gallup poll released on June 5 revealed that sentiment in favor of Roosevelt's reelection rose sharply after the German invasion of France. Early in September, George Gallup declared, "The election may be decided not so much by political campaigning as by Adolf Hitler." In post-election analyses, pollsters found "that the third term issue and domestic questions in general . . . [were] the issues on which Mr. Willkie gained most ground and, in fact, came close to actually winning." The President had been saved from defeat by strong support from urban voters and public confidence in his ability to strengthen national defense and manage foreign policy.[76]

Roosevelt, responsive as always to the vagaries of the public mood, recognized the importance of the war in assuring a

---

[75]See New Republic 103 (September 2, 1940), p. 325; Herbert H. Lehman, address to the New York State Democratic Convention, September 30, 1940, box 580-CA-408, Wagner papers, Georgetown University Library; J. B. Shannon, "Presidential Politics in the South," in Taylor Cole and John H. Hallowell, The Southern Political Scene, 1938-1948 (Gainesville, Fla., 1948), pp. 471-473; Donahoe, Private Plans and Public Dangers, pp. 175-177; Lash, Eleanor and Franklin, pp. 804-806. Quotation from Hopkins to President, August 22, 1940, President's Secretary's File 150, FDR papers, FDR Library. See also Wayne Coy to President, December 26, 1940, President's Personal File 1820, FDR papers, FDR Library.

[76]Quotations from New York Times, June 5, 1940, p. 18, September 4, 1940, p. 20, and November 10, 1940, p. 7. For the election results, see Barnes, Willkie, pp. 211-238; Burns, Lion and the Fox, p. 454; and Perrett, Days of Sadness, pp. 41, 53.

third term. On July 5, the President had admitted to James A.
Farley that if it were not for the war, "Willkie . . . would
be elected." The President believed, probably correctly, that
his mandate in 1940 covered defense and foreign policy, not a
continuation of reform. Consequently, Roosevelt had no intention of following the course advocated by New Dealers, who
spoke of an anti-fascist struggle for social and economic democracy at home as well as resistance to aggression abroad.
The President would do whatever was necessary to prepare the
nation for possible war with the Axis. All else he considered
secondary.[77]

The opposition, though it had lost the election, sensed
that attitude on the part of the President and the electorate,
and pressed relentlessly for measures to purify the defense
program of New Deal policies. Sporadically, Roosevelt resisted
the inroads made by enemies of the New Deal, but as a practical
politician he eventually acquiesced in much of the opposition
design for wartime America. He receded to that position because he believed, whether accurately or not, that only by
making concessions to opposition demands could the government
harness the established institutions of society and produce
quickly the greatest amount of armed strength with the least
amount of political conflict.[78]

The Legislative Agenda of the Opposition

Rearmament imparted new urgency to Congressional efforts
to revise New Deal measures like the National Labor Relations
and Fair Labor Standards Acts.[79] During the first session of
the 76th Congress (January 3 to August 5, 1939), critics of
the Fair Labor Standards Act had pushed steadily for amendments

---

[77] Quotation from Farley, Jim Farley's Story, pp. 252-253.
Roosevelt's views are revealed in Complete Presidential Press
Conferences 15-16: 1940, p. 15:492. See also Lash, Eleanor
and Franklin, pp. 781, 785, 787-788.

[78] Burns, Lion and the Fox, p. 417; John M. Blum, "'That
Kind Of A Liberal': Franklin D. Roosevelt After Twenty-Five
Years," Yale Review LX (Autumn, 1970), p. 19. For Eleanor
Roosevelt's assessment of her husband's intentions, see Eleanor
Roosevelt, This I Remember (New York, 1949), pp. 238-239 and
Sidney Baldwin, Poverty and Politics: The Rise and Decline of
the Farm Security Administration (Chapel Hill, N.C., 1968),
p. 366. See also John Taber to Richard B. Wigglesworth, Novem-
ber 12, 1940, box 62, Taber papers, Cornell University Library.

[79] Newsweek, April 15, 1940, pp. 58-60; New York Times,
May 3, 1940, p. 14; Perrett, Days of Sadness, pp. 72-73.

to that law. Two reliable New Dealers, Mary T. Norton (D., N.J.), Chairman of the House Committee on Education and Labor, and Adolph Sabath (D., Ill.), Chairman of the Rules Committee, had used parliamentary maneuvers to frustrate revision of the Act.[80] The leaders of the opposition, however, insisted that labor standards and labor relations policies lacked popular support and therefore were susceptible to redefinition. They continued to urge changes in the wages and hours law.

Late in April 1940, the anti-labor front in the House tried again to overhaul the Fair Labor Standards Act. Representative Graham Barden (D., N.C.) sponsored a set of amendments that limited the coverage of the law. Barden, however, was only a mouthpiece for Representative Eugene Cox, the real leader of the anti-labor forces. To facilitate revision of the law, "Cox's Army" of renegade Democrats and Republicans exploited the growing estrangement between farm state legislators and those representing urban, industrial districts. In the past, Democrats from the city and country had frequently collaborated to obtain House passage for the legislative objectives of both farmers and workers. New Deal farm leaders, such as Agriculture Secretary Wallace, justified that collaboration on the grounds that an increase in the purchasing power of labor would expand the market for farm commodities. Republicans retorted that organized labor was making economic gains at the expense of both businessmen and farmers, since higher wages increased the costs of manufactured goods which farmers purchased.[81]

"Cox's Army" took advantage of another source of tension between agricultural and urban representatives. Many rural districts contained no heavy industry, but a significant number of "sweated

---

[80]Norton to President, May 16, 1939, President's Secretary's File 138 and E. M. Watson to President, June 30, 1939, President's Secretary's File 113, FDR papers, FDR Library; John Taber to H. H. Griswold, May 20, 1939, and John Taber to C. S. Dudley, July 18, 1939, box 63, Taber papers, Cornell University Library.

[81]Quotation from Congressional Record, 76th Congress, 3rd Session, p. 5126. The House debate on amending the Fair Labor Standards Act of 1938 may be followed in the Congressional Record, 76th Congress, 3rd Session, pp. 5035-5052, 5120-5156, 5193-5228, 5255-5281, 5342-5370, 5436-5458, 5474-5500. On friction between rural and urban Congressmen, see Campbell, Farm Bureau and the New Deal, pp. 105, 116-117, 186 and Shannon, "Presidential Politics in the South," pp. 466-467. Wallace's position is explained in a letter to Representative Mary T. Norton, Congressional Record, 76th Congress, 3rd Session, p. 5123. See also Louis H. Bean, "Farm Income, Factory Payrolls and National Income," March 7, 1940, box 38, Bean papers, FDR Library; and Edward A. O'Neal to John Taber, April 25, 1940, box 67, Taber papers, Cornell University Library.

light industries" such as sawmills, pulpwood processing, tobacco
processing, pecan shelling, sugar, packing and canning companies.
Those operations had come under the jurisdiction of the Fair
Labor Standards Act, and employers protested vigorously against
the enforcement of minimum wages and maximum hours. Many representatives from rural districts responded to the pressure from
employers. Furthermore, opponents of the labor standards law
claimed that minimum wages in food processing industries added
to the final cost of agricultural commodities in retail outlets,
thereby discouraging consumption and constricting the market for
farm produce. In addition to the emerging conflict of interest
between rural and urban Congressmen, there were sectional considerations. Many Southerners, though not all, believed the Fair
Labor Standards Act deprived the South of its chief advantage
in attracting northern industry--wage differentials.[82]

The interaction of ideological, economic and sectional
interests generated considerable support for the Barden amendments to the wages and hours law. Representative Norton, the
chief protector of New Deal labor policy in the House, tried to
forestall consideration of the amendments. The Rules Committee,
controlled by the opposition and goaded by Representative Cox,
took the unusual step of submitting a special rule that would
extract the Barden amendments from Norton's New Deal-dominated
Labor Committee and bring them directly to the House floor. By
roll calls of 189-185 and 233-141, the House approved consideration of the Barden Bill, along with two other less-sweeping
proposals. The votes indicated that the bipartisan opposition,
assisted by some farm-state Democrats and those sensitive to
protests from the processors of agricultural commodities, had
more than enough strength to overhaul the wages and hours law.[83]

The Barden amendments ostensibly exempted "agriculture"
from the rulings and decisions of the Wages and Hours Administration. As Barden asserted on April 23, "the amendments attempt
to provide more protection for the agricultural situation and
for the producers of agricultural products." Representative
Sabath, defending the existing law, disagreed:

> All agricultural labor--that is, work done on the
> farm or by the farmer--is already exempt. The

---

[82]Irving Richter, "Four Years of the Fair Labor Standards
Act of 1938," Journal of Political Economy LI (1943), pp. 98-
99; Nation 150 (April 20, 1940), p. 498; Congressional Record,
76th Congress, 3rd Session, pp. 5048, 5350-5351, 5360; New
York Times, April 27, 1940, p. 1.

[83]New York Times, April 26, 1940, p. 1; Congressional Record, 76th Congress, 3rd Session, pp. 5045-5046, 5051-5052.
For House roll call votes on amendment of the Fair Labor Standards Act of 1938, see Appendix I, Guttman scaling table 2,
items 13, 15.

Barden bill is seeking these exemptions in the name
of the farmer but the farmer is not involved. It is
the packing, canning, sugar and cotton lobbies who
are seeking this legislation.

Richard Buckler, the lone Farmer-Labor representative from Wisconsin, deplored the effort to provoke a split between urban
and rural legislators. "As long as the special-privilege groups
can keep the farmers and the workers fighting each other," said
Buckler, "just that long will they be able to rob them both."
Representative John Coffee (D., Wash.) characterized the Barden
amendments as another example of the "frantic efforts being
exerted by predatory groups and their sympathizers, and by reactionary interests in general, to emasculate, eviscerate, or
abrogate in entirety progressive legislation."[84]

The pro-labor forces of the House, badly outnumbered, lost
nearly every roll call. But the effort to change the Fair Labor
Standards Act ultimately collapsed because the special rule permitting debate on the Barden Bill also allowed amendments from
the floor. Both the friends and enemies of labor riddled the
Barden Bill with so many exemptions and provisos that it became
a monstrosity. Barden himself asked the House to kill the measure, which it wisely did.[85]

The opposition sortie against the wages and hours law
failed as a result of poor parliamentary management. The assault on the fundamental principles of collective bargaining
was more successful, at least in the House of Representatives.
The National Labor Relations Act, called by one historian probably the most bluntly anti-corporation legislation the United
States has ever known," established the right of workers to
organize and bargain collectively through their own representatives.[86] Because it revolutionized national labor policy, it
became the target of hostile employer groups, industry lobbies,
trade associations and business apologists. Those anti-labor
forces blamed the law for the surge of labor militancy and rapid
growth of the Congress of Industrial Organizations. After the
Supreme Court upheld the Act, the anti-labor front pinned its
hopes for emasculation or repeal on the Special House Committee

---

[84] Quotations from _Congressional Record_, 76th Congress, 3rd
Session, pp. 4924, 5036, 5228, 5263.

[85] Riddick, "Third Session of the Seventy-sixth Congress,"
p. 300; Courtenay Dinwiddie, "Child Labor," in William M.
Schuyler, ed., _The American Year Book, 1940_ (New York, 1941),
p. 657; _New York Times_, April 28, 1940, p. 9 and April 29, 1940,
p. 6; _Time_, May 13, 1940, p. 20.

[86] Eric F. Goldman, _Rendezvous with Destiny_ (New York, 1952),
p. 365.

to Investigate the National Labor Relations Board, created during the "reactionary revolt" in the summer of 1939. A three-man majority on the committee--Democratic renegade Howard W. Smith, the chairman, and two Republicans, Charles A. Halleck of Indiana and Harry N. Routzohn of Ohio--brushed aside the protests of the two minority Democrats, and conducted an inquiry that confirmed the prejudices of the most extreme critics of the NLRB.[87] In a statement typical of their attitude, Representative Earl C. Michener (R., Mich.) charged that the National Labor Relations Board "conceived it to be its duty arbitrarily to organize labor throughout the country and set about the objective of organizing labor rather than presenting a forum whereby labor could organize itself." The hearings before the Smith Committee, concluded early in 1940, weakened public support for the Wagner Act and the NLRB. Even more damaging was the position of the American Federation of Labor, which accused the NLRB of favoring the rival CIO. William Green, President of the AFL, requested limited changes in the law.[88]

Encouraged by the split in the house of labor, Representative Smith, relentless foe of "radical" labor, submitted a package of amendments that would have abolished the existing board and turned labor policy sharply to the right. The House Education and Labor Committee tried to suppress the Smith proposals, but again the opposition, its resolve hardened by the onset of the defense program, had the votes to force the amendments to the floor.[89] Smith justified his bill on the grounds that the NLRB

---

[87]Kenneth G. Crawford, "Assault on the NLRB," Nation 149 (December 30, 1939), pp. 726-727; New Republic 102 (January 22, 1940), pp. 106-107; Newsweek, January 29, 1940, pp. 48-49; Time, March 18, 1940, pp. 13-14. See also "Record of Representative Howard Smith of Virginia," n.d., box 706-LA-719, Wagner papers, Georgetown University Library; Arthur D. Healy and Abe Murdock, statement on the Smith Committee, March 11, 1940, box 709-LA-720, Wagner papers, Georgetown University Library; James A. Robinson, The House Rules Committee (Indianapolis, 1963), pp. 82-83; Joel Seidman, American Labor from Defense to Reconversion (Chicago, 1953), pp. 67-68; Millis and Brown, From the Wagner Act to Taft-Hartley, pp. 30, 33, 281-285; U.S., Congress, House, Special Committee to Investigate the National Labor Relations Board, Intermediate Report, H. Rept. 1902, 76th Congress, 3rd Session, 1940; and Appendix I, Guttman scaling table 2, item 11.

[88]Quotation from Congressional Record, 76th Congress, 3rd Session, p. 4538. On the position of the AFL, see Newsweek, October 23, 1939, pp. 50-52, June 17, 1940, pp. 67-68; and Time, March 25, 1940, pp. 21-22.

[89]Congressional Digest 19 (1940), pp. 98, 162; New York Times, February 22, 1940, p. 1, March 9, 1940, p. 1, April 2,

fostered radicalism, punished business, and was staffed by bureaucrats who did not profess unqualified faith in capitalism.

> In conclusion [Smith told the House on June 6] let
> me say we are confronted by the greatest emergency
> of our national life. . . . today our first line of
> defense . . . is in the factories and shops and in
> the great industries of this country. Our safety as
> a nation depends upon their efficient operation. . . .
> above all, no agency of this Government must be per-
> mitted to stir up strife or to strafe, or hamstring,
> or persecute the industries of the country upon which
> our safety now depends.

Representative Clare Hoffman (R., Mich.), an anti-labor zealot,
agreed with Smith that the NLRB was hampering defense.

> I regret [said Hoffman] that the New Deal and its
> philosophy is so great a handicap in this our time
> of trial. . . . One of the greatest obstructions
> to . . . preparedness is the unfairness of the
> National Labor Relations Act and the arbitrary and
> unjust acts of the N.L.R.B.[90]

Loyal Democrats defended the board and the Wagner Act.
Representative Norton warned that the Smith amendments would
"practically repeal the law" and would destroy collective bargaining.[91] Representative Abe Murdock (D., Utah), one of the
minority members of the Smith Committee, denounced the opposition for smearing the NLRB. Murdock also rebutted the accusation that the board was interfering with defense. The experience of World War I, he said, proved the need for a labor
board to mediate industrial disputes and maintain uninterrupted
production. Another faithful New Dealer, Representative Frank
E. Hook (D., Mich.), declared that the Wagner Act symbolized

1940, p. 1, April 4, 1940, p. 1; Time, March 18, 1940, pp. 13-
14; Newsweek, March 18, 1940, pp. 59-60, April 15, 1940, pp.
58-60, April 29, 1940, p. 60; Congressional Record, 76th Congress, 3rd Session, p. 7518; Millis and Brown, From the Wagner
Act to Taft Hartley, pp. 351-352. See Roosevelt's comments,
Complete Presidential Press Conferences 15-16: 1940, pp. 15:
464-465.

[90]The House debate on amending the Wagner Act may be followed in the Congressional Record, 76th Congress, 3rd Session,
pp. 7506-7518, 7706-7739, 7771-7805. Quotations from Congressional Record, 76th Congress, 3rd Session, pp. 7715, 7720,
7723.

[91]Quotation from New York Times, March 9, 1940, p. 1.

the democratic values that made American society worth protecting against the Nazi peril:

> If we fail to defend the rights of free men and
> women in a democracy, if we take away the social
> legislation previously enacted, if we take away the
> labor legislation that has been placed on the stat-
> ute books, if we take away the rights of collec-
> tive bargaining, we are not defending democracy as
> it should be defended.[92]

Despite that impassioned appeal, on June 7, 116 orthodox and renegade Democrats, a majority of the party membership voting, joined 142 Republicans to pass a modified version of the Smith amendments, 258 to 129. On labor policy, the Democratic Party had cracked wide open. Seventy-five of the 100 Southern Democratic votes had been cast in favor of the Smith Bill, evidence of the growing tendency of the Southerners in the House to align themselves, on domestic issues, with the GOP.[93]

Disposition of the Smith amendments became the responsibility of the Senate, where the Administration retained a measure of control and support for the National Labor Relations Act remained stronger than in the House. Illustrative of that different mood was Senate passage on May 27 of the LaFollette-Thomas Oppressive Labor Practices Bill, aimed at eliminating some of the grosser anti-union tactics of large employers, including blacklists, industrial espionage and warfare, professional strike-breaking and yellow dog contracts. Prior to approval, the Senate had weakened the LaFollette-Thomas Bill, but its passage, even in truncated form, indicated the dim prospects for the Smith Bill.[94]

Representative Smith asked the Senate and the President to act speedily and favorably on his amendments. Other critics of the National Labor Relations Board joined him in urging the Senate to approve the Smith Bill. The secretary of the Ohio Chamber of Commerce advised Senator Taft that the Wagner Act

---

[92]Quotation from Congressional Record, 76th Congress, 3rd Session, p. 7799. See also Congressional Record, 76th Congress, 3rd Session, pp. 7718-7719.

[93]Benson, "The Year in Congress," American Year Book, 1940, p. 32; Riddick, "Third Session of the Seventy-sixth Congress," p. 301; Congressional Record, 76th Congress, 3rd Session, p. 7805. For House roll call votes on amendment of the Wagner Act, see Appendix I, Guttman scaling table 2, items 5, 8, 12.

[94]New York Times, May 24, 1940, p. 9 and May 28, 1940, pp. 1, 12; Newsweek, June 10, 1940, p. 36; Riddick, "Third Session of the Seventy-sixth Congress," p. 300.

"hangs over business like a pall," and implored him to exert every effort in behalf of pending amendments. Taft hoped to bring the Wagner Act changes to the Senate floor for a vote. But Senator Elbert D. Thomas (D., Utah), Chairman of the Education and Labor Committee, announced that the amendments would require exhaustive study and consigned them to lingering death in a committee pigeonhole.[95]

The Smith Committee continued to pillory the Wagner Act and the NLRB for the remainder of the session. Late in December, the committee's anti-labor majority produced a final report. An intemperate indictment of New Deal labor policy, the report repeated the criticisms that had been directed at the Wagner Act since its passage in 1935, served as a springboard for the activities of the anti-labor front during World War II, and presaged the Taft-Hartley Act of 1947. The report concluded that "coddling" of labor had caused violent, illegal strikes and the spread of working-class militancy. Revision of the National Labor Relations Act was necessary "lest industrial peace, and with it the entire program of national defense, be jeopardized."[96]

Senator Thomas and the majority of the Education and Labor Committee justified inaction on the Smith amendments to the Wagner Act because the Walter-Logan Bill, also pending before Congress, embodied similar provisions and made those applicable to all administrative agencies not specifically exempted. The Walter-Logan Bill became the most ambitious legislative attack on the New Deal prior to the 78th Congress (1943-44). It stemmed from anxiety over the proliferation of Federal bureaus whose decisions affected both persons and property.[97]

That concern antedated the New Deal. In 1932, James M. Beck, Solicitor General during the Harding Administration, and Ollie R. McGuire, a former counsel to the Comptroller General, published Our Wonderland of Bureaucracy, "an extreme but widely publicized expression of aversion to the administrative

---

[95] Congressional Record, 76th Congress, 3rd Session, p. 7716; George B. Chandler to Taft, June 8, 1940, box 640, New Deal-General, 1938-1940, Taft papers, Library of Congress; Congressional Digest 19 (1940), p. 257.

[96] Quotation from U.S., Congress, House, Special Committee to Investigate the National Labor Relations Board, Report, H. Rept. 3109, part 1, 76th Congress, 3rd Session, 1940, p. 1:152. See also Nation 152 (January 11, 1941), pp. 33-34; Newsweek, January 6, 1941, p. 39 and Millis and Brown, From the Wagner Act to Taft-Hartley, p. 353.

[97] Millis and Brown, From the Wagner Act to Taft-Hartley, p. 353; Crider, Bureaucrat, pp. 299-300, 304.

process."[98] The advent of the New Deal, with its manifold relief, recovery and reform apparatus, heightened the concern of
those, like Beck and McGuire, who feared the development of "administrative absolutism" and the eclipse of Constitutional government "of laws and not of men."[99]

In 1933, the American Bar Association established a special committee on administrative law to study the procedures
of regulatory commissions and quasi-judicial agencies. O. R.
McGuire became chairman of that committee in 1935 and coordinated "vigorous efforts" to insure "safeguards . . . such as
ample judicial review of administrative decisions and public
hearings before rules and regulations might be promulgated by
these regulatory governmental agencies." McGuire was also the
central figure in the drafting of the American Bar Association's
administrative law bill.[100] In January 1939, Senator M. M.
Logan (D., Ky.) assumed official sponsorship of McGuire's proposal, which was ultimately co-sponsored in the House by Representative Francis Walter (D., Pa.). The key provision of the
Walter-Logan Bill would permit unconditional judicial review of
all orders and decisions of affected Federal administrative
agencies.[101]

The Roosevelt Administration was not insensitive to the
growing pressure for a uniform code of administrative procedure.
Partly in response to the agitation of the American Bar Association, the President recognized the "need for procedural reform in the field of administrative law." On February 16, 1939,
he authorized Attorney General Frank Murphy to appoint a committee to make "A thorough and comprehensive study . . . of
existing practices and procedures with a view to detecting any

---

[98]Quotation from Ferrel Heady and Eleanor Tabor Linenthal,
"Congress and Administrative Regulation," Law and Contemporary
Problems XXVI (1961), p. 240. For an example of pre-New Deal
anti-bureaucratic literature, see Sterling E. Edmunds, The Federal Octopus in 1933 (Charlottesville, Va., 1933), pp. 42-78,
133-144.

[99]Quotations from O. R. McGuire, Americans on Guard (Washington, 1942), pp. 23, 216, 218.

[100]McGuire, Americans on Guard, pp. xv-xvi, 100-101, 196-
216, 227-231, 316-318. See also Robert M. Benjamin, "A Lawyer's
View of Administrative Procedure," Law and Contemporary Problems XXVI (1961), p. 208 and Frederick F. Blachly and Miriam E.
Oatman, Federal Regulatory Action and Control (Washington, 1940),
pp. 183-185.

[101]Congressional Record, 76th Congress, 1st Session, p.
5561; Blachly and Oatman, Federal Regulatory Action and Control,
pp. 185-188, 339-348.

existing deficiencies and pointing the way to improvements."[102] Meanwhile, without much deliberation, the Senate in July routinely passed the Walter-Logan Bill. Majority leader Alben Barkley (D., Ky.), not present when the bill was approved, understood the implications of the measure and coaxed his colleagues into recalling their hasty action. He promised that the Walter-Logan Bill would again be brought up for consideration before the expiration of the 76th Congress.[103]

In the aftermath of the initial approval and subsequent retraction by the Senate, the Walter-Logan Bill steadily gained adherents. Some of those who endorsed the measure were undoubtedly sincere in their desire for rationalization of administrative procedure and provision of judicial review. Yet the motives of other proponents were, from the first, suspect. McGuire, the chief author of the bill, was a reactionary who regarded with disfavor virtually every reform since the creation of the Interstate Commerce Commission in 1887. In the Walter-Logan Bill, McGuire had devised a way to paralyze the Securities and Exchange Commission, the Federal Power Commission, the Wages and Hours Administration, the National Labor Relations Board, and other arms of the Federal Government that implemented the policies of the New Deal. That fact was not lost on business organizations critical of Federal intervention in private economic activity. The business community soon joined bar associations in urging passage of the Walter-Logan Bill. And in Congress, the leaders of the opposition elevated the administrative law bill to a high place on their legislative agenda.[104]

The House Judiciary Committee, chaired by Hatton W. Sumners of Texas, an orthodox Democrat about to join the opposition, recommended passage of the Walter-Logan Bill. "The law," said the committee, "must provide that the governors shall be governed, and the regulators shall be regulated, if our present form of government is to endure." On February 7, 1940, the Rules Committee approved consideration of the administrative law

---

[102] President to Murphy, February 16, 1939, President's Official File 3594, FDR papers, FDR Library.

[103] Congressional Record, 76th Congress, 1st Session, pp. 7075-7078, 9389-9395, 9466-9468, 10621; Congressional Record, 76th Congress, 3rd Session, p. 13743.

[104] McGuire, Americans on Guard, pp. xv-xvi, 19-20, 128-130, 180-216, 259, 320-322, 351-361; Heady and Linenthal, "Congress and Administrative Regulation," p. 242; Blachly and Oatman, Federal Regulatory Action and Control, pp. 197-198; Congressional Digest 19 (1940), pp. 131-132; New York Times, January 27, 1940, p. 1. See also the materials in box 494, Bureaucracy, 1938-1940, Taft papers, Library of Congress.

bill. Supporters of the measure acknowledged that its purpose
was to curb the power of Federal boards and commissions, particularly the National Labor Relations Board and the Securities
and Exchange Commission. Representative Cox, in a speech on
March 21, accused the SEC of "rapidly falling to the low level
of the National Labor Relations Board." Unless "its behavior
is quickly improved," Cox admonished, "it will undergo the kind
of washing out that awaits the board."[105]

At a press conference on April 5, the President disclosed
his objections to the Walter-Logan Bill. He predicted that the
measure would cause long delays in handling government business
and would confer an unfair advantage on wealthy litigants.[106]
A report published by the Brookings Institution substantiated
both of those criticisms. The report, Federal Regulatory Action and Control, by Frederick F. Blachly and Miriam E. Oatman,
defended the existing system of regulatory agencies and explained the shortcomings of the Walter-Logan Bill. Blachly
and Oatman predicted "complete confusion in federal administrative law for years if the bill should be passed."

> The effect of the proposed change would be to bring
> about trials de novo on the administrative record.
> The courts then would be flooded with cases they
> should not be expected to handle.

According to their projection, the Walter-Logan Bill would impose a "judicial strait-jacket" on the executive branch of the
government.

> No progress would be made by seeking to substitute
> a real and all-pervading judicial absolutism for the
> imaginary 'administrative absolutism' which is
> charged but not proved by supporters of the judicial
> formula. . . . [The bill] is based on the moribund con-
> ception that law cannot prevail or justice be done
> except through the courts. . . . Because it looks
> backward and tries to revive the very system of judi-
> cial regulation of business and industry which proved
> so impossible as to lead to the establishment of ad-
> ministrative regulatory bodies, it should be discarded.

In place of the drastic Walter-Logan Bill, Blachly and Oatman

---

[105]Quotations from New York Times, February 8, 1940, p. 15
and March 22, 1940, p. 35. See also John Taber to L. J. Engle-
son, February 21, 1940, box 67, Taber papers, Cornell University Library.

[106]Roosevelt, Complete Presidential Press Conferences 15-
16: 1940, pp. 15:230-232; New York Times, April 6, 1940,
p. 1.

favored revision of current procedures to eliminate abuses of power by Federal regulatory agencies. That, presumably, was the objective of the Attorney General's Committee on Administrative Procedure, authorized by the President in his letter of February 16, 1939.[107]

The members of the Congressional opposition were in no temper to await the findings of the Attorney General's Committee. They pressed onward with the Walter-Logan Bill. Opening debate on April 15, Representative Walter insisted that there was no intention of hamstringing any agency. "But," he added, "it can never be admitted in this country that the administrative bureaucrats will control the legislative and judicial branches of this government." The bill was "a warning to those who are . . . intent on securing and exercising greater autocratic powers in the administration of laws than the Congress conferred upon them."[108] Other members echoed Walter's diatribe against Federal bureaucracy, "this Frankenstein which we as a Congress have created." In their view, the Walter-Logan Bill would rejuvenate Congressional authority, safeguard a government of laws, and restore freedom from "administrative absolutism."[109]

In advancing the measure as a check on bureaucracy, the spokesmen for the opposition were less than candid. Majority leader Rayburn exposed their real intentions by pointing out that the bill left much of the Federal bureaucracy untouched. "Why should the Federal Reserve Board . . . the Federal Deposit Insurance Corporation and the Interstate Commerce Commission" be exempt from the provisions of the bill, Rayburn asked, when the Federal Communications Commission and Securities and Exchange Commission were not? "It seems," he added, that most "of the agencies with whose establishment I had to do" were not exempt.[110] The majority leader sensed that the Walter-Logan Bill was designed to nullify New Deal policies by subjecting selected agencies to massive "judicial intervention." Other Administration supporters agreed with that assessment. Representative John Rankin (D., Miss.) charged that the bill was an

---

[107] Blachly and Oatman, Federal Regulatory Action and Control, pp. 225-226, 230. See also Heady and Linenthal, "Congress and Administrative Regulation," p. 242.

[108] Quotation from New York Times, April 16, 1940, p. 16. The House debate on the Walter-Logan Bill may be followed in the Congressional Record, 76th Congress, 3rd Session, pp. 4530-4548, 4590-4604, 4646-4675, 4722-4742.

[109] Congressional Record, 76th Congress, 3rd Session, pp. 4533-4544, 4647. See also Heady and Linenthal, "Congress and Administrative Regulation," p. 244.

[110] Quotations from Congressional Record, 76th Congress, 3rd Session, pp. 4531-4532.

assault on the public power policy embodied in the Tennessee Valley Authority and the Rural Electrification Administration. The Walter-Logan Bill, objected Representative Thomas F. Ford (D., Calif.), would mean "that the great and powerful groups . . . could employ batteries of high-priced lawyers who, by interposing unlimited objections, could thus block" the application of any law. Representative Kent E. Keller (D., Ill.) ridiculed the Walter-Logan measure as "The lawyers' emergency relief bill" whose purpose was "hamstringing the New Deal." Representative Morris Edelstein (D., N.Y.) condemned the bill as a device to thwart New Deal labor laws, the opponents of which, he said, "have not given up. Legislation which they could not prevent they seek to frustrate. . . . This bill represents still another and more ingenious method of frustration."111

As one expert on administrative law has written, proponents of the Walter-Logan Bill were "fully aware of its devastating character, for they exempted from its provisions the agencies whose work they were anxious to protect."112 Representative Cox forthrightly admitted that the measure was directed only against New Deal agencies. "There have been no complaints," he said, "against any of the old commissions. It is the new commissions that have been set up during the past few years." Cox castigated "these new agencies," particularly the SEC, NLRB, and the Wages and Hours Administration, because their "thinking is apparently rooted in doctrine that emanates from Russia." Representative Clarence Hancock (R., N.Y.), seconding Cox, grumbled that "Business in the United States is being strangled by Government interference . . . and must be set free."113

On April 18, Representative Emmanuel Celler (D., N.Y.), leader of those opposed to the Walter-Logan Bill, offered a motion to recommit the measure. Though majority leader Rayburn had belatedly announced his backing for Celler's motion, the Administration supporters lost, 106-272. The House then approved the bill, 282-96. The victorious coalition included 151 Republicans (99 percent of those voting), 75 Southern Democrats (82 percent of those voting), 54 non-Southern Democrats (42 percent of those voting), and 2 minor party members. Opposing the Walter-Logan Bill were 76 non-Southern Democrats, 16 Southern Democrats, 2 Republicans, and 2 minor party members. Like House votes on labor policy, the roll call on the Walter-Logan measure

---

111Quotations from Congressional Record, 76th Congress, 3rd Session, pp. 4600, 4654-4655. See also New York Times, April 17, 1940, p. 14.

112Kenneth C. Davis quoted in Heady and Linenthal, "Congress and Administrative Regulation," p. 244.

113Quotations from Congressional Record, 76th Congress, 3rd Session, pp. 4531, 4591-4592.

revealed a backlash against the New Deal among orthodox Democrats representing predominantly rural constituencies in southern, border, midwestern and plains states.[114]

After passage of the Walter-Logan Bill, a discouraged Representative Celler sent a warning to the President:

> Frankly, I never worked so hard during my eighteen
> years in Congress in opposition to any bill. Despite
> Sam Rayburn's help we were licked decisively. . . .
> if the bill is to be killed in the Senate, a great
> deal of work is to be done in importuning the Sena-
> tors, and you will forgive me for advising that this
> work must be done now.

Celler believed the Walter-Logan Bill would renew judicial harassment of New Deal policy and would "tie the bureaus into
endless knots." The bill, he told Roosevelt, "is nothing short
of a monstrosity and would kill most of the good work you have
done."[115]

As the Administration began "importuning the Senators" to
head off what was now a serious challenge to the New Deal, the
opposition intensified its own efforts in behalf of the Walter-
Logan Bill.[116] On April 22, Paul W. Walter, one of Senator
Taft's political lieutenants, counseled the Senator to fight
for Senate passage of the measure

> and build it into a popular issue. . . . It seems to
> me that a very carefully prepared speech, to be deliv-
> ered on the Senate floor, which carefully analyzes
> this bill and which might refer to the Bill of Rights
> and make the bill appear to be a warning sign on the
> highway to further dictatorship, might receive a very
> good response from the press throughout the country.[117]

---

[114]Riddick, "Third Session of the Seventy-sixth Congress,"
pp. 300-301; Benson, "The Year in Congress," American Year Book,
1940, p. 32; New York Times, April 18, 1940, p. 18, April 19,
1940, p. 1; Nation 150 (April 27, 1940), pp. 528-529; Congressional Record, 76th Congress, 3rd Session, pp. 4743-4744. For
House roll call votes on the Walter-Logan Bill, see Appendix I,
Guttman scaling table 2, items 6, 7.

[115]Celler to President, April 18, 1940, President's Personal File 2748, FDR papers, FDR Library.

[116]President to Thomas G. Corcoran, April 20, 1940, President's Personal File 2748, FDR papers, FDR Library.

[117]Walter to Taft, April 22, 1940, box 764, Walter-Logan
Bill, 1940, Taft papers, Library of Congress.

The press, especially the columnists hostile to the New Deal, had already grasped the significance of the Walter-Logan Bill. Hugh S. Johnson, Mark Sullivan, David Lawrence, Arthur Krock, and Frank R. Kent, among others, praised the passage of the bill by the House. The "little group of New Dealers who run things in Washington are in a state of fury over the passage by the House of the Walter-Logan Bill and the prospect of its passage by the Senate," wrote Kent.[118]

The inception of the national defense program added to the pressure for Senate passage of the Walter-Logan Bill. On June 22, the United States Chamber of Commerce asserted that a rapid expansion of defense production required not the imposition of new controls but the "removal of old ones which act as a brake on our industrial machine."[119] In the opinion of its supporters, the Walter-Logan Bill had become the most expeditious means available for removing the "brake from the industrial machine." The bill would eliminate obstacles to preparedness which supposedly arose from "the continued warfare carried on by the present administration against private enterprise, private capital, and private industry."[120]

The most provocative element in that alleged "warfare against private enterprise" was, as so often, New Deal labor policy. In order to accelerate production under the defense program, business organizations demanded "a modification of labor legislation which prevents smooth employer-employee relations."[121] Unions, on the other hand, steadfastly resisted the use of the national emergency to curtail their rights or to beat down labor standards. The Roosevelt Administration gave repeated assurances that it would protect the rights of labor. On September 1, the National Defense Advisory Commission issued a formal statement defining the Administration's attitude. The statement "affirmed support of the 40 hour week as contributing to the absorption of surplus and unemployed labor in the defense program" and asserted that all defense work must be carried on in compliance with the Walsh-Healey Act, Fair

---

[118] Quotation from Frank R. Kent, "The Great Game of Politics," n.d., box 764, Walter-Logan Bill, 1940, Taft papers, Library of Congress. See also New York Times, March 5, 1940, p. 22 and April 19, 1940, p. 20.

[119] New York Times, June 23, 1940, p. 14.

[120] Quotation from Congressional Record, 76th Congress, 3rd Session, pp. 8864-8865; see also New York Times, May 3, 1940, p. 14.

[121] Stone, Business As Usual, p. 261; Perrett, Days of Sadness, pp. 72-73. Quotation from New York Times, June 23, 1940, p. 14.

Labor Standards Act, and the National Labor Relations Act.[122] That position scarcely satisfied critics who believed "that France has shown it is impossible to carry out an effective defense program with a 40-hour week."[123]

The controversy over New Deal labor policy grew more heated in early October. Attorney General Robert Jackson issued a series of legal opinions which held "the findings of the National Labor Relations Board that an employer is in violation of the National Labor Relations Act are binding and conclusive upon the other agencies of the executive branch of the Government. . . ."[124] The Attorney General's ruling, if enforced, would deny defense contracts to such firms as the Ford Motor Company and Bethlehem Steel which had failed to comply with NLRB decisions. Industrialists, the press, and the Congressional opposition protested that Jackson had sanctioned a "blacklisting" of defense contractors that would impede rearmament. Said an outraged Representative Taber, "If a Republican had delivered such a ruling he would have been called a 'fifth columnist'. . . ."[125] Late in October, the Administration retreated and quietly abandoned the policy. Nevertheless, the opposition suspected New Dealers of endeavoring to unionize the entire labor force under the aegis of the defense program and the National Labor Relations Board. Because the provisions of the Walter-Logan Bill would render the NLRB impotent, the opposition escalated its agitation for Senate passage of the bill.[126]

Throughout the summer of 1940, Senators Barkley, Minton, and other Administration loyalists had parried the attempts of Republicans and renegade Democrats to bring up the Walter-Logan Bill. Finally, on September 20, an exasperated Senator Edward R. Burke (D., Neb.), one of the chief advocates of the measure, reminded Barkley that he had promised the bill would be

---

[122]Quotations from Witt Bowden, "Labor Conditions and Legislation," in William M. Schuyler, ed., The American Year Book, 1940 (New York, 1941), pp. 628, 642. See also Nation 152 (January 4, 1941), p. 4; and Seidman, American Labor, p. 28.

[123]Ralph Robey, "The Defense Program and Business," Newsweek, May 27, 1940, p. 62.

[124]New York Times, October 8, 1940, p. 1. Quotation from Bowden, "Labor Conditions and Legislation," p. 643.

[125]Quotation from Time, October 14, 1940, p. 30. See also Newsweek, October 14, 1940, p. 76.

[126]Perrett, Days of Sadness, p. 73, Bowden, "Labor Conditions and Legislation," pp. 644-645; New York Times, October 8, 1940, p. 1; Congressional Record, 76th Congress, 3rd Session, pp. 13221-13222.

considered prior to the expiration of the 76th Congress. Still
Barkley stalled, hoping Congress would adjourn before the Senate
acted. On November 19, the opposition in the House, joined by
isolationists suspicious of Roosevelt's foreign policy, refused
to adjourn and compelled the Senate to deal with the Walter-
Logan Bill.[127]

The decision not to adjourn was undoubtedly influenced by
a strike of the United Automobile Workers at the Vultee aircraft plant at Downey, California. The strike, which lasted
from November 15 to November 26, "occurred during the C.I.O.
convention and at a time when there was widespread alarm from
talk of a serious lag in the defense program."[128] The Congressional opposition pointed to the Vultee strike as proof that
"coddling" of labor by the Administration was undermining national defense. Said Representative Jennings Randolph, orthodox
Democrat of West Virginia, "If these strikes . . . continue, we
should take proper steps to see that such conditions are reme-
died by law if necessary." The "remedy by law" that lay closest to hand was the Walter-Logan Bill, which proponents now
touted as a rebuke to labor.[129]

Union leaders were aware of the destructive implications
of the measure. According to John L. Lewis, President of the
CIO, the Walter-Logan Bill "imposes on workers seeking protection of Federal rights a prohibitive expense and allows those
who deny these rights the easy opportunity to defend their vio-
lations by obstructive litigation and tactics." Lewis claimed
enactment of the bill would render labor's rights fictitious,
"because the slender resources of workers can not support the
burden of lengthy proceedings and consequent delay."[130]

---

[127] New York Times, May 6, 1940, p. 8, May 7, 1940, p. 1,
May 9, 1940, p. 14, May 31, 1940, p. 21, September 21, 1940,
p. 1 and September 22, 1940, p. 9; Congressional Record, 76th
Congress, 3rd Session, pp. 13660-13661, 13743-13744; Time,
December 2, 1940, pp. 14-15; Congressional Digest 19 (1940),
pp. 289-290; Benson, "The Year in Congress," American Year Book,
1940, p. 32. For House roll call vote on adjournment, see
Appendix I, Guttman scaling table 1, item 5.

[128] Quotation from Bowden, "Labor Conditions and Legislation," p. 631. See also New York Times, December 9, 1940, p.
13 and Congressional Record, 76th Congress, 3rd Session,
pp. 13774-13776.

[129] New York Times, December 13, 1940, p. 1. Quotations
from Congressional Record, 76th Congress, 3rd Session, pp. 13701
and 13964. See also Congressional Record, 76th Congress, 3rd
Session, p. 13750.

[130] Quotations from Bowden, "Labor Conditions and Legislation," p. 645.

Against that background, the Senate voted, 34-21, to consider the Walter-Logan Bill. Barkley, almost worn out by his dogged resistance, again asked his colleagues to await the report of the Attorney General's Committee on Administrative Procedure. But Republicans and renegade Democrats, convinced that New Deal labor policy was hampering defense, would not be denied. On November 26, the Senate wearily approved the measure, 27-25, with 43 not voting. Twenty-four Democratic Senators, over one-third of the party's membership, were among those absent, which gave the bill's supporters, 16 Republicans, 6 orthodox Democrats, 4 renegade Democrats, and 1 Farmer-Laborite, a temporary numerical superiority. Most of the powerful orthodox Democrats, including Senators Byrnes, Harrison, and 9 other Southerners, stayed with the Administration, but in the unusual circumstances brought about by extensive absenteeism, the measure passed. A few days later, the House concurred in minor Senate amendments and sent the Walter-Logan Bill to the President.[131]

Both opposition members and Administration loyalists anticipated a veto. Roosevelt did not disappoint them, for on December 18, he returned the bill without his signature. "I could not," the President told Congress, "conscientiously approve any bill which would turn the clock backward and place the entire functioning of the Government at the mercy of never-ending lawsuits and subject all administrative acts and processes to the control of the judiciary. . . ." Then Roosevelt addressed the real issue:

> The very heart of modern reform administration is
> the administrative tribunal. . . . Great interests,
> therefore, which desire to escape regulation rightly
> see that if they can strike at the heart of modern
> reform by sterilizing the administrative tribunal
> which administers them, they will have effectively
> destroyed the reform itself.[132]

The struggle over the Walter-Logan Bill was not yet finished, for Roosevelt had to make his veto stick. While the

---

[131] Senate debate on the Walter-Logan Bill may be followed in Congressional Record, 76th Congress, 3rd Session, pp. 13660, 13719, 13721, 13726, 13743, 13748, 13750, 14026-14040. For Senate roll call votes on the Walter-Logan Bill, see Congressional Record, 76th Congress, 3rd Session, pp. 13726, 13748; and Appendix II, Guttman scaling table 1, items 31, 33.

[132] Quotations from Rosenman, Public Papers and Addresses of FDR 9: 1940, p. 619. See also Time, December 9, 1940, p. 14; New York Times, December 12, 1940, p. 20, December 17, 1940, p. 17; and Heady and Linenthal, "Congress and Administrative Regulation," pp. 244-245.

Senate seemed sure to sustain the President, early indications
were that the House would override. Such a setback, coming
just before the convening of the new Congress, would further
weaken Presidential authority and damage party discipline.
The Administration wanted to avert an override, if at all possible. Yet Speaker of the House Rayburn "made no secret of
the fact that. . . . the House would pass" the bill over the
President's veto. Rayburn had "left Washington in disgust" and
persuaded Lyndon Johnson (D., Tex.), that talented conciliator,
to accompany him. The Democratic leadership in the House would
evidently stand by helplessly while the opposition humiliated
the President.[133]

At that juncture, Tom Corcoran performed his last major
service for Roosevelt. Corcoran convinced majority leader John
McCormack (D., Mass.) "that a fight ought to be made" even if it
was hopeless. McCormack, John Dempsey (D., N. Mex.), and Adolph
Sabath began to rally the loyal Democratic membership in the
House. The heads of Federal departments and agencies were encouraged to lobby "with some of the Congressmen who had voted
for the Bill." Rayburn and Johnson returned to Washington and
went to work on doubtful members.[134] Though late in starting,
the Administration supporters were effective, as Representative
Sumners ruefully conceded: "Some of the boys . . . have had a
good deal of heat put on them in the last few days."[135]

On December 18, the House failed to override the veto of
the Walter-Logan Bill, 153-127, with 141 not voting. Democratic defections to the opposition had been dramatically reduced. Perhaps because the President's prestige and authority
were at stake, only 36 Democrats joined the Republicans and
most of those were renegades with a long record of consistent
opposition to the Administration and to Roosevelt. The veto
was saved by 32 orthodox Democrats who had backed the original
passage of the Walter-Logan Bill, but who now changed their
votes to sustain the President. Many of those who switched
sides were Southerners. Twenty-six Southern Democrats still
favored the bill, but 25 voted to sustain the veto. The increase in the percentage of Southern Democrats supporting the

---

[133] New York Times, December 14, 1940, p. 11. Quotations
from Harold Ickes to President, December 19, 1940, President's Secretary's File 73, FDR papers, FDR Library.

[134] President to Corcoran, April 30, 1940, President's
Personal File 2748, FDR papers, FDR Library. Quotations from
Harold Ickes to President, December 19, 1940, President's
Secretary's File 73, FDR papers, FDR Library.

[135] Quotation from Congressional Record, 76th Congress,
3rd Session, p. 13951.

Administration indicated that party loyalty was not a negligible factor in the tug-of-war between the President and his adversaries.[136]

The outcome of the struggle over the Walter-Logan Bill pleased Roosevelt. Though he had been forced to expend some of his limited stock of influence, he had avoided a potentially damaging reversal just prior to the convening of the new Congress. The failure to override demonstrated that even in the House of Representatives, the Democrats retained sufficient cohesion to continue working with the President on some matters. Areas of cooperation included the protection of Roosevelt's prestige and authority as President, as well as such substantive issues as foreign policy, national defense, agricultural policy, and appropriations.[137]

Nevertheless, the President recognized the fundamental hostility toward the New Deal that had divided House Democrats, particularly on labor and regulatory policy. He was also disturbed by the defeatist attitude of the House leadership, which he believed augured ill for the future. On December 23, he lectured Speaker Rayburn,

> Because of our long-time friendship and intimate association I know you will not mind if I write you . . . some thoughts which come to me since the failure of the Republicans, and certain Democrats, to override the veto of the Walter-Logan Bill. Courage--just sheer courage--brought that about.

Roosevelt wrote that he understood the "inclination on the part of the Democrats--the friendly kind--the 'cooperation' kind, to feel, ten days ago, that the veto would be over-ridden." But, he continued, "When all is said and done that inclination amounted to a yielding to a probable defeat. . . ."

> You and I and John McCormack are facing a very difficult session. On the success of that session will depend the future reputation of the President and the Speaker and the Majority Leader. It will not help any of the three to meet with a series of defeats in the next Congress. . . .

---

[136] Benson, "The Year in Congress," _American Year Book, 1940_, p. 32; _Congressional Record_, 76th Congress, 3rd Session, p. 13953. For House roll call vote on motion to override the President's veto, see Appendix I, Guttman scaling table 1, item 4. See also George B. Galloway, _Congress at the Crossroads_ (New York, 1946), pp. 242-243.

[137] Riddick, "Third Session of the Seventy-sixth Congress," pp. 291-295.

> The vote last Wednesday is proof. . . . [that]
> A very large number of prospective defeats--not all--
> can be turned into victory by carrying on a real
> honest-to-goodness fight thereby cutting down the per-
> centage of defeats. . . .
> You and John have an opportunity to salvage much
> that would otherwise be lost in the coming session.
> . . .138

The President's letter acknowledged that the political momentum had passed into the hands of the opposition. No longer
did the Administration propose to Congress. It now strove to
defeat legislation initiated by the enemies of its domestic
policies. In vetoing the Walter-Logan Bill, Roosevelt had
acted for the first time "as protector, as defender, wielder
of the veto against encroachments" on the New Deal.139 Confronted by the growing strength of the Congressional opposition, the President foresaw that his future role, and that of
the loyal Democrats, would be "to salvage much that would otherwise be lost." Even as the Roosevelt Administration concentrated more and more on the defense of the United States against
those it identified as foreign enemies, it faced a continuing
struggle with its domestic opposition.

138President to Rayburn, December 23, 1940, President's
Secretary's File 138, FDR papers, FDR Library.

139Quotation from Richard E. Neustadt, "Extending the
Horizons of Democratic Liberalism," in J. Joseph Huthmacher,
ed., The Truman Years (Hinsdale, Ill., 1972), p. 96.

CHAPTER 3

THE STRUGGLE FOR FISCAL CONTROL

The appropriations for national defense approved by Congress
in 1940 and 1941 had significant implications for the American
economy and Federal fiscal policy. At the beginning of the Congressional session of 1940, opposition members had demanded an
end to deficit finance. After German armies overran western
Europe, not one responsible spokesman quibbled over the unbalanced budget. Compensatory spenders, frustrated during the late
1930s, had their theories tested on a huge scale. Yet the unin-
tended triumph of the new economics proved a pyrrhic one for the
Keynesian reformers of the Roosevelt Administration. Even
though Federal expenditures soared, fiscal policy remained a
controversial issue.[1]

Patriotism Plus Ten Percent: The Revenue Acts of 1940

As of January 1940, the Federal debt stood at about $42
billion, within $3 billion of the statutory limit. By the end
of May, the Treasury Department recognized that the debt ceiling
would have to be raised so that the government could meet some
of the costs of defense through additional borrowing. Secretary of the Treasury Henry Morgenthau, Jr., was also eager to
bolster the revenue side of the Federal ledger.[2]

The Administration based its tax policy on principles identified with the New Deal. The Treasury Department and the
President favored a progressive tax program that would confiscate

---

[1]John M. Blum, From the Morgenthau Diaries, vol. II: Years
of Urgency, 1938-1941 (Boston, 1965), p. 278; Randolph E. Paul,
Taxation in the United States (Boston, 1954), pp. 253-254; Herbert Stein, The Fiscal Revolution in America (Chicago, 1969),
p. 169; Robert LeKachman, The Age of Keynes (New York, 1966),
pp. 149-151; Robert A. Gordon, Economic Instability and Growth:
The American Record (New York, 1974), pp. 80-82; Roy Blough,
The Federal Taxing Process (New York, 1952), pp. 242-249; Stuart
Chase, Idle Money, Idle Men (New York, 1940), p. 3.

[2]William J. Carson, "National Finance and the Public Debt,"
in William M. Schuyler, ed., The American Year Book, 1940 (New
York, 1941), p. 250; Paul, Taxation, pp. 256-257; Blum, Years
of Urgency, pp. 278-279, 284-285; Morgenthau Diary, vol. 230,
pp. 335-336 and vol. 266, p. 281, FDR Library.

excessive profits arising from defense expenditures and avoid
the perversion of public investment for private gain. In Roosevelt's words, the Administration wanted new revenue to come
"from that group that can afford to pay it the most."[3]

Yet the President had always been braver in words than in
deeds when formulating tax policy. Moreover, the war in Europe
distracted his attention, increased his responsibilities, and
caused him to hoard his dwindling influence with Congress for
strategic military and foreign policies. Since 1937, the Senate
Finance and House Ways and Means Committees had framed revenue
legislation according to their own principles. In the clash of
philosophic outlooks on taxation, the advantage lay with the
Congressional opposition.[4]

The business community, emboldened by the need for armament
production, argued that new taxes on profits from defense contracts would retard both preparedness and recovery. Corporate
management "refused the war" and would not proceed with contracts while under the threat of profit limitations and unfavorable amortization provisions. As journalist I. F. Stone wrote,
"Behind the smokescreen of publicity, industry . . . was carrying on a sitdown strike for special tax privileges."[5] The Wall
Street Journal had warned, "Industry will demand many concessions in the way of tax exemptions, amortization policies, re-
laxation of labor laws, et cetera" in exchange for a rapid expansion of production. New Dealers considered those demands a
form of blackmail, but the Congressional opposition, convinced
that the New Deal had strangled business initiative, was ready
to enact such concessions into law.[6]

---

[3]Morgenthau Diary, vol. 157, p. 114, FDR Library; Paul,
Taxation, p. 255. Quotation from Blum, Years of Urgency, p. 284.

[4]Blum, Years of Urgency, p. 284; Paul, Taxation, pp. 208-
220.

[5]I. F. Stone, Business As Usual: The First Year of Defense (New York, 1941), p. 159. See also Blum, Years of Urgency,
p. 279; Harold M. Fleming, "The Politics of Profits," in Ray F.
Harvey and others, The Politics of This War (New York, 1943),
pp. 84-88; and Lewis Corey, The Unfinished Task: Economic Reconstruction for Democracy (New York, 1942), pp. 39-40.

[6]Quotation from Geoffrey Perrett, Days of Sadness, Years
of Triumph (New York, 1973), p. 72. For the business point of
view, see Burnham Finney, Arsenal of Democracy: How Industry
Builds Our Defense (New York, 1941), pp. 89-97; Jesse H. Jones,
Fifty Billion Dollars: My Thirteen Years with the RFC (New
York, 1951), p. 320; and Donald Nelson, "What Industry Did," in
Jack Goodman, ed., While You Were Gone: A Report on Wartime
Life in the United States (New York, 1946), p. 214.

Within parameters dictated by Congressional attitudes and Presidential impatience, the tax committees drafted and Roosevelt accepted a revenue bill that increased the national debt limit from $45 billion to $49 billion, levied special defense excise and income taxes, and reduced income tax exemptions by 20 percent. The latter provision added 2,000,000 low-income taxpayers to the Federal rolls. The bill also boosted surtax rates on individual incomes ranging between $6,000 and $100,000, and instituted small increases in corporate rates.[7] The bill was far removed from the progressive tax program that the President and the Secretary of the Treasury said they desired. At least one Administration economist, Mordecai Ezekiel, protested to Budget Director Harold Smith "that the new tax bill" struck too hard at the "lower levels of income." There was "little comfort . . . I could give Dr. Ezekiel," Smith wrote, "since the committees of Congress . . . have gone ahead" with a regressive tax measure. In deference to Senator Pat Harrison (D., Miss.), Chairman of the Senate Finance Committee, no excess profits tax had been included in the bill. Harrison was not opposed to what he considered the right kind of excess profits measure, but he wanted to postpone action until after the November election.[8]

On June 11, the House of Representatives passed the revenue bill by a vote of 396 to 6. The Senate moved with more deliberation. Senator Robert M. La Follette, Jr. (Prog., Wis.), spokesman for anti-interventionist progressives, was appalled that the bill did not contain a tax to prevent the business community from profiting by war.[9] On June 19, La Follette told the Senate "that this tax bill will go down in history not only as a sham and a delusion but also as one of the most inequitable tax measures ever passed by Congress." In its present form, he continued, the revenue measure amplified

> the inequities in our tax structure by tremendously
> increasing the burden which is levied without regard
> to ability to pay . . . [and by failing] to adopt an
> excess profits tax to reach those who will profit out
> of the huge defense expenditures which Congress has
> voted. . . .

---

[7] Paul, Taxation, pp. 256-258; Blum, Years of Urgency, pp. 286-287; George C. S. Benson, "The Year in Congress," in William M. Schuyler, ed., The American Year Book, 1940 (New York, 1941), p. 35.

[8] Quotation from Harold D. Smith, Daily Memoranda, June 8, 1940, Smith papers, FDR Library. For Harrison's views, see Blum, Years of Urgency, p. 287.

[9] Paul, Taxation, pp. 259-260; Benson, "The Year in Congress," American Year Book, 1940, p. 35; Blum, Years of Urgency, p. 288; New York Times, June 12, 1940, p. 14, June 16, 1940, p. 22.

Following up on La Follette's remarks, Senator Burton K. Wheeler (D., Mont.) reminded his colleagues "that some of those who will profit by making war munitions are saying that if heavy taxes are imposed on them. . . . they will not cooperate." That threat moved Senator Homer T. Bone (D., Wash.) to heights of sarcasm. "These patriotic businessmen," he said, "these fellows who are waving flags and bellowing to high heaven about their Americanism and patriotism . . . said to us . . . 'If we cannot make that much profit, of course, our enthusiasm will wane.'" Bone heaped on scorn:

> These businessmen suggested to us . . . that they felt very sure that they could not do a very good job if their profits were cut down to 7 or 8 percent. . . . Their stockholders would not like it. God would be insulted. The angels in heaven would wear their wings at half mast if we did such an atrocious thing to them.[10]

Though less flamboyant than Senator Bone, La Follette also rejected the argument that business might not cooperate if heavily taxed. He cited "our experience during 1917, 1918, 1919, 1920, and 1921," when a steeply graduated excess profits tax did not prevent private industry from manufacturing munitions for the government. Senator Alexander Wiley (R., Wis.) retorted that low corporate taxes were an incentive to economic growth and that corporations needed large reserves as a cushion against future depression. La Follette, unswerving in his purpose, referred to England's stringent excess profits tax and said he could not

> justify reaching the long arm of the Treasury into the pockets of people who pay the excise taxes and at the same time refuse to increase the taxes upon those corporations which, directly and indirectly, will profit by . . . [defense] expenditures.

He introduced an amendment to the pending revenue bill which levied an immediate excess profits tax on all earnings above eight percent return on invested capital.[11]

Senator Walter F. George (D., Ga.), who was rapidly becoming Congress's most prestigious voice on revenue legislation, opposed

---

[10]Quotations from Congressional Record, 76th Congress, 3rd Session, pp. 8596-8597, 8621. See also Joseph P. Lash, Eleanor and Franklin (New York, 1973), pp. 809-810; Stone, Business As Usual, pp. 159-161; U.S. Congress, Senate, Committee on Naval Affairs, Hearings before the Committee on Naval Affairs on H.R. 9822, 76th Congress, 3rd Session, 1940, p. 20; and Congressional Record, 76th Congress, 3rd Session, pp. 8624-8625.

[11]Congressional Record, 76th Congress, 3rd Session, pp. 8594-8598, 8600-8601.

the La Follette amendment, as did a majority of renegade and orthodox Democrats and Republicans. But New Dealers, assisted by some fiscal conservatives who favored increased revenues, won approval of the provision by a vote of 41 to 31. That victory for progressive taxation was short-lived, for the House-Senate conference committee on the revenue bill excised the La Follette amendment. To satisfy those who favored excess profits taxation, the conferees promised that such a tax would be enacted "as soon as possible." The revenue bill then passed the Senate, 75-5.[12]

The First Revenue Act of 1940 contained no excess profits tax, but Congress and the Administration shared an obligation to enact such a tax at the earliest possible date. The crucial issue was whether it would be an authentic excess profits measure or a fraud. In late June, the President told the Secretary of the Treasury to "make it tough." Morgenthau did his best to follow Roosevelt's instructions.[13]

The Congressional opposition had other plans. In response to pressure from organized industry, the National Defense Advisory Commission urged favorable adjustment of amortization privileges and repeal of the Vinson-Trammel Act, which limited profits on defense contracts in the shipbuilding and aircraft industries to 8 percent. Opposition spokesmen enthusiastically endorsed those recommendations. Roosevelt and Morgenthau, on the other hand, insisted that the changes should come after enactment of a steeply graduated excess profits tax. "Any effort to separate the favors to business from the new tax, . . . [Roosevelt] warned, would invite a veto, for if business got what it wanted, its spokesmen in Congress could very probably defeat what it did not want."[14]

---

[12]Quotation from Paul, Taxation, p. 262. For Senate roll call vote on the La Follette amendment, see Congressional Record, 76th Congress, 3rd Session, p. 8614; and Floyd M. Riddick, "Third Session of the Seventy-sixth Congress," American Political Science Review XXXV (1941), p. 296. The revenue bill is analyzed in Roy G. and Gladys C. Blakey, "The Two Federal Revenue Acts of 1940," American Economic Review XXX (1940), pp. 724-728. See also Congressional Record, 76th Congress, 3rd Session, p. 8585.

[13]Quotation from Blum, Years of Urgency, p. 289. See also Paul, Taxation, pp. 260-263.

[14]Benson, "The Year in Congress," American Year Book, 1940, p. 35; Stone, Business As Usual, pp. 162-165; Perrett, Days of Sadness, p. 72; Harold Ickes, The Secret Diary of Harold Ickes, vol. III: The Lowering Clouds, 1939-1941 (New York, 1954), p. 315. Quotation from Blum, Years of Urgency, p. 291. See also Oscar Cox, Diary, July 12, 1940, box 145, Cox papers, FDR Library.

As a consequence of the struggle over excess profits, the opposition kept a second revenue bill locked up in committee through July. Finally, the President gave in. Though Roosevelt publicly denied that there was a sitdown strike by businessmen, industry was not producing arms, and the President was forced to surrender to business pressure for higher profits, favorable amortization privileges, and other incentives. Anxious for "an excess profits bill this session," he agreed to leave "the details of the bill" to Harrison and Doughton of the Finance and Ways and Means Committees. The Treasury alerted Roosevelt that Harrison and Doughton "were thinking . . . of a face-saving bill, and not one that will really get the revenue on an equitable basis."[15] But the President no longer cared. Secretary of War Henry L. Stimson, Secretary of the Navy Frank Knox, and NDAC production chief William S. Knudsen had convinced him that delay in formulating amortization provisions was impeding rearmament. If corporate management did not get what it wanted on taxes, they argued, businessmen would not sign defense contracts. Roosevelt came to share the view of Stimson, Knox and Knudsen that maximum arms production required large profits for industry.[16]

Late in August, the House Ways and Means Committee produced a second revenue bill that granted a package of concessions to business and provided for an ineffectual excess profits tax. The Senate Finance Committee further diluted the tax. Its draft called for a flat instead of a graduated schedule. Under the Senate bill, each business could choose between two methods of calculating a tax credit to offset its excess profits liability. It could calculate a credit based on return from invested capital or based on previous average earnings. That option would allow corporations with enormous capital structures (like large steel companies) and those with a recent upsurge in earnings (like aircraft manufacturers) to escape the tax.[17]

The Treasury, unhappy with such attentiveness to the desires of industry, now collaborated with Senator La Follette on

---

[15]Franklin D. Roosevelt, Complete Presidential Press Conferences of Franklin D. Roosevelt, vols. 15-16: 1940 (New York, 1972), pp. 16:93, 155, 161. Quotations from Blum, Years of Urgency, p. 291.

[16]For Stimson's views, see Elting E. Morison, Turmoil and Tradition: A Study of the Life and Times of Henry L. Stimson (Boston, 1960), pp. 512-516; and Henry L. Stimson and McGeorge Bundy, On Active Service in Peace and War (New York, 1947), pp. 352-354. See also Blum, Years of Urgency, pp. 291-292; and Ickes, Diary III, pp. 289-290.

[17]Paul, Taxation, pp. 263-268; Blum, Years of Urgency, pp. 293-294; Roy G. and Gladys C. Blakey, "Two Federal Revenue Acts of 1940," pp. 731-732.

an amendment to put more teeth into the bill. But Roosevelt,
though privately sympathetic, considered the La Follette amendment a hopeless cause. He would not support the proposal and
without his assistance, the last chance for an equitable tax
expired. On the floor of the Senate, La Follette flayed the
bill offered by "genial" Senator Harrison as a travesty that
gutted "every principle of sound taxation." The Senate listened to La Follette's appeal and then rejected his amendment,
41-20.[18]

The Second Revenue Act of 1940, given final Congressional
approval on October 8, was a delusive measure. It called for
a 50 percent tax on excessive business profits but still contained loopholes which limited the utility of that tax. The
act also suspended the profit limitation sections in the Vinson-
Trammel Act and the Merchant Marine Act and provided for 60-
month amortization, out of tax-free earnings, of the total
costs of properly certified emergency defense facilities. Those
provisions constituted a defeat for the principles of tax reform advocated by the Treasury Department.[19]

The First and Second Revenue Acts of 1940 bore the imprint
of the Congressional opposition to the New Deal. Roosevelt reluctantly accepted the legislation because he believed that
concessions had to be made to assure maximum arms production
with a minimum of friction. Yet other approaches were available. The British, for example, had levied a 100 percent tax
on excess profits and had tried to divide the sacrifices of war
as equally as possible. To enlist the wholehearted support of
the working class and the Labor Party, the British coalition
government was endeavoring to wage a "People's War." The Revenue
Acts of 1940 ensured that the American defense effort would not
be a "People's War" on the British model but would instead mag-
nify the entrenched economic power of consolidated units of finance and industry.[20]

---

[18] Blum, Years of Urgency, pp. 294-295. For Senate roll
call vote on the La Follette Amendment, see Congressional Record,
76th Congress, 3rd Session, p. 12172; and Riddick, "Third Session of the Seventy-sixth Congress," pp. 296-297. Quotations
from Congressional Record, 76th Congress, 3rd Session, pp.
12068-12081.

[19] Perrett, Days of Sadness, p. 72; Benson, "The Year in
Congress," American Year Book, 1940, pp. 35-36; Paul, Taxation,
pp. 269-270; Roy G. and Gladys C. Blakey, "Two Federal Revenue
Acts of 1940," pp. 728-731.

[20] Angus Calder, The People's War: Britain, 1939-1945
(New York, 1972), pp. 20-22, 100-124; Stone, Business As Usual,
p. 162; Congressional Record, 76th Congress, 3rd Session,
p. 7722; Perrett, Days of Sadness, pp. 72, 178-179.

Some government officials dissented from the policy of capitulating to big business. Thurman Arnold, head of the anti-trust division of the Department of Justice, warned against relying so heavily on "management by private monopoly." He believed that "the vast government spending for war production . . . .created a great opportunity for conspiratorial agreements between businessmen with respect to prices, bidding, consolidations and mergers." The result of those "conspiratorial agreements," said Arnold, was restriction of production in national defense industries and artificially high prices for defense materials.[21] But Arnold came to be thought of as a dangerous fanatic by those "who feel that industry will not cooperate in national defense unless they are completely let alone." Those were "the same kind of people," Arnold commented, "who thought industry wouldn't cooperate in economic recovery unless it was let alone." As an antidote to oligopolistic behavior, he urged continued enforcement of the anti-trust laws, but pressures were already building, as early as the summer of 1940, which eventually halted Arnold's anti-trust prosecutions for the duration of the war.[22]

Like the anti-trust division of the Department of Justice, the Temporary National Economic Committee sounded a cautionary note. Its experts believed that oligopolistic practices had aggravated the depression and, by stifling competition, made recovery more difficult. According to TNEC, the defense program threatened to exacerbate the problem of oligopoly by funneling huge appropriations into the coffers of dominant firms. As of February 1941, reported TNEC, "45 percent of all contracts, amounting to about $13,000,000,000, were awarded to 6 closely interrelated corporate groups." For that reason, TNEC warned,

It is quite conceivable that the democracies might attain a military victory over the aggressors only to find themselves under the domination of economic

---

[21] Quotations from Thurman Arnold, Fair Fights and Foul (New York, 1965), p. 144; and U.S.,Congress, Temporary National Economic Committee, Final Report and Recommendations, 77th Congress, 1st Session, 1941, p. 99.

[22] Quotations from Arnold to President, May 17, 1941, President's Secretary's File 146, FDR papers, FDR Library. See also U.S., Congress, Temporary National Economic Committee, Final Report and Recommendations, 77th Congress, 1st Session, 1941, p. 100; James H. Rowe to President, August 15, 1940, President's Secretary's File 146, FDR papers, FDR Library; Morison, Turmoil and Tradition, p. 513; Richard Polenberg, War and Society: The United States, 1941-1945 (Philadelphia, 1972), p. 78.

authority far more concentrated and influential than
that which existed prior to the war.[23]

But TNEC, a relic of the New Deal, soon terminated its investigation. Its final report, released at a time when "the attention of the American people . . . was focused on external affairs," received scant notice from the Administration, the Congress, the press or the public.[24]

In the event of war, the special Senate committee investigating the munitions industry had warned in 1936, preventing
business aggrandizement would be almost impossible. Efforts to
control profiteering, the committee declared, would "be in direct conflict with the efforts to stimulate production; it is
the former rather than the latter which must be sacrificed."
The revenue legislation of 1940 seemed to bear out that asser-
tion. Powerful Congressional factions and some senior officials of the Roosevelt Administration believed that the New
Deal had devitalized private enterprise during the 1930s and
were determined to compensate during the defense period for New
Deal policies. In the pungent phrases of Secretary of War
Henry L. Stimson, "If you are going to . . . prepare for war,
in a capitalist country, you have got to let business make
money out of the process or business won't work." Under unrelenting pressure from those who held that view, the Roosevelt
Administration handed the defense economy to big business and
commissioned it to turn out weapons. Henceforth, the defense
effort would operate on "patriotism plus 10%."[25]

The Battle of the Budget

The tax policy embodied in the Revenue Acts of 1940 was a
victory for the program of business appeasement long supported
by critics of the New Deal. In the words of Harold Ickes,

---

[23]U.S., Congress, Temporary National Economic Committee,
Final Report and Recommendations, 77th Congress, 1st Session,
1941, pp. 3-4.

[24]Jerome B. Cohen, "The Forgotten T.N.E.C.," Current History I (September, 1941), p. 46.

[25]Quotations from U.S., Congress, Senate, Special Committee
on Investigation of the Munitions Industry, Report on War Department Bills S. 1716-S. 1722 Relating to Industrial Mobilization in Wartime, S. Rept. 944, part 4, 74th Congress, 2nd Session, 1936, p. 9; Polenberg, War and Society, p. 12; and Perrett, Days of Sadness, p. 182. See also U.S., Congress, Senate,
Special Committee on Investigation of the Munitions Industry,
Preliminary Report on Wartime Taxation and Price Control, S.
Rept. 944, part 2, 74th Congress, 1st Session, 1935, pp. 3-52.

"This is abandoning advanced New Deal ground with a vengeance."[26]
As a corollary to that tax policy, the Congressional opposition
once again renewed its drive to slash non-military spending.
The last such effort to reduce expenditures, initiated early in
1940, had faltered prior to the fall of France and the President's request for additional funds for rearmament. Yet the
attack on spending was so constant a refrain in the repertoire
of fiscal conservatives, that they were not long in reverting to
it. The appropriations for defense and the prospect of higher
taxes gave their position added force. Economizers argued, not
without justification, that the defense program necessitated cutbacks in other categories of government spending, an argument
that the Roosevelt Administration partially accepted.[27]

In the van of the opposition drive against New Deal "extravagance" was Senator Harry F. Byrd (D., Va.), perhaps the
Administration's most persistent detractor. On May 30, 1940,
Byrd announced that he would propose an amendment to the pending
relief appropriation which would mandate a minimum 10 percent
reduction in each appropriation already voted for activities
other than national defense. The Senator insisted that regular
expenditures constituted a source of funds which could be
channeled into the defense program. The cutbacks would total
over $400,000,000 and should be made, he said, before the enact-
ment of higher taxes.[28]

A horizontal 10 percent reduction in non-military expenditures would have seriously hindered the operations of the
Federal government. As introduced in the Senate on May 31,
Byrd's amendment would have compelled a reduction in the pay of
Federal employees or the outright furlough of some of them.
Furthermore, a horizontal reduction of 10 percent would have
required deep cuts in relief and agricultural appropriations
and, as Byrd well knew, would have caused suffering among the
needy. The defense program had not yet created any substantial
reemployment and the sums appropriated for Federal aid to the
unemployed were, as usual, inadequate. Even with Federal aid,
state and local governments still had difficulty meeting the
requirements of public assistance.[29]

---

[26]Ickes, Diary III, p. 295.

[27]During the debate on the First Revenue Act of 1940,
House Republicans offered their standard charges about wasteful
New Deal spending. See Paul, Taxation, p. 257.

[28]New York Times, May 30, 1940, p. 8, May 31, 1940, p. 9.

[29]Fred K. Hoehler, "Public and Private Social Work," in
William M. Schuyler, ed., The American Year Book, 1940 (New
York, 1941), pp. 607-610; Congressional Record, 76th Congress,
3rd Session, pp. 7256, 8477.

The President recognized those realities and attempted to deflect Byrd's rigid proposal. According to Budget Director Smith, Roosevelt "felt that there was some sentiment in Congress for a reduction" in the "expenses of the Government other than those for national defense."[30] But he objected to mandatory legislation. On June 3, Roosevelt met with the Congressional leadership and announced a more flexible plan for curtailing non-military expenditures. It was difficult, he told the press on June 4, to distinguish between defense and non-defense spending. The rearmament program would throw a greater burden on many regular departments of the government. An across-the-board cutback was too drastic, but the President promised to establish reserves and impound funds whenever possible.[31]

Senator Byrd did not trust Roosevelt to execute a voluntary cutback in spending. He was joined by Senator Arthur Vandenberg (R., Mich.), a like-minded ally, and the National Economy League, a business lobby, in demanding a mandatory 10 percent reduction. On June 9, Byrd asked the Senate to adopt his proposal: "Congress should feel impelled," he said, "to eliminate every present extravagance in our National Government . . . so that such savings can be diverted to the cost of national defense."[32]

Byrd lacked the votes to attach his amendment to the relief appropriation. He turned to a friendlier forum, the Senate Finance Committee, dominated by Senators Harrison and George. Aware of certain technical defects in his resolution, Byrd requested Harrison's assistance in perfecting the language of the amendment. On June 10, they conferred with Budget Director Harold Smith and Under Secretary of the Treasury Daniel Bell. Smith wrote of the conference, "We [Smith and Bell] felt that there should not be a 10 percent cut, but if 10 percent was what the Senator was insisting upon," then "we would . . . attempt to draft . . . a practical, workable resolution without . . . committing ourselves to it." The Budget Director suggested that Byrd revise his resolution so that the President would be directed to reduce the total of all non-defense appropriations for fiscal 1941 by at least 10 percent. The change in wording would allow the President to decide which appropriations should be left untouched and which should be cut.[33]

---

[30] Harold D. Smith, Memorandum of Conference with the President, June 3, 1940, Smith papers, FDR Library.

[31] New York Times, June 4, 1940, p. 13; Roosevelt, Complete Presidential Press Conferences 15-16: 1940, pp. 15: 439-442; Harold D. Smith, Memorandum of Conference with the President, June 3, 1940, Smith papers, FDR Library.

[32] Quotation from New York Times, June 10, 1940, p. 1.

[33] New York Times, June 12, 1940, p. 14; Congressional Record, 76th Congress, 3rd Session, p. 8477; Harold D. Smith, Daily Memoranda, June 10, 1940, Smith papers, FDR Library.

Byrd and Harrison submitted the revised amendment to the Finance Committee, which paused in its exertions on the First Revenue Act of 1940 and adopted the Byrd proviso by a vote of 16 to 4. That action conformed to the committee's curious notion of equality of sacrifice. Though unwilling to support an excess profits levy, the committee was ready to slash the work relief and farm programs.[34]

That plan offended Senators supporting the Administration. Majority leader Alben Barkley (D., Ky.) objected that the Byrd amendment to the revenue bill "might result in a greater reduction in the relief appropriations than 10 percent in order to arrive at the average of 10 [percent]." Senator Richard Russell (D., Ga.), a dogged defender of agricultural interests, concurred: "it seems to me that [Senator Byrd] . . . has excluded and exempted until he has placed all the burden of the reduction squarely on the agricultural program and on the relief bill. . . ." Senators Homer Bone (D., Wash.) and John Bankhead (D., Ala.) complained that the Byrd amendment would delegate Congress' Constitutional power over appropriations to the President. Said Bone, "We ought to do the pruning and cutting of the Budget, instead of passing the Budget, having it become a law, and then dumping it on the lap of the President and having him do what the Constitution says he cannot do."[35]

When it suited his purpose, Byrd often castigated Roosevelt for exceeding the constraints of the Constitution. Though he recognized the inconsistency of his present position, he defended his amendment, whether unconstitutional or not, because "it would be impractical to return to the appropriating committees the job of revising" various appropriations. Byrd admitted that "Congress is passing the buck to the President," but he argued that such a course was justified by "the crisis which confronts the country."[36]

Byrd was fighting a losing battle. New Deal and orthodox Democrats, particularly those from farm states, and Senators averse to Presidential impoundment of appropriations, banded together. By a vote of 41 to 36, they rejected the mandatory language of the Byrd proviso. The Senate had "cut the heart

---

[34]New York Times, June 16, 1940, p. 22; Newsweek, June 24, 1940, p. 35.

[35]Quotations from Congressional Record, 76th Congress, 3rd Session, pp. 8477, 8479, 8492. See also New York Times, June 19, 1940, p. 13.

[36]Quotations from Harold D. Smith, Daily Memoranda, June 10, 1940, Smith papers, FDR Library; and Congressional Record, 76th Congress, 3rd Session, p. 8492.

out of the amendment," lamented Byrd, who was ready to ask that the remnant of his plan be excised from the revenue bill.[37]

At that point, Senator Millard Tydings (D., Md.), another Democratic renegade, took up the cause. He introduced an amendment calling for a mandatory reduction of 5 percent. That proposal, too, was defeated by a vote of 47 to 33. Undeterred, Tydings offered a 3 percent mandatory reduction. Majority leader Barkley, visibly angry, reminded Tydings that the Finance Committee had not levied heavy taxes on the wealthy or on the excess profits of corporations.

> I want to . . . [take] the revenue from those who are . . . able to bear the burden, and not press down more unjustly upon those who are the unfortunate part of our people.
> We cannot save 10 percent, we cannot save 5 percent, we cannot even save 3 percent . . . without taking the larger part of it from those to whom I have referred.[38]

Tydings made one last attempt to win approval for a mandatory reduction, this time of 4 percent. The Senate rejected it by a vote of 41 to 32, whereupon Byrd asked that the useless remnant of his original amendment be removed from the revenue bill and that was done by a vote of 63 to 14.[39]

Rejection of the Byrd and Tydings amendments scarcely dampened the campaign to reduce non-defense expenditures. Throughout the remainder of 1940, fiscal conservatives continued to demand that the President eliminate all "nonessential" spending.[40] Roosevelt responded to that escalation of political pressure with gestures that he hoped would pacify the economizers. But Senator Byrd and his allies had little faith in Presidential intentions. If sweeping reductions were to be made, they felt sure Congress would have to make them.

In place of his original scheme, Byrd now concentrated on an alternative plan, the establishment of a joint appropriations committee. Such an entity, if dominated by anti-New Deal

---

[37]Congressional Record, 76th Congress, 3rd Session, pp. 8499-8500.

[38]Congressional Record, 76th Congress, 3rd Session, pp. 8500-8508.

[39]Congressional Record, 76th Congress, 3rd Session, pp. 8586-8587. For Senate roll call votes on non-defense spending, see Appendix II, Guttman scaling table 4, items 4, 5, 7.

[40]New York Times, September 21, 1940, p. 1.

factions, could give the Congressional opposition a measure of control over expenditures similar to that which it already exerted over taxation. At the beginning of the current session, Senator Harrison had proposed a joint appropriations committee. The House of Representatives had refused to go along with Harrison's scheme because of the House's special role under the Constitution. All appropriations bills originated there, and House members feared that a joint committee might undermine their prerogatives. As long as that attitude persisted, Byrd and his supporters, it seemed, would have difficulty winning House acceptance of a Congressional budget agency.[41]

Meanwhile, wrote Harold Smith, the Roosevelt Administration grappled "with the problem of setting up reserves against the appropriations in order to save money on so-called non-defense items." Smith thought there was considerable misunderstanding about the problem of non-defense spending. It was "not an easy matter," he commented, "to make reductions after the appropriations had been made; . . . in many cases a very tight budget had been submitted in the first place, and . . . Congress had made other cuts, in the activities of the Government." Despite the "considerable difficulty" involved, Smith ordered his budget examiners "to determine what proposed expenditures might be delayed or eliminated."[42]

Even as the Administration stepped up impoundment of appropriations, economy advocates in Congress kept up a steady stream of complaints against alleged waste in non-military appropriations. On September 23, for example, Senator Robert A. Taft (R., O.) declared: "I believe that $2,000,000,000 can be cut out of our domestic expenditures." And on October 13, Senator Alva B. Adams (D., Colo.) urged a scaling down of non-defense spending. The latest wave of economy talk crested on November 7, only two days after Roosevelt's reelection, when Byrd denounced Secretary Morgenthau for asking that the national debt limit be lifted to allow the Treasury the latitude to finance defense on the most favorable terms possible. Such a policy, said Byrd, would be an "incentive for further extravagance."

In the face of gigantic expenditures for national defense universally approved by the nation the Federal

---

[41]Congressional Record, 76th Congress, 3rd Session, p. 8573. On the Harrison plan, see the New York Times, January 7, 1940, p. 1, January 8, 1940, p. 1, January 9, 1940, p. 13, January 11, 1940, p. 1, January 14, 1940, p. 21; and Congressional Digest 19 (1940), p. 35. For Roosevelt's views on a Congressional budget agency, see President to James J. Davis, February 10, 1940, President's Official File 79, FDR papers, FDR Library.

[42]Harold D. Smith, Memorandum of Conference with the President, June 3, 1940, and Daily Memoranda, June 25, 1940, Smith papers, FDR Library.

government is still spending approximately the same huge amounts for strictly non-defense and non-essential peacetime activities of the government.

The time had come, Byrd insisted, "to reduce non-essential non-defense spending to the absolute minimum and devote consequent savings to financing the defense program."[43]

Shortly thereafter, the Roosevelt Administration began to hint that further cuts in non-military spending were forthcoming. Those hints were timed to coincide with the admission that more tax revenue would be needed by the Federal government. On November 20, 1940, Representative Robert Doughton (D., N.C.) conferred with the President and afterward told reporters that higher taxes were inevitable. Doughton pointedly linked his remarks about tax increases to anticipated reductions in relief spending, made possible, he said, because of increasing reemployment by private industry.[44]

On November 26, the President conceded the necessity for further economies in non-defense spending. He told a press conference that his "general policy" for "this coming budget" would be to "cut down to the bone on non-military public works." The President wanted planning on public works to continue, so that

when this great employment on defense comes to an end. . . . as fast as people are thrown out of work in munitions factories, we will be able to take projects . . . off the shelf and put the people who have been working on defense . . . back on useful public works . . . thereby taking up the slack and preventing a serious depression.

Roosevelt hoped that the pronouncement of his budget principles would reassure "a lot of Congressmen and Senators" who had been clamoring for cuts in non-defense expenditures.[45] But some remained skeptical. Representative Joseph Martin (R., Mass.), House minority leader, dismissed the President's pledge of greater economy as "the same old stuff." "He just talked about it, didn't he," said Martin.[46]

---

[43] New York Times, September 24, 1940, p. 13, October 14, 1940, p. 7, November 8, 1940, p. 13.

[44] New York Times, November 21, 1940, p. 1.

[45] Roosevelt, Complete Presidential Press Conferences 15-16: 1940, pp. 16: 326-327. See also U.S., Congress, House, Committee on Appropriations, Hearings before a subcommittee of the House Committee on Appropriations on the Independent Offices Appropriations Bill, 77th Congress, 1st Session, 1941, p. 742.

[46] Quotation from New York Times, November 28, 1940, p. 14. For the views of another distrustful Republican, Representative

While members of the opposition grumbled about the lack of
Administration action on non-military spending, private organizations issued strong statements demanding cuts in all but defense outlays. On December 3, the committee on government finance of the National Association of Manufacturers urged elimination of "astronomical" domestic expenditures. A few days
later, the Chamber of Commerce of the United States endorsed
the establishment of a Congressional agency to review expenditure policy. "It is believed," said the Chamber, "that savings
of hundreds of millions of dollars could be made without difficulty in non-defense expenditures." On December 11, the Brookings Institution declared that domestic spending must be curbed
in order to preserve economic stability. Still another private
group, the National Economy League, claimed that a saving of
more than $2,000,000,000 could be made in the next fiscal year.[47]

Partly in response to continuing agitation for reductions
in spending, the President on December 18 ordered the curtailment of office building construction by the Federal government.
But neither that move, nor the announcement of his fiscal 1942
budget satisfied his enemies. The budget called for the expenditure of $17.5 billion, of which $10.8 billion, or 62 percent, had been allocated for national defense. Fixed commitments, such as interest payments, pensions, completion of public
works projects, and similar items, accounted for $3,196,000,000.
The remainder, $3,478,000,000, was earmarked for civil depart-
ments and agencies, agricultural programs, public works, social
services, and relief. In that last category, the President
claimed to have reduced non-defense expenditures "by 600 million
dollars or 15 per cent" as compared to fiscal 1941. Roosevelt
told his press conference on January 7, 1941, that he was
"rather happy" with a 15 percent reduction. But the saving in
which he took such pride fell far short of the $2,000,000,000
being demanded by Senator Taft, the National Economy League,
and others who favored drastic retrenchment.[48]

On Capitol Hill, the President's budget provoked a new
flurry of interest in some form of Congressional budget control
and prompted Taft to comment, "The President still believes in
spending money as if it were water." Representative Clifton

Robert F. Rich of Pennsylvania, see Congressional Record, 76th
Congress, 3rd Session, p. 13766.

[47]New York Times, December 4, 1940, p. 22, December 9,
1940, p. 14, December 12, 1940, p. 43, December 30, 1940, p. 13.

[48]New York Times, December 19, 1940, p. 19. Quotations
from Franklin D. Roosevelt, Complete Presidential Press Conferences of Franklin D. Roosevelt, vols. 17-18: 1941 (New York,
1972), pp. 17: 10, 16, 21, 23. See also Samuel I. Rosenman,
ed., The Public Papers and Addresses of Franklin D. Roosevelt,
vol. 9: 1940, War and Aid to Democracies (New York, 1941),
p. 654.

Woodrum (D., Va.), who frequently spoke for fiscal conservatives in the House, suggested that Congress devise its own machinery for cutting domestic expenditures. Woodrum urged the establishment of a House budget committee, which would include the majority and minority leaders, the chairmen of Appropriations and Ways and Means, and ranking members of the two committees. Their function, as described by Woodrum, would be to set an upper limit on expenditures, to determine the spending priorities within that limit and to act as a check on the logrolling of appropriations which threatened to exceed the limit.[49]

Representative Allen T. Treadway (R., Mass.) advanced a similar plan for a joint budget committee drawn from both House and Senate. But all such proposals proved abortive. For the moment, at least, the Congressional opposition acquiesced, albeit unhappily, in the existing budget process and made no serious effort to establish a mechanism to revise the President's estimated expenditures.[50]

Yet the idea of some form of Congressional budget control was not quite dead. When the Senate on February 14, 1941, approved a bill raising the national debt limit to $65 billion, Senator Byrd offered a resolution to establish a joint commission of six Senators and six Representatives to examine the government's fiscal policy and make recommendations aimed at the elimination of all nonessential Federal expenditures. Until non-defense spending was reduced, said Byrd, "we face the dilemma of adding every dollar for national defense and every dollar of aid to Great Britain and other countries to the national debt." Not only concern over the mounting Federal debt, but also the prospect of still higher taxes gave life to Byrd's latest version of the joint committee plan.[51]

According to Roosevelt's annual budget message of January 8, 1941, the projected deficit for fiscal 1942 would be $9,210,000,000.[52] That figure made no allowance for possible lend-lease appropriations, the legislation for which was submitted to Congress on January 10. After a difficult struggle occupying the next two months, the factions of the Democratic Party coalesced to pass the lend-lease bill by a vote of 260 to 165 in the House and 60 to 31 in the Senate. Lend-lease, one of

---

[49] Quotation from New York Times, January 9, 1941, p. 1. For the Woodrum proposal, see the New York Times, December 4, 1940, p. 1, December 5, 1940, p. 1, December 6, 1940, p. 14, December 11, 1940, p. 1, December 31, 1940, p. 8, January 3, 1941, p. 11, January 5, 1941, p. 1, and January 6, 1941, p. 1. See also Congressional Record, 76th Congress, 3rd Session, p. 14008.

[50] New York Times, January 9, 1941, p. 1.

[51] Quotation from New York Times, February 15, 1941, p. 1.

[52] Rosenman, Public Papers and Addresses of FDR 9: 1940, p. 659.

those strategic policies for which Roosevelt had carefully con-
served his influence with Congress, required additional appropriations which, in turn, would further inflate the deficit.[53]

Secretary of the Treasury Morgenthau believed that taxation "should meet two-thirds of the costs of the federal government, including expenditures for defense and Lend-Lease."
Guided by that proposition, the Treasury estimated that it needed
at least $3,500,000,000 in additional taxes to offset the bur-
geoning costs of national defense and lend-lease.[54] A tax bill
of that size would be the largest single revenue measure in
national history and would bring the total of tax revenues to
about $13,000,000,000. Senator Tom Connally (D., Tex.) joked
that the Revenue Bill of 1941 would "jerk 'em out of their shoes,"
and many Congressmen seemed genuinely shocked at the stiff increases in individual and corporate rates contemplated by the
Treasury.[55] On March 24, 1941, Representative Thomas A. Jenkins
(R., O.), a member of the Ways and Means Committee, wrote Budget
Director Smith that the new revenue measure

> will be the heaviest tax bill ever imposed on the
> American people at any one time. . . . The people
> are demanding that a saving of at least a billion
> dollars a year be made from unnecessary expendi-
> tures by the Government before this tremendous
> additional burden is levied.

Other members of the Ways and Means Committee agreed with Jenkins
that cutbacks in non-military spending should precede further increases in taxation.[56]

---

[53]Rosenman, Public Papers and Addresses of FDR 9: 1940,
pp. 668, 674-675; James M. Burns, Roosevelt: The Soldier of
Freedom (New York, 1970), pp. 24-25, 43-49; Blum, Years of Ur-
gency, pp. 198-228; Paul, Taxation, p. 272; Floyd M. Riddick,
"First Session of the Seventy-seventh Congress," American Polit-
ical Science Review XXXVI (1942), pp. 293, 297, 301; George
C. S. Benson, "The Year in Congress," in William M. Schuyler,
ed., The American Year Book, 1941 (New York, 1942), pp. 23-24;
Congressional Digest 20 (1941), pp. 65, 97; Roosevelt, Complete
Presidential Press Conference 17-18: 1941, pp. 17: 12-14.

[54]Roy G. and Gladys C. Blakey, "The Revenue Act of 1941,"
American Economic Review XXXI (1941), p. 810; Blum, Years of
Urgency, p. 304; Samuel I. Rosenman, ed., The Public Papers and
Addresses of Franklin D. Roosevelt, vol. 10: 1941, The Call to
Battle Stations (New York, 1950), pp. 144-146.

[55]Paul, Taxation, p. 272.

[56]Jenkins to Smith, March 24, 1941, General Records of the
Director, series 39.27, box 37, Records of the Bureau of the
Budget, Record Group 51, National Archives.

At that juncture, the call for economy came not from Congress, but from within the Administration. Secretary Morgenthau wished to devote every available dollar to national defense and foreign aid, to hold the deficit to a manageable level, and to avert a disastrous wartime inflation. Always an advocate of economy, he told the Ways and Means Committee on April 24 that non-military expenditures should be reexamined "with a magnifying glass." Morgenthau stressed "that we must continue to provide for those in want, those who face old age without means of their own, or who are otherwise in urgent need of relief." But he thought it unwise "to spend in . . . non-defense and non-relief fields as if we had no emergency defense program." Morgenthau listed the farm program, particularly soil conservation and parity payments, the Civilian Conservation Corps, the National Youth Administration and public roads construction as areas where as much as a billion dollars could be saved.[57]

Morgenthau's testimony touched off a debate over which branch of government had primary responsibility for reducing non-defense expenditures--Congress or the Administration. Early in May 1941, members of the Ways and Means Committee asked that a cut of $1,000,000,000, the sum recommended by Morgenthau, accompany the $3,500,000,000 revenue measure. Representative A. Willis Robertson (D., Va.), one of the leading Democratic renegades, wrote:

When the Secretary of [the Treasury]. . . presented to the Ways and Means Committee a three and one-half billion dollar tax bill and told us it should be accompanied by a cut of a billion dollars in non-defense items he put all the members of our committee on the spot. We know he was right but, unfortunately, we don't control the appropriations. The President would make our task far easier if he would publicly support the Morgenthau recommendation, and also send his House leaders a plan to effect that recommendation.[58]

Roosevelt clung to his budget, which embodied the Administration's priorities for the distribution of Federal resources. In that budget, national defense took precedence over all other considerations. Yet the President had allocated sufficient funds for domestic purposes to continue New Deal agencies,

---

[57] Quotations from New York Times, April 25, 1941, p. 1. See also Blum, Years of Urgency, pp. 305-307.

[58] New York Times, May 3, 1941, p. 9. Quotation from Robertson to E. M. Watson, May 5, 1941, President's Official File 137, FDR papers, FDR Library.

though at a reduced level of operation. He thought that additional reductions of the size sought by the opposition would be premature and would force the Administration to abandon many of the domestic functions assumed by the Federal government in the 1930s. Instead of a drastic cutback, Roosevelt favored a gradual curtailment of domestic spending as economic conditions made necessary and desirable.[59]

Republicans criticized the President's unwillingness to support drastic retrenchment. Many of those who were clamoring the loudest for large savings, like Representative Everett Dirksen (R., Ill.), were scarcely paragons of fiscal restraint. In March and early April, they had participated in a successful effort to increase the agricultural appropriation bill. The Senate Appropriations Committee exceeded Roosevelt's budgetary estimate by $303,651,822.[60] After that performance, Budget Director Smith commented that "the President must put the pressure on members of Congress to keep them from exceeding his Budget. This is quite in contrast to the popular conception that if Congress were left alone it would make substantial cuts in the Federal budget."[61]

The tussle over non-military spending continued into the early summer. Congress managed a few reductions in Roosevelt's budget, especially in the emergency relief appropriation.[62] But the final total for non-defense expenditures, $6,436,000,000, was only slightly less than the figure projected by the President in January. On July 5, Budget Director Smith defended the Administration's record on domestic spending. He told reporters that it was virtually impossible to separate defense and

---

[59] Roosevelt, Complete Presidential Press Conferences 17-18: 1941, pp. 17: 321-324; Rosenman, Public Papers and Addresses of FDR 9: 1940, pp. 654-657. See also Harold D. Smith, Memorandum of Conference with the President, September 15, 1941, Smith papers, FDR Library.

[60] New York Times, May 9, 1941, p. 22. For Republican efforts in behalf of larger agricultural appropriations, see the New York Times, March 4, 1941, p. 1, March 6, 1941, p. 1, March 7, 1941, p. 13, March 16, 1941, p. 38, March 18, 1941, p. 15, and March 28, 1941, pp. 18, 32.

[61] Harold D. Smith, Memorandum of Conference with the President, April 18, 1941, Smith papers, FDR Library.

[62] For the continuing debate over non-defense spending, see Morgenthau Diary, vol. 398, p. 322, FDR Library; Roosevelt, Complete Presidential Press Conferences 17-18: 1941, pp. 17: 321-325; and New York Times, May 13, 1941, pp. 12-13, May 14, 1941, p. 15, May 15, 1941, p. 1, May 18, 1941, section IV, p. 3, May 17, 1941, p. 1, May 22, 1941, p. 24, May 23, 1941, p. 17, June 4, 1941, pp. 6, 33, June 6, 1941, p. 24, July 1, 1941, p. 17.

non-defense items and insisted that the Administration had
practiced fiscal restraint.[63]

Despite the contention of the Administration that significant savings had been made, critics asserted that more had to be
done. In testimony before the House Ways and Means Committee and
later before the Senate Finance Committee, spokesmen for business lobbies and other private groups pleaded for reductions in
expenditures that they hoped would lessen the need for higher
tax rates proposed in the pending revenue bill.[64] Early in
July, the lobbying effort in behalf of retrenchment led to the
establishment of the Citizens Emergency Committee on Non-Defense
Expenditures. The National Association of Manufacturers, the
National Industrial Conference Board, the old Liberty League,
and the Republican Party were well represented on the new committee, which became one of the most important anti-New Deal
fronts of the war years. The chairman of the Citizens Emergency
Committee, Henry M. Wriston, President of Brown University and
vigorous opponent of Roosevelt's reelection in 1940, castigated
the Administration for proceeding "on the principle of 'business
as usual.'" All "the new demands upon the public treasury occa-
sioned by the international crisis," he said, "have been pyra-
mided on top of an already staggering load."[65]

That argument was repeated with a partisan twist when the
Ways and Means Committee formally reported the $3,500,000,000
revenue bill to the House of Representatives. On July 25, Republican members of the committee submitted a minority report that
blamed New Deal spending for the heavy tax burden being imposed
on the American people: "The nation's finances are in a critical state, due to the extravagant spending and reckless borrowing under the New Deal Administration during the past eight
years." During that time, the statement said, New Deal "wastrels"
had spent over $66 billion and, as a consequence, 13 tax measures
had been enacted by Congress. The Republicans demanded that all
"unnecessary and wasteful expenditures" be eliminated.

> If the government is going "all out" for national de-
> fense and "all out" for taxes upon the people, it is
> compelled both by necessity and by a regard for its

[63] New York Times, July 6, 1941, p. 17.

[64] U.S., Congress, House, Committee on Ways and Means,
Hearings before the Committee on Ways and Means on Revenue Revision of 1941, 77th Congress, 1st Session, 1941, pp. 622, 844,
1017.

[65] Quotations from New York Times, July 20, 1941, p. 24. On
Wriston and the Citizens Emergency Committee, see the New York
Times, September 9, 1940, p. 10 and July 8, 1941, pp. 1, 10.

obligations to the taxpayers of the country to also
go "all out" for economy.[66]

In the ensuing debate on the revenue bill, opposition spokesmen used those criticisms to good advantage. According to Representative Daniel Reed (R., N.Y.), for eight years New Dealers had
pointed with pride to Federal expenditures in various Congressional districts. But the Revenue Bill of 1941 meant that "every
day is payday for the taxpayers," said Reed. The pork barrel
was beginning to emit "an unpleasant stench" and might prove to
be a greater liability than asset at the polls. Republican members made no secret of their hope that voters would punish the
Democrats for not paring non-defense spending before levying new
taxes.[67]

Even as the opposition labored to pin the blame for higher
taxes on New Deal spending, Congress passed the so-called defense
highways bill, which appropriated more than $300,000,000 for
highway construction. The President objected both to the sum
appropriated, far more than the Administration had requested, and
to a provision of the bill which apportioned the money by states
instead of by need. On August 2, Roosevelt vetoed the bill,
which he said had been transformed into Congressional pork barrel disguised as defense. Four days later the Senate voted to
override the veto, 57 to 19. Senators Vandenberg, Bailey and
Byrd, three of the chief proponents of economy, supported Roosevelt, but others, such as Senators Adams, George, Glass, Smith
and Tydings, revealed their inconsistency by voting to override
the President's veto. On August 8, the House sustained Roosevelt by two votes, but a large majority of both Republicans and
Democrats voted to override. The defense highways bill provided further proof that many Congressional critics were hypo-
critical in their denunciation of Administration spending.[68]

---

[66]Quotations from U.S., Congress, House, Committee on Ways
and Means, The Revenue Bill of 1941, H. Rept. 1040 to accompany
H.R. 5417, 77th Congress, 1st Session, 1941, pp. 71-74. See
also Paul, Taxation, pp. 272-273; and New York Times, July 26,
1941, p. 30.

[67]Quotations from Paul, Taxation, p. 274.

[68]Congressional Record, 77th Congress, 1st Session, p. 6658.
For House and Senate roll call votes on motion to override the
President's veto, see Congressional Record, 77th Congress, 1st
Session, pp. 6810, 6895-6897. See also Carlton Jackson, Presi-
dential Vetoes, 1792-1945 (Athens, Ga., 1967), pp. 216-217;
Riddick, "First Session of the Seventy-seventh Congress," p.
301; Lawrence H. Curry, Jr., "Southern Senators and Their Roll
Call Votes in Congress, 1941-1944" (Ph.D. dissertation, Duke
University, 1971), pp. 149-150; and New York Times, August 5,
1941, p. 11, August 7, 1941, p. 13, August 8, 1941, p. 7.

Following the controversy over defense highways, attention turned back to the Revenue Bill of 1941. In the Senate, the debate followed lines already marked out in the House. On August 8, Secretary Morgenthau appeared before the Senate Finance Committee to urge a strengthening of the excess profits tax, broadening of the income tax system, and reduction of non-defense expenditures. When asked what specific savings he recommended, Morgenthau replied that specific cuts were a matter for the Bureau of the Budget and Congress. Senator Bailey interrupted to say that Congress would enforce reductions "if some effort is made as to leadership and coordination" by the executive branch. Senator Byrd told Morgenthau, "Reduction in expenditures necessarily must start with the President's recommendations to Congress." Morgenthau reminded the Senators that he had once suggested the creation of a special Congressional committee which would consult with the Treasury and the Bureau of the Budget and help determine the government's fiscal program. Perhaps, the Secretary implied, something might be accomplished through such a committee.[69]

Two days later, Senator George, who had become Chairman of the Finance Committee when Harrison died on June 22, hinted that his committee was seriously considering moves to restrain non-defense spending. George regarded proposed tax increases as "staggering." Even with them, a huge deficit would remain. "It has become more and more apparent," he said, "that we must effect some reductions in non-defense spending."[70]

With the Congressional climate growing more favorable toward some form of budgetary control, the indefatigable Senator Byrd once again advanced his proposal to create a special committee on reduction of non-essential Federal expenditures. On August 28, the Finance Committee unanimously approved Byrd's plan, which was embodied in an amendment to the Revenue Bill of 1941. The Finance Committee also ratified Byrd's resolution requiring the Bureau of the Budget to furnish estimates on how savings of $1 billion, $1.5 billion, and $2 billion could be achieved in the next fiscal year. Praising those two actions, Senator Byrd repeated his long-standing argument that it was "outrageous" to impose heavy new taxes without first making "a sincere effort" to reduce domestic expenditures.[71]

---

[69] Quotations from U.S., Congress, Senate, Committee on Finance, Hearings Before the Committee on Finance on H.R. 5417, 77th Congress, 1st Session, 1941, pp. 16-18; and New York Times, August 9, 1941, p. 1.

[70] Quotations from New York Times, August 11, 1941, p. 6.

[71] New York Times, August 29, 1941, p. 1.

Early in September, the full Senate approved the Byrd amendment to the revenue bill. Senate passage pleased economy advocates, though some cautioned that the House might reject the
amendment, just as it had killed the Harrison plan in January
1940. Perhaps because the Byrd proposal provided for a committee whose recommendations would not be binding, the House
accepted it. On September 17, Congress gave final approval to
the Revenue Act of 1941, thereby creating a Joint Committee on
Reduction of Nonessential Federal Expenditures. The new committee,
fiscal conservatives hoped, would strengthen Congressional control over domestic spending. An exultant Senator Taft described
it as "a Congressional Budget Committee such as I have frequently
suggested." That was pardonable hyperbole, for the committee
was an advisory body only, though it would actively supplement
and coordinate the work of House and Senate Appropriations Committees.[72]

The Byrd Committee

As the author of the amendment which established the committee, Senator Byrd became chairman. Formation of the committee marked the pinnacle of his Congressional career. He had
attempted to convert an earlier inquiry, the Special Committee
to Investigate the Executive Agencies of the Government, created
February 24, 1936, into an assault on the New Deal. The President had thwarted that earlier project. This time Byrd could
claim a mandate to cut the budgets of agencies and programs
that he had always opposed.[73]

---

[72]Congressional Record, 77th Congress, 1st Session, pp.
7274-7275; New York Times, September 4, 1941, pp. 1, 12, Septem-
ber 5, 1941, p. 8, September 8, 1941, p. 29, September 18, 1941,
p. 1; John H. Crider, The Bureaucrat (Philadelphia, 1944), pp.
59-60. Quotation from Robert A. Taft, transcript of speech,
September 19, 1941, box 1257, Taft papers, Library of Congress.
For Byrd's account of the formation of the committee, see U.S.,
Congress, Senate, Committee on Education and Labor, Hearings on
S. 2295, 77th Congress, 2nd Session, 1942, pp. 56-57. See also
Roy G. and Gladys C. Blakey, "Revenue Act of 1941," pp. 810-811,
817.

[73]For Byrd's earlier foray against the New Deal, see Harold
Ickes, The Secret Diary of Harold Ickes, vol. II: The Inside
Struggle, 1936-1939 (New York, 1954), pp. 8, 48; "Report on Gov-
ernment Financial Agencies Prepared by the Brookings Institution,"
Correspondence, 1935-1942, AD 140-01, box 108, Records of the
Farm Security Administration, Record Group 96, National Archives;
Washington Post, March 9, 1939, pp. 1, 4; and box 692, Reorgani-
zation, 1937-1939, Taft papers, Library of Congress. See also
the biographical sketch of Byrd in John A. Perkins, "National
Personalities," William M. Schuyler, ed., The American Year Book,
1942 (New York, 1943), p. 25.

Many in the Administration, including Marriner Eccles and Frederic Delano, mistrusted Byrd's motives as a champion of government economy. In their view, Byrd was a reactionary who was incapable of intelligent criticism.[74] The possibility that he might some day head an economy investigation had worried Administration insiders, who feared he would transform Congressional hearings into an inquisition against the New Deal. On March 10, 1939, for example, Henry Morgenthau had cautioned Presidential Secretary Stephen Early that the membership of a Congressional economy committee must be carefully selected so as not to "get the committee loaded with Harry Byrd and his friends." Yet in September 1941, the Administration could not prevent "Harry Byrd and his friends" from forging a new weapon in their struggle against Roosevelt.

Policy conflicts between Byrd and the President made Budget Director Smith reluctant to comply with the Finance Committee resolution requiring him to furnish a schedule of hypothetical reductions in domestic expenditures. That request, approved at the same time as the joint committee plan, "asked the Budget Director to submit . . . proposals as if he . . . had been asked to cut the Budget one billion, one billion and a half, and two billion dollars." Roosevelt, Smith noted, had been "occupied with international affairs" and "had overlooked this Resolution," though it endangered his program. Considering "the fixed charges," Smith said, "a two-billion cut might mean as much as 50 per cent" in domestic spending. The President "thought such proposals ridiculous." Nevertheless, the Byrd Resolution "had been so carefully drawn in connection with the Budget and Accounting Act that requires the Budget Director to supply information upon request to the Appropriations and Finance Committees of Congress that there was no way of dodging the issue." Even if the resolution could not be evaded, Roosevelt did not want Smith put "in the position of making recommendations" that would undercut Administration policy. The Budget Director promised he would offer nothing that "would be used against the President" and left Roosevelt with the hope that

> the submission of information to show what such cuts
> would mean would be a blessing in disguise in that
> it might afford an opportunity to educate the people
> of the country concerning the Federal Budget and put
> at rest some of the misinformation about the Budget.[76]

---

[74]Frederic A. Delano, "Draft Statement on Recent Editorial Comments on 'Government Spending,'" January 19, 1939, Fiscal and Monetary Advisory Board 766, Records of NRPB, Record Group 187, National Archives.

[75]Morgenthau Diary, vol. 168, pp. 292-293, FDR Library.

[76]Harold D. Smith, Memorandum of Conference with the President, September 15, 1941, Smith papers, FDR Library.

Grudgingly, the Bureau of the Budget compiled the information required by the Byrd Resolution and on October 15 submitted a report to the Senate Finance Committee. The report assumed "that the Committee had in mind a hypothetical approach involving a broad review of Federal programs to achieve arbitrary reductions of $1 billion, $1.5 billion and $2 billion." Those arbitrary reductions could be achieved by more efficient management; by reducing economic and social aid programs; and by curtailing or eliminating government functions. The first possibility, according to the Bureau's report, would yield only minor savings. If significant reductions were to be made, then they would have to be accomplished by curtailing social and economic programs and terminating certain functions currently performed by the Federal government. A saving of $1 billion, the Bureau reported, would require a 28.6 percent reduction in aids to agriculture, a 51 percent cutback in youth assistance, and a 31.6 percent decrease in work relief. An arbitrary reduction of $1.5 billion would compel cuts of 44.1 percent, 67.5 percent, and 49.3 percent in the agriculture, youth and work relief programs. A $2 billion figure would translate into reductions of 45.5 percent, 94.8 percent and 73.9 percent in those same programs.

The report warned that cuts of the magnitude specified would disrupt the operations of civil departments and agencies which had a "greatly increased workload" as a result of the defense effort. Proposed decreases in agricultural appropriations, declared the Budget Bureau, would require "curtailment of the funds available for the stamp plan, free school lunches, etc." Hardest hit of all would be the youth assistance program, which had already been contracted. Further disruption would be unwise, according to the report, for "there can be little doubt that some sort of youth program will be necessary in the post-defense period." In sum, the Bureau believed that "many of the indicated downward revisions would seriously impair the defense effort and other vital Government activities."[77]

Budget Director Smith continued to hope that his report to the Finance Committee would "educate the people" to the complexities of the Federal budget and persuade many that too drastic reductions would wreck the orderly conduct of the government's business.[78] But at least one newspaper, the Kansas City Times, was outraged by the justification of domestic spending

---

[77]"Byrd Report," October 15, 1941, General Records of the Director, series 39.27, box 37, Records of the Bureau of the Budget, Record Group 51, National Archives; "Three Economy Plans Offered to Congress," Washington Star, October 18, 1941, entry 17, "Campaign Against NYA," Records of the National Youth Administration, Record Group 119, National Archives.

[78]Harold D. Smith, Memorandum of Conference with the President, October 14, 1941, Smith papers, FDR Library.

offered by the Bureau of the Budget. "The impression created," said the _Times_, "was that the whole accumulated spending of the last eight or nine years was both necessary and patriotic."[79] Like the _Times_, Senator Byrd rejected that argument. He intended to use the Bureau's report as a basis on which his new committee would recommend cuts in "nonessential" spending.

The membership of the committee insured that Byrd's viewpoint would dominate. Serving with him were Senators Carter Glass (D., Va.), Kenneth McKellar (D., Tenn.), Gerald Nye (R., N.D.), Walter George (D., Ga.), Robert La Follette (Prog., Wis.), and Representatives Robert Doughton (D., N.C.), Thomas Cullen (D., N.Y.), Clarence Cannon (D., Mo.), Clifton Woodrum (D., Va.), John Taber (R., N.Y.) and Allen Treadway (R., Mass.). Of that formidable concentration of bipartisan Congressional influence, only La Follette was a reliable supporter of the New Deal. Glass, George, Woodrum, Treadway and Taber, along with Byrd, were leaders of the Congressional opposition. McKellar, Doughton and Cannon were orthodox Democrats retreating rapidly from New Deal principles. The composition of the committee would allow opposition members to control the proceedings.[80]

No one recognized that fact more clearly than Harold Smith. The Revenue Act of 1941 made the Budget Director and the Secretary of the Treasury members of the Byrd Committee. Smith was reluctant to collaborate with a joint committee of Congress, especially since the intentions of that group conflicted with Administration policy. At the committee's first meeting on October 29, he announced that as long as he was working on the President's budget, he would not submit any information on estimated expenditures for fiscal 1943. During the ensuing quarrel "over what [the committee] . . . could get out of the Director of the Budget," only Senator La Follette sided with Smith. The rest of the committee put the Budget Director "in a corner."[81]

Smith's efforts to defend the Administration against its Congressional adversaries received little or no encouragement from the Secretary of the Treasury. Morgenthau rather enjoyed Smith's discomfiture at the hands of Byrd and other opposition members. Unlike the Budget Director, Morgenthau was ready to cooperate with the joint committee in revising the budget. Six months earlier, he had urged a reduction of $1 billion, a

---

[79]Quotation from Morgenthau Diary, vol. 458, p. 47, FDR Library.

[80]Sidney Baldwin, _Poverty and Politics: The Rise and Decline of the Farm Security Administration_ (Chapel Hill, N.C., 1968), p. 347.

[81]Quotations from Morgenthau Diary, vol. 455, pp. 151-152, FDR Library.

statement that infuriated Smith because of "the implication
[that] the President and the Budget Director did a very poor job
of budget-making." Shortly after Morgenthau's comments, Smith
had written, "If the pronouncement had come from the United States
Chamber of Commerce or the National Economy League, it would have
been in character, but to come from a cabinet member of this Administration" smacked of disloyalty. "It is also clear," Smith
went on, "that the Secretary of the Treasury is not in sympathy
with the particular programs he slates for the knife." Morgenthau had injured the President's cause, for he gave "the impression that there is a billion dollars of water in the Budget."[82]

Morgenthau continued, both publicly and privately, to favor
a billion dollar cutback. The Secretary realized he spoke without the approval of the President, but Morgenthau felt so strongly
about non-defense economy that he was prepared to risk Roosevelt's disfavor. On November 10, the Secretary discussed with
his staff the prospects for successful cooperation with the Byrd
Committee. Under Secretary Daniel Bell predicted that Morgenthau would become "Harry Byrd's catspaw and goat, and he is going
to get all the publicity out of it and you are going to do all
the work and get all the blame." Despite that blunt warning
from a trusted aide, Morgenthau remained determined to press for
sweeping reductions. "I am going to make some recommendations,"
he said, "even though I get fired." To forestall inflation and
promote defense financing, the Secretary insisted "we've got to
move on economy."[83]

In spite of misgivings on the part of his own staff, the
overt hostility of Harold Smith, and the possible disapproval
of the President, Morgenthau sealed his alliance with Senator
Byrd. On the afternoon of November 10, he met with Byrd and
Doughton, the chairman and vice-chairman, to consider what
course the joint committee should follow. Morgenthau told the
two Congressmen "that the only way to economize effectively" was
to eliminate certain functions currently performed by the Federal government and in that way "stop the waste and unnecessary
expenditure" which was no longer needed for "pump-priming." To
that end, he promised to appear before the next meeting of the
Byrd Committee and offer concrete proposals for savings in the
non-defense budget.[84]

---

[82]Morgenthau Diary, vol. 455, pp. 151-152, FDR Library.
Quotations from Smith to President, May 1, 1941, Miscellaneous
White House Memoranda, Smith papers, FDR Library.

[83]Morgenthau Diary, vol. 458, p. 134, vol. 459, pp. 88-89,
93-94, 108-111, 117-118, 123, FDR Library.

[84]Morgenthau Diary, vol. 458, pp. 133-136, vol. 459, pp.
2-5, 128, 131-139, 141-153, FDR Library.

On November 14, Secretary Morgenthau delivered a lengthy prepared statement to the Joint Committee on Reduction of Non-essential Federal Expenditures. He called for the postponement of all reclamation, river and harbor, flood control, soil conservation, and highway projects. In addition, the Secretary argued that "the regular activities of the Civilian Conservation Corps and National Youth Administration must conflict with the more important defense program, and should be eliminated." Further, he asserted that "at this time we could well afford to make drastic cuts in our agricultural expenditures." The Secretary wanted it understood "that in making the suggestion that . . . farm expenditures should be re-examined, I do not refer to the bulk of activities undertaken by the Farm Security Administration, inasmuch as the need for much of their expenditures is, in my opinion, still urgent." Morgenthau also exempted from his recommendations the Surplus Marketing Administration, which administered the distribution of surplus commodities to needy families.[85]

Morgenthau's statement was generally well received by the committee, although some members showed more interest in abolishing NYA, CCC and WPA than in curtailing public works, roads, and agricultural subsidies. Senator McKellar, for example, vehemently defended "public roads projects." Morgenthau replied that "all the projects subject to economies are popular and have adherents." The committee, he said, should press for reductions distributed evenly among all categories of non-defense expenditures.[86]

The Secretary of the Treasury, sincerely committed to balanced reductions in domestic spending, soon discovered that opposition members had a different conception of the committee's task. They preferred to cut selectively and their list of vulnerable items seemed limited to New Deal programs that they had never supported. Under Secretary Daniel Bell, substituting for Morgenthau at the Byrd Committee meeting on November 18, quickly grasped the situation. "McKellar," he told the Secretary, "went into . . . [another] long rigamarole on roads. . . . Roads were certainly a defense item and shouldn't be touched. . . . So I think they'll cut everything except the [programs]. . . . they're interested in."[87]

---

[85]"Economy Suggestions Submitted by Secretary Morgenthau to the Joint Committee on Reduction of Non-Defense Expenditures," November 14, 1941, General Records of the Director, series 39.27, box 37, Records of the Bureau of the Budget, Record Group 51, National Archives. See also Morgenthau Diary, vol. 461, p. 130, FDR Library; and Morgenthau to President, November 17, 1941, President's Official File 119, FDR papers, FDR Library.

[86]Morgenthau Diary, vol. 462, pp. 66-69, FDR Library.

[87]Quotation from Morgenthau Diary, vol. 463, pp. 41-42, FDR Library.

Committee members were eager to slash funds for New Deal agencies, but Budget Director Smith urged them to wait until budget examiners "familiar with . . . [those] organizations and their appropriations" could appear before the committee. Then, said Smith, the committee should permit representatives of affected agencies to defend their programs.[88] Byrd and his colleagues accepted that procedure and for the next three weeks, listened to testimony concerning the Civilian Conservation Corps, National Youth Administration and Work Projects Administration. The committee also pondered possible cuts in the budgets of other agencies, including the Department of Agriculture. Among the Congressional members, only Senator La Follette defended New Deal agencies and resisted the effort to curtail assistance to lower-income groups while the government was spending billions on defense contracts that enriched inadequately-taxed corporations.

The committee's majority displayed its prejudices in the treatment accorded spokesmen for the Bureau of the Budget, CCC, NYA and WPA. On November 28, B. S. Beecher, one of Harold Smith's budget examiners, testified that declining CCC enrollments had enabled the Budget Bureau to impound $95,000,000 of the original $246,000,000 appropriation for fiscal 1942. But the saving failed to placate Taber, Byrd and McKellar. They were so relentless in pursuit of suspected waste and inefficiency in the CCC, that they began to bully the unfortunate budget examiner as though he were responsible for the policies of the Corps. Blaming the agency for absorbing rural youths needed as farm workers, committee members cross-examined Beecher about the effect of CCC enrollments on the agricultural labor supply. McKellar charged that agency personnel had engaged in promotional advertising to entice recruits into the organization and reverse the downward trend of enrollments. "Why is it," he truculently demanded of Beecher, "that you go around and drum up boys to get them in the CCC?" Budget Director Smith, annoyed by McKellar's misdirected petulance, reminded the committee that "Mr. Beecher is connected with the Budget. . . . He is not connected with the agency."[89]

Beecher's ordeal served as a dress rehearsal for the appearance on December 4 of the Director of the Civilian Conservation Corps, James J. McEntee. The Director, bluff and outspoken, began his statement to the committee with a challenge. I know, he said,

---

[88]Quotation from Morgenthau Diary, vol. 465, pp. 18-20, FDR Library.

[89]U.S., Congress, Joint Committee on Reduction of Nonessential Federal Expenditures, Hearings, 77th Congress, 1st Session, 1941, part 1, pp. 1-6; Morgenthau Diary, vol. 466, pp. 253-258, FDR Library.

the value of the work the Corps has done and its value
to the Nation. I feel that Congress, if the work of
the Corps were to be stopped now, would undoubtedly appropriate money to have the work performed in some other
way, or by some other agency.

Senator McKellar regarded that "as a threat" and admonished
McEntee, "I do not like that kind of language." Representative
Doughton, also rankled by McEntee's tactless opening, asked if
the director thought the CCC "should be made permanent"? "I
think the type of work," replied McEntee, "that is being carried on is vital enough to be made a permanent part of the work
program of this Government." Did the Director feel that way,
inquired Doughton, because of the value of the CCC as a relief
agency? No, answered McEntee, to the committee's surprise,
"I do not think today, from a relief standpoint, there is a
scintilla of reason for carrying on this Corps."[90]

The CCC began, McEntee explained, as a relief organization,
became a conservation and work organization, and, at the express
direction of Congress, assumed some of the functions of a social
service and rehabilitation agency. Though the CCC had a repu-
tation "more or less as a relief organization," its work, conservation, and rehabilitation functions had become more important than relief. The Corps engaged in soil erosion control,
reforestation, road building, fire fighting and fire prevention,
fish and wildlife conservation, and national park maintenance.
The organization also endeavored to rehabilitate enrollees by
providing them work experience, vocational training, remedial
education, and basic health care. Two factors, said the Director, "justify the operation of this Corps; one is the amount
of work that it is doing; the other is the benefit that the
Corps is to the young men."[91]

In his summary of CCC activities, McEntee challenged the
committee to consider the Corps not as a temporary relief agency,
but as a program of long-term value, a desirable blend of social
service, soil and water conservation, and public works. But
most members still viewed CCC as a relief organization that had
outlived its usefulness. Representative Taber asserted that CCC
enrollees were undisciplined and lazy. McKellar agreed. The
"most important [thing] . . . that I saw those boys do, he said,
was "thumbing rides to get into town." McKellar belittled the

---

[90]U.S., Congress, Joint Committee on Reduction of Nonessential Federal Expenditures, Hearings, 77th Congress, 1st Session,
1941, part 1, pp. 265-266; Morgenthau Diary, vol. 468, pp.
274-275.

[91]U.S., Congress, Joint Committee on Reduction of Nonessential Federal Expenditures, Hearings, 77th Congress, 1st Session,
1941, part 1, pp. 267-281.

educational and vocational training efforts of the CCC, and declared, "You have not educated the boys at all."[92]

Committee members also disparaged the value of the work performed by the Corps. McKellar said he did "not believe there has been one single solitary cent of improvement of the national wealth or national economy in any manner, shape or form." Faced with such obduracy on the part of his inquisitors, McEntee had a difficult time defending the Corps' operation. At last, exasperated by continued badgering and barracking, he conceded "that if in the judgment of Congress the work being performed and the rather intangible values in connection with this Corps do not justify this expenditure, we ought to stop the entire expenditure." That was the only sentence McEntee uttered which pleased the committee's majority.[93]

The Byrd Committee was equally uncompromising in its attitude toward the National Youth Administration. The Bureau of the Budget had already impounded $28,400,000 of the $151,767,000 NYA appropriation and the agency had substantially contracted its program of youth assistance. In the current year, testified Deputy Administrator Dillard B. Lasseter, the number of youths receiving financial aid from NYA had dropped by about one-half. Lasseter, who appeared before the committee on December 2, explained that NYA furnished financial support so that impoverished high school and college youth could continue their formal education. For "those who have already left school," he said, NYA provided "work experience and training." Since the beginning of the defense program, the agency had concentrated on training young workers, increasingly blacks and women, for employment in defense industries, an activity that Lasseter claimed was essential to greater production.[94]

Lasseter's testimony had little impact on the committee's majority, which adjudged NYA an obsolete relief agency, tinged with an ill-defined but nonetheless dangerous radicalism. Representative Doughton insisted that "All ambitious young boys and girls have adequate facilities right in their reach. It is not a question of whether they are poor or wealthy, it is a

---

[92]U.S., Congress, Joint Committee on Reduction of Nonessential Federal Expenditures, Hearings, 77th Congress, 1st Session, 1941, part 1, pp. 271, 281.

[93]U.S., Congress, Joint Committee on Reduction of Nonessential Federal Expenditures, Hearings, 77th Congress, 1st Session, 1941, part 1, p. 284.

[94]U.S., Congress, Joint Committee on Reduction of Nonessential Federal Expenditures, Hearings, 77th Congress, 1st Session, 1941, part 1, pp. 177-214; Morgenthau Diary, vol. 467, pp. 259-262, FDR Library.

question of whether or not they will avail themselves of it."
In his opinion, there was no justification, and perhaps had
never been, for the NYA program.[95]

As committee members received testimony covering CCC and
NYA, their demeanor was that of men who had made up their minds
and listened only to ascertain what arguments would be used in
defense of affected agencies. So it was also with the Work
Projects Administration. According to figures furnished by
the Bureau of the Budget, the work relief appropriation for
fiscal 1942 was $886,000,000, or $464,000,000 less than fiscal
1941. The savings resulted from a decrease in unemployment,
which had declined from 7,900,000 in October 1940 to 3,900,000
in October 1941. The Budget Bureau expected the downward trend
to continue and had already impounded $15,040,000 of the WPA
appropriation for fiscal 1942.[96]

Most members of the Byrd Committee thought the sum impounded
was insufficient. They believed work relief could be abolished,
now that the defense program had brought about substantial reemployment. Speaking for WPA, Deputy Administrator Francis
Dryden explained that defense employment varied from one lo-
cality to the next. Conversion to defense production displaced workers in non-defense industries, thereby creating isolated pools of unemployment. Some workers, particularly blacks
and other minorities, had not yet benefitted from the defense
boom. For those reasons, said Dryden, WPA would be needed to
ease the transition to a wartime economy. Work relief would
dwindle as private industry gradually absorbed WPA workers.[97]

McKellar, openly skeptical of any voluntary curtailment,
interjected, "We are obliged to cut this thing down now."
"This is supposed to be the most prosperous year that the United
States has ever experienced," he went on, and therefore was "the
best time" to terminate a function which the Federal government
had assumed only because of the Great Depression. Public service employment "wasn't necessary prior to 1929," said McKellar,
and it should not "be necessary now." Dryden disagreed. Elimination of WPA would say to the unemployed, "You, because you

---

[95]U.S., Congress, Joint Committee on Reduction of Nonessential Federal Expenditures, Hearings, 77th Congress, 1st Session,
1941, part 1, pp. 201, 215-263.

[96]U.S., Congress, Joint Committee on Reduction of Nonessential Federal Expenditures, Hearings, 77th Congress, 1st Session,
1941, part 1, pp. 74, 111, 121-122; Morgenthau Diary, vol. 467,
pp. 68-72, FDR Library.

[97]U.S., Congress, Joint Committee on Reduction of Nonessential Federal Expenditures, Hearings, 77th Congress, 1st Session,
1941, part 1, pp. 304-305, 320-321.

are in need . . . out of this whole defense program you are the one that is to be picked out. We can spend our money to meet our defense needs but we cannot spend money to support a part of our population." The committee was not moved by Dryden's plea for equitable treatment.[98]

The agriculture program was the remaining category of government expenditure in which significant reductions might be achieved. Of $1,244,410,104 appropriated for agriculture in fiscal 1942, the Bureau of the Budget had impounded $167,631,864. On December 17, Senator Byrd solicited the views of Representative Cannon, Chairman of the House Appropriations Committee, on the possibility of further reductions in agricultural expenditures. Cannon, a tenacious defender of the interests of commercial agriculture, opposed any cuts in appropriations for parity and soil conservation payments. Those items, which benefitted organized commercial farmers, totaled over $700,000,000, or approximately 57 percent of the entire agricultural appropriation for fiscal 1942. Since Cannon would countenance no cuts in parity or soil conservation payments, the remainder of the farm program would have to bear the brunt of contemplated reductions.[99]

Byrd, McKellar and Doughton endorsed Cannon's position and on December 18 questioned Secretary of Agriculture Claude Wickard about possible reductions of $300,000,000 to $600,000,000 in the fiscal 1943 appropriation. Wickard doubted that such savings were possible. There were "items in the Department of Agriculture," committee members insisted, "which undoubtedly could be cut." Byrd and McKellar mentioned the Surplus Marketing Administration, which distributed surplus commodities to needy families, the Rural Electrification Administration, and the Farm Security Administration as agencies that might be terminated in order to effect economies.[100]

The predisposition of the hearings was plain. Using the level of Federal activity in 1929 as a rough benchmark, the Byrd Committee was ready to pare expenditures by amputating New Deal agencies. Most members felt little sympathy for the underdogs of American society who might suffer from abrupt abandonment of

---

[98] U.S., Congress, Joint Committee on Reduction of Nonessential Federal Expenditures, Hearings, 77th Congress, 1st Session, 1941, part 1, pp. 317-319, 321-322; Morgenthau Diary, vol. 468, pp. 276-277, FDR Library.

[99] U.S., Congress, Joint Committee on Reduction of Nonessential Federal Expenditures, Hearings, 77th Congress, 1st Session, 1941, part 1, pp. 129-152; Morgenthau Diary, vol. 474, pp. 31-33, FDR Library.

[100] Morgenthau Diary, vol. 474, pp. 159-165, FDR Library.

Federal public assistance and social service policies. Doughton, for example, believed that poverty, in the prosperous year of 1941, existed only in "some isolated cases," while Senator McKellar accused the beneficiaries of CCC, NYA and WPA of wanting "to get on where they don't have to do any . . . work."101

Equally important, committee members were sensitive to the backlash, real or imagined, that had developed against increased taxation. As Doughton said on December 4, "people all over the country are clamoring . . . 'I know we need additional revenue, but you must cut out these nondefense expenditures that are un-necessary.'" He could not see "how we will ever enact another tax law unless we can convince the taxpayers that we are doing something to remove this burden they think they are carrying." That sentiment clinched the case against vulnerable agencies.102

On December 16, the Byrd Committee considered what recom-mendations it would submit to Congress. Representative Treadway urged restraint. If the committee "should be too drastic in its recommendations for the abolishment of agencies," he said, it might be difficult to secure Congressional support. But Morgen-thau observed that he "had found it much easier to abolish bur-eaus than it was to make cuts in the amounts appropriated for such bureaus." The draconian approach satisfied most members, who authorized a subcommittee to write a preliminary report embodying the views of the majority.103

The Byrd Committee report, released on December 24, con-tained six major recommendations. First, the committee urged that "no new adventures or commitments in public works or costly government programs be undertaken during the period of the war emergency," a sensible policy that the Roosevelt Admin-istration had already adopted. Second, the report recommended that the Civilian Conservation Corps and National Youth Admin-istration be abolished and that defense training programs carried on by those organizations be consolidated in some suit-able agency. Again, the Administration had already curtailed the regular activities of those two agencies but had not abol-ished them. Third, the committee advocated rapid curtailment of WPA and recommended an appropriation of "not more than $50,000,000 per month for 3 months beginning July 1, 1942."

101U.S., Congress, Joint Committee on Reduction of Non-essential Federal Expenditures, Hearings, 77th Congress, 1st Session, 1941, part 1, pp. 319-320.

102U.S., Congress, Joint Committee on Reduction of Non-essential Federal Expenditures, Hearings, 77th Congress, 1st Session, 1941, part 1, p. 319; Morgenthau Diary, vol. 474, p. 164, FDR Library.

103Morgenthau Diary, vol. 473, pp. 290-295, FDR Library.

Fourth, the report urged every possible saving in the administrative overhead of civil departments and agencies. Fifth, the
committee proposed a reduction of $100,000,000 in the appropria-
tion for the Surplus Marketing Administration, abolition of the
farm tenant program and the Farm Security Administration, and
deferment of Rural Electrification Administration expansion.
Last, the committee recommended "that during the emergency one-
half of the Federal highway appropriations and authorizations
be deferred, at a saving of $64,000,000."[104]

Only Smith, Morgenthau and La Follette dissented from the
Byrd Committee report. The Budget Director still thought he
"could not serve the President and a Congressional committee on
the same subject at the same time" and therefore refused to en-
dorse the recommendations of the committee. The Secretary of
the Treasury, though he accepted most of the report, disagreed
with the recommendations regarding agriculture. On December 22,
before release of the report, he wrote Byrd that he opposed
abolition of the Farm Security Administration. Morgenthau
favored "cuts in our agricultural expenditures" but not in programs designed to assist poverty-stricken tenant farmers and
the ill-nourished who depended on distribution of surplus commodities. Instead, soil conservation and parity payments should
be reduced because commercial farmers were receiving their fair
"share of the total expenditures made by the Government as the
increase in . . . net [farm] income indicates."[105]

The sternest criticism of the Byrd Committee came from
La Follette, who appended a lengthy minority statement to the
preliminary report. "The sweeping recommendations of the majority of the committee," he charged, were "hasty and unwarranted." After only ten hours of hearings, the Senator continued, the committee proposed to reverse national policies
that had received "consistent and steadfast" support from Congress. Allegations against CCC, NYA, WPA, FSA and other New
Deal agencies, La Follette dismissed as largely unsubstantiated
rumor and gossip. The committee's majority, he claimed, had
made "a 'whipping boy' of minor abuses and deficiencies in established Federal social programs which have proved their worth."
He agreed "with the general objective of reducing waste and
all nonessential expenditures," but the committee wanted to
achieve economy by sacrificing programs that aided the bottom
strata of American society. "Congressional approval of the
recommendations," he said, "would knock some of the major props
of Federal support out from under . . . the lower income levels."

[104]U.S., Congress, Joint Committee on Reduction of Nonessential Federal Expenditures, Preliminary Report, S. Doc. 152,
77th Congress, 1st Session, 1941, pp. 1-7.

[105]U.S., Congress, Joint Committee on Reduction of Nonessential Federal Expenditures, Preliminary Report, S. Doc. 152,
77th Congress, 1st Session, 1941, pp. 8-9.

The Senator thought it was "sheer folly to build up the
military defenses and at the same time neglect the problems of
hunger and privation of millions of our Nation." War expenditures would create jobs, but they were "no answer to the problems of public assistance." He defended CCC, NYA, WPA and FSA
as agencies that had "waged war with some success" against
"poverty and underprivilege." He deplored the proposal to curtail the Surplus Marketing Administration, which would mean a
"reduction of almost 45 percent in the total funds available
this year . . . for the food stamp plan, cotton stamp plan,
school-lunch programs, and direct distribution of surplus commodities to needy people." Destruction of Federal agencies that
administered public assistance would not only be unfair, wrote
La Follette, but would also deprive the nation of the means to
cope with pressing postwar problems. Postwar needs, he predicted, "will require, more than ever before, well-perfected machinery to cope with post-war social and economic problems."
Acceptance of the committee's recommendations, he concluded,
would be a "grave error."[106]

As La Follette contended, the Byrd Committee report constituted a counterbudget, a set of proposals fraught with consequences for the future of national policy. The recommendations, if enacted, would overhaul the President's budget and re-
allocate Federal resources. Economy in non-defense expenditures was not the only issue at stake, for the Roosevelt Administration had already accomplished substantial savings in non-
defense spending. Bureau of the Budget impoundments promised
additional reductions as circumstances warranted. The Byrd
Committee report went beyond economy to propose abolition or
debilitation of programs identified with the New Deal commitment
to the lower third of society. The President had already conceded the need for reductions in the regular activities of agencies like NYA and CCC. But he remained convinced those agencies would have a role to play, especially in the postwar era,
and therefore he resisted efforts to extinguish them entirely.[107]

Pearl Harbor and Politics As Usual

The Japanese air raid on Pearl Harbor temporarily eclipsed

[106]U.S., Congress, Joint Committee on Reduction of Nonessential Federal Expenditures, Preliminary Report, S. Doc. 152,
77th Congress, 1st Session, 1941, pp. 10-23.

[107]Harold D. Smith, Memoranda of Conferences with the
President, November 17, 1941, November 24, 1941, December 18,
1941, Smith papers, FDR Library. See Marriner Eccles' warning
against too severe cuts in domestic spending, U.S., Congress,
House, Committee on Ways and Means, Hearings before the Committee on Ways and Means on Revenue Revision of 1941, 77th Congress, 1st Session, 1941, vol. 1, pp. 688-689.

all political calculations. On Capitol Hill, legislators responded to that sudden, sickening defeat by rallying around the
flag and President. Politics would be adjourned for the duration, they proclaimed, and perhaps in the immediate aftermath of
Pearl Harbor they actually meant what they said. On December
16, Representative Clare Hoffman (R., Mich.), avowed adversary
of Roosevelt and the New Deal "labor government," announced his
support for the Chief Executive: "Out of the sky came a vicious
assault by a skillful and determined enemy and ere it was ended
a representative of the Democratic Party, who was President, became our President."[108]

Others, either more honest or more realistic, refused to
renounce partisanship. On December 26, Senator Taft defended
the right of the Congressional opposition to criticize Administration policies and proposals. Under cover of war, Taft
argued, New Dealers would try to alter permanently the social
and economic structure of the nation. "The Government," he remarked, "is getting more and more into business. . . . Many of
the new industrial plants will be owned by the Government.
Whether they will ever be returned to private industry . . .
may well be doubted." Equally disturbing, in Taft's view, was
"an unsound fiscal policy [which] may bring the country to bank-
ruptcy and complete inflation." He identified the Administration's primary economic policy makers as "Mr. Eccles, Mr. Henderson, Mr. Currie, and Mr. Mordecai Ezekiel." They were among
"The Government economists at the heart of the New Deal. . . .
[whose] only regret about the $20,000,000,000 increase in debt
during the thirties is that it was not sufficiently large."

> The National Resources Planning Board [Taft con-
> tinued] is already preparing a program of great pub-
> lic works to be undertaken after the war. . . . That
> is the kind of nonsense which inspires the present
> post-war planning within the administration and af-
> fects its present fiscal policy. If that kind of
> philosophy does dominate the Government's policy, we
> will be ruined long before the war is over.

While Congress could not "assume to run the war," declared
the Senator, it must forestall policies that threatened American
capitalism. "In particular," he asserted, "we must subject any
proposals for the period after the war to the most intense public discussion." Only in that way could the Congressional opposition "preserve an underlying condition which will permit . . .
[the restoration of] the American system [of free enterprise]
. . . in which we believe." For the immediate future, Taft
advised "a strong fiscal policy" characterized by deep cuts in

---

[108]Quotation from Congressional Record, 77th Congress, 1st
Session, p. 9856. See also Congressional Record, 77th Congress,
1st Session, pp. 9505-9521.

non-war expenditures. "I believe that within 6 months we can abolish Work Projects Administration and Civilian Conservation Corps and National Youth Administration."[109]

Taft, acknowledged as the guiding intelligence of Senate Republicans, outlined a program that guaranteed a continuation of partisan strife. Indeed, he welcomed political conflict, for "as a matter of general principle . . . criticism in time of war is essential to the maintenance of any kind of democratic government." Taft relished partisan conflict for another reason as well. With New Deal strength on the wane, the onset of war gave the Congressional opposition tactical advantages that the Administration and its supporters lacked. Republicans, and their like-minded Democratic auxiliaries, could support essential war measures and take credit for their patriotism. Simultaneously, opposition leaders could blame New Deal policies for interfering with the war effort. Restrictions and regulations accompanying the war would revitalize shopworn arguments against bureaucracy and regimentation. With minimal effort, Republicans would gain the support of those irritated by the stress and inconvenience of war.[110]

Despite platitudes about national unity, few politicians expected a lasting moratorium on internal conflict. Only a day after Pearl Harbor, the Senate became embroiled in a brief but nasty quarrel over labor policy. A series of industrial disputes, dating back to the Vultee aircraft strike of November 1940, had aroused the ire of the anti-labor front in Congress. Brief shutdowns of the bituminous coal mines occurred in September, October and November 1941, and the inability of the National Defense Mediation Board to settle those strikes caused angry Congressmen to press harder for legislative action. On December 8, Senator Byrd demanded enactment of either the Smith Bill or the Connally Bill, both of which regulated strikes and the union shop. The Smith Bill had already passed the House by a vote of 252 to 136, a roll call that replicated the alignment on Wagner Act revision in June 1940. But Administration loyalists in the Senate staved off action on the Smith Bill, Connally Bill and analogous measures. On January 12, 1942, the President established the National War Labor Board to replace the defunct National Defense Mediation Board and that cooled, for a time, enthusiasm for punitive legislation.[111]

---

[109] Quotations from Congressional Record, 77th Congress, 1st Session, pp. A5709-A5711. See also Robert A. Taft, transcript of speech, December 19, 1941, box 1258, Taft papers, Library of Congress.

[110] Quotation from Congressional Record, 77th Congress, 1st Session, p. A5709. See also Roland A. Young, Congressional Politics in the Second World War (New York, 1956), p. 13; and Frank E. Gannett, address, January 24, 1942, box 17, Gannett papers, Cornell University Library.

[111] Congressional Record, 77th Congress, 1st Session, pp. 9318-9361, 9363-9395, 9514-9516. For House roll call vote on

Labor policy was only one of the divisive issues in the
weeks after Pearl Harbor. Equally disruptive was the problem
of price stabilization. In April 1941, Roosevelt had created
the Office of Price Administration and Civilian Supply, with
New Deal economist Leon Henderson as Administrator. That agency
had endeavored, through voluntary agreements, to control price
increases. But prices of consumer goods, especially food, continued to rise rapidly. In July 1941, the President sent Congress a message requesting prompt action on price stabilization.[112] For the next six months, the House and Senate engaged
in lengthy debate over the form of price control legislation.
Opposition members considered Henderson antagonistic to business
and refused to grant as much discretionary authority to OPA as
the Administration thought necessary. Farm state Congressmen
resisted the imposition of ceilings on commodity prices. The
interests of the farm bloc and business spokesmen overlapped,
and on November 28, 1941, the House passed a price control bill
that amounted to a defeat for Roosevelt and his supporters. To
supervise the unpopular Henderson, who carried the double stigma
of consumer advocate and New Dealer, the House bill created a
five-member board of review which could overrule the Price Administrator. Representatives from agricltural districts inserted a number of options for computing ceiling prices on farm
products. One hundred-ten percent of parity became the minimum
ceiling, while other options would allow farm prices to reach
200 to 300 percent of the 1941 level.[113]

the Smith Bill, see Congressional Record, 77th Congress, 1st Session, pp. 9396-9397; and Appendix III, Guttman scaling table 2,
item 2. On establishment of the War Labor Board, see Samuel I.
Rosenman, ed., The Public Papers and Addresses of Franklin D.
Roosevelt, vol. 11: 1942, Humanity on the Defensive (New York,
1950), pp. 42-48; and Polenberg, War and Society, pp. 155-156.
For labor disputes and anti-strike legislation, see Benson, "The
Year in Congress," American Year Book, 1941, p. 25; Congres-
sional Digest 20 (1941), pp. 99-129; Young, Congressional Poli-
tics, pp. 56-58; and Wesley McCune, "The Politics of Labor in
Wartime," in Ray F. Harvey and others, The Politics of This War
(New York, 1943), pp. 172-181.

[112]Rosenman, Public Papers and Addresses of FDR 10: 1941,
pp. 99-107, 284-289. See also Fred Warner Neal, "The Politics
of Price-Fixing," in Ray F. Harvey and others, The Politics of
This War (New York, 1943), pp. 194-201.

[113]Young, Congressional Politics, pp. 90-93; Alfred D. Stedman, "The Politics of the Farmers in Wartime," in Ray F. Harvey
and others, The Politics of This War (New York, 1943), pp. 146-
147; Mabel G. Benson, "The Year in Congress," in William M.
Schuyler, ed., The American Year Book, 1942 (New York, 1943),
pp. 33-34; Wesley McCune, The Farm Bloc (New York, 1943),
pp. 60-64.

In the Senate, Administration supporters eliminated the five-member board of review, in spite of efforts by Taft and some Republicans to retain that provision. The Administration was less successful in revising sections of the bill pertaining to agricultural prices. Bipartisan collaboration among farm state Senators prevented the delegation of effective power over commodity prices to OPA. On January 27, 1942, the bill received final approval.[114] In the months that followed, its deficiencies became apparent. The control of inflation, which involved decisions adversely affecting powerful producer groups, continued to cause friction between the Administration and its Congressional critics.[115]

The sale of war bonds and increased taxation were other devices employed by the government to restrain inflation. Taxes proved a constant source of discord on Capitol Hill. In his budget message of January 5, 1942, Roosevelt projected a deficit of $35 billion, but the pace of the war effort made it likely that the deficit would approach $60 billion for fiscal 1943. A huge inflationary gap separated the dwindling amount of goods and services available for civilian consumption and the purchasing power in the hands of the American people. Higher taxes, in conjunction with bond sales, were necessary to reduce purchasing power and ease inflationary pressures which endangered price stability.[116]

The Administration favored revenue legislation that embodied New Deal principles of equitable taxation. But the Congressional tax committees, as the Revenue Acts of 1940 illustrated, had become antagonistic to New Deal revenue policy. Everyone agreed that inflation had to be curbed, but opposition members and Democrats of orthodox economic views rejected Treasury Department recommendations and followed their own course. Chief points of difference between the Administration and the Congressional committees were the amount of additional

---

[114]Congressional Record, 77th Congress, 2nd Session, pp. 239, 242, 725; Neal, "Politics of Price-Fixing," pp. 201-203; Curry, "Southern Senators and Their Roll Call Votes in Congress," pp. 189-191; Appendix IV, Guttman scaling table 1, items 1, 30. See also Rosenman, Public Papers and Addresses of FDR 11: 1942, pp. 67-73; and Burns, Soldier of Freedom, pp. 196-197.

[115]Young, Congressional Politics, p. 93; Polenberg, War and Society, pp. 30-31; Neal, "Politics of Price Fixing," pp. 203-204.

[116]Rosenman, Public Papers and Addresses of FDR 11: 1942, pp. 6-20; Paul, Taxation, pp. 279-291; John M. Blum, From the Morgenthau Diaries, vol. III: Years of War, 1941-1945 (Boston, 1967), pp. 16-17; Benson, "The Year in Congress," American Year Book, 1942, pp. 36-37.

revenue to be raised and the income strata that would bear the burden.[117] In a nationwide address on April 27, 1942, Roosevelt appealed for heavier taxes. "Profits must be taxed to the utmost limit consistent with continued production," the President told Congress. He stated bluntly that no citizen should have an income after taxes of more than $25,000 a year. But Roosevelt's goading could not overcome the configuration of forces within Congress. Almost no support surfaced for the proposed limit on incomes and the tax committees displayed continuing hostility toward both tax reform and the size of tax increases sought by the Administration.[118]

The reluctance of dominant factions on Capitol Hill to raise adequate revenue ill conformed with their professed desire for a "strong fiscal policy" that would avert inflation. The Roosevelt Administration advocated greater personal and corporate taxes to close the inflationary gap, while opposition members recoiled from that approach. Instead, they proposed to fight inflation by carrying out the recommendations of the Byrd Committee report. The further reduction of non-war expenditures, according to Senator Byrd and his allies, would enable Congress to get by with lower taxes and still ease inflationary pressure. The argument was specious, for total non-war expenditures in fiscal 1943, excluding fixed charges, were not more than $3 billion, and even if everything had been deleted, that would not have been much of an offset to a deficit of almost $60 billion. What was needed was more revenue. Yet fiscal conservatives believed they had found an expedient alternative to that necessity.[119]

Abolition of the CCC

Of the Federal agencies marked for elimination by the Byrd Committee, the Civilian Conservation Corps was perhaps most vulnerable. Since the inception of the defense program, CCC had presented the Roosevelt Administration with a dilemma. Continuation of the agency as if the defense program did not exist would have been unreasonable. On the other hand, the President

---

[117]Paul, Taxation, pp. 294-299; Blum, Years of War, pp. 33-36; Harold M. Fleming, "The Politics of War Financing," in Ray F. Harvey and others, The Politics of This War (New York, 1943), pp. 247-248.

[118]Rosenman, Public Papers and Addresses of FDR 11: 1942, pp. 216-217; Polenberg, War and Society, pp. 24-28, 89; Burns, Soldier of Freedom, p. 256.

[119]Stein, Fiscal Revolution, p. 182; Young, Congressional Politics, p. 124; Paul, Taxation, p. 300; William J. Carson, "National Finance and the Public Debt," in William M. Schuyler, ed., The American Year Book, 1942 (New York, 1943), p. 247.

did not want the Corps abolished. He evidently intended for it to become a permanent instrument of national policy, for in 1939 he had separated CCC and NYA from the emergency work relief program and transferred those agencies to the newly-created Federal Security Agency.[120]

The Administration responded to the predicament by gradually curtailing CCC and by modifying the agency's function. In September 1940, for example, Administration officials implemented a plan to train CCC enrollees for employment in defense industries. Basic army drill and other military subjects were also incorporated into the Corps' program. The new emphasis on pre-military and vocational training oriented CCC toward the fulfillment of defense needs.[121]

In other ways Administration officials tried to change the purpose of the agency. Perhaps the most important effort to alter the structure and function of CCC occurred late in 1940. Certain junior officials of the Department of Agriculture conceived a plan to convert the Corps from a temporary relief agency into a full-fledged social service organization for American youth. Dissatisfied with what they considered an unimaginative program, the well-intentioned reformers hoped to develop new leadership for CCC. They recommended that young men from major universities be trained as camp commanders who would then supplant the Army reserve officers currently in charge. An unused camp at Mt. Sharon, Vermont, would become the first such "staff college" for the Corps.[122]

The plan might never have come to fruition without the intervention of the President's wife. Eleanor Roosevelt had made youth her special concern, and she had long considered the CCC program inadequate. The First Lady welcomed the Department of Agriculture proposal and enlisted the aid of Harry Hopkins to persuade her husband that the plan had merit. For his part, the President realized the Army was already withdrawing its better officers from the CCC and reassigning them to strictly military

---

[120] Roosevelt, Complete Presidential Press Conferences 17-18: 1941, pp. 17: 34-35, 322-323; Lash, Eleanor and Franklin, pp. 711, 718; Harold D. Smith, Memorandum of Conference with the President, November 30, 1940, Smith papers, FDR Library.

[121] John A. Salmond, The Civilian Conservation Corps, 1933-1942: A New Deal Case Study (Durham, N.C., 1967), pp. 194-199; Harold D. Smith, Daily Memoranda, July 29, 1940, Smith papers, FDR Library; Roosevelt, Complete Presidential Press Conferences 15-16: 1940, pp. 15: 389, 402, 426, 437, 16: 42.

[122] J. F. Scott and L. W. A'Hearn to Harold D. Smith, February 6, 1941, General Records of the Director, series 39.27, box 42, Records of the Bureau of the Budget, Record Group 51, National Archives.

duty. The time seemed propitious for a new departure. On September 18, 1940, Roosevelt approved the creation of "a special training agency" to prepare future camp commanders.[123]

The Mount Sharon experiment attracted adverse comment from sources hostile to the New Deal. On December 28, 1940, the New York Herald Tribune, no friend of the Administration, informed the public and the Congress of the existence of Mt. Sharon. Republicans immediately censured the Administration for enrolling Harvard and Dartmouth students, representatives of the "more privileged" classes, in a CCC camp intended for relief of unemployed youth. Representative Albert J. Engel (R., Mich.), who had never before shown much sympathy for the poor, charged that "the pampered sons of rich families are usurping a form of relief meant only for the nation's underprivileged." The clamor for a full investigation caused Representative Malcolm Tarver (D., Ga.), Chairman of the Labor-Federal Security Appropriations Subcommittee, to ask for all CCC files pertaining to the Mt. Sharon experiment.[124]

Facing a potentially damaging Congressional inquiry, the Roosevelt Administration retreated. On February 3, 1941, Secretary of War Henry Stimson advised the Bureau of the Budget that he opposed "the establishment of experimental camps." Stimson wanted CCC used only "in connection with National Defense." Federal Security Administrator Paul V. McNutt questioned "whether the procedures contemplated [at Mt. Sharon] can be adopted within the statutory framework of the Civilian Conservation Corps and the current appropriation act." On February 15, Budget Director Smith warned the President that the experiment would "be susceptible to considerable criticism." Convinced at last, Roosevelt allowed CCC Director McEntee to close down the "staff college." By March 19, regular enrollees had replaced the college students at Mt. Sharon.[125]

Politically, the Mt. Sharon project proved a serious blunder. Incensed Congressmen thought the Administration had attempted, without the approval of Congress, to transform the Corps. With

---

[123]Eleanor Roosevelt to President, December 26, 1940, General Records of the Director, series 39.27, box 42, Records of the Bureau of the Budget, Record Group 51, National Archives; Lash, Eleanor and Franklin, pp. 698-721; Salmond, Civilian Conservation Corps, pp. 202-205.

[124]Salmond, Civilian Conservation Corps, pp. 205-206.

[125]Quotations from Henry L. Stimson to Harold D. Smith, February 3, 1941, Paul McNutt to Harold D. Smith, February 4, 1941, Harold D. Smith to President, February 15, 1941, General Records of the Director, series 39.27, box 42, Records of the Bureau of the Budget, Record Group 51, National Archives. See also Salmond, Civilian Conservation Corps, p. 206.

the future of CCC increasingly uncertain, the unfavorable publicity aided those who favored termination. CCC Director
McEntee informed the Bureau of the Budget that "several Congressmen called him up telling him they now feel that they have finally 'got something' on the Corps." Representative Clifton
Woodrum (D., Va.) told McEntee that the Corps was "on the spot."
The Mt. Sharon experiment, said Woodrum, would "have a decided
effect on 1942 appropriations for the Corps."[126]

The Mt. Sharon incident betrayed a fundamental inconsistency in the Administration's effort to convert CCC into something more than a temporary relief agency. By emphasizing vocational and pre-military training for CCC enrollees, the Administration had associated the organization with the national defense effort. At Mt. Sharon, however, government officials ex-
perimented with a new kind of youth program not related to the
immediate requirements of defense. The Mt. Sharon episode suggested that the Administration was still pursuing reform objectives at the expense of national security. Taft, Byrd,
McKellar, Taber, and other opposition members relied heavily on
that accusation in their campaign to abolish CCC.[127]

On January 5, 1942, Senator John Bankhead (D., Ala.) informed the President of a concerted effort by opposition leaders
to carry out the recommendations of the Byrd Committee report.
"I hope the President will not allow Senator Byrd and his gang
of anti-New Dealers to destroy such outstanding New Deal measures as the Youth Administration, the CCC, and particularly
Farm Security," Bankhead told Presidential secretary "Pa"
Watson. "They opposed these measures when they were proposed,
and they are trying now to destroy them." Already alert to the
danger, Roosevelt, though preoccupied with the war, tried to
protect CCC. He believed the Corps should become part of "a
future youth training program."[128]

By the end of 1941, however, the vicissitudes affecting
CCC had reached a critical stage. The agency had less than
160,000 enrollees in 900 camps, as compared to 300,000 ten
months earlier. Six thousand youths were leaving the Corps

---

[126] Quotations from L. W. A'Hearn to Martin, January 25,
1941, General Records of the Director, series 39.27, box 42,
Records of the Bureau of the Budget, Record Group 51, National
Archives.

[127] Salmond, *Civilian Conservation Corps*, pp. 207-208.

[128] Quotations from E. M. Watson to President, January 5,
1942, President's Secretary's File 187, FDR papers, FDR Library;
and Harold D. Smith, Memorandum of Conference with the President, December 6, 1941, Smith papers, FDR Library.

each month to take jobs in private industry.[129]   After Pearl
Harbor, conversion to war production accelerated and, for the
first time, the American economy faced a potential manpower
shortage. That shortage was not yet a "labor famine," such as
imperiled British war production, but it was becoming serious,
nonetheless. As the number of unemployed declined, CCC enrollments decreased correspondingly. On December 18, 1941, the
President decided to provide "only a minimum of appropriations"
for CCC. Budget Director Smith raised the possibility "that
the CCC might temporarily even drop out of the picture, except
for the lowest age groups, veterans, territorials, and Indians."[130]
In his budget message of January 5, 1942, Roosevelt admitted
that wartime conditions necessitated "a considerable reduction
in the program of the Civilian Conservation Corps and the National Youth Administration." Still, the President affirmed
that a much-reduced CCC had a function to perform. The Corps,
he later told a press conference, should continue its essential
conservation work, like fighting forest fires, and serve as a
training organization for youths not old enough for the Army.[131]

     In spite of Roosevelt's determination to maintain a rump
program, primarily for its postwar implications, practical difficulties threatened the continued operation of CCC. The
President told reporters on February 13, 1942, that the Administration was "cutting down on the CCC . . . because the boys are
not applying."[132] Enrollees consisted increasingly of blacks,
Indians, and the very young, who suffered from discriminatory
hiring practices by private industry.[133] Under those circumstances, continuation of a shrunken CCC for the duration of the

---

[129]Salmond, Civilian Conservation Corps, p. 210.

[130]Harold D. Smith, Memorandum of Conference with the President, December 18, 1941, Smith papers, FDR Library.

[131]Rosenman, Public Papers and Addresses of FDR 11: 1942,
pp. 11-12; Franklin D. Roosevelt, Complete Presidential Press
Conferences of Franklin D. Roosevelt, vols. 19-20: 1942 (New
York, 1972), pp. 19: 139-142, 283-285.

[132]Roosevelt, Complete Presidential Press Conferences
19-20: 1942, p. 19: 141.

[133]Harold D. Smith, Memorandum of Conference with the President, December 18, 1941, Smith papers, FDR Library; Salmond,
Civilian Conservation Corps, p. 209; Polenberg, War and Society,
pp. 79-80. See also William A. Aery, "Negro Education," in
William M. Schuyler, ed., The American Year Book, 1940 (New York,
1941), p. 1038; and Allan G. Harper, "American Indian Affairs,"
in William M. Schuyler, ed., The American Year Book, 1942 (New
York, 1943), pp. 554-555.

war would entail disproportionately high administrative costs in order to service fewer and fewer youths. To reduce administrative expenses, Roosevelt considered consolidating CCC with the National Youth Administration. Proponents of consolidation claimed it might save as much as $100,000,000 each year and satisfy the need for economy in money and manpower while preserving the CCC program for potential expansion after the war ended.[134]

At the President's request, the Bureau of the Budget drafted a bill to consolidate the Corps with the Youth Administration. "[T]his legislation," reported Budget Director Smith on March 14, "looks more and more like a youth program for the post-war period, and I feel definitely that it will be murdered if presented to Congress at this time." Because the Administration no longer controlled Congress, said Smith, the measure merging CCC and NYA would have to be abandoned. He recommended that Roosevelt "maintain . . . a skeleton program for the CCC during the war period" and consolidate the Corps with the Youth Administration "by Executive Order rather than attempt the legislative route." That strategy would enable the Administration to preserve the nucleus of a "fundamental program" even though "CCC is rapidly fading out of the picture."[135] On March 17, the President endorsed Smith's plan. "In regard to C.C.C.," he wrote, "I would keep a skeleton organization going here in Washington" and take "boys under twenty, giving preference to those who need physical rehabilitation in order to fit them for service in the army."[136]

Meanwhile, Senators McKellar and Byrd pressed for Congressional approval of the Byrd Committee report. On February 23, McKellar introduced a bill providing for abolition of CCC and NYA. By including both youth agencies in his bill, he committed a tactical error. Substantial sentiment for termination of CCC had surfaced in Congress, but the Youth Administration was a different matter. Roosevelt had confined NYA "almost exclusively to . . . defense training," and many Congressmen considered

---

[134]Roosevelt, Complete Presidential Press Conferences 17-18: 1941, pp. 18: 344-345; Pete Jarman to President, November 5, 1941, President's Official File 268, FDR papers, FDR Library; Harold D. Smith, Memorandum of Conference with the President, December 6, 1941, Smith papers, FDR Library; Salmond, Civilian Conservation Corps, p. 209. See also Orlie M. Clem, "Secondary Education," in William M. Schuyler, ed., The American Year Book, 1941 (New York, 1942), p. 971.

[135]Smith to President, March 14, 1942, Miscellaneous White House Memoranda, Smith papers, FDR Library.

[136]President to Smith, March 17, 1942, President's Official File 268, FDR papers, FDR Library.

it an important war agency supplying thousands of trained workers for essential war industries.[137]

On March 13, Senator Elbert D. Thomas (D., Utah), Chairman
of the Education and Labor Committee and a faithful Presidential
supporter, advised Roosevelt that the committee would have to
hold hearings on McKellar's bill.[138] Three days later, the
President asked McKellar to "come down and talk with me before
anything more is done about S. 2295, which in effect provides
for terminating the CCC and the NYA. At the present time," Roosevelt continued, "both of these agencies are engaged mostly in
essential war work." McKellar replied that he would "be glad
to come down any time . . . and talk to you about this matter,"
but the tenor of his letter conveyed the inflexibility of his
resolve.[139]

McKellar's bill, coupled with a Gallup poll showing that 54
percent of the American people now favored abolition of CCC,
sapped the confidence of Corps' officials. CCC Director McEntee
said "it would be better to fold up" the Corps immediately,
rather than have Congress force an end. Others believed CCC
could still survive and wanted to fight McKellar.[140] The President, though the matter ranked far down on his list of wartime
priorities, continued to favor retention of a skeleton force and
consolidation with NYA by Executive Order.[141]

Congressional supporters of the Civilian Conservation Corps
won the first skirmish with McKellar and Byrd. Senator Thomas'
Education and Labor Committee was packed with such reliable New
Dealers as Senators James Murray (D., Mont.), Claude Pepper

---

[137]President to Smith, March 17, 1942, President's Official
File 268, FDR papers, FDR Library; Congressional Record, 77th
Congress, 2nd Session, p. 4914. See also Salmond, Civilian Con-
servation Corps, p. 212; and J. O. Keller and H. G. Pyle, "Adult
Education," in William M. Schuyler, ed., The American Year Book,
1942 (New York, 1943), pp. 981-982.

[138]Thomas to President, March 13, 1942, President's Official File 268, FDR papers, FDR Library.

[139]President to McKellar, March 16, 1942, and McKellar to
President, March 17, 1942, President's Official File 268, FDR
papers, FDR Library.

[140]Salmond, Civilian Conservation Corps, p. 213.

[141]President to James J. McEntee, March 15, 1942, President's Personal File 2265, FDR papers, FDR Library; and President to Harold D. Smith, March 17, 1942, President's Official
File 268, FDR papers, FDR Library; Harold D. Smith, Daily
Memoranda, March 23, 1942, Smith papers, FDR Library.

(D., Fla.), Allen Ellender (D., La.), and Lister Hill (D., Ala.). From March 23 to April 17, the committee held hearings on the McKellar Bill but then refused to report the measure to the Senate.[142]

Stymied by the Education and Labor Committee, McKellar, Byrd, Taber and their allies resorted to another method of liquidating the Civilian Conservation Corps. On May 4, 1942, the President requested $49,101,000 to operate 150 CCC camps. A supplemental estimate raised the figure to $80,118,000 for 350 camps.[143] In the House of Representatives, opposition members urged the Appropriations Committee to reject Roosevelt's request and follow the Byrd Committee recommendation instead. A subcommittee left the CCC item intact, but on June 3, the full committee voted, 15 to 12, with 13 absent, to deny further funds to the Corps.[144]

On June 4 and 5, Administration loyalists in the House strove to restore the appropriation. Presenting the case for CCC, majority leader John McCormack (D., Mass.) emphasized that the War Department utilized the Corps for construction of roads and similar facilities on Army reservations. "If we do not appropriate money" for CCC, said McCormack, "we must appropriate it to hire somebody do the very thing the boys in these camps would be doing."[145] Representative Malcolm Tarver (D., Ga.) reminded his colleagues that CCC provided essential fire protection for national forests. "I know," he said,

---

[142] Paul McNutt to President, March 18, 1942, and President to Paul McNutt, March 18, 1942, President's Official File 268, FDR papers, FDR Library. For the composition of the Senate Education and Labor Committee, see Curry, "Southern Senators and Their Roll Call Votes in Congress," p. 166. See also U.S., Congress, Senate, Committee on Education and Labor, Hearings before the Committee on Education and Labor on S. 2295, 77th Congress, 2nd Session, 1942, pp. 56-59, 69, 253, 270, 334, 519-552; Salmond, Civilian Conservation Corps, pp. 213-215; and John A. Salmond, "Postscript to the New Deal: The Defeat of the Nomination of Aubrey W. Williams as Rural Electrification Administrator in 1945," Journal of American History LXI (September 1974), pp. 422-423.

[143] Congressional Record, 77th Congress, 2nd Session, pp. 3934, 4419.

[144] Congressional Record, 77th Congress, 2nd Session, p. 4832; Salmond, Civilian Conservation Corps, p. 215; Congressional Digest 21 (1942), p. 163.

[145] Congressional Record, 77th Congress, 2nd Session, p. 4939.

we all have been subject to a tremendous barrage by
people who are evidently acting in coordination, seeking
to have us support the conclusions of what is known as
the Byrd committee. The Byrd committee . . . is composed very largely of gentlemen who never were in favor
of these activities which in their report they propose
to have eliminated. They would be opposed to the continuance of those activities in normal times and under
normal conditions.

At the end of the war, Tarver declared, "we will have . . . millions of people in this country out of employment, including
millions of boys who are returned from the armed services of the
country." In that event, he concluded, "there may be need for
a very largely expanded C.C.C."[146]

Tarver's remarks caused Representative Charles Halleck
(R., Ind.) to charge that the Administration really wanted to
retain CCC for its postwar program, not because the Corps was
essential to the war effort.[147] The Administration's policy,
Representative Albert Engel (R., Mich.) asserted, was to cut
the budget of CCC but retain the agency. That policy, he continued, would incur large overhead expenses while distributing
few benefits. Abolition of the Corps' bureaucracy would be
more economical.[148] Representative John Cochran (D., Mo.) replied,

There is something else back of this fight. There
is politics back of this. . . . The President has
made it known, or at least it has leaked out, that
it is his purpose, by Executive Order, to place the
C.C.C. and the N.Y.A. together. The effort to destroy the C.C.C. right now is an effort to prevent
the President from consolidating the two organizations. Members have spoken about overhead, but let
the President put them together and when he does
consolidate them, then the overhead is reduced automatically.[149]

Opposition members retorted that the Administration had introduced "politics" into the issue by seeking to preserve an agency

---

[146] Congressional Record, 77th Congress, 2nd Session,
pp. 4927-4928.

[147] Congressional Record, 77th Congress, 2nd Session,
p. 4928.

[148] Congressional Record, 77th Congress, 2nd Session,
pp. 3286, 4906-4907.

[149] Congressional Record, 77th Congress, 2nd Session,
p. 4932.

that had lost its raison d'etre. "The original reason for the establishment of the C.C.C. was to provide for unemployment," said Representative William Whittington (D., Miss.). "The reason for the establishment of the C.C.C. camps no longer exists."[150]

Some Republicans would not admit that there had ever been a justification for the Civilian Conservation Corps. Representative Taber, perhaps the most zealous critic of the Corps, denounced the agency as "the most wasteful and the most destructive" organization in the government. It was a "dangerous antidefense activity." He demanded immediate liquidation of the CCC. On June 5, 1942, the House voted, 158-121, not to appropriate any more money for the Corps.[151]

Administration supporters hoped the Senate would overrule the House, as had happened frequently during past appropriation fights.[152] The President instructed Budget Director Smith to "make it clear, on my behalf, to the Appropriations Committee in the Senate that the elimination of the CCC will call for a wholly separate appropriation to take its place in two of the CCC activities."

The first is the need for forest fire protection, especially on the Pacific Coast and back as far as the Rockies, where we must guard against Japanese incendiary bombs and incendiary fires during the dry season. This is essential for our national future.

"The second," he continued, "is the building of roads and other facilities for [military] camps. These have to be built by someone and I shall have to ask for a special appropriation to let the work out by contract instead of having it done by the CCC." Roosevelt concluded, "Make it clear that the abolishing of the CCC saves the nation no money."[153]

---

[150] Congressional Record, 77th Congress, 2nd Session, p. 5800.

[151] Congressional Record, 77th Congress, 2nd Session, p. 4935. For House teller vote on CCC appropriation, see Congressional Record, 77th Congress, 2nd Session, p. 4940. See also Salmond, Civilian Conservation Corps, pp. 215-216.

[152] Unsigned memorandum to Marvin H. McIntyre, n.d., President's Official File 268, FDR papers, FDR Library.

[153] President to Smith, June 17, 1942, President's Official File 268, FDR papers, FDR Library.

The Budget Director relayed the President's message to
Senator Patrick McCarran (D., Nev.), chairman of the subcommittee which would consider CCC funds. McCarran tried to persuade his subcommittee to restore the item for the Corps. But
first that group and then the full Appropriations Committee
refused to go along.[154] McCarran, with White House backing,
carried the fight to the Senate floor. Chances for success appeared poor. Organized private interest groups, including the
United States Chamber of Commerce, National Association of
Manufacturers, American Farm Bureau Federation, and Citizens
Emergency Committee on Non-Defense Expenditures, favored termination of the Corps. With only a few exceptions, the nation's
newspapers had applauded the House vote denying funds for CCC.
On the other hand, support for the Corps was relatively frag-
mented and ineffective.[155] To surmount that handicap, McCarran
made the most of Roosevelt's backing and attempted to rally
Administration forces. On June 26, the Senate voted on
McCarran's amendment providing money for 350 camps. When the
roll call was completed, 32 Senators--16 New Deal reliables, 13
orthodox Democrats, 2 Republicans and 1 Independent--had voted
to retain the Civilian Conservation Corps. An equal number of
Senators, 10 orthodox Democrats, 14 Republicans, and 8 renegade
Democrats, had voted to abolish the Corps. Vice President
Henry A. Wallace broke the tie. He voted to continue CCC. By
the narrowest of margins, the Corps survived.[156]

A split in the faction of orthodox Democrats caused the
tie vote. Administration loyalists voted as a bloc in favor of
CCC, while Republicans and Democratic intractables united in
opposition. The swing group, the orthodox Democrats, divided
along sectional lines. Of the 13 supporting CCC, 8 represented
states west of the Mississippi River (California, Arizona, New
Mexico, Nevada, and Oklahoma). Of the 10 orthodox Democrats
opposing CCC, 8 represented states east of the Mississippi River
(Massachusetts, Connecticut, Delaware, Maryland, South Carolina,
Alabama, Tennessee). In fact, of the 18 Democratic Senators
who voted against CCC, only Senators Clark (Mo.), Connally (Tex.),
and Wheeler (Mont.) represented states west of the Mississippi.

---

[154]U.S., Congress, Senate, Committee on Appropriations,
Hearings before a Subcommittee on Appropriations on H.R. 7181,
77th Congress, 2nd Session, pp. 289-300; Congressional Record,
77th Congress, 2nd Session, p. 5601.

[155]Salmond, Civilian Conservation Corps, p. 216.

[156]For Senate roll call votes on the CCC appropriation,
see Congressional Record, 77th Congress, 2nd Session, pp. 5612-
5613; Curry, "Southern Senators and Their Roll Call Votes in
Congress," pp. 232-233; and Appendix IV, Guttman scaling table
4, items 3, 4. See also John P. Robertson to T. W. Womack, tray
102, box 2, Norris papers, Library of Congress.

That sectional alignment may be explained by the estimated distribution of CCC camps. According to figures furnished by Senator McCarran, 10 New England and mid-Atlantic states would receive only 26 camps, while 11 western and Pacific Coast states would have 85 camps. Evidently, some Democratic Senators from eastern states resented the allocation of so many CCC camps to western states. Conversely, Senators from the Mountain West and Pacific Coast--areas directly affected by the need for forest fire protection--gave strong support to the Corps.[157]

The Senate had granted CCC only a temporary reprieve. The House clung to its position that the Corps should be liquidated. Senate and House conferees wrangled over CCC until House members agreed to put the issue up for another vote. On June 30, 1942, a solid majority of 230 Representatives, 93 Democrats and 137 Republicans, refused to accept the Senate's action on the CCC appropriation. Orthodox Democrats from southern, border, midwestern and plains states, areas where complaints that CCC aggravated the agricultural labor shortage were widespread, joined renegade Democrats and Republicans to defeat funds for the agency.[158] After that roll call, "which was quite overwhelming," McCarran concluded that further efforts were futile. On June 30, the Senate receded from its previous stand and agreed to terminate the Civilian Conservation Corps.[159]

Like the Revenue Acts of 1940 and the creation of the Byrd Committee in 1941, termination of CCC was a victory for the campaign to reverse New Deal policies. The President wanted the Corps to become part of a postwar program but was reluctant to put the issue forward on that basis. With victory over the Axis powers at least two or three years away, the Administration feared that dominant Congressional factions would consider discussion of postwar domestic policies premature and would automatically reject such recommendations. The strategy adopted by the Administration was to maintain a skeleton CCC organization for the duration of the war and integrate that skeleton force into the war program.

Opposition leaders easily penetrated the President's artifice. Publicly, they justified elimination of the Corps on the grounds of non-war economy. The saving, however, amounted to

[157] *Congressional Record*, 77th Congress, 2nd Session, pp. 5601-5613.

[158] For House roll call vote, see *Congressional Record*, 77th Congress, 2nd Session, pp. 5802-5803; and Appendix III, Guttman scaling table 4, item 1.

[159] *Congressional Record*, 77th Congress, 2nd Session, pp. 5788-5789; Salmond, *Civilian Conservation Corps*, p. 217; Benson, "The Year in Congress," *American Year Book, 1942*, p. 36.

little more than $62,000,000, a negligible offset to a deficit of almost $60,000,000,000. Privately, Representative Taber admitted that he and his allies believed CCC "should be dropped, not only for the duration of the war, but forever after."[160]

In mid-1942, liquidation of CCC had few immediate consequences of any substance. Conversion of the economy to war production had already forced the President to reduce the Corps to "nominal levels." That may have doomed CCC, for the closing of camps during 1941 and early 1942 left many Congressmen with no vested interest in continuing the Corps. Yet the defeat suffered by the Administration indicated the growing vulnerability of the New Deal legacy. Previously loyal supporters had become unpredictable and many orthodox Democrats, already estranged from the New Deal, had emerged as consistent adversaries of the President. The struggle for fiscal control had ended unfavorably for Roosevelt and he could no longer prevent encroachments by the Congressional opposition. As the Byrd Committee later gloated, abolition of CCC was "the first complete dismantling of a major depression agency." That initial success invited attacks on other New Deal agencies marked for elimination by the Joint Committee on Reduction of Nonessential Federal Expenditures.[161]

---

[160]Congressional Record, 77th Congress, 2nd Session, pp. 5624-5625. Quotation from John Taber to Ray P. Chase, January 15, 1942, box 87, Taber papers, Cornell University Library.

[161]Quotations from Harold D. Smith, Memorandum of Conference with the President, January 16, 1942, Smith papers, FDR Library; and U.S., Congress, Joint Committee on Reduction of Nonessential Federal Expenditures, Supplemental Report, S. Doc. 152, 77th Congress, 2nd Session, 1942, p. 6. See also Congressional Record, 77th Congress, 2nd Session, p. 4937.

CHAPTER 4

ASCENDANCY OF THE OPPOSITION

In 1942, the Congressional opposition wrested control of
domestic expenditures from the Roosevelt Administration and
its supporters. As abolition of the Civilian Conservation
Corps illustrated, that control could be used to terminate New
Deal programs which the President wanted to maintain on stand-
by status for possible reactivation at the end of the war.
Roosevelt's adversaries continued to press for the liquidation
of remaining relief programs, such as the National Youth Administration and the Work Projects Administration, because
those agencies, like CCC, seemed to have outlived their usefulness in a fully mobilized war economy. But opposition leaders
did not limit their legislative attacks to NYA and WPA. Agencies that combined wartime functions and reform purposes, like
the Office of Civilian Defense and the Farm Security Administration, also became targets of Republicans and renegade Democrats. The Byrd Committee continued to serve as the principal
forum for their activities.[1]

"Reform Still Clings Like a Leech"

On January 23, 1942, Senator Byrd announced that his committee would investigate complaints against the Farm Security
Administration, the government agency that loaned money and
offered assistance to impoverished farmers, sharecroppers and
migrant workers. The Byrd Committee had already recommended
liquidation of FSA.[2] On February 6, committee members heard
Judge Robert K. Greene of the Probate Court of Hale County,
Greensboro, Alabama, accuse local Farm Security officials of
paying "the back and current poll taxes" of white borrowers, a
practice that violated the laws of Alabama. The issue was
sensitive, for eight southern states relied on poll taxes, in

---

[1]U.S., Congress, Joint Committee on Reduction of Nonessential Federal Expenditures, Preliminary Report, S. Doc. 152,
77th Congress, 1st Session, 1941, p. 3; Ray F. Harvey, "The
Politics of Politics," in Ray F. Harvey and others, The Politics of This War (New York, 1943), pp. 315-317; Richard Polenberg, War and Society: The United States, 1941-1945 (Philadelphia, 1972), p. 80.

[2]Morgenthau Diary, vol. 487, p. 301, vol. 491, p. 402-A,
FDR Library; U.S.,Congress, Joint Committee on Reduction of
Nonessential Federal Expenditures, Preliminary Report, S. Doc.
152, 77th Congress, 1st Session, 1941, pp. 4-7.

conjunction with literacy tests and other devices, to disen-
franchise blacks and low-income whites.[3]

Farm Security Administrator C. B. "Beanie" Baldwin, an
avowed New Dealer, denied that FSA had ever directly paid poll
taxes for any individual in any state. In granting a supervised
loan, he explained, agency personnel drafted a budget for the
low-income farm family and permitted the borrower to include
his poll tax and other taxes as part of the family's necessary
expenses. The borrower paid his poll tax out of other income
he received, from the sale of crops, for example, and not out
of money from FSA. Baldwin submitted an opinion by Mastin G.
White, solicitor of the Department of Agriculture, which held
that FSA had not transgressed any state or Federal laws.[4]

Baldwin's explanation, later corroborated by Secretary of
Agriculture Claude Wickard, failed to satisfy Senators Byrd,
McKellar, and Glass, who subjected Baldwin to an angry cross-
examination. The three Senators were sure that FSA enabled poor
whites to vote, and they feared that the practice might some day
be extended to blacks. They also believed that Farm Security
was organizing a subservient clientele that would pressure Congress for larger appropriations. During the questioning, Byrd
became so strident that Senator La Follette interceded for
Baldwin and reminded the chairman that he was not conducting
"an inquisition."[5]

The poll-tax complaint opened the way for a carefully
planned assault on the entire Farm Security program. The next
witness before the Byrd Committee was a persistent detractor of

---

[3]U.S., Congress, Joint Committee on Reduction of Nonessential Federal Expenditures, Hearings, 77th Congress, 2nd Session,
1942, pp. 699-711. Quotation from Morgenthau Diary, vol. 493,
pp. 98-99, FDR Library. See also Thomas L. Stokes, "The Congress," in Jack Goodman, ed., While You Were Gone: A Report on
Wartime Life in the United States (New York, 1946), pp. 140-151;
Sidney Baldwin, Poverty and Politics: The Rise and Decline of
the Farm Security Administration (Chapel Hill, N.C., 1968), p.
350; and New Republic 107 (September 14, 1942), p. 301.

[4]U.S., Congress, Joint Committee on Reduction of Nonessential Federal Expenditures, Hearings, 77th Congress, 2nd Session,
1942, pp. 711-715; Morgenthau Diary, vol. 493, p. 99, FDR Library. For Baldwin's recollection of this incident, see Studs
Terkel, Hard Times: An Oral History of the Great Depression
(New York, 1971), pp. 299-300.

[5]U.S., Congress, Joint Committee on Reduction of Nonessential Federal Expenditures, Hearings, 77th Congress, 2nd Session,
1942, pp. 715-724; Morgenthau Diary, vol. 493, p. 99, FDR
Library.

the agency, Edward A. O'Neal of Alabama, President of the American Farm Bureau Federation. O'Neal, chief spokesman for organized commercial agriculture, opposed Farm Security because its activities diverted funds from soil conservation and parity payments, deprived landowners of their sharecroppers and day labor, kept small farmers in production, and increased competition with larger, established farms. Furthermore, O'Neal believed FSA officials promoted collective farming, land reform, and other radical experiments which threatened traditional patterns of land ownership. That was reason enough for him to condemn the agency, but he also suspected FSA of seeking a New Deal for Negroes in the black belt areas of the South. The close ties between Farm Security and the National Farmers Union, a small but growing rival to the Farm Bureau, constituted still another reason for O'Neal's hostility.[6]

In his statement to the Byrd Committee, O'Neal indicted FSA "for waste, extravagance, and indefensible practices." He urged Congress to abolish the agency. The Committee's majority, relishing that testimony, agreed to hear "concrete, definite evidence" which O'Neal claimed he could produce to substantiate his accusations.[7] The "evidence," presented on February 10, consisted of reports written by Farm Bureau officials, scarcely impartial investigators. The reports "appeared to be isolated cases and not generally applicable to all FSA activities," in the opinion of William Heffelfinger of the Treasury Department.[8]

O'Neal's charges of waste, political corruption, inefficiency, and "socialized farming" provoked an indignant rejoinder

---

[6]U.S., Congress, Joint Committee on Reduction of Nonessential Federal Expenditures, Hearings, 77th Congress, 2nd Session, 1942, pp. 742-746; Morgenthau Diary, vol. 493, p. 100, FDR Library. See also Wesley McCune, The Farm Bloc (New York, 1943), pp. 29-31, 165-221; Alfred D. Stedman, "The Politics of the Farmers in Wartime," in Ray F. Harvey and others, The Politics of This War (New York , 1943), p. 163; Baldwin, Poverty and Politics pp. 173-174, 279-284, 298-303, 336-344; and Lawrence H. Curry, Jr., "Southern Senators and Their Roll-Call Votes in Congress" (Ph.D. dissertation, Duke University, 1971), pp. 209-210.

[7]U.S., Congress, Joint Committee on Reduction of Nonessential Federal Expenditures, Hearings, 77th Congress, 2nd Session, 1942, pp. 742-746, 757; Morgenthau Diary, vol. 493, p. 100, FDR Library.

[8]Quotation from Morgenthau Diary, vol. 495, p. 86, FDR Library. See also U.S., Congress, Joint Committee on Reduction of Nonessential Federal Expenditures, Hearings, 77th Congress, 2nd Session, 1942, pp. 792-838; McCune, Farm Bloc, pp. 190-191; and Baldwin, Poverty and Politics, pp. 349-350.

from the Farm Security Administrator. The Farm Bureau leadership, Baldwin exclaimed, exhibited "the most severe prejudice" against his agency and the poor farmers it served. "Mr. O'Neal cannot,by any stretch of the imagination, be considered as representing the interest of the low income farm family." A furious argument, a "grand circus performance" according to one observer, then ensued between Baldwin and O'Neal and forced Byrd to adjourn the hearings.[9]

On February 13, Baldwin presented a detailed refutation of charges made by O'Neal. The FSA, he declared, tried "to perpetuate the small farm" by assisting poor families who deserved government protection much more than "large operators" who belonged to the Farm Bureau and received the bulk of Federal benefit payments and subsidies.[10] Baldwin's spirited defense received support from other witnesses. James G. Patton, President of the National Farmers Union, told the committee that the Farm Bureau had never shown the slightest concern for low-income farmers. The vendetta against FSA, suggested Patton, resulted from the desire of commercial farmers to suppress smaller competitors and achieve higher agricultural prices through scarcity.[11]

The most effective statement in behalf of Farm Security was that of Howard R. Tolley, chief of the Bureau of Agricultural Economics. Tolley maintained tnat "the Farm Security Administration is engaged in one of the most needed activities that is being carried on by the Department of Agriculture, and is doing one of the best jobs. . . . If the Farm Security program were abolished," he continued, "I feel sure that we would have a great deal more distress and poverty among the farmers of the country than we do now. . . ." Equally important, abolition of FSA "would have a very adverse effect upon the food for victory program," the wartime production drive sponsored by the Department of Agriculture. Tolley insisted that the "work of the Farm Security Administration with low income farmers" was necessary to attain food production goals because FSA

---

[9]Quotations from Morgenthau Diary, vol. 493, p. 100, FDR Library; and U.S., Congress, Joint Committee on Reduction of Nonessential Federal Expenditures, Hearings, 77th Congress, 2nd Session, 1942, pp. 840-946.

[10]U.S., Congress, Joint Committee on Reduction of Nonessential Federal Expenditures, Hearings, 77th Congress, 2nd Session, 1942, pp. 847-904; Morgenthau Diary, vol. 496, pp. 174-175, FDR Library.

[11]U.S., Congress, Joint Committee on Reduction of Nonessential Federal Expenditures, Hearings, 77th Congress, 2nd Session, 1942, p. 916; Morgenthau Diary, vol. 496, p. 175, FDR Library.

provided credit, supervision, and technical expertise which enabled small farmers to increase yields.[12]

Nevertheless, Byrd, McKellar, Taber and other opposition
members demanded termination of FSA. The Farm Security program, they argued, was another instance of nonessential New Deal
spending which should be eliminated because of the war. That
argument, plausible in the case of CCC, seemed inappropriate
when applied to FSA. As Representative Laurence F. Arnold (D.,
Ill.) observed on February 22, 1942, "Whatever agricultural
programs stabilize and strengthen our production of vital foodstuffs must be supported as indispensable tools for victory."
The Farm Security Administration could "energize the little
farmer and fit him into the food production program."[13] Even
Secretary of the Treasury Henry Morgenthau, Jr., the chief Administration advocate of non-war economy, exempted Farm Security
from his recommendations. But FSA had incurred the enmity of
powerful organized private interest groups and violated the
conception of proper agricultural policy held by important
leaders of the opposition. For those reasons, FSA encountered
a series of determined attacks by its enemies.[14]

Early in February 1942, Representative Harold Cooley (D.,
N.C.) had introduced a resolution creating a select committee
to investigate Farm Security. Department of Agriculture officials believed the Cooley resolution, like the charges aired
before the Byrd Committee, was intended to harass FSA at a time
when Congressional supporters were trying to protect the
agency's appropriation. Hard work by Administration leaders
in the House prevented Cooley from receiving a rule for his
resolution.[15]

---

[12]U.S., Congress, Joint Committee on Reduction of Nonessential Federal Expenditures, Hearings, 77th Congress, 2nd Session, 1942, pp. 911-913; Morgenthau Diary, vol. 496, p. 175,
FDR Library.

[13]Laurence F. Arnold, "Food Will Win," February 22, 1942,
Correspondence, 1935-42, AD-071, box 55, Records of the Farm
Security Administration, Record Group 96, National Archives.
See also Howard R. Tolley, The Farmer Citizen at War (New York,
1943), pp. 31-32, 61; and McCune, Farm Bloc, p. 275.

[14]Congressional Record, 77th Congress, 2nd Session, pp.
A840-A841; Baldwin, Poverty and Politics, pp. 325, 335-349.

[15]Congressional Record, 77th Congress, 2nd Session,
p. 1005; Gardner Jackson to Marvin H. McIntyre, March 11, 1942,
President's Personal File 3453, FDR papers, FDR Library.

Farm Security still faced a difficult appropriations fight.
A House subcommittee had already cut direct appropriations and
loan funds for FSA below the current year's figure. Led by
Representative Everett Dirksen (R., Ill.), the agency's adversaries attempted a further reduction. On March 13, Dirksen offered an amendment to the agricultural appropriations bill which
slashed FSA direct appropriations from $50,319,557 to
$25,319,557.[16]

That was a crippling reduction in administrative funds
available to the agency. High administrative costs had often
exposed Farm Security to attack. As one official explained,
"the operation of the low income farmer has to be constantly
supervised and requires a large staff of field agents to go from
farm to farm keeping an eye on these operations and servicing
the loans."[17] Once before, in 1938, Senator Byrd and his allies
had attempted to wreck the Farm Security program by limiting
funds for administrative overhead. At that time, Secretary of
Agriculture Henry A. Wallace and the President had persuaded
Congress to reject Byrd's ploy.[18]

Now the Dirksen amendment received the blessing of Representative Clarence Cannon (D., Mo.), Chairman of the House Appropriations Committee. "The hearings before . . . the Joint
Committee on the Reduction of Nonessential Federal Expenditures
last month are convincing proof of the necessity of reducing
this top-heavy appropriation for administrative expense," said
Cannon. Representative Clifford Hope (R., Kans.), one of a
handful of Republicans supporting FSA, disagreed: "If you cut
$25,000,000 . . . you will practically put [Farm Security] . . .
out of business." Crippling the program would jeopardize increased food production, added Representative Malcolm Tarver
(D., Ga.). If Cannon, Dirksen, Taber and other opponents of
FSA were so anxious to cut nonessential spending, Representative Reid F. Murray (R., Wisc.) said, then they should limit
the subsidies paid to "large landowners and large corporation
farmers" instead of curtailing the assistance granted low-
income farmers.[19]

Those arguments did not deter either Cannon or the American
Farm Bureau Federation. On March 13, the House voted, 142-119,

---

[16]Congressional Record, 77th Congress, 2nd Session, p.
2415.

[17]Gardner Jackson to Marvin H. McIntyre, March 11, 1942,
President's Personal File 3453, FDR papers, FDR Library.

[18]Baldwin, Poverty and Politics, pp. 318-319.

[19]Quotations from Congressional Record, 77th Congress,
2nd Session, pp. 2375-2376, 2415, 2418, 2426.

to cut FSA funds.[20]   One loyal New Dealer, Representative Frank
E. Hook (D., Mich), accused "Edward O'Neal, head of the Farm
Bureau Federation . . . [of] directing the efforts of those on
the floor of the House to sabotage" the Farm Security program.
Hook criticized his fellow Democrats for lacking the "organization and . . . united will to save those things that we . . .
have fought for in the years past." Then he castigated the
enemies of the New Deal.

> True to the character of all wars, the present war
> placed into the hands of the Tory minority increased
> powers of obstruction. Ever since America was re-
> quired to go all-out for arms production this self-
> ish group could command a high price for its co-
> operation.

President Roosevelt, Hook continued, "paid the price that was
demanded and that was the control of the defense program" and
abandonment of reform. The Byrd Committee had led the "work
of destruction" by clamoring "for further cuts as war expenditures rise and the peril of inflation threatens us." Obstructionists had "fought price control, rationing, and adequate . . .
taxes, but they are the ones now that demand that inflation be
halted by slashing appropriations for agencies . . . necessary
to the war program."[21]

The Dirksen amendment had cut funds for Farm Security far
below the figure requested by the President in his January
budget message. Roosevelt had told reporters on February 10,
"Our whole food situation for the duration of the war is intimately connected with it [FSA]. Furthermore, the whole problem
of security for a large number of individual families is at
stake. Of course it is essential."[22] Subsequently, the President and other Administration officials "were very much impressed by the presentation of the Secretary of Agriculture,"
who said "that perhaps his greatest opportunity for expansion
in farm production, necessary in the war effort, was in the low-
income farm group served by the Farm Security program." According to Budget Director Harold D. Smith, "Congress would
probably be touchy to an expansion of . . . Farm Security," but
"in view of the possible shortage of foodstuffs for ourselves
and our allies, we felt compelled to recommend this program . . .

---

[20]Congressional Record, 77th Congress, 2nd Session, p.
2427. See also Baldwin, Poverty and Politics, p. 355.

[21]Congressional Record, 77th Congress, 2nd Session, pp.
2427-2428.

[22]Franklin D. Roosevelt, Complete Presidential Press Conferences of Franklin D. Roosevelt, vols. 19-20: 1942 (New
York, 1972), p. 19: 124.

for presentation to this Congress." In the case of Farm Security, reform seemed consonant with the requirements of war. While providing a greater measure of security for the "low-income farm group," FSA would help produce "Food for Victory."[23]

On May 1, the President decided to submit a supplemental budget request that would substantially expand the Farm Security program. The revised budget estimate went to the Senate, where Democratic loyalists hoped to reverse the unfavorable House action on FSA. A Senate subcommittee, though it did not accede to the President's request for an enlarged program, did restore cuts made by the House. When the appropriation came before the full Senate, Administration supporters parried efforts by Senators Byrd and McKellar to inflict new reductions. In a speech on May 18, Byrd asserted that the Farm Security program was really a form of communism, because it included "collective farming projects similar to those in Communist Russia," a reference to cooperative farming experiments inherited from the old Federal Emergency Relief Administration and the Resettlement Administration. Less than four hundred families were involved in cooperative farming, out of a million and a half farm families aided by FSA. Byrd's irresponsible tactics reflected a growing willingness to label the New Deal "red." In that spirit, Senator McKellar declared that Farm Security Administrator Baldwin was a communist, an accusation that elicited forceful rebuttals from Senators Bankhead (D., Ala.), Russell (D., Ga.), Hill (D., Ala.), and Pepper (D., Fla.), all of whom defended FSA and rebuked McKellar for his unwarranted characterization of Baldwin.[24]

When the floor fight ended on May 20, the Senate had approved $52,319,557 in direct appropriations and $165,000,000 in RFC loan authorizations for the Farm Security program. The figures represented an increase of $25,750,000 in direct appropriations and $70,000,000 in loans over the House amounts. Two months elapsed before Senate and House conferees reconciled the conflict over FSA. They finally compromised on $38,625,000 in direct appropriations and $130,000,000 in RFC loan authorizations.[25] The aggregate fell about $125,000,000 below the

[23]Quotations from Harold D. Smith, Memorandum of Conference with the President, May 1, 1942, Smith papers, FDR Library. See also Baldwin, Poverty and Politics, pp. 354-355.

[24]Congressional Record, 77th Congress, 2nd Session, pp. 4283, 4286, 4312-4314. See also Gardner Jackson to Marvin H. McIntyre, March 11, 1942, President's Personal File 3453, FDR papers, FDR Library; and Baldwin, Poverty and Politics, p. 358.

[25]Congressional Record, 77th Congress, 2nd Session, pp. 5059, 5559-5560, 5625, 6171-6172, A3025. See also Baldwin, Poverty and Politics, p. 359; and Curry, "Southern Senators and Their Roll-Call Votes in Congress," pp. 212-213.

President's original request for FSA and negated Administration plans for an expanded Farm Security program. Fewer low-income farmers would receive assistance and would produce less milk, pork, chicken, eggs, and soybeans. Equally disturbing to supporters of FSA, the budget cuts would undermine efforts "to perpetuate the small farm" and a democratic structure in agriculture. They feared the destruction of Farm Security would leave rural America dominated by "corporate and large-scale commercial farming." In a letter of protest to the President, James G. Patton of the National Farmers Union, Murray Lincoln of the Ohio Farm Bureau, William Green, President of the American Federation of Labor, and Philip Murray, President of the Congress of Industrial Organizations, warned "that what happens now in agriculture will shape what happens after victory has been won." FSA still survived, but the reductions in its budget foreshadowed the eventual termination of the New Deal for the small farmer.[26]

After its brief but sensational investigation of the Farm Security Administration, the Byrd Committee turned to the Office of Civilian Defense. The President had created that agency by executive order in May 1941, to coordinate local, state and Federal preparations against air raids, sabotage and similar contingencies.[27] Roosevelt had other purposes in mind as well. Many dedicated proponents of social reform, especially those close to Eleanor Roosevelt, believed the defense effort would disrupt the fabric of society. To cope with inevitable dislocations and to bolster public morale, they favored the channeling of volunteer energies into social service activities that would protect and advance the welfare of the American people.[28] English wartime experience had already demonstrated the utility of innovative social service endeavors, such as commnal feeding facilities, emergency housing, child care and health services. The "enormous new range of social safety nets"

---

[26]Quotations from James G. Patton and others to President, June 20, 1942, President's Official File 1568, FDR papers, FDR Library. See also Congressional Record, 77th Congress, 2nd Session, pp. 5558-5559; Baldwin, Poverty and Politics, pp. 360-361; and Polenberg, War and Society, pp. 84-86.

[27]Samuel Rosenman, ed., The Public Papers and Addresses of Franklin D. Roosevelt, vol. 10: 1941, The Call to Battle Stations (New York, 1950), pp. 162-172; Jessie C. Bourneuf, "The Office of Civilian Defense," July 15, 1943, pp. 1-5, series 41.3, no. 227, Records of the Bureau of the Budget, Record Group 51, National Archives; John A. Tillema, "Federal Administrative Agencies," in William M. Schuyler, ed., The American Year Book, 1941 (New York, 1942), pp. 61-62.

[28]Joseph P. Lash, Eleanor and Franklin (New York, 1973), pp. 823-824.

erected in England had given citizen volunteers an opportunity to participate in the war and had helped sustain civilian morale during the darkest days of the blitz.[29] Mrs. Roosevelt and her circle, mindful of England's "Voluntary Services for Civil Defense," wanted to create a similar "American Social Defense Organization." The President, initially skeptical of his wife's plans, eventually accepted her approach to civil defense problems. He gave OCD broad powers in the fields of civil morale, hygiene, diet, mental and physical fitness.[30]

Serious flaws in personnel and organization plagued the civilian defense program. The President appointed Fiorello LaGuardia, Mayor of New York City, as Director of OCD. In part, Roosevelt was paying off a political debt to the mayor and in part he was counting on LaGuardia's acknowledged talents as promoter and showman to dramatize civilian defense and rally public support. LaGuardia proved a bad choice. He had so many other responsibilities that he could give little or no direction to OCD. Worse, LaGuardia was interested almost exclusively in air raid protection and ignored the broader role assigned OCD.[31] In despair over the shortcomings of the program, Eleanor Roosevelt consented to become assistant director of OCD in charge of volunteer participation. When she began work in September 1941, Mrs. Roosevelt hoped to make OCD "a yeasty force for interagency action at the Federal level and for effective community organization throughout the country." She had in mind improved nutritional, health, child care, physical fitness and related emergency welfare services.[32]

The social reformist tinge of OCD, deepened by the association of Mrs. Roosevelt with the agency, invited a Congressional

---

[29] Angus Calder, The People's War: Britain, 1939-45 (New York, 1972), p. 225.

[30] Rosenman, Public Papers and Addresses of FDR 10: 1941, p. 26; Lash, Eleanor and Franklin, pp. 825-826. See also Ralph E. Spear, "Public and Private Social Services," in William M. Schuyler, ed., The American Year Book, 1942 (New York, 1943), pp. 565-566.

[31] Harold D. Smith, Memoranda of Conferences with the President, April 4, 1941, May 19, 1941, and May 29, 1941, Smith papers, FDR Library; Jessie C. Bourneuf, "The Office of Civilian Defense," July 15, 1943, pp. 6-12, series 41.3, no. 227, Records of the Bureau of the Budget, Record Group 51, National Archives; Lash, Eleanor and Franklin, pp. 826-828.

[32] Jessie C. Bourneuf, "The Office of Civilian Defense," July 15, 1943, pp. 14-15, series 41.3, no. 227, Records of the Bureau of the Budget, Record Group 51, National Archives; Lash, Eleanor and Franklin, pp. 829, 831-834.

investigation. By December 1941, opposition members were baying
on the track of the civilian defense program. The first complaints were directed against the "part-time" administration of
LaGuardia.[33] The mayor, however, was already on the way out.
On December 13, Wayne Coy of the Office of Emergency Management
and Harold Smith of the Bureau of the Budget had advised the
President, "Your committee on Civilian Defense is despondent and
despairing of the activities of that organization." Mrs. Roosevelt agreed that LaGuardia would have to go. The President
responded by appointing James M. Landis, a former head of the
Securities and Exchange Commission and then dean of the Harvard
Law School, as executive officer of OCD. He would administer
the agency and LaGuardia would remain only as a figure head.[34]

On January 8, 1942, the day before the White House disclosed the forthcoming reorganization of OCD, the House voted,
187 to 169, to abolish the Office of Director of Civilian Defense and transfer all authority and funds to the Secretary of
War. The opposition coalition comprised 47 Democrats, mostly
renegades, 138 Republicans, and 2 minor party members. Supporting OCD were 164 Democrats and 5 Republicans. Of the
Southern Democrats voting, 30 favored the abolition of OCD
while 56 backed the Administration.[35] The vote reflected irritation with LaGuardia's inept administration and suspicion
among Republicans and renegade Democrats that OCD was a cloak
for wartime New Dealism.[36]

The appointment of Landis, announced on January 9, temporarily blunted Congressional criticism of OCD. Administration
supporters in the Senate restored funds and authority to the
agency, and on January 19, the House voted, 172 to 167, to

[33] Congressional Record, 77th Congress, 1st Session, pp.
9990, 10148; Jessie C. Bourneuf, "The Office of Civilian Defense," July 15, 1943, pp. 17-18, series 41.3, no. 227, Records of the Bureau of the Budget, Record Group 51, National
Archives.

[34] Quotation from Coy and Smith to President, December 13,
1941, President's Official File 79, FDR papers, FDR Library.
See also Harold D. Smith, Memoranda of Conferences with the
President, December 15, 1941, December 19, 1941, and January
2, 1942, Smith papers, FDR Library; and Lash, Eleanor and
Franklin, pp. 836-837.

[35] For House roll call vote on OCD, see Congressional Record, 77th Congress, 2nd Session, p. 153; and Appendix III,
Guttman scaling table 1, item 28.

[36] Congressional Record, 77th Congress, 2nd Session, pp.
135-152; Lash, Eleanor and Franklin, p. 837; Roland Young, Congressional Politics in the Second World War (New York, 1956),
p. 47.

abandon its amendment eliminating the Office of Director.[37]
However, opposition spokesmen sensed that the civil defense
issue could be exploited, and they soon returned to the attack.

After first trying to discredit Landis, whom Representative Leland M. Ford (R., Calif.) described as "very pink,"
Congressional critics concentrated on Eleanor Roosevelt and
some of the people she had appointed to positions in the Volunteer Participation Division of OCD.[38] On February 6, Representative John Taber (R., N.Y.) condemned as "leeches on the
United States Treasury" Melvyn Douglas, an actor who headed
the Arts Council of OCD, Joseph P. Lash, a member of the Youth
Division, Malcolm Cowley and others affiliated with OCD who
held pronounced leftist views. According to the House Special
Committee on Un-American Activities, chaired by Martin Dies
(D., Tex.), those individuals were dangerous subversives who
belonged to communist-front organizations. Representative
Phillip Bennett (R., Mo.) agreed that OCD was riddled with
"pinks, downright 'reds' and political hacks." Under LaGuardia,
Mrs. Roosevelt and Landis, the agency had become "a haven" for
such people, declared Representative Paul Shafer (R., Mich.).[39]

To those charges of communist infiltration were added
others of waste, inefficiency and "do-goodism." Congressional
critics regarded the volunteer welfare services planned by OCD
as "frills and nonsense." Civil defense did not require "an
extensive and general 'uplift program,'" said Representative
Shafer. It involved protection against military action.[40]
Anything else was boondoggling, and many Congressmen thought
the biggest boondoggle of all was the employment of Mayris
Chaney, a professional dancer, by the physical fitness division
of OCD. According to her job description, Miss Chaney, a friend
of Mrs. Roosevelt, was "responsible for planning a program

---

[37]Congressional Record, 77th Congress, 2nd Session, pp.
478-479; Appendix III, Guttman scaling table 1, item 25. See
also Jessie C. Bourneuf, "The Office of Civilian Defense," July
15, 1943, p. 19, series 41.3, no. 227, Records of the Bureau of
the Budget, Record Group 51, National Archives.

[38]Congressional Record, 77th Congress, 2nd Session, pp.
258-259; Lash, Eleanor and Franklin, p. 838.

[39]Congressional Record, 77th Congress, 2nd Session, pp.
1094-1095, 1110, 1153; Lash, Eleanor and Franklin, p. 838;
Congressional Digest 21 (1942), pp. 65-66. See also Morgenthau
Diary, vol. 495, p. 426, FDR Library.

[40]Quotations from Congressional Record, 77th Congress, 2nd
Session, pp. 1096, 1153; and Lash, Eleanor and Franklin, p. 839.

designed to further the health and well-being of the nation through the medium of the dance. . . ."[41]

In a slap at the First Lady and the Administration, a majority of the House voted on February 6 to prohibit the use of agency funds for "aesthetic diversions," such as instruction in "physical fitness by dancers, fan dancing, street shows, theatrical performances, or other public entertainments." The opposition had handed the Roosevelt Administration a domestic "Pearl Harbor," lamented Representative Clarence Cannon (D., Mo.), who was defending OCD. Republicans had used the civilian defense issue, said Cannon, to "gain partisan advantage in the Congressional elections this fall." The "Republican blitzkrieg" had succeeded, he judged, because Democrats lacked the cohesion and discipline to protect the Administration from embarrassment.[42]

Samuel Grafton, a newspaper columnist sympathetic to the Roosevelt Administration, had his own explanation of the relentless pursuit of OCD, Mayris Chaney, and Mrs. Roosevelt. "They burnt Mayris Chaney at the stake in Congress last week," Grafton wrote. Hiring Miss Chaney had been unwise, he went on, but that did not account for the outpouring of abuse and vilification "They've needed you, girl. For down below, the thing is still smoldering, the hatred of the last eight years, of the galling march of social change, so intimately connected with the name of Roosevelt."[43]

The storm in Congress, declared Mrs. Roosevelt on February 10, was "purely political and made by the same people who have fought NYA, CCC, WPA, [and] Farm Security. . . ." Nevertheless, she felt she must exit as gracefully as possible. Because of her reform proclivities, Mrs. Roosevelt personified much that the Congressional opposition detested. Her continued involvement with OCD endangered the entire program. On February 17, she resigned.[44]

---

[41]Jessie C. Bourneuf, "The Office of Civilian Defense," July 15, 1943, p. 20, series 41.3, no. 227, Records of the Bureau of the Budget, Record Group 51, National Archives. See also Congressional Record, 77th Congress, 2nd Session, pp. 1146-1147.

[42]Quotations from Congressional Record, 77th Congress, 2nd Session, pp. 1116, 1366; Jessie C. Bourneuf, "The Office of Civilian Defense," July 15, 1943, p. 21, series 41.3, no. 227, Records of the Bureau of the Budget, Record Group 51, National Archives; and Young, Congressional Politics, pp. 48-49.

[43]Quotations from Lash, Eleanor and Franklin, p. 839.

[44]Quotation from Lash, Eleanor and Franklin, p. 841. See also Polenberg, War and Society, p. 187; and Jessie C. Bourneuf, "The Office of Civilian Defense," July 15, 1943, p. 25, series 41.3, no. 227, Records of the Bureau of the Budget, Record Group 51, National Archives.

After that, the furor gradually subsided, although critics still sniped intermittently at OCD. On February 27, the
Byrd Committee cross-examined Landis and tried to elicit
pledges that he would "abolish all frills in his organization
and confine its activities to the basic problem of training the
people in protective features necessary in the event of air
raids."[45] Landis replied that the executive order creating OCD
gave the agency broad responsibilities for health, welfare and
morale. The committee's majority, led by Senator McKellar, refused to accept that interpretation and accused Landis of evading
the prohibition against "frills and nonsense." The committee
impressed on Landis the deep-seated Congressional disapproval
of the Volunteer Participation Division and its activities.
Senator Byrd and Representative Taber seemed particularly both-
ered by the "racial program" of OCD. Mrs. Roosevelt was well-
known as an advocate of Negro advancement and even though she
had departed, they worried that the "Racial Relations Unit"
would embody her views. Byrd strongly implied that Landis
should terminate the race relations program.[46]

In effect, the Byrd Committee issued Landis an ultimatum:
Eliminate all but civilian protection from the purview of OCD
or face continuing harassment and possible termination of
funds. Landis had little choice but to comply. During the
reorganization that followed, the Volunteer Participation Division and non-protection activities steadily diminished in importance. Mrs. Roosevelt had hoped OCD would become a "people's
war" agency mobilizing the energies of millions of volunteers
in social service activities.[47] A remnant of her policy survived in the Office of Defense Health and Welfare Services,
which assumed sundry functions that OCD was prohibited from

---

[45]Morgenthau Diary, vol. 502, p. 54, FDR Library.

[46]U.S., Congress, Joint Committee on Reduction of Nonessential Federal Expenditures, Hearings, 77th Congress, 2nd Session,
1942, pp. 1062-1063, 1066-1067, 1070, 1074-1075, 1123. See
also Morgenthau Diary, vol. 502, pp. 53-56, FDR Library; Jessie
C. Bourneuf, "The Office of Civilian Defense," July 15, 1943,
p. 25, series 41.3, no. 227, Records of the Bureau of the Budget, Record Group 51, National Archives; and Lash, Eleanor and
Franklin, p. 839.

[47]Jonathan Daniels to Marvin H. McIntyre, June 23, 1943,
President's Official File 4422, FDR papers, FDR Library; Harold
D. Smith to President, August 19, 1943, General Records of the
Director, series 39.27, box 18, Records of the Bureau of the
Budget, Record Group 51, National Archives; Jessie C. Bourneuf,
"The Office of Civilian Defense," July 15, 1943, pp. 21-26,
series 41.3, no. 227, Records of the Bureau of the Budget,
Record Group 51, National Archives; Lash, Eleanor and Franklin,
pp. 842-843.

performing. The Office of Defense Health and Welfare Services provided emergency education, health, nutrition, child care, housing and recreation services that occasionally assisted troubled Americans during the war years.[48]

The House debate on OCD revealed the enduring character of Congressional hostility toward reform. As Representative Eugene E. Cox (D., Ga.), leader of the Democratic renegades, observed:

> For years we have run along under a split or double program, recovery and reform. Recovery, of course, has been displaced by defense, but reform still clings like a leech. Those who have heretofore been active in the effort to make over this country are taking advantage of the stress we now are in to promote and advance their scheme of collectivism.[49]

Difficulties with the civilian defense program gave credence to Cox's oft-repeated argument that a continuation of New Deal reform interfered with the war effort. Yet the problems of OCD had little to do with New Dealism. Modeled on the English experience, the Office of Civilian Defense had hastily improvised arrangements and procedures to cope with possible emergency conditions. If the emergency—sabotage, air raids, invasion—had eventuated, both civilian protection and the social service activities planned by OCD would have become "indispensable functionally and probably invulnerable politically." When no bombs fell on American cities, the Office of Civilian Defense looked ridiculous, just as English civil defense services had appeared ludicrous during the "phony war" of September 1939 to April 1940. Because World War II remained a foreign war for the United States, the Office of Civilian Defense became an accessible target for those who sought the destruction of the New Deal.[50]

---

[48]For the Office of Defense Health and Welfare Services, later the Office of Community War Services, see Geoffrey Perrett, Days of Sadness, Years of Triumph (New York, 1973), p. 352; and Samuel I. Rosenman, ed., The Public Papers and Addresses of Franklin D. Roosevelt, vol. 11: 1942, Humanity on the Defensive (New York, 1950), pp. 289-292.

[49]Congressional Record, 77th Congress, 2nd Session, p. 1147.

[50]Quotation from Young, Congressional Politics, p. 47. See also Henry F. Pringle, "The War Agencies," in Jack Goodman, ed., While You Were Gone: A Report on Wartime Life in the United States (New York, 1946), p. 179; Calder, The People's War, pp. 58-78; and Lash, Eleanor and Franklin, p. 842.

To Hold the Political Trench

Administration supporters watched with dismay the growing frequency and ferocity of opposition attacks. "It is very evident," wrote Pennsylvania Democratic National Committeewoman Emma Guffey Miller, "that reactionary influences throughout the country have begun a systematic campaign to break down the New Deal. . . ."[51] The Byrd Committee investigation, the undermining of Farm Security, and the harassment of OCD seemed to bear out that observation. Accordingly, New Dealers attempted to regroup their forces. Early in March 1942, about 100 Administration supporters held a political rally to celebrate the start of the tenth year of Roosevelt's Presidency and to rekindle flagging spirits. Held under the auspices of the New Republic, the meeting at Washington's Cosmos Club included Supreme Court Justice Hugo Black, labor director Sidney Hillman of the War Production Board, Senators Lister Hill (D., Ala.), James Mead (D., N.Y.), Claude Pepper (D., Fla.), Theodore F. Green (D., R.I.), James E. Murray (D., Mont.), Representatives John M. Coffee (D., Wash.) and Thomas H. Eliot (D., Mass.). Attorney General Francis Biddle admonished the assembled faithful to fight for New Deal principles "because the opposition is going to fight whether you do or not." Reformers must "hold the political trench."[52]

Biddle's speech was a defensive reaction to inroads already made by opponents of New Deal policies, but critics interpreted his remarks as proof of the Administration's perfidious intentions. New Dealers were plotting "an aggressive fight for New Dealism . . . during the war," exclaimed columnist David Lawrence. "Determination to keep the New Deal intact, no matter how long it postpones victory in the war, has been reached by the militant band of New Dealers who surround the President and influence his decisions," he wrote. Those comments were quoted approvingly by Representative Clare E. Hoffman (R., Mich.), one of those, like Lawrence, who believed the pursuit of victory called for elimination of the New Deal.[53]

Supporters of the Administration's domestic policies feared the New Deal was already on the verge of being eliminated. Some looked to the President for dramatic action that would reaffirm

---

[51]Miller to Eleanor Roosevelt, November 5, 1941, General Records of the Director, series 39.27, box 37, Records of the Bureau of the Budget, Record Group 51, National Archives.

[52]New York Times, March 7, 1942, p. 15; Time, March 16, 1942, p. 13. See also the newspaper clippings in box 640, New Dealism & Truce, 1942, Taft papers, Library of Congress.

[53]Quotations from Congressional Record, 77th Congress, 2nd Session, pp. A938-A939.

his commitment to reform and expose the motives of the opposition. On March 11, 1942, Gardner Jackson, assistant to the Under Secretary of Agriculture, wrote Presidential secretary Marvin H. McIntyre:

> The nature and vehemence of the castigation of the Office of Civilian Defense, the nature of the outpourings of the Dies Committee through Martin Dies, . . . the attempt of Representative Harold Cooley of North Carolina . . . to investigate Farm Security Administration--all of those fit into a pattern of designed discrediting of the Administration.

The "Harry Byrd economy committee," Jackson concluded, was also "a part of the design, and an important part."[54] On March 24, Secretary of the Interior Harold Ickes expressed similar views in a letter to Roosevelt. Ickes warned that power on Capitol Hill had passed "into the hands of men fundamentally opposed to your leadership and to the basic democratic principles for which we are fighting." Your enemies, the Secretary continued,

> are constantly seeking for every possible weakness in your armor. Your leaders in Congress sit tongue-tied, while vicious attacks are made upon various of your policies which, if successful, will weaken you and expose you to more direct attack as the enemy grows . . . bolder with success.

Ickes "detected an increasing note of concern on the part of those who . . . could be called New Dealers" and advised Roosevelt to "start something immediately . . . an active campaign of education" which would salvage the deteriorating political situation and save New Deal policies that might otherwise be undone.[55]

The importuning of aides and supporters caused Roosevelt briefly to consider a public defense of the domestic policies of the Administration. On March 14, he asked WPA Commissioner Howard O. Hunter to compile material "on the WPA, the NYA, and the Farm Security Administration." Hunter responded a few days later with the draft of a speech blasting the campaign "unleashed against those agencies of the Federal Government that were created to help people"--a campaign, in the words

---

[54] Jackson to McIntyre, March 11, 1942, President's Personal File 3453, FDR papers, FDR Library.

[55] Ickes to President, March 24, 1942, President's Secretary's File 73, FDR papers, FDR Library.

of the proposed speech, carried on by "domestic Blackout Boys."[56]

Hunter's draft was never used. The President decided not to answer his detractors, for reasons he explained in a letter to Representative Mary T. Norton (D., N.J.). Congresswoman Norton had implored Roosevelt to make a "fireside chat" defending Administration labor policy, which was under fire from opposition leaders. "I am appealing to you dear friend as the only person who can combat this surge of misinformation," she wrote on March 23.[57] In his reply the following day, Roosevelt told Norton,

> for the duration of the war, there are going to be periods of hysteria, misinformation, volcanic eruptions, etc., and if I start the practice of going on the air to answer each one, the value of my going on the air will soon disappear. I think this particular anti-labor outburst is already beginning to diminish--and will continue to do so unless some new circumstance develops.

The President had to conserve his ability to persuade the public just as he had to hoard his influence with Congress. If he became "a platitude to the public," Roosevelt might find himself unable to generate popular and Congressional support at some critical stage of the war.[58] During his press conference on March 13, the President had declared flatly that "Politics is out" and portrayed himself as a chief of state acting in behalf of the national interest, not petty factional, partisan or group advantage. A passionate defense of the Administration's domestic policies would contradict that pose.[59]

---

[56] Quotations from Hunter to Grace Tully, March 16, 1942, and "Memorandum on Work Projects Administration, National Youth Administration, and Farm Security Administration," n.d., President's Personal File 1820, FDR papers, FDR Library.

[57] Norton to President, March 23, 1942, President's Secretary's File 138, FDR papers, FDR Library. For criticism of the Administration's labor policy, see Congressional Digest 21 (1942), pp. 98, 131-160.

[58] President to Norton, March 24, 1942, President's Secretary's File 138, FDR papers, FDR Library. See also Elliott Roosevelt, ed., F.D.R.--His Personal Letters, 1928-1945, vol. II: 1938-1945 (New York, 1950), pp. 1300-1301.

[59] Roosevelt, Complete Presidential Press Conferences 19-20: 1942, p. 19: 203; James M. Burns, Roosevelt: The Soldier of Freedom (New York, 1970), p. 273.

Poll Taxes and Price Control

Roosevelt's stance gave his supporters little comfort. Their concern about the domestic political situation continued to mount. In Congress, divisive issues, particularly poll taxes and agricultural price control, disrupted the Democratic Party and weakened further the Administration's position.

The Servicemen's Absentee Voting Bill, designed to facilitate absentee voting in the 1942 Congressional elections by men and women in the armed services, provoked controversy because of an amendment eliminating the payment of any poll tax as a requirement for voting under the bill. The anti-poll tax amendment, which raised the question of Negro voting rights, offended Southern Democrats.[60]

Senator Wayland Brooks (R., Ill.) had submitted the anti-poll tax amendment. His purpose may have been to arouse resistance among Southerners in order to defeat the absentee voting bill. That would prevent soldiers, drawn from an age group which tended to vote Democratic, from casting ballots in the upcoming election. Brooks claimed he wanted only to remove "a complication and inconvenience" to those in the service of their country. For their part, Southerners complained that anti-poll tax "crusaders" were trying to force their will on states which required payment of the tax. Some non-Southern Democrats criticized the amendment because they feared it might imperil passage of the entire bill. In spite of those protests, the Senate adopted the provision by a vote of 33 to 20. Only 2 Southerners, Claude Pepper (D., Fla.) and Robert Reynolds (D., N.C.), joined 17 other Democrats, 12 Republicans, one Progressive and one Independent in supporting the amendment. Seven Southerners voted with 13 other Democrats against the anti-poll tax rider.[61]

As Brooks may have intended, the poll-tax issue set off an intra-party dispute among Senate Democrats. It had identical consequences in the House. Representative Stephen M. Young (D., O.), speaking in favor of the anti-poll tax amendment to the absentee voting bill, charged that "The idea behind the

---

[60]Mabel G. Benson, "The Year in Congress," in William M. Schuyler, ed., The American Year Book, 1942 (New York, 1943), pp. 30-31; Congressional Digest 21 (1942), pp. 259-288; New Republic 107 (September 14, 1942), p. 301; Robert A. Garson, The Democratic Party and the Politics of Sectionalism, 1941-1948 (Baton Rouge, La., 1974), pp. 25-26.

[61]Quotations from Congressional Record, 77th Congress, 2nd Session, pp. 6931-6938. For Senate roll call vote on the poll-tax amendment, see Congressional Record, 77th Congress, 2nd Session, p. 6971.

poll tax is to keep the poor from voting or to keep Negroes
from voting, or both." Representative Hatton W. Sumners (D.,
Tex.) replied that the anti-poll tax amendment would "strengthen
the stranglehold of this great Federal bureaucracy upon the
throats of the States." On September 9, a group of 50 Southern
Democrats attempted to recommit the absentee voting bill, but
the House, by a vote of 56 to 244, refused to kill the measure,
which it then passed.[62]

The anti-poll tax amendment divided the Democratic Party
into southern and non-southern factions. An issue equally destructive of Democratic unity was the question of agricultural
price regulation. A part of the broad problem of wartime economic stabilization, farm price control was a major source of
controversy throughout the second session of the 77th Congress
(January 6-December 16, 1942). To deal with a scarcity of
goods and an excess of consumer purchasing power, the Roosevelt
Administration formulated "a coordinated anti-inflationary
program" comprising heavy taxation, bond sales, rationing, priorities, allocations, wage stabilization, and extensive price
regulation.[63] A Congressional majority had balked implementa-
tion of two parts of that program. The first, according to
the President's anti-inflation message of April 27, 1942, was
adequate taxation. The second item was regulation of agricultural prices, which the Emergency Price Control Act, signed
January 30, 1942, had failed to cover effectively. As Roosevelt noted, "Under a complicated formula in the existing law,
prices for farm products . . . may rise to 110 percent of
parity or even higher . . . this can mean a dangerous increase
in the cost of living for the average family over present
prices."[64]

---

[62]Quotations from Congressional Record, 77th Congress, 2nd
Session, p. 7065. For House roll call vote on the Servicemen's
Absentee Voting Act of 1942, see Congressional Record, 77th
Congress, 2nd Session, p. 7078; and Appendix III, Guttman scaling
table 2, item 14. For a slightly different account of the pas-
sage of the Servicemen's Absentee Voting Act of 1942, see Young,
Congressional Politics, pp. 83-84.

[63]Quotation from Harold D. Smith to President, July 23, 1941,
Miscellaneous White House Memoranda, Smith papers, FDR Library.
See also Harold D. Smith, Memoranda of Conferences with the
President, April 1, 1942, April 4, 1942, and April 9, 1942,
Smith papers, FDR Library; Rosenman, Public Papers and Addresses
of FDR 10: 1941, pp. 284-289; Benson, "The Year in Congress,"
American Year Book, 1942, pp. 33-35; and Polenberg, War and So-
ciety, pp. 88-89.

[64]Rosenman, Public Papers and Addresses of FDR 11: 1942,
pp. 220, 222. See also Young, Congressional Politics, pp. 92-94.

Members of the Congressional farm bloc had inserted the "complicated formula" into the Emergency Price Control Act at the urging of the American Farm Bureau Federation, National Grange, National Cooperative Milk Producers Federation, and National Council of Farmer Cooperatives, the "big four" farm [65] lobbies representing the interests of commercial agriculture. Administration officials feared that proposed increases in agricultural prices would set in motion other inflationary disturbances, particularly demands for higher wages. On April 27, Roosevelt therefore asked for legislative authority to control agricultural prices.[66]

The President's request encountered resistance from organized commercial agriculture and its spokesmen in Congress, who exhibited an "ugly attitude" toward stiffer price control legislation, according to Price Administrator Leon Henderson. Farm bloc Congressmen, said Henderson, felt "that there was no restraint . . . on wages or profits and therefore . . . had decided . . . to do something for the farmer."[67] Leaders of agricultural organizations complained about the shortage and cost of farm labor, a problem created both by induction of rural youths into military service and by high industrial wages and plentiful employment opportunities which attracted farm labor into war jobs. Because of wartime restrictions, farmers found it impossible to replace scarce hired help with mechanized equipment. To pass along the higher cost of agricultural labor and to capture a larger share of the national income for farmers, agricultural lobbies pressed for higher commodity prices even as the Administration stressed the need to control those prices.[68]

---

[65] Leon Henderson to President, December 26, 1941, January 12, 1942, and James F. Byrnes to President, December 31, 1942, President's Official File 327, FDR papers, FDR Library; Fred Warner Neal, "The Politics of Price-Fixing," in Ray F. Harvey and others, The Politics of This War (New York, 1943), pp. 199-203; McCune, Farm Bloc, pp. 60-64; and Curry, "Southern Senators and Their Roll-Call Votes in Congress," pp. 184-194.

[66] Rosenman, Public Papers and Addresses of FDR 11: 1942, pp. 221-222; Harold D. Smith, Memoranda of Conferences with the President, April 5, 1941, and April 18, 1941, Smith papers, FDR Library.

[67] Leon Henderson, "Brief Notes of Meeting in Cabinet Room, The White House," April 10, 1942, Smith papers, FDR Library.

[68] Eugene Casey to President, n.d., President's Secretary's File 145, FDR papers, FDR Library; Martin Krost and Kenneth Williams, memorandum on farm prices, March 12, 1943, box 25, Lubin papers, FDR Library; Congressional Record, 77th Congress, 2nd Session, p. 7349; Alfred D. Stedman, "The Politics of the Farmers in Wartime," in Ray F. Harvey and others, The Politics of This War (New York, 1943), p. 149.

For four months after the President's anti-inflation message of April 27, the issue of agricultural price control hung
fire in Congress. Meanwhile food and fiber prices continued to
rise and union leaders agitated for wage increases to keep pace
with the cost of living. In his Labor Day message of September
7, Roosevelt renewed his appeal for statutory authority to regulate farm prices. He told Congress, "It is impossible for the
cost of living to be stabilized while farm prices continue to
rise. You cannot expect the laborer to maintain a fixed wage
level if everything he wears and eats begins to go up drastic-
ally in price." The President warned that runaway inflation
could jeopardize the successful prosecution of the war. "Therefore, I ask the Congress to pass legislation under which the
President would be specifically authorized to stabilize the cost
of living, including the price of all farm commodities." Roosevelt then added an electrifying pledge: "I ask the Congress to
take this action by the first of October. . . . In the event
that the Congress should fail to act, and act adequately, I
shall accept the responsibility, and I will act."[69]

The President's message incensed many Congressmen who
thought the Chief Executive was dictating to the legislative
branch. Faced with a deadline of October 1, Congress could
choose among three different responses to Roosevelt's ultimatum.
Some advised that it do nothing and let the President use his
war powers to stabilize farm prices and industrial wages. But
allegiance to Constitutional processes, as Roosevelt himself
had pointed out, made some sort of enabling legislation desirable. In considering legislation, Congress could approve a
bill authorizing the President to do whatever was necessary to
stabilize the cost of living. That would be the simplest solution, favored by Administration leaders, but a majority of Congress was too restive to delegate such sweeping power over the
domestic economy. Congress chose instead to frame a detailed
set of guidelines within which Roosevelt and Price Administrator
Henderson would have to operate. The decision to write a detailed bill provoked an intense struggle between the Administration and the farm bloc.[70]

---

[69] Quotations from Rosenman, Public Papers and Addresses of
FDR 11: 1942, pp. 356, 358, 364. See also Roosevelt, Complete
Presidential Press Conferences 19-20: 1942, pp. 20: 66-72;
Congressional Digest 21 (1942), pp. 195-224; Neal, "Politics of
Price-Fixing," pp. 205-213; Burns, Soldier of Freedom, pp. 260-
261; and Ernest S. Griffith, Congress: Its Contemporary Role
(New York, 1951), pp. 11-12.

[70] Rosenman, Public Papers and Addresses of FDR 11: 1942,
pp. 364-365; Congressional Record, 77th Congress, 2nd Session,
pp. 7338, 7342; Young, Congressional Politics, pp. 94-96;
McCune, Farm Bloc, pp. 59-60.

In the House of Representatives, Administration supporters
introduced an Emergency Anti-Inflation Bill providing that ceilings on agricultural prices could be fixed either at parity or
at the highest levels prevailing between January 1, 1942, and
September 15, 1942, whichever was higher. Those provisions, if
enacted, would empower the Office of Price Administration to
regulate nearly all previously exempt grocery items. On September 23, farm bloc members offered an amendment that would
"do something for the farmer" by revising the parity formula to
include all costs of production, including the costs of hired
and family labor. Instead of allowing OPA to regulate farm
prices, the amendment, sponsored by Representative Paul Brown
(D., Ga.), would permit another rise in the cost of living. Upward revaluation of parity became a test of strength between
Administration supporters and farm bloc members in the House.[71]

The debate on the Brown amendment exposed the resentments
harbored by agricultural spokesmen. Roosevelt's Labor Day message on inflation, "which the Farm Bureau deliberately and vi-
ciously distorted and misrepresented," reported Presidential
assistant Eugene Casey, seemed to accuse farmers of selfish insistence on higher commodity prices and make farmers responsible for inflation.[72] Representative H. Carl Andersen (R.,
Minn.) dismissed the notion that farmers had caused inflation
as "rot!" Farmers were victims of inflation, not the cause of
it, according to Representative George A. Dondero (R., Mich.).
All the farmers wanted, said Representative William M. Whittington (D., Miss.) was "equality of treatment."[73]

The anger of the farm lobbies and their Congressional
spokesmen reflected the conviction, reported by Presidential
assistant Eugene Casey, "that the 'political high command' of
the New Deal has 'thrown agriculture to the dogs' and is relying
on the city vote, especially the labor vote . . . to win elections." If ceilings were imposed on agricultural prices, urban
consumers would pay less for their groceries. That was only
one instance, wrote Casey, of what farm lobbies considered
Administration "coddling" of organized labor "at the expense of
agriculture and at the expense of the national welfare."[74]

---

[71]Congressional Record, 77th Congress, 2nd Session, pp.
7338-7355; Young, Congressional Politics, p. 97; McCune, Farm
Bloc, p. 64.

[72]Casey to President, n.d., President's Secretary's File
145, FDR papers, FDR Library.

[73]Quotations from Congressional Record, 77th Congress,
2nd Session, pp. 7343-7344, 7348.

[74]Casey to President, n.d., President's Secretary's File
145, FDR papers, FDR Library.

Farm bloc antagonism toward organized labor dominated the
House debate on the Brown amendment. Representative Andersen
attacked the Administration for "permitting union labor to run
hog wild . . . making it impossible for agriculture to endure
. . . Congress wanted last January to clap a just, fair ceiling
on labor," said Andersen,

> but Administration pressure killed that proposal.
> Now with labor in defense plants receiving unheard
> of wages the President very unkindly tries to blame
> the farmer and the Congress for the situation for
> which nobody but himself and his advisers are re-
> sponsible.

Andersen's remarks prompted Representative Frank E. Hook (D.,
Mich.) to defend the President against an alliance of "the
chambers of commerce tying in together with the big farm organizations headed by the commercial farmers sending their tele-
grams and orders . . . advising . . . their Congressmen to vote
for . . . the Paul Brown inflation amendment." Replying to
Hook and other Administration loyalists, Representative Clare
E. Hoffman (R., Mich.) denounced Roosevelt for his "policy of
yielding to the demands of labor organizations." Farmers, said
Hoffman, worked 60, 70, and even 80 hours per week, "from day-
light to dark," while industrial workers received "premium
pay" for time in excess of the 40-hour week. The President,
Hoffman charged, had favored trade unions "at the expense of
the farmer, the businessman . . . and all those who live on
so-called fixed incomes." In contrast, Representative Thomas
F. Ford (D., Calif.) declared, "all this bluster about additional price is just political bunk on the part of the farm
bloc . . . you boys who want parity for farmers do not know
what the h--- you are talking about. The Brown amendment is
vicious and inflationary."[75]

In the midst of those charges and countercharges, the House,
by a vote of 205 to 172, adopted the Brown amendment to the
Emergency Anti-Inflation Bill. The victorious farm bloc coalition consisted of 106 Democrats, 98 Republicans, and 1 Progressive, while 118 Democrats, 53 Republicans, and 1 American
Labor Party member rejected the Brown proviso. The roll call
revealed some partisan division, since 65 percent of Republicans
voting favored the amendment and 53 percent of Democrats voting
opposed it. More striking, though, was the sectional alignment.
The strongest support, without regard to party, came from the
nation's farming regions--the Plains, South, Mountain West, and
agricultural Midwest. The strongest opposition came from the
urban, industrial East--New England, the mid-Atlantic and eastern
border states. Representatives from 7 eastern states (Massachusetts,

---

[75]Quotations from Congressional Record, 77th Congress, 2nd
Session, pp. 7348-7349, 7363, 7394.

Connecticut, Rhode Island, New Hampshire, Maine, West Virginia, and Maryland) unanimously opposed the Brown amendment, while members from 12 southern and western states (Alabama, Florida, Mississippi, Arkansas, Kansas, South Dakota, Nebraska, New Mexico, Idaho, Wyoming, Montana and Nevada) unanimously favored it. On the issue of farm price regulation, the agricultural South and West had attracted sufficient Republican votes to constitute a majority of the House.[76]

With the threat of a Presidential veto hanging over the Brown amendment, the Senate eventually rejected the upward re-valuation of parity approved by the House. That action per-mitted a compromise between the farm bloc and the Administra-tion. The Emergency Anti-Inflation Act, signed October 2, 1942, gave Roosevelt most of what he wanted. It authorized the President to stabilize all wages, prices and salaries affecting the cost of living. OPA could impose ceilings on agricultural prices at parity or the highest prices prevailing between Janu-ary 1, 1942, and September 15, 1942. In return, farm state Congressmen won a floor under commodity prices of 90 percent of parity and an Administration commitment to consider farm labor costs in determining price ceilings.[77]

The struggle over agricultural price control damaged the Democratic Party. The harmonious relationship of farmers and workers, formed during the depression when both groups sought government assistance, had weakened in the late 1930s and now threatened to dissolve under the strains of a fully mobilized war economy. To curb inflation, the Administration through the War Labor Board had persuaded union leaders to limit wage de-mands in return for a general stabilization of the cost of living, especially of food costs. The promised stabilization of food prices required the Administration to restrict sums received by farmers for their commodities. That anti-inflation strategy caused a clash between Democrats representing agri-cultural constituencies and those from urban districts.[78]

---

[76]For House roll call vote on the Brown amendment to the anti-inflation bill, see Congressional Record, 77th Congress, 2nd Session, pp. 7397-7398. See also McCune, Farm Bloc, p. 64.

[77]Rosenman, Public Papers and Addresses of FDR 11: 1942, pp. 396-407; McCune, Farm Bloc, pp. 65-69; Young, Congressional Politics, pp. 97-98; Floyd M. Riddick, "The Second Session of the Seventy-Seventh Congress," American Political Science Re-view XXXVII (1943), p. 305; Benson, "The Year in Congress," American Year Book, 1942, p. 35.

[78]On problems of economic stabilization, see Harold D. Smith, Memoranda of Conferences with the President, April 4, 1942, and April 18, 1942, Smith papers, FDR Library; Martin Krost and Kenneth Williams, memorandum on farm prices, March 12,

Republicans, too, had divided over the issue of agricultural price regulation, but the GOP still seemed more receptive to the demands of farm leaders than the Roosevelt Administration. At least one Roosevelt sympathizer, M. W. Thatcher of the National Farmers Union, thought the big four farm lobbies led by the Farm Bureau were seeking an anti-Administration alliance with big business and the Republican Party. Thatcher condemned Farm Bureau chief Ed O'Neal for "playing the game of the anti-New Deal democrats and Republicans . . . for the Congressional elections of '42 and the National election of '44." Instead of lining up with business and the Republicans, Thatcher wanted farmers to continue their partnership with labor and the Democrats, but wartime circumstances made that an unnatural relationship.[79]

The issues of agricultural price control and poll taxes disrupted the New Deal coalition which Roosevelt had forged in 1936 and was striving to maintain. That electoral coalition--composed of urban workers, ethnics, racial minorities, southern, midwestern, and western farmers, and middle class reformers--became increasingly unstable as clashes over economic policy and racial questions pitted organized labor against organized agriculture, and southern segregationists against northern politicians seeking black votes.[80] The continued breakdown of Democratic Party cohesion cast doubt on the ability of the President to command a Congressional majority even on economic policies he considered vital to the war effort. With the 1942 elections at hand, the situation was ripe for exploitation by the Republican minority.

Elections of 1942

"TRULY DO WE REACH THE RUBICON IN NOVEMBER, 1942," Presidential assistant Eugene Casey wrote Roosevelt on November 26, 1941. "The 1942 elections will be lost," he predicted, unless the nation was "immediately informed and enlightened" about the

---

1943, box 25, Lubin papers, FDR Library; Rosenman, Public Papers and Addresses of FDR 11: 1942, pp. 42-48, 171-173, 221-222, 369-374; Stedman, "Politics of the Farmers in Wartime," pp. 148-151, 161-167; and Polenberg, War and Society, pp. 25-26, 35-36.

[79] Thatcher to President, April 21, 1941, President's Official File 899, FDR papers, FDR Library. See also Martin Krost and Kenneth Williams, memorandum on farm prices, March 12, 1943, box 25, Lubin papers, FDR Library; and Congressional Record, 77th Congress, 2nd Session, p. 2431.

[80] Polenberg, War and Society, pp. 91-92; Garson, Democratic Party and the Politics of Sectionalism, pp. 16-30.

Administration's domestic and foreign policies.[81] Secretary
of the Interior Harold Ickes shared Casey's view of the upcoming elections. Ickes depicted the 1942 campaign as a crucial turning point both in the conduct of the war and in domestic policy. "[I]f we should lose on the political front next
November," he warned the President on February 2, 1942, "the
going thereafter . . . would be very difficult indeed . . . a
real fight will be made by the opposition to capture the House
of Representatives this year. Undoubtedly you have this in
mind and are preparing to meet the enemy at the polls." He reiterated the point on March 24. "We are fighting an internal
war against those who have been your enemies from the beginning
and who have not ceased to be such," he told Roosevelt. "The
groups that we have known variously as 'big business,' or 'concentrated wealth,' or 'economic royalists,' might now be called
American Fascists and that is how I classify them," Ickes wrote.

> These forces . . . would rather destroy you than win
> the war. And if they should carry the House of
> Representatives, to say nothing of making inroads in
> the Senate, why would not they have the right to in-
> sist they have a clear mandate from the people?[82]

The President listened to those warnings of disaster, but
he did not act upon what he heard. In accordance with his role
as war leader, he had decided to maintain a non-partisan posture.
When Democratic National Chairman Edward J. Flynn suggested on
February 2, 1942, that Americans could support the war effort by
electing Democrats to Congress, Roosevelt rebuffed him. "[W]e
want Congressmen, regardless of party--get that--to back up the
Government of the United States," the President informed the
press on February 6.[83] Remembering Woodrow Wilson's controversial and ineffective appeal for a Democratic Congress in 1918,
Roosevelt evidently wanted to avoid a similar gamble which, if
lost, could be interpreted as a popular rejection of his leadership. He refused to assign much significance to the campaign.
When the Union for Democratic Action and New Republic implied
that preservation of the New Deal and the possibility of a

---

[81]Casey to President, November 26, 1941, President's Secretary's File 112, FDR papers, FDR Library.

[82]Ickes to President, February 2, 1942, and March 24, 1942,
President's Secretary's File 73, FDR papers, FDR Library.

[83]Roosevelt, Complete Presidential Press Conferences 19-20:
1942, pp. 19: 113-114. See also Burns, Soldier of Freedom,
pp. 273-276; Congressional Record, 77th Congress, 2nd Session,
pp. A352-A353; and Clarence A. Berdahl, "Political Parties and
Elections," American Political Science Review XXXVII (1943),
p. 76.

liberal postwar society would hinge on the fall elections, "the most important congressional election since the close of the Civil War," Roosevelt characterized that statement as "perfectly silly." Privately, he was not so unconcerned, but his public stance remained that of the Commander-in-Chief, not the party chieftain.[84]

The President's non-involvement left the Democratic campaign in the hands of National Chairman Flynn and Representative Patrick H. Drewry (D., Va.), head of the Congressional Elections Committee. Drewry, a renegade with greater affinity for the Republicans than for Roosevelt, could not inspirit the campaign. Flynn had been a skillful leader in the Bronx, his local fiefdom, but the job of national chairman "is altogether too big for him," as Harold Ickes observed. With little central direction and few issues on which Congressional Democrats agreed, the party's campaign devolved, like most off-year campaigns, into a series of local contests.[85]

Meanwhile, the electorate displayed considerable dissatisfaction with the management of the war effort. Discontent arose over the unfavorable course of the war, alleged Administration favoritism toward organized labor, irritation with wartime controls and regulations, and apparent confusion and muddling in Washington. Clumsy mistakes in the first rationing programs--sugar, coffee, gasoline--had made the Office of Price Administration seem obsessed with restrictive and pointless red tape. OPA quickly became the most unpopular of the war agencies.[86]

More damaging to public confidence than bungling by OPA were production bottlenecks, especially the squabble over national rubber policy. Japan had blocked at least 90 percent of America's prewar supply of natural rubber. With stockpiles insufficient to meet civilian and military needs, government and industry had to initiate a synthetic rubber program. One group of politicians, chemists and business executives coalesced

---

[84]Quotation from New Republic 106 (May 18, 1942), p. 683; and Roosevelt, Complete Presidential Press Conferences 19-20: 1942, p. 19: 326.

[85]Quotation from Ickes to President, March 24, 1942, President's Secretary's File 73, FDR papers, FDR Library. See also Eugene Casey to President, November 26, 1941, President's Secretary's File 113, FDR papers, FDR Library; Burns, Soldier of Freedom, pp. 276, 280; and John Harding, "The 1942 Congressional Elections," American Political Science Review XXXVIII (1944), pp. 47-48.

[86]Neal, "Politics of Price-Fixing," pp. 212-213; Perrett, Days of Sadness, pp. 133-134, 247; Burns, Soldier of Freedom, p. 280; New Republic 107 (September 7, 1942), p. 271.

around the oil industry and urged a synthetic rubber process
based on petroleum. Another group backed a process based on
alcohol manufactured from grain. While the Administration
vacillated, agricultural lobbies and their Congressional mouth-
pieces pushed the alcohol process. In the summer of 1942, they
secured passage of a bill creating a separate rubber agency and
giving preference to alcohol. Roosevelt vetoed the bill and
appointed a special commission headed by Bernard Baruch to investigate the rubber problem. But the "rubber mess" contributed to an unflattering picture of confusion and inefficiency
in the midst of a great war.[87]

Highly publicized quarrels among government officials also
gave an impression of discord and incompetence in high places.
On February 17, 1942, Representative John J. Cochran (D., Mo.),
a loyal New Dealer, advised the President that "this guerilla
warfare" among his subordinates was causing "a very bad situation not only . . . [in Congress] but also around the Country."[88]
Roosevelt finally became convinced that interagency conflict
undermined public confidence. On August 21, he instructed
heads of Federal agencies and departments to refrain from public criticism of other agencies. "Officials divert to quarrels
with each other the time and energy they ought to be devoting
to fighting the enemy," wrote the President. "The people, con-
fused by these contradictory voices, are apt to obtain the
false impression that the Government as a whole is uncertain as
to its objectives and general method and that it does not know
its job."[89]

Though Roosevelt could mute quarrelsome subordinates, he
could not dispel the feeling that the government was bungling.
That feeling was beginning to cost the Administration public
support. Throughout the summer and fall of 1942, pollster
Hadley Cantril sampled political attitudes for the President.
Cantril found popular support shifting toward the Republicans.
Surveys by the Gallup organization revealed the same trend.
Had the Congressional elections been held in June, the Democrats
would have gained some 20 seats in the House. By September,
polls showed that Republicans would gain more than 20 seats.[90]

---

[87] Rosenman, Public Papers and Addresses of FDR 11: 1942,
pp. 265-268, 271, 312-322; Stedman, "Politics of the Farmers in
Wartime," pp. 164-165; Young, Congressional Politics, p. 38;
Alan S. Milward, War, Economy and Society, 1939-1945 (London,
1977), p. 179.

[88] Cochran to President, February 17, 1942, President's
Personal File 1820, FDR papers, FDR Library.

[89] Rosenman, Public Papers and Addresses of FDR 11: 1942,
pp. 331-333.

[90] See the New York Times, June 21, 1942, p. 33, August 16,
1942, p. 40, September 30, 1942, p. 27; New Republic 107

Republican candidates effectively exploited discontent with the conduct of the war. In a speech at Omaha on September 3--typical of many delivered by Republicans during the campaign--Senator Hugh Butler (R., Neb.) recounted the case against the Roosevelt Administration. Alluding to American defeats in the Pacific, he accused the Administration of failing "to develop a policy of effective military action." The United States was losing because the President and his advisors treated the war as "just another boondoggling project." Instead of organizing for victory, "those influences back of this administration . . . have invariably chosen to maintain its social programs and its political machinery--even at the expense of the war effort." The Administration had not taken "the lead in demanding retrenchment of non-essential expenditures," but had "fought to the last ditch against every effort to abolish those pet social agencies. . . ." Levelling his "most serious" criticism at the President's labor policy, Butler described the Administration as "a government of one class only--labor. It is, in fact, what would be called in England or on the Continent a Labor Government. . . ." Favoritism toward labor, said Butler, entailed discrimination against businessmen and farmers, particularly in the regulation of prices.[91]

Finally, Butler addressed "post-war economic problems." He warned that "many of the bright young bureaucrats" in war agencies were "not planning to give up their jobs without a struggle. 'Once we get this economic system organized, it will never get away from us again,' they say." Butler conceded that "vast war powers over our economy" were necessary, "but . . . we must watch over their use, and we must be ready to take them back after the emergency, if we expect to keep the free American system for which we are fighting." Because "decisions made today" would determine the postwar order, the Republican Party had to resist wartime policies that might effect permanent changes in the traditional social and economic system.[92]

Republicans viewed the war as a struggle for supremacy at home and abroad. At home, the enemy was reform. Like Senator Butler, Senator Robert Taft thought that "many powers have been sought [by the Roosevelt Administration] for the sake of domestic policy, with the war as a mere excuse." The task of the Congressional opposition, he said, was to keep "the war

---

(September 28, 1942), p. 379; Burns, Soldier of Freedom, p. 280; and Perrett, Days of Sadness, p. 247.

[91]Congressional Record, 77th Congress, 2nd Session, pp. A3226-A3227.

[92]Congressional Record, 77th Congress, 2nd Session, p. A3227.

effort along lines which will not after the war require any
permanent change in the fundamentals of the American system."
According to Taft, the war provided an opportunity to dismantle
the New Deal and thus permit reestablishment of the traditional
American system of unfettered private enterprise at the end of
the war. The title of Hugh Butler's Omaha address, "Our War
Effort Versus the New Deal," expressed the attitude that per-
vaded the Republican campaign in 1942.[93]

The attitude of the Congressional opposition forced proponents of reform to rally to the Roosevelt Administration as a
bulwark against recrudescent reaction. The left-of-center press,
liberal intellectuals, organized labor, and other pro-New Deal
groups recognized the deficiencies of Roosevelt's deliberately
non-political posture. They criticized his reluctance to fight
for the advanced ground of the New Deal. James G. Patton of
the National Farmers Union, the only major farm group to back
the Administration's domestic policies, complained to Roosevelt in April 1941 "that advances which have been made during
your administrations" were in danger of being lost. Senator
George Norris (I., Neb.), one of the most consistent and coura-
geous Senate progressives, told Harold Ickes in November 1941
that "we might win the war and lose everything else that we
have gained in the last eight years." Mrs. Emma Guffey Miller,
energetic Democratic National Committeewoman from Pennsylvania,
wrote the President on January 9, 1942, that she was "interested not only in a total victory in the war but in a Democratic Peace as well" and cautioned Roosevelt that his appeasement of the opposition meant "surrender . . . to the enemy."
On March 4, Nelson P. Poynter of the Office of Government Reports wrote Robert E. Sherwood, "On the domestic front we have
stopped preaching the idea of liberalism upon the assumption
that we could thus better maintain 'national unity.' This
assumption," said Poynter, "has proved illusory. The enemies
of liberalism, since the shock of Pearl Harbor has worn off,
have again taken up their tom-toms and war clubs. They have
not hesitated to attack liberal ideas and institutions in the
name of national defense." Because the President had offered
only half-hearted and sporadic resistance to those attacks on
New Deal principles, reformers worried that he had "surrendered
to the reactionaries."[94]

---

[93] Robert A. Taft, "Republican Policy--1942," box 640, New
Dealism & Truce, 1942, Taft papers, Library of Congress; Congressional Record, 77th Congress, 1st Session, pp. A5709-A5711;
and Robert A. Taft, transcripts of speeches, January 15, 1942,
and May 7, 1942, box 1259, Taft papers, Library of Congress.

[94] Quotations from Patton to President, April 7, 1941,
President's Official File 899, FDR papers, FDR Library; Harold
Ickes, The Secret Diary of Harold Ickes, vol. III: The Lowering
Clouds, 1939-1941 (New York, 1954), p. 652; Miller to President,

For all their misgivings, New Dealers and reformers could not visualize any practical alternative to Roosevelt. The realities of American politics made them captives of the President. Bad as the Administration's lapses might be, the possibility of a Republican victory seemed worse.[95] In any event, the Roosevelt Administration retained just enough of the old New Deal tinge to hold the loyalty of most advocates of reform. So it was that the President had repeatedly insisted that incomes during the war should be limited to a maximum of $25,000 after taxes.[96] That proposal, which resembled the redistributive revenue policies of the New Deal, aroused the ire of the opposition. "It is pure communism," wrote newspaper columnist George Rothwell Brown. Reformers, however, applauded and cited the $25,000 limitation on incomes as proof "that the New Deal banner still waves."[97]

The writings and speeches of Vice President Henry A. Wallace provided further evidence of a continuing commitment to reform. The Vice President, like others who wanted to preserve and build on the legacy of the New Deal, believed the death and destruction of war would be futile unless a more humane and equitable social order emerged from the global conflict. A military victory which left the old regime unchanged would not be enough. "[W]e are writing the postwar world as we go along," Wallace admonished Roosevelt on February 24, 1942. What happened during the war would shape the structure of America's political economy after victory was won. Hence, he urged public policies that would promote "economic democracy" for the common man.[98]

January 9, 1942, General Records of the Director, series 39.27, box 43, Records of the Bureau of the Budget, Record Group 51, National Archives; Poynter to Sherwood, March 4, 1942, Correspondence of the Director, 1936-1943, box 43, Records of the Office of Government Reports, Record Group 44, Federal Records Center; New Republic 107 (October 26, 1942), p. 543.

[95] New Republic 107 (October 5, 1942), p. 435. See also Oswald Garrison Villard, "The Collapse of the War Liberals," Christian Century LXI (October 25, 1944), pp. 1227-1228.

[96] Rosenman, Public Papers and Addresses of FDR 11: 1942, pp. 15, 221, 374.

[97] Quotations from Congressional Record, 77th Congress, 2nd Session, p. A3876; and New Republic 107 (October 26, 1942), pp. 543-544.

[98] John M. Blum, ed., The Price of Vision: The Diary of Henry A. Wallace, 1942-1946 (Boston, 1973), pp. 32, 55.

In "Foundations of the Peace," an article for the Atlantic Monthly published in January 1942, Wallace spelled out what he meant by "economic democracy." He deplored the prewar economy of organized scarcity caused by tariffs and other barriers inhibiting international trade, by maldistributions of income, and by oligopolistic business arrangements which kept production and consumption artificially low and profits artificially high. In place of that prewar system, the Vice President wanted to establish an economy of "widely distributed abundance." The means to achieve that goal was expansionary fiscal policy. Wallace proposed public investment in "development of undeveloped areas," in reequipment of "our own industrial and transportation system," and in "better housing, schooling, and recreation." He recommended tax and expenditure policies that would reduce "inequalities in incomes, so that a higher and more stable demand for consumers' goods will be attained." And he suggested a comprehensive social security program: "Certain minimum standards of food, clothing, and shelter ought to be established, and arrangements ought to be made to guarantee that no one should fall below those standards." The result of such efforts would be full employment and a more equitable sharing of the fruits of prosperity.

The Vice President had taken the Keynesian reform program of the late New Deal, the philosophy that had underlain the Self-Liquidating Projects Bill of 1939, recast it, and made it his prescription for post-war America. "A 'new order' is truly waiting to be created . . . a new order of democracy. . . . This is the new frontier, which Americans in the middle of the twentieth century find beckoning them on," he wrote. Americans could achieve an economy of abundance if they planned for it even as they accelerated their "drive for victory."[99]

Four months later, Wallace elaborated on themes he had introduced in "Foundations of the Peace." On May 8, 1942, he delivered an address to the Free World Association entitled "The Price of Free World Victory." This celebrated speech, reprints of which were widely distributed by public and private agencies, stated Wallace's faith that war against fascism could become an engine of positive social and economic change. World War II, he said, was a crucial stage in a worldwide "people's revolution." Here at home, the New Deal had been only the first battle, for the people's revolution "has not been completed, either here in the United States or in any other nation in the world. We know that this revolution cannot stop until freedom from want has actually been attained. . . . The peace must mean a better standard of living for the common man. . . ." Though the temptation would be great, the postwar era should not be an "American Century," a kind of

---

[99] Henry A. Wallace, "Foundations of the Peace," Atlantic Monthly 169 (January 1942), pp. 34-41.

benevolent imperialism. "I say that the century on which we are entering--the century which will come out of this war-- can be and must be the century of the common man."[100]

Wallace's statement of American war aims disturbed those who thought it portended abolition of the private enterprise system. The President of the National Association of Manufacturers, W. P. Witherow, retorted, "I am not making guns or tanks to win a 'people's revolution.' I am making armament to help our boys save America. . . . I am not fighting . . . for governmental handouts of free Utopia."[101] Reformers, however, were elated by Wallace's vision of a new postwar order. The Vice President became the hero of the left-of-center press, the CIO, the National Farmers Union, the National Resources Planning Board Keynesians, and other supporters of the New Deal.[102]

Realization of Wallace's goals depended upon the election of reformist candidates. On May 18, 1942, the New Republic, one of the principal left-of-center journals, and the Union for Democratic Action, a pro-New Deal lobby whose slogan was "A two-front fight for democracy, at home and abroad," published jointly a handbook for the fall elections entitled "A Congress to Win the War." Winning the war meant not just a military victory but preservation of New Deal policies and further reform of America's social and economic system. The New Republic warned that the Congressional opposition had seized upon "the war situation . . . as an excuse for destroying the social program of the government." Illustrative of those destructive intentions, the New Republic wrote, were liquidation of the Civilian Conservation Corps, harassment of the Rural Electrification Administration, Wages and Hours Administration, and other New Deal agencies. Predicting that those developments provided only a foretaste of what would occur if the opposition won control of the House of Representatives, the New Republic and UDA asked for defeat of 16 Republicans and 9 renegade Democrats. Among the "obstructionists" named by the New Republic were key leaders of the bipartisan opposition, including Representatives Howard W. Smith (D., Va.), Eugene E. Cox (D., Ga.), and Clare E. Hoffman (R., Mich.).[103]

---

[100]Blum, Price of Vision, pp. 636-638.

[101]New York Times, December 3, 1942, p. 14.

[102]Edward L. and Frederick H. Schapsmeier, Prophet in Politics: Henry A. Wallace and the War Years, 1940-1965 (Ames, Ia., 1970), pp. 24-37, 50-83; Norman D. Markowitz, The Rise and Fall of the People's Century: Henry A. Wallace and American Liberalism, 1941-1948 (New York, 1973), pp. 36-58; Blum, Price of Vision, pp. 25, 32-35.

[103]New Republic 106 (May 18, 1942), pp. 683-711.

Publication of "A Congress to Win the War" angered opposition members who recalled the "purge" of 1938, feared another,
similar campaign, and began to retaliate by identifying reform
with communism. As Senator Taft remarked on August 8,

> There is a distinct propaganda movement today,
> headed up in New York, with a lot of branches like
> the Union for Democratic Action, which has a strong
> Communist tinge. This group is circularizing every
> congressional district in the United States with
> a 30-page pamphlet denouncing a large percentage of
> the Congressmen seeking reelection. . . . It is vi-
> tally important that we have Congressmen who will
> stand up against many of the administration's pro-
> posals, supposed to relate to the war, but actually
> having far more effect on domestic affairs.[104]

Representative J. Parnell Thomas (R., N.J.), one of those
singled out by the New Republic and UDA, echoed Senator Taft's
complaint. Thomas attempted to discredit "A Congress to Win
the War" by describing it as "the keynote of the now famous
purge campaign of Members of Congress which the Communists and
their dupes sought to bring about."[105]

Taft and Thomas need not have worried. The efforts of the
New Republic and Union for Democratic Action had few discernible
results. A few Democratic renegades were defeated in the primaries, but their seats seemed likely to go Republican in the
general election.[106] In the southern primaries, where victory
was tantamount to election, Representative Luther Patrick (D.,
Ala.) and Senator Wall Doxey (D., Miss.) were beaten by men
less sympathetic to reformist policies. The campaign tactics
of James O. Eastland, Doxey's replacement, revealed the new
Senator from Mississippi to be both racist and reactionary.
Another newcomer, Charles E. McKenzie, the victor in the fifth
district of Louisiana, held views indistinguishable from those
of Eastland. The results of the 1942 primaries left the northern Democratic Party with a New Dealish complexion, but the
southern wing was moving in the opposite direction. The trend
of southern politics indicated a preference for preserving
the status-quo, particularly in relations between the races.[107]

---

[104]Robert A. Taft, transcript of speech, August 8, 1942,
box 1259, Taft papers, Library of Congress.

[105]Congressional Record, 77th Congress, 2nd Session,
pp. A3710-A3711.

[106]New Republic 107 (October 5, 1942), pp. 415-416.

[107]New Republic 107 (September 21, 1942), p. 348, (September 28, 1942), p. 380. On Eastland, see Blum, Price of

As the general election approached, the prospect of a low voter turnout enhanced Republican chances and diminished those of Administration supporters. Perhaps the only event that could have rescued Democratic candidates was a sensational military victory. The battle of Midway Island, June 4-7, had marked the resurgence of American sea power in the Pacific, but the government could not yet reveal either the devices that accounted for the victory or the extent of the Japanese defeat. On August 7, American marines landed on Tulagi and Guadalcanal in the southern Solomon Islands. But the battle for Guadalcanal turned into a bloody stalemate, with American forces grimly hanging on while the Japanese Imperial Navy and a United States fleet slugged away at each other.[108] In the European Theater, the President planned an invasion of North Africa to take place some time in October. According to James McGregor Burns, Roosevelt's biographer, the President, while discussing the North African landing with General George C. Marshall, Chief of Staff, "held up his folded hands in mock prayer and said, 'Please make it before Election Day.'" But for logistical reasons, the operation's commander, General Dwight D. Eisenhower, postponed the invasion until November 8, a few days after the election.[109]

"The Republican Party is primarily interested in the election of a majority in the House of Representatives in 1942," Senator Taft had written on May 8.[110] Republicans did not quite achieve that goal, but they gained 42 House seats and nine in the Senate. They also captured governorships in New York, Pennsylvania, Ohio, Michigan, and California. The Republican tide engulfed outspoken New Deal Democrats and progressives, including Representative Knute Hill (D., Wash.), advocate of Roosevelt's $25,000 limitation on incomes, Representative Frank E. Hook (D., Mich.), ardent defender of organized labor, Senator Josh Lee (D., Okla.), a reliable Presidential supporter, and Senator Prentiss M. Brown (D., Mich.), floor manager of the Administration's Emergency Anti-Inflation Bill.[111]

Vision, p. 83; and biographical sketch in Curry, "Southern Senators and Their Roll-Call Votes in Congress," pp. 75-80. See also Polenberg, War and Society, p. 192; and Garson, Democratic Party and the Politics of Sectionalism, p. 26.

[108] Gordon Wright, The Ordeal of Total War, 1939-1945 (New York, 1968), p. 43; Burns, Soldier of Freedom, pp. 255, 283-285; and Perrett, Days of Sadness, pp. 207-215.

[109] Burns, Soldier of Freedom, p. 290; Perrett, Days of Sadness, p. 254.

[110] Taft to S. W. Craiger, May 8, 1942, box 27, Taft papers, Library of Congress.

[111] For results of the 1942 Congressional elections, see the New York Times, November 4, 1942, pp. 1, 6; Thomas N. Hoover,

In Nebraska, Senator George Norris had received a ringing
Presidential endorsement--Roosevelt's only overt intrusion into
the campaign--but Republican Kenneth S. Wherry soundly defeated
the aging progressive.[112] Connecticut exemplified the national
trend. Prior to the election, Democrats held all five House
seats in that state. Republicans swept the delegation, thereby
retiring such consistent New Dealers as Representatives James
Shanley and Herman Koppelman. In the farm belt, Republicans
made equally impressive gains. GOP candidates won five previously Democratic seats in Missouri. According to Senator Harry
S Truman (D., Mo.) his state and "the Middle West had gone
Republican partly because of the way in which Leon Henderson had
administered livestock prices and partly because of the shortage
of manpower on the farm." Iowa, the home state of Vice President Wallace, "went 100 per cent Republican--Governor, Senator,
entire Congressional delegation."[113]

In mid-1942, the Senate had 65 Democrats, 29 Republicans,
1 Progressive and 1 Independent. The House had 262 Democrats,
166 Republicans, 2 Progressives, 1 Farmer-Labor member and 1
American Labor Party member. The new Congress would have 57
Democrats, 38 Republicans, and 1 Progressive in the Senate and
222 Democrats, 208 Republicans, 2 Progressives, 1 Farmer-Labor
member and 1 American Labor Party member in the House. The
position of the Administration was worse than those figures
indicated, for the 40 or so renegade Democrats who voted consistently with the Republicans would give the opposition effective
control of the House.[114]

Republican leaders, surprised by the magnitude of their
victory, exulted. On December 9, Frank Gannett, assistant

"Elections of 1942," in William M. Schuyler, ed., The American
Year Book, 1942 (New York, 1943), pp. 66-85; Harding, "The 1942
Congressional Elections," p. 41; and Polenberg, War and Society,
pp. 187-188. See also Congressional Record, 77th Congress, 2nd
Session, pp. 7255-7256, 7311.

[112]For Roosevelt's endorsement of Norris, see Rosenman,
Public Papers and Addresses of FDR 11: 1942, pp. 432-433; and
Burns,Soldier of Freedom, pp. 279, 281.

[113]Quotations from Eliot Janeway, "Trials and Errors,"
Fortune XXVI (December 1942), p. 30; and Blum, Price of Vision,
p. 134.

[114]Congressional Directory, 77th Congress, 2nd Session,
June 1942 (Washington, 1942), pp. 145-147; Congressional Direc-
tory, 78th Congress, 1st Session, January 1943 (Washington,
1943), pp. 145-147; Congressional Digest 21 (1942), pp. 289-290;
Jonathan Daniels, White House Witness, 1942-1945 (Garden City,
N.Y., 1975), p. 73.

chairman of the Republican National Committee, wrote Senator
Taft: "As a matter of fact, the victory we won is amazing. We
could have won ten more districts with just a little more support and effort." Gannett's estimate of ten more seats may
have been an exaggeration. Still, a change of less than a
thousand votes in the closest Congressional districts would have
given the Republicans five more House seats. As Gannett saw it,
"the Republican party is on the march. I am sure we shall meet
our increased responsibility, end the New Deal, and preserve our
form of government."[115]

Surveying the wreckage, Democrats sought an explanation
for the setbacks they had received. Edwin W. Pauley, secretary
of the Democratic National Committee, prepared a memorandum
listing the primary causes of the debacle. Resentment against
government bureaucracy, dissatisfaction with the conduct of the
war, with OPA and Leon Henderson, irritation with Administration labor policy headed his list.[116]

Congressional Democrats agreed with Pauley's assessment.
They blamed "the President and his Administration for what has
happened to the party," according to Eliot Janeway, in a post-
election analysis for _Fortune_. "They feel that the people, unable to reach his appointees, have made them the scapegoats."[117]
The 77th Congress, despite a fractious attitude toward taxes,
OCD, FSA, and price control, had made a positive record. Congress had appropriated every dollar for military purposes which
the Administration had requested. It had granted the President
sweeping emergency powers. In many respects, the 77th Congress
was entitled to be known as the "Victory Congress."[118] Yet the
voters had punished incumbents. As Senator Tom Connally (D.,
Tex.) explained on November 5,

> The only visible sign of the Federal Government is
> the Representative or the Senator. . . . If something
> goes wrong . . . the people cannot do anything to the
> [bureaucrats] . . . but they see their Representative
> in Congress when he comes home, or they see their
> Senator and they say "Here is the guy we are looking
> for. Swat him. He did it. . . ."[119]

---

[115]Gannett to Taft, December 9, 1942, box 27, Taft papers,
Library of Congress. See also Hoover, "Elections of 1942,"
p. 66.

[116]Pauley to President, December 14, 1942, President's Personal File 1820, FDR papers, FDR Library.

[117]Janeway, "Trials and Errors," p. 32.

[118]Perrett, _Days of Sadness_, pp. 247-249, 253-254.

[119]_Congressional Record_, 77th Congress, 2nd Session,
p. 8709.

Congressional Democrats had suffered for discomforts arising
from restrictions, regulations, rationing, higher taxes, the
draft, Pearl Harbor and subsequent defeats, the war itself.[120]

The election had unquestionably strengthened the bipartisan
opposition in Congress. That it signaled a mass repudiation of
"recent social progress," as some liberals feared, was less
clear.[121] A light turnout produced most of the Republican gains.
Of 80,000,000 potential voters, only 28 million voted, 8 million
less than in 1938 and almost 22 million fewer than in 1940. In
district after district, the total vote for Republican candidates remained constant or declined slightly while the total for
Democratic candidates fell precipitously. A significant proportion of low-income and young people, who tended to vote Democratic, had not gone to the polls. Young men serving in the
armed forces found voting difficult if not impossible. Many
workers employed in war industries could not vote because they
had recently relocated and could not meet residency requirements. Even if they qualified, war workers were reluctant to
sacrifice wages by taking time off to vote. Those on night
shifts or overtime found voting inconvenient.[122]

The wartime reversion to the "politics of prosperity" also
injured Democratic candidates. "[L]arge numbers of the poor
who for a decade had seen a very direct connection between a
Democratic victory and their daily lives were now making enough
money to feel temporarily secure and to indulge in political
indifference," Hadley Cantril concluded.[123] Former Senator
Lewis Schwellenbach agreed. "The Democrats have been in power
for ten years and the people always get tired after that length
of time," he said. With jobs plentiful, wages high, farm income rising, a complacent electorate had forgotten who helped
them during the depression. "These people who were out of work

---

[120]See, for example, "The Case Against the 77th Congress,"
Fortune XXV (May 1942), pp. 73-75, 150, 152, 155-156, 158, 160;
and Berdahl, "Political Parties and Elections," pp. 78-80.

[121]Albert Guerard, "A National Government?" New Republic
108 (February 1, 1943), p. 150.

[122]Hadley Cantril and John Harding, "The 1942 Elections:
A Case Study in Political Psychology," Public Opinion Quarterly
VII (Summer 1943), pp. 222-241; Harding, "The 1942 Congressional Elections," pp. 41-58; Polenberg, War and Society, pp.
189-190. See also Stokes, "The Congress," pp. 138-139; and
Knute Hill to John Carmody, September 12, 1942, box 57, Carmody
papers, FDR Library.

[123]Cantril and Harding, "The 1942 Elections," pp. 232-233.

in 1930 have good jobs now. I'll bet half the people on WPA
wouldn't admit that fact if they were asked."[124]

Presidential Strategy for the Home Front

Roosevelt seemed relieved that the campaign had ended.
Publicly, he dismissed the election results as of little consequence. Pressed by reporters for an assessment of Democratic
losses, the President ducked. "I knew very little about this
election." A newsman persisted: "Mr. President, will it make
any difference in your attitude toward Congress?" "Why should
it," Roosevelt answered. The sole objective of his Administration was "winning the war" as quickly as possible, and all
the successful candidates for Congress endorsed that goal.[125]

Roosevelt's replies were disingenuous. In spite of his
disclaimer, the election returns did affect his attitude. They
confirmed his belief that ancillary issues would have to be
subordinated to the lowest common denominator of national
unity--a military victory speedily won. The Vice President
and other reform leaders portrayed the war as a "people's revolution" which compelled attention, at home and abroad, to a
wide range of social and economic concerns. The adverse political trend convinced Roosevelt that those concerns would
evoke resistance from his domestic opposition and imperil his
leadership. Therefore, he was ready to sacrifice reformist
policies, even if they abetted the war effort. Only that which
was absolutely necessary for a military victory mattered.
Roosevelt's actions, since the outbreak of war in September
1939, had gradually conformed to that "necessitarian" strategy.
The election results only verified his instincts. Throughout
1943, he followed the line of least political resistance on the
home front.[126]

In an address to the New York Herald Tribune forum on
November 17, 1942, Roosevelt advertised his willingness to ac-
commodate the opposition. "[I]n time of war," the President
declared, "the American people know that the one all-important
job before them is fighting and working to win. Therefore, of
necessity," he continued, "while long-range social and economic

---

[124]Schwellenbach to Joseph Guffey, January 14, 1943,
President's Personal File 1820, FDR papers, FDR Library.

[125]Roosevelt, Complete Presidential Press Conferences 19-
20: 1942, pp. 20: 200-201. See also Burns, Soldier of Freedom, p. 281.

[126]John H. Crider, The Bureaucrat (Philadelphia, 1944),
pp. 174-175; Perrett, Days of Sadness, p. 287; Blum, Price of
Vision, p. 26; Burns, Soldier of Freedom, pp. 300-301.

problems are by no means forgotten, they are a little like books
which for the moment we have laid aside in order that we might
get out the old atlas to learn the geography of the battle
areas."[127] James G. Patton of the National Farmers Union immediately protested Roosevelt's apparent disavowal of reform. "I
was deeply disturbed to read tonight your words about laying
aside 'long range social and economic problems' for the atlas
of war," Patton telegraphed the White House. "Your personal
and political enemies led by Harry Byrd, will, I believe, inter-
pret this statement as a repudiation of the great constructive
works of your administration which are more important than ever,
now that we are engaged in a global war for freedom and democracy." In his reply on November 19, the President attempted to
reassure Patton, but he conceded that his Administration would
not "move forward on our progressive path" until after the war
was over.[128]

Roosevelt's decision regarding government personnel provided another hint of his readiness, while the war lasted, to
appease his adversaries. On February 17, 1942, the Senate had
approved a resolution offered by Senator Millard Tydings of
Maryland, a leading Democratic renegade, to create a special
appropriations subcommittee empowered to investigate the
number of employees in the various executive departments and
agencies.[129] The resolution reflected Congressional antagonism
toward Federal bureaucracy, which had expanded enormously as a
consequence of the war. Opposition leaders were especially
alarmed by "ballooning bureaucracy," because they feared government control of private enterprise--"a planned economy" in
Senator Taft's phrase--and preferred that government play a
minor role in postwar affairs.[130] Tydings argued that overstaffing by government agencies drained manpower from vital war
and agricultural production. The Tydings Committee, along with
the Byrd Committee, pressed for severe cuts in government personnel and redeployment of employees into essential war agencies,
war industry jobs, or the armed forces.[131]

---

[127]Rosenman, Public Papers and Addresses of FDR 11: 1942,
p. 483.

[128]Patton to President, November 17, 1942, and President to
Patton, November 19, 1942, President's Official File 899, FDR
papers, FDR Library. See also Congressional Record, 77th Congress, 2nd Session, p. A4158.

[129]Congressional Record, 77th Congress, 2nd Session, pp.
1189, 1311.

[130]Robert A. Taft, "Price Fixing A Necessary Evil," box
1257, Taft papers, Library of Congress. See also Harold D.
Smith, Daily Record, January 27, 1943, Smith papers, FDR Library.

[131]U.S., Congress, Senate, Committee on Appropriations,
Transfer of Employees Conserving Office Space, Relief in Housing

The recommendations of the Tydings Committee annoyed Roosevelt, but he recognized that overstaffing had occurred in some instances. The President directed the Bureau of the Budget to formulate a policy on draft deferment of government workers, hiring practices by Federal agencies, and other personnel problems accompanying civilian control of the war economy. Then, on November 17, he announced a new policy toward selective service deferments for government workers. Henceforth, he declared, there would be no "blanket exemptions" of young men because of employment by the Federal Government.[132] Budget Director Smith dissented vigorously. "After reading your release on deferment yesterday," he wrote, "I confess that I went home last night literally mumbling, I was so dumbfounded. After months of struggle with Civil Service and Manpower," Smith continued, "we finally developed a procedure and a deferment policy for the Government. . . . This morning the situation is complete chaos, and that is not too extravagant a word." The Budget Director contended that "the release seems to deny. . . . the importance of civilian government. I am sure that you do not want the military to run this country. Yet, the effect may be just that, if we attempt to maintain a Federal Service composed of inexperienced, untrained, older persons." Smith reminded Roosevelt that "the morale in the civil service, with all the sniping against 'bureaucracy' that is going on, is as low as a snake's belly. I think we need to do something fast to recover morale. . . ."[133] The President remained adamant. "We have in the Government an enormous number of men who ought to be with the fighting forces," he replied on November 19. "The only way to get at this problem is to reconsider the whole matter of exemptions from active military or naval service. . . . The fact remains," Roosevelt concluded, "that it is being said by

---

Conditions and Promotion of Economy and Efficiency, S. Rept. 1554, 77th Congress, 2nd Session, 1942; U.S. Congress, Joint Committee on Reduction of Nonessential Federal Expenditures, Supplemental Report, S. Doc. 152, part 2, 77th Congress, 2nd Session, 1942. See also Congressional Digest 21 (1942), pp. 65-66; and "A Million Men for the Army," March 11, 1943, box 526, Taft papers, Library of Congress.

[132] Quotation from Rosenman, Public Papers and Addresses of FDR 11: 1942, p. 477. See also Wayne Coy to Samuel Rosenman, July 13, 1942, President to Wayne Coy, July 30, 1942, Wayne Coy to President, August 3, 1942, Wayne Coy to Harold D. Smith, August 6, 1942, General Records of the Director, series 39.27, box 37, Records of the Bureau of the Budget, Record Group 51, National Archives.

[133] Smith to President, November 18, 1942, President's Secretary's File 116, FDR papers, FDR Library.

thousands throughout the country that the best refuge during this war is a Government job."[134]

At a conference with the Budget Director on December 4, the President elaborated his position. The Administration, he said, "was under attack for its deferment policy" by the Tydings Committee and other critics. Smith retorted that "no case had been made against the policies now employed in the Government with respect to deferment." Roosevelt admitted "that was probably true," but the situation was "purely political" and he wanted to forestall further criticism from the opposition.[135]

That same day, the President abolished the Work Projects Administration. The Byrd Committee had repeatedly demanded liquidation of the old relief agency, and Roosevelt may have terminated WPA as another sop to the opposition. Publicly, the President said only that the vast expansion of employment caused by the war had made "a national work relief program . . . no longer necessary." Few doubted that the manpower shortage had obviated the need for WPA. As with CCC, however, some New Dealers wanted WPA temporarily suspended so that it could be reactivated as part of the Administration's postwar program. Instead of a "wartime furlough," Roosevelt gave the agency an "honorable discharge."[136]

Yet another indication of the President's post-election spirit of accommodation was the replacement of Price Administrator Leon Henderson. As chief of OPA, Henderson had perhaps the most difficult job in the entire government. Because of his determination to control agricultural prices, the farm bloc had subjected him to incessant criticism. Businessmen condemned the Price Administrator because OPA restrained the levels of profit. Moreover, Henderson's long service to Roosevelt had made him synonymous with New Deal economic policies. The Price Administrator was proud that "OPA's top staff are 100 percent Roosevelt and New Deal."[137] That circumstance probably increased

---

[134]President to Smith, November 18, 1942, President's Secretary's File 116, FDR papers, FDR Library.

[135]Harold D. Smith, Memorandum of Conference with the President, December 4, 1942, Smith papers, FDR Library. See also Washington Post, December 13, 1942, p. 14.

[136]Quotations from Rosenman, Public Papers and Addresses of FDR 11: 1942, pp. 505-506; and Polenberg, War and Society, p. 81.

[137]Henderson to President, December 15, 1942, President's Secretary's File 159, FDR papers, FDR Library. See also Congressional Record, 77th Congress, 2nd Session, pp. A2355, 2399-2400; and Chester Bowles, Promises to Keep: My Years in Public Life (New York, 1971), p. 41.

hostility toward OPA and Henderson on Capitol Hill, hostility
so great that it caused a protracted struggle over adequate appropriations for OPA. On December 2, Representative F. Edward
Hebert (D., La.), one of the Democratic intractables, asserted
that "the greatest contribution to the war effort in this
country would be for the President to fire Leon Henderson if he
does not resign."[138] As Chester Bowles, himself head of OPA
from July 1943 to June 1946, later wrote, Henderson "had coura-
geously and successfully led the fight for a stable economy.
He had thrown all his energies and abilities into the task and
in the process had brought down upon his head the wrath of
every economic group in the country." Suffering from ill health
and under pressure from Democratic politicians unhappy with his
performance as Price Administrator, Henderson resigned on
December 17. The President replaced him with former Senator
Prentiss M. Brown, evidently in order to improve OPA's poor relations with Capitol Hill.[139]

Not only was Roosevelt seeking better relations with Congress, he was equally interested in restoring a degree of harmony to the Democratic Party. In the aftermath of the election,
renegades like Representative Eugene E. Cox (D., Ga.) were
openly promoting a merger of Southern Democrats and the newly
enlarged Republican minority.[140] Southerners were particularly
restive at this time because certain prominent Democratic
leaders and Administration officials, like Vice President Wallace,
Mrs. Roosevelt, Aubrey Williams of NYA, and Beanie Baldwin of
FSA, had espoused the cause of racial equality.[141] In a speech
before the Congress of American-Soviet Friendship delivered
November 8, 1942, the Vice President had advocated "ethnic
democracy," which "means merely that the different races and
minority groups must be given equality of economic opportunity."
The President, Wallace observed, "was guided by principles of
ethnic democracy when in June of 1941 he issued an executive

---

[138]Congressional Record, 77th Congress, 2nd Session, p.
9232. See also New Republic 107 (July 13, 1942), p. 39; and
Congressional Record, 77th Congress, 2nd Session, pp. A2657-A2658.

[139]Quotation from Bowles, Promises to Keep, p. 41. See
also Young, Congressional Politics, p. 105.

[140]Congressional Record, 77th Congress, 2nd Session, pp.
8765, 8806, 9100-9101, 9246; New York Times, November 25, 1942,
p. 13. See also Garson, Democratic Party and the Politics of
Sectionalism, pp. 27-30.

[141]Lash, Eleanor and Franklin, pp. 668-697; Baldwin, Poverty
and Politics, pp. 272, 282-284; John A. Salmond, "Postscript to
the New Deal: The Defeat of the Nomination of Aubrey W. Williams as Rural Electrification Administrator in 1945," Journal
of American History LXI (September 1974), pp. 419-420.

order prohibiting racial discrimination in the employing of workers by national defense industries."[142] Wallace referred to the Fair Employment Practices Committee, which Roosevelt had reluctantly created in response to pressure from black leaders. Southerners resented the existence of such a Federal agency. To them it symbolized a policy "to break down and destroy the segregation laws" of the entire South, as Eugene "Bull" Connor of Birmingham, Alabama, had written the President on August 7, 1942. Connor heaped special abuse on the National Youth Administration which he said had "preached social equality and stirred up strife." Nearly all white Southern politicians supported racial segregation. Efforts to rehabilitate the social and economic status of blacks inevitably alienated Democratic Congressmen from southern states.[143]

Roosevelt, in the opinion of Vice President Wallace, was "very sensitive as to what the southern senators feel."[144] Revival of the poll-tax issue in mid-November destroyed any change the President might have had to placate Southern Democrats. Anti-poll tax enthusiasts in the House introduced a bill abolishing the poll tax as a qualification for voting in Federal primary and general elections. The House passed the bill, 254 to 84.[145] In the Senate, Claude Pepper (D., Fla.), the foremost southern New Dealer, pushed hard for adoption of the anti-poll tax measure. Pepper received no assistance from other New Dealers representing southern states, like Senators Lister Hill (D., Ala.), Allen Ellender (D., La.), and Theodore Bilbo (D., Miss.), who was the most blatant racist in the Senate. They joined the rest of their southern brethren in a nine-day filibuster against the anti-poll tax bill. On November 23, the Senate voted on cloture, which required a two-thirds majority. The motion failed, 37 to 41, an outcome that reflected, in part, Southern Democratic-Republican collaboration. The vote, as Senator Ellender remarked, "put the bill to sleep for the remainder of the present Congress."[146]

[142] Vital Speeches 9 (November 15, 1942), pp. 72-73.

[143] Connor to President, August 7, 1942, President's Official File 444-d, FDR papers, FDR Library. See also Rosenman, Public Papers and Addresses of FDR 10: 1941, pp. 233-237; Garson, Democratic Party and the Politics of Sectionalism, pp. 18-27; and Burns, Soldier of Freedom, pp. 264-265.

[144] Blum, Price of Vision, p. 131.

[145] Congressional Record, 77th Congress, 2nd Session, pp. 8070-8079, 8091-8094, 8095-8096, 8120-8174.

[146] Congressional Record, 77th Congress, 2nd Session, pp. 8814-8849, 8897-8922, 8925-8947, 8949-8971, 9005-9033, 9043-9050, 9052-9059, 9060-9065. For Senate roll call vote on cloture, see Congressional Record, 77th Congress, 2nd Session,

The poll-tax controversy aggravated the strain between Southern and non-Southern Democrats. Reviewing the situation on December 14, Roosevelt "spoke very vigorously about Claude Pepper" to Vice President Wallace "and said that Pepper ought to be paddled for bringing up the poll tax legislation at this time."[147] The effort to abolish the poll tax had touched the sensitive nerve of white supremacy and had awakened many Southern Democrats to the implications of New Deal gestures toward the black vote in northern cities.[148]

Republicans, sensing the widening rift between Southern Democrats and the Administration, tried to turn the division to their advantage. On December 16, Representative Karl Mundt (R., S.D.) encouraged Southerners to withdraw from the party of the New Deal and form a "Dixie Party or a group under some other name" which would "provide an opportunity for the South once again to find expression for its policies and principles." Mundt continued, "the South is stirring uneasily and beginning to manifest unwillingness to permit the New Deal planners and schemers to completely take over . . . the management of the Democratic Party."[149]

Southern politicians, while still Democrats, needed little urging to declare their independence. Governor Frank M. Dixon of Alabama, for one, accused the New Deal of "dynamiting" the social structure of the South. In a speech delivered in New York on December 11, Dixon declared, "It is their own party administration which sought to knife [Southern Democrats] . . . with Federal control of elections, with the Fair Employment Practices Committee. . . ." The South would not meekly submit to such outrages. "Suggestions are rife as to the formation of a Southern Democratic Party. . . . Ways and means are being discussed daily to break our chains. We will find some way . . . if this senseless attack keeps up," he concluded.[150] On January 15, 1943, southern Congressmen caucused to discuss future strategy. The next day, Representative Charles E. McKenzie (D., La.) denounced New Deal efforts "to sabotage the white people of the South." Southern Democrats, restless for some

---

p. 9065; and Appendix V, Guttman scaling table 5, item 5. See also Riddick, "Second Session of the Seventy-Seventh Congress," p. 299.

[147]Blum, Price of Vision, p. 145.

[148]Polenberg, War and Society, p. 192; Garson, Democratic Party and the Politics of Sectionalism, pp. 24-26.

[149]Congressional Record, 77th Congress, pp. A4395-A4396.

[150]New York Times, December 12, 1942, p. 34; Washington Post, December 12, 1942, p. 4.

time, now emerged as a cohesive, anti-Administration force in Congressional politics.[151]

If southern Congressmen were in revolt, New Dealers and reformers were hardly less upset with the President. They interpreted his post-election appeasement of the opposition as a further shift to the right-of-center. Already New Dealers felt that businessmen, mostly Republicans, in the War Production Board and other agencies had taken over the war effort. The attitude of those business executives, reported Presidential assistant James H. Rowe, was, "When the New Dealers were in power they didn't include us; now that we are in power we won't include them."[152] On November 26, 1942, Vice President Wallace told Roosevelt "the liberals were finding themselves in an increasingly difficult position. Many officials," said Wallace, "were putting out the story . . . that men in uniform were going to run the country for the next 10 years. Businessmen in Commerce and their kindred souls in State Department were increasingly getting the idea that big corporations were going to run the country." The President expressed sympathy but took no action.[153]

Tennessee Valley Authority Chairman David E. Lilienthal shared the feeling of discouragement that had prompted Wallace's complaint. "Liberal forces are disorganized and defeatist," Lilienthal noted on December 9. "The President apparently feels that the time to take the initiative, on his part, has not come. New Deal supporters," he added, "say, in sadness and bitterness, that the New Deal is dead, that it has been betrayed." On December 10, Lilienthal went to the White House to discuss "the application of TVA principles to the post-war world" and discovered that Roosevelt "had decided to give up everything except winning a military victory." The President evidently wanted to bury questions of social and economic reform. He had, Lilienthal felt, abandoned the broad purposes for which reformers believed the war was being fought.[154]

---

[151] New York Times, January 17, 1943, p. 40. See also J. Donald Kingsley, "Congress and the New Deal," Current History IV (March 1943), pp. 28-29.

[152] Quotation from Rowe to President, January 23, 1941, President's Secretary's File 150, FDR papers, FDR Library. See also Rowe to President, February 6, 1941, and March 6, 1941, President's Secretary's File 142, FDR papers, FDR Library; Perrett, Days of Sadness, p. 287; and Polenberg, War and Society, pp. 89-91.

[153] Blum, Price of Vision, p. 137.

[154] David E. Lilienthal, The Journals of David E. Lilienthal vol. I: The TVA Years, 1939-1945 (New York, 1964), pp. 566, 569-572.

Yet Roosevelt, as usual, was playing a double game. When Lilienthal returned some hours later for another conference with the President, he found renewed elan. The message to the new Congress, Roosevelt said, would pledge a postwar program of economic security. "Those boys on Guadalcanal and in Africa--does this Congress propose to tell them they are going to come back to fear about jobs, fear about the things a man can't prevent, like accident, sickness, and so on?" The President declared firmly, "I am going to fight back. . . . I'm really going to tell this next Congress."[155]

Roosevelt's display of combativeness buoyed Lilienthal's hopes. "It may be the turning of the tide of reaction, if he will press forward from this point," the TVA Chairman later wrote. But Lilienthal was not sure. Presidential strategy for the home front made military victory the preeminent concern. Expediency demanded the postponement of social and economic issues for the duration of the war. The Administration would acquiesce in a rollback of New Deal programs by the Congressional opposition. Those programs were expendable, in Roosevelt's view, because new and better programs could roll again at the end of the war when he resuscitated reform.[156]

That strategy only partially satisfied reformers. They believed wartime policies would dictate the shape of postwar society. Abandonment of reform during the war, they contended, would make a postwar revival of the New Deal difficult if not impossible. But Roosevelt's intentions, molded by his sensitive assessment of political possibilities, left New Dealers to struggle on their own for appropriate public policies. Not until victory over the Axis was at hand, would the President commit his prestige to the battle. Disheartened by that attitude, New Dealers foresaw, in Lilienthal's words, a "catastrophe, the greatest that can befall us, the tragedy of a futile, barren war."[157]

---

[155] Lilienthal, Journals I, pp. 570-571.

[156] Lilienthal, Journals I, p. 583.

[157] Lilienthal, Journals I, p. 583.

CHAPTER 5

THE BATTLE OF WASHINGTON

The continuous policy disputes of the war years culminated in the 78th Congress (1943-44). Already the bipartisan opposition had made inroads on the New Deal legacy. In the new Congress, the President's adversaries continued to inflict a retroactive revenge on the New Deal but concentrated as well on issues with postwar implications. Those implications had always been present, even in the struggle over depression-era agencies like the Civilian Conservation Corps and wartime agencies like the Office of Civilian Defense. They emerged more starkly as victory drew nearer. By 1943, opposition leaders were ready to use their control of Congress to shape the contours of postwar public policy.[1]

The President, too, was thinking of the postwar. He had promised David Lilienthal, "I'm really going to _tell_ this next Congress," and true to his word, his annual message, delivered January 7, 1943, outlined a postwar program of full employment and economic security. Roosevelt began by dwelling on military events. Applause punctuated his commentary on the progress of the war, but silence greeted him when he turned to domestic concerns. He praised workers, farmers and business executives for contributions to the war effort. He apologized for shortcomings in economic mobilization. And he spoke briefly of the postwar world. It "would be inconceivable," the President said, "it would, indeed, be sacrilegious--if this Nation and the world did not attain some real lasting good out of all these efforts and sufferings and bloodshed and death." When the war ended, the men and women in the armed forces should "have the right to expect full employment--full employment for themselves and for all able-bodied men and women in America who want to work." Indeed, Americans wanted "assurance against the evils of all major economic hazards--assurance that will extend from the cradle to the grave. And this great Government can and must provide this assurance." What the people did not want was "a postwar America which suffers from undernourishment or slums--or the dole." He admitted,

---

[1]See Blair Moody, "The Politics of Domestic Strategy," in Ray F. Harvey and others, The Politics of This War (New York, 1943), p. 31; and Marquis Childs, I Write From Washington (New York, 1942), p. 5.

I have been told that this is no time to speak
of a better America after the war. I am told it is
a grave error on my part.
I dissent.
And if the security of the individual citizen, or
the family, should become a subject of national debate, the country knows where I stand.
I say this now to this Seventy-Eighth Congress,
because it is wholly possible that freedom from want--
the right to employment, the right of assurance against
life's hazards--will loom very large as a task of
America during the coming two years.[2]

Roosevelt harbored no illusions about the 78th Congress.
The elections of 1942 had produced the largest bipartisan oppo-
sition he had yet faced.[3] In a confidential memorandum of
December 14, 1942, Edwin W. Pauley, secretary of the Democratic
National Committee, accurately forecast the attitude of various
Congressional factions toward major issues. Pauley told Roosevelt that the 78th Congress would be militantly anti-labor.
"Practically all the old opponents of . . . organized labor,"
he wrote, "are still more determined in their opposition." The
estrangement of organized labor and organized agriculture would
cause a majority of rural Southern Democrats, who now held almost half the Democratic seats in the House, to support legislation rescinding rights granted trade unions by the Wagner Act
and other New Deal statutes. The anti-labor front, Pauley predicted, would constitute a large majority of the House and pos-
sibly the Senate, as well.[4]

The outlook for Administration farm policy was equally
bleak. "Except for the South the Democratic Party has been
practically wiped out in the entire farm belt," wrote Pauley.
Republicans from agricultural districts would join forces with
"the agricultural bloc in the South" and try to force the Administration to accept an upward revaluation of parity. That
would destroy the Administration's anti-inflation policy, for

---

[2] Samuel I. Rosenman, ed., The Public Papers and Addresses
of Franklin D. Roosevelt, vol. 12: 1943, The Tide Turns (New
York, 1950), pp. 21-31. See also James M. Burns, Roosevelt:
The Soldier of Freedom (New York, 1970), pp. 305-307.

[3] Mary S. Benson, "The Year in Congress," in William M.
Schuyler, ed., The American Year Book, 1943 (New York, 1944),
p. 24; Lawrence H. Curry, Jr., "Southern Senators and Their
Roll-Call Votes in Congress, 1941-1944" (Ph.D. dissertation,
Duke University, 1971), pp. 240-241.

[4] Pauley to President, December 14, 1942, President's Per-
sonal File 1820, FDR papers, FDR Library. See also Richard
Polenberg, War and Society: The United States, 1941-1945
(Philadelphia, 1972), p. 192.

it would "remove all real control on farm prices." The farm bloc "will be in the saddle."[5]

Only "needed war legislation," Pauley wrote, would meet little resistance. Otherwise, opposition leaders would attempt to countermand Administration policies and enact their own. In drafting revenue legislation, for instance, Congressional tax committees would likely ignore Treasury Department recommendations. Republicans and renegade Democrats would vigorously oppose postwar planning by the executive branch, especially if such plans embodied reform purposes. The President could still wield his veto to protect Administration policy and to prevent encroachments on the New Deal legacy. However, a major veto like that of the Walter-Logan Bill in December 1940, might not again be sustained. Because the elections of 1942 had altered the balance of power between the Roosevelt Administration and the opposition, the 78th Congress could probably override the President.[6]

As Pauley's memorandum made clear, the Administration faced a difficult session. Roosevelt's adversaries interpreted the 1942 elections as a mandate to crush the New Deal and forestall a postwar revival of reform. The election, declared Representative Robert F. Rich (R., Pa.), was "a flag waving to this administration--the New Deal administration--telling them, 'You have got to pursue another course. You cannot go on the way you have and save America and win this war. . . .'" The American people, he said, wanted Republicans and like-minded Democrats to "stop waste, stop extravagance . . . throw out the incompetent in government, get rid of the radicals, and get back to constitutional government." Representative Carter Manasco (D., Ala.) agreed that Congress had to defeat the New Deal on the home front in order to defeat the foreign foe. "We cannot win the war against the Axis," he argued, "until we win the battle of Washington."[7] Representative Charles L. Gifford (R., Mass.) expressed those sentiments more succinctly: "we must win the war from the New Deal."[8]

---

[5]Pauley to President, December 14, 1942, President's Personal File 1820, FDR papers, FDR Library.

[6]Pauley to President, December 14, 1942, President's Personal File 1820, FDR papers, FDR Library. See also Curry, "Southern Senators and Their Roll-Call Votes in Congress," p. 241.

[7]Quotations from Congressional Record, 77th Congress, 2nd Session, pp. 8713, 8718. See also Robert A. Garson, The Democratic Party and the Politics of Sectionalism, 1941-1948 (Baton Rouge, La., 1974), p. 31.

[8]Congressional Record, 78th Congress, 1st Session, p. 56. See also Roland Young, Congressional Politics in the Second World War (New York, 1956), pp. 22-23.

Reprisals Against the Bureaucracy

The Congressional assault on reform commenced in early 1943 with harrying actions against Federal administrative agencies, especially those concerned with domestic affairs. Republicans and their Democratic auxiliaries suspected the existence of a conspiracy involving "the bureaucrats, the crackpots, the Communists and the New Dealers" in the Federal service who intended "to remake America," as Representative Clare E. Hoffman (R., Mich.) phrased it. "The American people," said Representative Fritz G. Lanham (D., Tex.), "discern the well-organized efforts of a subversive group--and they think they detect some of them in important positions . . . who are seeking to destroy our system of free enterprise and foist upon us the ideology of foreign regimes hostile to our basic and traditional purposes." Already the New Deal had "substituted government by bureaus for government under the Constitution," charged one Republican Senator. The war was a convenient "smoke screen behind which these new dealers hide their schemes for socializing the country," and unless Congress prevented it, Roosevelt's "post-war superworld planners" would impose state socialism by bureaucratic edict.[9]

To thwart the "crackpot plans and schemes of the starry-eyed New Deal dreamers," said Representative Hoffman, Congress had to recover policy-making functions usurped by executive agencies. Further, the Congressional opposition had to conduct a "thorough house cleaning" of the Federal service. Those actions would help ensure that "our American system of free enterprise" was not "displaced by some form of totalitarianism" after the war ended.[10]

In the vanguard of the Congressional campaign against New Dealers was the House Special Committee to Investigate Un-American Activities. Under its chairman, Representative Martin Dies (D., Tex.), that committee had already become the chief persecutor of reformers employed by the Federal government. Instead of investigating un-American activities, observed Representative J. Bayard Clark (D., N.C.), the committee had "come to be more of a supervisor of executive departments." This "whole thing is a drive at the executive department of this Government," agreed Representative James F. O'Connor (D., Mont.). The committee, said Representative Richard P. Gale (R., Minn.) was

----

[9]Quotations from Congressional Record, 78th Congress, 1st Session, pp. 460-461, 550, 555, 698.

[10]Quotations from Congressional Record, 78th Congress, 1st Session, pp. 53, 135, 697. See also Lawrence Sullivan, Bureaucracy Runs Amuck (Indianapolis, 1944), p. 77.

conducting a "cheap smear campaign" against New Dealers.[11]

Dies dismissed those charges as witting and unwitting efforts to protect communism by discrediting his committee. He was especially eager to retaliate against those, like the New Republic and the Union for Democratic Action, who had tried to defeat "obstructionists" in the recent primary and general elections. Many bureaucrats, said Dies, were "linked up with the effort to smear Members of Congress." In fact, "a gigantic bureaucracy" that planned "to take over this country" was part of a "united front of radicals and crackpots." He promised that his committee would drive those dangerous elements out of the Federal government.[12]

The official tenure of the Dies Committee had expired at the close of the previous Congress. In early February, Representative Eugene Cox (D., Ga.) submitted a resolution continuing the committee for another two years. The "people of this country are waging two wars," Cox told the House, "one against a foreign foe and one against enemies here at home." The Dies Committee should be continued to combat "the enemy within our own borders."[13] On February 10, by a vote of 302-94, the House approved Cox's resolution extending the committee. Seventy-eight Democrats, 13 Republicans, and 3 minor party members opposed the resolution, but 178 Republicans (93 percent of those voting), 80 Southern Democrats (87 percent of those voting), 43 non-Southern Democrats (39 percent of those voting), and 1 minor party member gave the committee overwhelming support.[14] As one Representative ruefully admitted, many Congressmen were afraid to vote against the resolution because their position would be misconstrued as "a vote for communism."[15]

The Congressional drive against reformers in the Federal government did not confine itself to strident rhetoric. While

---

[11]Quotations from Congressional Record, 78th Congress, 1st Session, pp. 796, 801, 803. See also Polenberg, War and Society, pp. 193-194.

[12]Congressional Record, 78th Congress, 1st Session, pp. 478, 482, 485.

[13]Congressional Record, 78th Congress, 1st Session, pp. 795-796.

[14]For House roll call vote on the Dies Committee, see Congressional Record, 78th Congress, 1st Session, pp. 809-810; and Appendix VI, Guttman scaling table 3, item 7.

[15]Congressional Record, 78th Congress, 1st Session, p. 803. See also Benson, "The Year in Congress," American Year Book, 1943, p. 31.

the Dies Committee resolution was still pending, opposition members moved to discharge 39 Federal employees accused by Representative Dies of communist and other radical affiliations.[16]
So implacable was the mood of the House that the effort would
have succeeded had not majority leader John McCormack (D.,
Mass.) and Representative Clarence Cannon (D., Mo.) intervened.
Cannon said he did not want to participate in a "lynching bee,"
and suggested that a special appropriations subcommittee investigate allegations against the 39 named individuals.[17]

On May 18, the special subcommittee presented a report ex-
onerating all but three of the persons named by Dies. According
to Representative Clinton P. Anderson, a member of the subcommittee, the dismissal of most of the charges was a rebuke to
Dies and other irresponsible communist hunters. However, the
subcommittee did recommend summary discharge and disqualifica-
tion of three Federal officials, Robert Morss Lovett, U.S. Government Secretary of the Virgin Islands, Goodwin D. Watson and
William E. Dodd, Jr., both of the Federal Communications Commission. There was no evidence proving that Lovett, Watson and
Dodd were communists, but because of their connections with
left-wing groups, the subcommittee offered an amendment to the
pending deficiency appropriation bill that would bar them from
further government service.[18]

Constitutional scholars like Representative Sam Hobbs (D.,
Ala.) described that amendment as a "bill of attainder," a legislative act inflicting punishment without judicial trial in violation of article I, section 9 of the Constitution. Hobbs predicted that the Supreme Court would invalidate the amendment.
Others protested that Lovett, Watson and Dodd were being punished for their political views, for exercising "their right of
free speech." Unmoved, the House approved the amendment by a
vote of 318 to 62.[19]

---

[16]Congressional Record, 78th Congress, 1st Session, pp.
645-652. See also Young, Congressional Politics, pp. 49-50.

[17]Congressional Record, 78th Congress, 1st Session, pp.
653, 713-714.

[18]Congressional Record, 78th Congress, 1st Session, pp.
4581-4584, 4602. See also Polenberg, War and Society, p. 194;
Wilfred E. Binkley, President and Congress (New York, 1947),
p. 270; and Frederick L. Schuman, "Bill of Attainder in the 78th
Congress," American Political Science Review XXXVII (1943),
pp. 819-829.

[19]Quotations from Congressional Record, 78th Congress, 1st
Session, pp. 4595-4597. For House roll call vote on the discharge amendment, see Congressional Record, 78th Congress, 1st
Session, p. 4605; and Appendix VI, Guttman scaling table 3,
item 1.

Both the Senate and the President objected to the "purge amendment." The Senate voted to delete the provision because most members considered it an unconstitutional form of "legislative assassination."[20] But the House insisted, and finally the Senate yielded because the deficiency appropriation was urgently needed to carry on the war. The President, in turn, condemned the rider as an attempt to disqualify Lovett, Watson and Dodd "for Federal employment because of political opinions attributed to them." He predicted the Supreme Court would declare the attached bill of attainder unconstitutional, but on September 14, signed the deficiency appropriation bill under protest, in order "to avoid delaying our conduct of the war."[21]

Congressional animosity toward reform-minded officials took other forms as well. Opposition members sought restraints on executive agencies that were supposedly escaping legislative oversight. They backed a resolution establishing a committee to investigate and regulate Federal agencies whose intentions were suspect on Capitol Hill. Introduced by Representative Howard W. Smith (D., Va.), one of the chief Democratic renegades, the resolution was "forced through the Committee on Rules by those Democrats opposed to the President with the aid of Republican members," reported Adolph Sabath (D., Ill.), Chairman of the Rules Committee. Some supporters of the President also favored the creation of an oversight committee. They wanted, in the words of Representative Jerry Voorhis (D., Calif.), "a continuing review of special agencies" to see that "their work is being carried on in accordance with the intent of Congress." Other members, particularly Roosevelt's adversaries, wanted the committee to monitor Federal agencies that might, in the hands of reformers, constitute a threat to existing institutions. "This Congress has a job to do to preserve our constitutional form of government, our industrial system of free enterprise, and our American way of life," said one Republican who favored the proposed committee.[22] On February 11, 1943, the House approved the Smith resolution by a vote of 294-50. Those opposing the proposal did so because they feared the new committee would hamper effective operation of the executive branch. They were crushed by a coalition of 154 Republicans (100 percent of those

---

[20] Congressional Record, 78th Congress, 1st Session, p. 6693. See also Curry, "Southern Senators and Their Roll-Call Votes in Congress," pp. 252-253.

[21] Rosenman, Public Papers and Addresses of FDR 12: 1943, pp. 385-388. See also Polenberg, War and Society, p. 195; and Young, Congressional Politics, pp. 51-53.

[22] Quotations from Congressional Record, 78th Congress, 1st Session, pp. 60, 872, 883. See also Harold Ickes to President, January 2, 1943, President's Secretary's File 73, FDR papers, FDR Library; and Young, Congressional Politics, pp. 107-108.

voting), 86 Southern Democrats (95 percent of those voting), 52 non-Southern Democrats (54 percent of those voting) and 2 minor party members.[23]

Representative Smith became Chairman of the Select Committee to Investigate Acts of Executive Agencies Beyond the Scope of Their Authority. As that gracelessly precise title suggested, the Smith Committee assumed that administrative agencies had willfully misinterpreted the intent of Congress, abused powers granted by law, and usurped powers not granted. The committee focused its inquiry on the Office of Price Administration, of all wartime agencies the most pervasive in impact and the most unpopular. Smith and his colleagues accused New Dealers in OPA of trying to force changes in the "business practices, cost practices and distribution practices" of private enterprise.[24]

As the Smith Committee proceeded with its investigation of OPA, Congressional feeling against that agency peaked. On June 18, the House adopted an amendment sponsored by Representative Everett Dirksen (R., Ill.) that arbitrarily reduced funds for OPA from $165,000,000 to $130,000,000.[25] A majority of the House was prepared to go further. Many opposition members had repeatedly called for a "house cleaning" of OPA. They disliked Federal control of business practices and distrusted the OPA staff, especially the New Deal economists and lawyers employed by the agency. Republicans and renegade Democrats denounced young Keynesians like John Kenneth Galbraith, deputy administrator for price, and Richard V. Gilbert, chief economic advisor to the Price Administrator, as "theorists, crackpots, left-wingers, college professors . . . incompetent, inexperienced

---

[23]For House roll call vote on the Smith resolution, see Congressional Record, 78th Congress, 1st Session, p. 884; and Appendix VI, Guttman scaling table 1, item 3.

[24]U.S., Congress, House, Select Committee to Investigate Acts of Executive Agencies Beyond the Scope of Their Authority, Second Intermediate Report, H. Rept. 862, 78th Congress, 1st Session, 1943, p. 11. See also Sullivan, Bureaucracy Runs Amuck, pp. 47-48; Young, Congressional Politics, pp. 107-108; Garson, Democratic Party and Politics of Sectionalism, p. 32; Chester Bowles, Promises to Keep: My Years in Public Life (New York, 1971), p. 46; Ray F. Harvey, "The Politics of Politics," in Ray F. Harvey and others, The Politics of This War (New York, 1943), p. 311; and John H. Crider, The Bureaucrat (Philadelphia, 1944), pp. 129-149.

[25]Congressional Record, 78th Congress, 1st Session, p. 6140.

dreamers and planners" lacking "any business experience."[26] To drive them from OPA, Representative Dirksen offered an amendment that prohibited payment of salaries to OPA officials who lacked at least five years business experience in the industries they regulated. On June 18, the House accepted the Dirksen amendment by a vote of 189 to 144. Because OPA was considered essential to the war effort, only 24 Democrats, mostly renegades, deserted the Administration, but nearly unanimous support by Republicans ensured adoption of the "anti-professor" proviso.[27]

The Dirksen amendments and other reprisals carried out against the executive branch underscored the institutional nature of legislation passed by the 78th Congress. Under the American system of divided powers, a degree of jealous rivalry between legislative and executive branches of the Federal government was a natural condition. The Great Depression had magnified the potential for institutional conflict because Congress, confronted by an economic emergency, delegated enormous power to the President and his agents. The war, necessitating still greater centralization of power, further amplified tension. Congressmen, whose importance depended on the significance of Congress as an institution, resented the accretion of discretionary authority in administrative agencies. Legislators of all factions believed they had to insist on Congress's rightful place in the framework of American government or meekly accept an irreversible decline in their prestige and power.[28]

Opposition leaders synchronized legislative attacks on Administration policies with the institutional conflict that was occurring simultaneously. As early as 1940, the opposition had presented the Walter-Logan Bill as the means to reestablish Congressional power and curb administrative agencies. Yet the clear intent of that legislation was to paralyze the New Deal. After failing to override the President's veto of the Walter-Logan Bill, the opposition relied instead on legislative oversight to exert pressure against such agencies as the National Labor Relations Board, the Farm Security Administration, and the Office of Civilian Defense. Those earlier efforts to discipline executive agencies and dictate policy culminated in

---

[26] Congressional Record, 78th Congress, 1st Session, pp. 97. 135, 6117.

[27] For House roll call vote on the Dirksen amendment, see Congressional Record, 78th Congress, 1st Session, p. 6141; and Appendix VI, Guttman scaling table 1, item 14.

[28] On the institutional clash between legislative and executive branches, see Harvey, "The Politics of Politics," pp. 309-312; Curry, "Southern Senators and Their Roll-Call Votes in Congress," pp. 235, 268; and Herman Finer, "Critics of Bureaucracy," Political Science Quarterly LX (1945), pp. 100-112.

1943 with the renewal of the Dies Committee, passage of the "purge amendment," creation of the Smith Committee, and adoption of the Dirksen OPA amendments. The Congressional opposition, by refurbishing and asserting the powers of the legislative branch, sought to become a continuous participant in guiding adminis-trative conduct and in defining the acceptable limits of policy. The powers that Congress had delegated to executive agencies with one hand, the Congressional opposition tried to revoke or cir-cumscribe with the other. That ambivalence toward delegation of power, in large measure, accounted for the collision between Congress and President during the war years.[29]

The Salary Limit Dispute

Of the President's wartime domestic policies, none seemed more insidious to the Congressional opposition than his effort to limit personal incomes to a maximum of $25,000 per year after taxes. In the annual budget message of January 5, 1942, and again in his anti-inflation message of April 27, 1942, Roosevelt had thrown his support behind Treasury Department pro-posals for heavy, progressive taxation. He also recommended that personal incomes after taxes be limited to $25,000 a year for the duration of the war.[30] His proposed limit on individ-ual incomes sprang from determination to prevent profiteering like that which had occurred during World War I, when public money had created thousands of war millionaires. With that scandal in mind, New Dealers and reformers demanded that the burdens of war be equalized and that no individual be permitted to enrich himself on account of the war. As Senator Lister Hill (D., Ala.) wrote Roosevelt on April 22, 1942,

Those of us who served in the armed forces during the last war solemnly covenanted that if our country was forced to go to war again, we [would] make cer-tain that there was . . . equal burdens and equal sacrifices for all the people, and with no person making profit from the war.

[29] See, for example, the remarks of Representative Eugene E. Cox (D., Ga.), Congressional Record, 78th Congress, 1st Session, p. 10. See also Arthur W. Macmahon, "Congressional Oversight of Administration: The Power of the Purse--I," Political Sci-ence Quarterly LVIII (1943), pp. 161-190.

[30] Samuel I. Rosenman, ed., The Public Papers and Addresses of Franklin D. Roosevelt, vol. 11: 1942, Humanity on the Defen-sive (New York, 1950), pp. 13-17, 219-221; Franklin D. Roosevelt, Complete Presidential Press Conferences of Franklin D. Roosevelt, vols. 19-20: 1942 (New York, 1972), pp. 19: 65-66; John M. Blum, From the Morgenthau Diaries, vol. III: Years of War, 1941-1945 (Boston, 1967), p. 35.

Hill asked for "a tax measure that will . . . take all income above $15,000 per year of every individual."[31] The President agreed that a ceiling on individual incomes should be part of a comprehensive approach embodying "equality of sacrifice." Instead of a limit of $15,000, Roosevelt settled on $25,000, a figure popularized by the leadership of the CIO.[32]

The Treasury Department, caught unawares by the President, never developed much enthusiasm for a ceiling on personal incomes. Treasury officials believed the larger problem was limitation of excessive corporate profits. Nevertheless, Secretary Morgenthau and his aides loyally endorsed the Presidential initiative. They recognized that some business executives were receiving unreasonably large bonuses and salaries. The department began work on a special 100 percent supertax that would capture all individual income, from whatever source derived, above $25,000 per year.[33]

On Capitol Hill, those Congressmen who dominated revenue legislation refused to consider the $25,000 ceiling on individual incomes a serious proposal. It was dismissed, Randolph Paul has written, as "just a bit of Roosevelt whimsy."[34] Undeterred by that adverse reaction, the President, in his Labor Day message on the cost of living, again recommended "a top limit on an individual's net income after taxes, approximating $25,000."[35] Congress proved no more receptive to the idea in September than it had been earlier. However, the Emergency Anti-Inflation Act of October 2, 1942, authorized the President to adjust wages and salaries in order to correct gross inequities. Roosevelt thought it was patently inequitable to draft men into the Army without imposing a ceiling on the salaries of individuals not conscripted. In a few cases, those salaries exceeded $500,000 a year. On October 3 he issued Executive Order 9250 establishing an Office of Economic Stabilization to coordinate the system of controls that the government had imposed

---

[31]Hill to President, April 22, 1942, President's Secretary's File 1820, FDR papers, FDR Library. See also Bowles, Promises to Keep, pp. 30-31.

[32]Rosenman, Public Papers and Addresses of FDR 11: 1942, p. 224. See also New York Times, April 28, 1942, p. 12; Polenberg, War and Society, pp. 24-25; and Burns, Soldier of Freedom, p. 256.

[33]Randolph E. Paul, Taxation in the United States (Boston, 1954), pp. 301-302; Blum, Years of War, pp. 39-40, 60.

[34]Paul, Taxation, p. 301.

[35]Rosenman, Public Papers and Addresses of FDR 11: 1942, p. 367.

on the economy. The executive order also provided that no salary would be permitted that exceeded $25,000 after the payment of taxes. In effect, the President ordered the reduction of "grossly inequitable" salaries and froze other salaries at existing levels. Under tax schedules then current, an annual salary of $67,200 became the maximum allowed, for that sum, after taxes, would yield a net income of approximately $25,000.[36]

Roosevelt recognized the inadequacy of the executive order, for it failed to reach incomes derived from sources other than salaries. In the annual budget message of January 6, 1943, he reminded Congress that "the receipt of very large net incomes from any source constitutes a gross inequity undermining national unity." He appealed again for a special supertax that would extend the principle of his salary limit order to all incomes, especially those resulting from private investments.[37]

The 78th Congress, as Roosevelt undoubtedly realized, was far more likely to rescind the order affecting salaries than it was to broaden the limitation. The President's action had provoked a ferocious response from his adversaries.[38] Most considered the salary limit a revival of earlier New Deal schemes to "soak-the-rich" and "share-the-wealth." Former Under Secretary of the Treasury John W. Hanes cited the "$25,000 limitation upon salaries" as "one more proof of the fact that our Government has been captured by a minority of European-minded Social Democrats--more intent upon winning the class war at home than the world war abroad."[39] Senator Robert A. Taft, calling Roosevelt's action "Demagoguery rampant," claimed that the salary limit would destroy "incentive and the free enterprise system," private philanthropy, the capital market, and "new enterprise after the war."[40]

Opposition to the President's limit on salaries mounted steadily. In January 1943, anti-Administration members of the House Ways and Means Committee prepared an amendment to the pending public debt bill that would revoke the offending

---

[36] Rosenman, Public Papers and Addresses of FDR 12: 1943, pp. 160-161, 398-399. See also Young, Congressional Politics, pp. 99, 101.

[37] Rosenman, Public Papers and Addresses of FDR 12: 1943, pp. 19-20.

[38] Young, Congressional Politics, pp. 102-103.

[39] John W. Hanes, statement on salary limit order, n.d., box 763, Taft papers, Library of Congress.

[40] Robert A. Taft, notes on salary limit order, n.d., box 763, Taft papers, Library of Congress.

provision of Executive Order 9250. That amendment was an effective contrivance because the President could not veto a bill raising the national debt ceiling without endangering the Treasury's war-financing program.[41]

Roosevelt objected to any Congressional action nullifying the salary limit order. "I could not," he wrote Ways and Means Chairman Robert Doughton (D., N.C.) on February 15, "exercise the discretion vested in me by the Congress to adjust salaries without finding that it is a gross inequity in wartime to permit one man to receive a salary in excess of $67,200 a year while the Government is drafting another man and requiring him to serve with the armed forces for $600 per year." He reiterated his request for "a special war supertax on net income" that would extend the principle of equality of sacrifice "to the coupon clipper as well as the man who earns the salary." If Congress would enact that 100 percent supertax or an equivalent, he would "immediately rescind the section of the Executive Order in question." But without such a levy, the President concluded, Congress should not "rescind the limitation and permit the existence of inequities that seriously affect the morale of soldiers and sailors, farmers and workers, imperiling efforts to stabilize wages and prices and thereby impairing the effective prosecution of the war."[42]

Roosevelt's letter had no effect on the Ways and Means Committee. Led by Representative Wesley E. Disney (D., Okla.), long-time adversary of the New Deal, a committee majority of 10 Republicans and 5 renegade Democrats attached a rider to the public debt bill that severely modified the President's order. If accepted by both houses of Congress, the Disney amendment would permit continued payment of salaries in excess of $67,200 and, while workers' wages remained stabilized, would allow other salaries to rise.[43]

House debate on the controversial Disney amendment began on March 11. The members of the opposition contended that Roosevelt's order limiting salaries contravened Congressional intent. Their argument depended on the meaning of the Emergency

---

[41]Congressional Record, 78th Congress, 1st Session, pp. A1253-A1254. See also Polenberg, War and Society, p. 89.

[42]Rosenman, Public Papers and Addresses of FDR 12: 1943, pp. 67-68, 90-94.

[43]Congressional Record, 78th Congress, 1st Session, pp. 1862, 1864, 1870-1871. See also Morgenthau Diary, vol. 610, p. 367, FDR Library; and Garson, Democratic Party and Politics of Sectionalism, p. 34.

Anti-Inflation Act of October 2, 1942.[44] While that legislation was pending, some members of the House Banking and Currency
Committee had suggested that the bill authorized the President
to set a limit. But the Chairman of the Banking and Currency
Committee, Representative Henry B. Steagall (D., Ala.), held
that the bill did not grant such authority. He did "not believe that the President of the United States would deliberately go against a clearly disclosed opinion of Congress."[45]

By issuing the order of October 3, 1942, Roosevelt exposed
himself to the charge that he had, in fact, flouted the will of
Congress. The President, asserted Representative Hamilton Fish
(R., N.Y.), had "deliberately violated and disregarded" the
wishes of a Congressional majority. In defense of Roosevelt,
Representative Albert Gore (D., Tenn.) suggested that Congress
had left the question of salary limitation up to the Chief Executive. The intent, said Gore, "was to get rid of a hot potato
by turning it over to the President. And now after he exer-
cises it, we come and complain." Interpreted literally, the
wording of the Act in question empowered the President to freeze,
reduce and limit salaries. Many Congressmen, perhaps a majority, had not expected Roosevelt to exercise that authority.
Here was another instance of the Congressional opposition endeavoring to take back with one hand the power Congress had
given with the other.[46]

The President's adversaries clamored for repeal of the
salary limit order for another reason. The limit was "un-
American," declared Representative Eugene Cox (D., Ga.), because it would destroy "individual initiative, and private enterprise." The purpose of the limit on salaries was "perfectly
plain," added Representative Ranulf Compton (R., Conn.). The
President was furthering his "program to redistribute the
wealth . . . the object is not revenue . . . but it is 'social
reform.'" Republicans discovered that "the Communist Party
in 1928 had recommended in its program a limitation of $25,000."
More recently, "certain C.I.O. leaders" and Eleanor Roosevelt
had advanced the same idea. "What is its real objective?"
asked Representative Disney. "Is it akin to Huey Long's wealth
sharing crusade? Is its effect to abort our American system?"
Republicans and anti-administration Democrats feared that the
salary limit order, though presented as a temporary wartime

---

[44]Congressional Record, 78th Congress, 1st Session, pp.
1862-1893.

[45]Congressional Record, 78th Congress, 1st Session, p.
1866. See also Young, Congressional Politics, pp. 101-102.

[46]Congressional Record, 78th Congress, 1st Session, pp.
1863, 1868, 1870.

measure, might become a permanent policy.[47]

Administration supporters tried to rebut those accusations. Stripped "to the cold realities," said Representative A. Leonard Allen (D., La.), the Disney proviso "simply becomes a move to raise the salaries of the big industrial executives of this country at a time when everybody else is called upon to economize and save." The contested executive order did not stem from some alien ideology but from demands by "the American Legion and other patriotic organizations and individuals . . . that the profi be taken out of war." Instead of weeping over "the boys who sit up in the air-conditioned offices to the tune of half-a-million-dollar salaries," Congress should "say today by our votes that men shall not profit out of the sacred blood . . . [spilled] in defense of America."[48]

Another critic of the Disney amendment, Representative Jere Cooper (D., Tenn.), attempted to remove the provision from the public debt bill.[49] On March 12, the House rejected Cooper's motion, 145-212, and then voted, 268-129, to pass the bill with the Disney amendment intact. Favoring the measure were 187 Republicans (96 percent of those voting), 43 Southern Democrats (48 percent of those voting) and 38 non-Southern Democrats (35 percent of those voting). Seventy-one non-Southern Democrats, 46 Southern Democrats, 8 Republicans and 4 minor party members resisted the Disney amendment to the end.[50]

In the Senate, debate on the issue was perfunctory. The Finance Committee, chaired by Senator Walter F. George (D., Ga.), replaced the Disney amendment with a slightly different provision revoking the President's authority to reduce salaries in excess of $67,200 but permitting him to freeze salaries for the duration.[51] Senator George, who possessed immense prestige on fiscal policy, argued that an arbitrary ceiling on salaries accomplished "no purpose save the fanciful purpose of producing a state of equality." Equality in earnings, he proclaimed,

---

[47] Quotations from Congressional Record, 78th Congress, 1st Session, pp. 1864, 1873, 1877, 1885.

[48] Congressional Record, 78th Congress, 1st Session, pp. 1962-1963.

[49] Congressional Record, 78th Congress, 1st Session, p. 1890.

[50] For House roll call vote on Disney amendment, see Congressional Record, 78th Congress, 1st Session, pp. 1968-1969; and Appendix VI, Guttman scaling table 2, item 1. See also Young, Congressional Politics, p. 102.

[51] Congressional Record, 78th Congress, 1st Session, pp. 2330-2331.

"has its place in no economy save the communistic state."[52] On March 23, the Senate ratified the Finance Committee amendment. After the House concurred, the measure went to the President.[53]

Forced to sign the Public Debt Act because of the urgency of war financing, Roosevelt sharply criticized the "irrelevant and unwarranted rider" attached to the measure. "If the circumstances were otherwise," he told Congress on April 11, "I should veto the bill." Congress had rescinded his limit on excessive salaries "without even attempting to offer a substitute." Though he knew his appeal was doomed, Roosevelt insisted that Congress should impose a war supertax on net income. "I still believe," he declared firmly, "that the Nation has a common purpose--equality of sacrifice in wartime."[54]

The degree of sacrifice required by the salary limit order would have been mild, for $25,000 a year after taxes was hardly an uncomfortable maximum. Moreover, the executive order had affected less than 4,000 persons and had allowed for exceptions to avoid undue hardship. To the President, the salary limit symbolized the commitment of his Administration to democratic principles. To the Congressional opposition, it seemed both a usurpation of power and yet another indication of Roosevelt's proclivity for soaking the rich. The President's adversaries were determined to prevent any reforms during the war that might lead to permanent changes after the war was over. In their view, equalization of incomes would have set a dangerous precedent for postwar public policy.[55]

The Quarrel Between Agriculture and Labor

Like the salary limit order, the Administration's position on agricultural price control provoked a noisy debate over Presidential power. As in 1942, so again in 1943 government regulation of farm prices proved an irritant that divided Congressional Democrats and left those representing rural constituencies at odds with the Administration. Underlying the latest dispute was the continuing tension between organized labor and organized agriculture.

---

[52] Congressional Record, 78th Congress, 1st Session, p. 2334.

[53] Congressional Record, 78th Congress, 1st Session, p. 2347.

[54] Rosenman, Public Papers and Addresses of FDR 12: 1943, pp. 157-162. See also Young, Congressional Politics, pp. 102-103.

[55] See Polenberg, War and Society, p. 89.

In the compromise that permitted passage of the Emergency
Anti-Inflation Act of October 2, 1942, farm state Congressmen
thought they had won a commitment to allow higher ceilings on
agricultural prices. The President, who had to consider the
effect of higher food and fiber prices on union labor, urban
consumers, and those living on fixed incomes, strove to prevent
further inflation. His executive order of October 3, 1942, the
same order that authorized the limitation on salaries, contained a provision freezing most commodity prices at existing
levels.[56]

That section of the executive order reopened the feud between the farm bloc and the White House. Claiming they had been
double-crossed, agricultural leaders clamored for legislative
retaliation against Roosevelt and Economic Stabilization Director James F. Byrnes.[57] Early in the first session of the 78th
Congress, Senator John Bankhead (D., Ala.), a leading proponent
of higher farm prices, introduced a bill specifically repealing
the offending provision of the President's executive order.[58]
The angry champions of the farmer accused Roosevelt of willfully
disregarding the intent of Congress. Senator Clyde Reed (R.,
Kan.) thought the issue involved was the same as in the salary
limitation dispute. Senators "who have the feeling that the
President had exceeded his powers in both instances," he said,
should vote for the Bankhead Bill.[59] Evidently most Senators
so believed for the Democratic leadership made no effort to
block the measure and it passed on February 25 by a vote of
78-2.[60]

The House took up the Bankhead Bill on March 24. Farm
bloc members had already won approval, five days earlier, of
the Pace Bill incorporating all farm labor costs into the cal-
culation of parity prices. The Bankhead Bill also seemed
assured of passage. Outnumbered Administration loyalists, resigned to defeat, worried about the inflationary consequences

---

[56]Eugene Casey to President, n.d., President's Secretary's
File 145, FDR papers, FDR Library; Young, Congressional Politics, p. 98.

[57]Congressional Record, 77th Congress, 2nd Session, pp.
8110-8111; Congressional Record, 78th Congress, 1st Session,
pp. 1299-1301; Wesley McCune, The Farm Bloc (New York, 1943),
pp. 69-73.

[58]Congressional Record, 78th Congress, 2nd Session, pp.
571, 1299-1301.

[59]Congressional Record, 78th Congress, 1st Session, p.
1308. See also Young, Congressional Politics, pp. 98-99.

[60]For Senate roll call vote on the Bankhead Bill, see Congressional Record, 78th Congress, 1st Session, p. 1308.

of such legislation. If Congress, through the Pace Bill and the Bankhead Bill, insisted on higher food prices, said Representative Adolph Sabath (D., Ill.), labor unions would be justified in demanding higher wages. Representative Estes Kefauver (D., Tenn.) agreed. The pressure on wages would be "almost irresistible if this bill goes through," he declared.[61]

Those and similar warnings were ignored. A large majority of the House not only favored higher ceilings on farm prices but also wanted to reprimand the President for issuing the contested executive order. "Since this Seventy Eighth Congress convened," said Representative Charles Halleck (R., Ind.),

> we have been required to spend a great deal of our time undoing executive and administrative acts which were outside and clearly beyond the scope of the authority contained in many measures enacted by Congresses preceding this one.

The action "required here today," Halleck continued, "is necessary because of an Executive order which I say flies right straight in the face of the mandate and will and the intention of the Congress."[62] As expected, the House passed the Bankhead Bill without a record vote.

On April 2, Roosevelt returned the Bankhead Bill with a stinging veto message. He warned that the legislation would ignite a firestorm of "wartime inflation and postwar chaos."[63] Even before the veto, Roosevelt was considering a "hold-the-line" executive order that would absolutely forbid "any further increases in prices affecting the cost of living or further increases in general wage or salary rates."[64] When news leaked out that stronger Presidential action against inflation was pending, support for the Bankhead Bill eroded. Farm bloc leaders now discovered a distinct reluctance to override the President's veto. On April 7, the Senate killed the Bankhead Bill by recommitting it to the Committee on Agriculture and Forestry.[65]

---

[61]Congressional Record, 78th Congress, 1st Session, pp. 2272, 2414, 2423.

[62]Congressional Record, 78th Congress, 1st Session, p. 2418.

[63]Rosenman, Public Papers and Addresses of FDR 12: 1943, pp. 135-143.

[64]Rosenman, Public Papers and Addresses of FDR 12: 1943, pp. 148, 150. See also Burns, Soldier of Freedom, pp. 340-341.

[65]Congressional Record, 78th Congress, 1st Session, p. 2959; Bowles, Promises to Keep, pp. 30, 41.

The Senate made no attempt to override the veto of the
Bankhead Bill because a majority did not want to accept responsibility for undermining the economic stabilization program.
For the same reason, the Senate failed to act on the House-ap-
proved Pace Bill, another device to raise farm prices. A work
stoppage in the bituminous coal mines was imminent and Senators
feared that a legislated rise in agricultural prices would ag-
gravate demands by coal miners and other trade unions for wage
increases. Even those Senators who still favored higher farm
prices grudgingly conceded that passage of the Pace Bill would
be untimely.[66]

The strife over the Bankhead and Pace Bills, though neither
became law, widened the breach between the farm bloc and the
Roosevelt Administration. Farm leaders, reported Presidential
assistant Eugene Casey, thought the "refusal to adjust price
ceilings," the veto of the Bankhead Bill, and a threatened veto
of the Pace Bill proved that the President favored organized
labor at the expense of "farmers' activities and interests."[67]
The mood of commercial farmers and their spokesmen was not improved by the issuance, on April 8, of the famous "hold-the-
line" executive order that endeavored to halt the "upward
spiral" of prices, salaries and wages.[68] At the same time, the
Administration instituted a program of consumer subsidies to
keep retail food prices from rising above existing levels.
Consumer subsidies became the bone of contention in a climactic
struggle over agricultural price control.[69]

Though the program itself was complicated, the principle
of consumer subsidies was simple. The Federal government purchased foodstuffs at market prices or higher than market prices
and resold them to distributors at less than cost. The loss
incurred was a subsidy to consumers that enabled the government
to stabilize and even roll back the retail prices of many commodities.[70]

---

[66] Franklin D. Roosevelt, Complete Presidential Press Conferences of Franklin D. Roosevelt, vols. 21-22: 1943 (New York,
1972), p. 21: 257; Rosenman, Public Papers and Addresses of
FDR 12: 1943, pp. 188-190; Young, Congressional Politics, p. 103.

[67] Casey to President, n.d., President's Secretary's File
145, FDR papers, FDR Library.

[68] Rosenman, Public Papers and Addresses of FDR 12: 1943,
p. 150.

[69] Young, Congressional Politics, p. 109.

[70] Bowles, Promises to Keep, pp. 41, 55-56; Sullivan, Bureaucracy Runs Amuck, p. 190; Burns, Soldier of Freedom, p. 341.

The consumer subsidy program was a logical extension of the agricultural policy followed by the Administration since May 1941. At that time, the President and his advisers decided against allowing food prices to rise to demand level, which would penalize consumers, but instead to provide larger income for farmers by continuing parity payments out of the Federal budget, wherein "the cost is distributed among tax payers more nearly in accordance with ability to pay."[71] Two years later, commodity prices had risen to parity or above. Agricultural spokesmen now insisted that prices had to go still higher to attain maximum food production. The Administration therefore inaugurated a program of consumer subsidies to reconcile the seemingly contradictory aims of greater incentives for food production and stable food prices at the retail level. The incentive payments for food production would come from the Federal budget, not out of the pockets of consumers. The program, it was hoped, would hold down the cost of living and thereby preserve labor peace. That ingenious solution to an apparently unsolvable dilemma had only two flaws. Congress had never authorized the consumer subsidy program, a fact that many members resented. And agricultural organizations opposed the effort to maintain retail food prices at artificially low levels. Because labor unions had urged a roll-back of food prices, farm leaders considered consumer subsidies yet another example of White House acquiescence to "the demands of labor."[72]

The Reconstruction Finance Corporation and Commodity Credit Corporation--both relatively independent of the Congressional appropriation process--furnished the money for subsidy payments. In June 1943, the law under which CCC operated came up for renewal. In the House, a coalition of farm state representatives and members who questioned the legality of the program inserted a provision prohibiting payment of any more subsidies.[73] On June 26, the Senate also voted, 39-37, to terminate the program. Twenty-four Republicans (86 percent of those voting), 7 Southern Democrats (39 percent of those voting) and 8 non-Southern

---

[71]Harold D. Smith to President, May 10, 1941, Miscellaneous White House Memoranda, Smith papers, FDR Library.

[72]Eugene Casey to President, n.d., President's Secretary's File 145, FDR papers, FDR Library; Harold D. Smith, Memorandum of Conference with the President, June 3, 1943, Smith papers, FDR Library; Morgenthau Diary, vol. 612, p. 75, vol. 672, pp. 286-290. FDR Library; Congressional Record, 78th Congress, 1st Session, pp. 3908, 6521-6522; Arthur P. Chew, "Conditions in Agriculture," in William M. Schuyler, ed., The American Year Book, 1943 (New York, 1944), pp. 432-433; Young, Congressional Politics, pp. 109-112.

[73]Congressional Record, 78th Congress, 1st Session, p. 6521; Young, Congressional Politics, p. 112.

Democrats (28 percent of those voting) opposed consumer subsidies, while 21 non-Southern Democrats, 11 Southern Democrats, 4 Republicans and 1 Progressive favored their continuation.[74]

On July 2, Roosevelt vetoed the CCC Bill because it terminated subsidy payments. The bill "blacks out the program to reduce the cost of living," he told Congress, and would "become law only over my strenuous objection and protest."[75] The same day the House tried to override the veto but failed, 228-154. The motion to override was supported by 179 Republicans (96 percent of those voting), 33 Southern Democrats (36 percent of those voting), 13 non-Southern Democrats (13 percent of those voting) and 3 minor party members, while 87 non-Southern Democrats, 59 Southern Democrats, 7 Republicans and 1 American Labor Party member backed the President.[76] Had the matter ended there, the Commodity Credit Corporation would have ceased to exist, but few Congressmen wanted to destroy the Corporation, for it maintained a floor under farm commodity prices. Therefore, Congress extended the CCC for six months and the subsidy program continued.[77]

That outcome marked the President's outstanding victory in domestic policy during the 78th Congress. Though Roosevelt could never have secured passage of a bill explicitly authorizing consumer subsidies, the Administration had sufficient votes to prevent its adversaries from killing the program. The price of that victory was further embitterment of agricultural groups and their spokesmen who expressed indignation that the Federal government should increase "the bonded debt of the Nation in order to pay the grocery bills for people whose salaries and wages are at levels never known before in the history of the country." Farm leaders concluded once again that the Administration was pursuing a political strategy that sacrificed agriculture to urban and labor interests.[78]

---

[74] For Senate roll call vote on consumer subsidies, see Congressional Record, 78th Congress, 1st Session, pp. 6558-6559; and Appendix VII, Guttman scaling table 9, item 6.

[75] Rosenman, Public Papers and Addresses of FDR 12: 1943, pp. 278, 281.

[76] For House roll call vote to override the President's veto, see Congressional Record, 78th Congress, 1st Session, pp. 7054-7055; and Appendix VI, Guttman scaling table 1, item 7.

[77] Floyd M. Riddick, "The First Session of the Seventy-Eighth Congress," American Political Science Review XXXVIII (1944), pp. 307-308; Benson, "The Year in Congress," American Year Book, 1943, p. 25; Young, Congressional Politics, pp. 112-113.

[78] Quotation from Congressional Record, 78th Congress, 1st Session, p. 6521. See also Harold D. Smith, Memorandum of

Because it engendered that·belief, the struggle over agricultural price regulation contributed, in some measure, to the
passage of the Smith-Connally Act, the wartime labor law that
represented the first step backward from New Deal collective
bargaining policy. Since 1939, anti-labor forces had sought repeal or revision of the Wagner Act of 1935. The House and
Senate Labor Committees had sidetracked those earlier efforts.
But public discontent with strikes in wartime, Republican gains
in the elections of 1942, and the feeling that the government
was "coddling" labor permitted a breakthrough by the anti-
labor front.[79]

The proximate cause of the Smith-Connally Act was a series
of strikes in the bituminous coal industry. Shortly after
Pearl Harbor, the representatives of organized labor had agreed
to refrain from strikes, but John L. Lewis, powerful head of
the United Mine Workers, declared that he did not consider the
"no-strike" pledge binding. Claiming that coal miners were
underpaid, in May and June 1943, he ordered shutdowns intended
to extract higher wages from the coal industry and the National
War Labor Board. Those strikes angered a large proportion of
the American people, who opposed work stoppages in essential
war industries and blamed Lewis for delaying victory and
costing the lives of American soldiers. Public outrage helped
goad Congress into passing legislation to curb labor unions.[80]

Bills of varying severity were already pending in the Senate.[81] By dexterous parliamentary maneuvering, Senator Tom
Connally (D., Tex.) had had the bill he sponsored referred to
the Judiciary Committee instead of the Labor Committee, which

Conference with the President, October 20, 1943, Smith papers,
FDR Library; Eugene Casey to President, n.d., President's Secretary's File 145, FDR papers, FDR Library; and Garson, Democratic Party and Politics of Sectionalism, p. 38.

[79]Harry A. Millis and Emily Clark Brown, From the Wagner
Act to Taft-Hartley (Chicago, 1950), pp. 284, 332-334, 346-
354; Young, Congressional Politics, p. 57.

[80]Hadley Cantril and others, "Suggestions for Reversing
the Adverse Trend of Public Opinion on the Administration's
Conduct of Domestic Affairs," July 20, 1943, pp. 2-5, President's Personal File 1820, FDR papers, FDR Library; Millis and
Brown, From the Wagner Act to Taft-Hartley, p. 294; Polenberg,
War and Society, p. 165; Young, Congressional Politics, pp. 58,
63; Garson, Democratic Party and Politics of Sectionalism,
pp. 38-39.

[81]See "Memo on Bills Now Pending Before the Senate Education and Labor Committee with Respect to Strikes," n.d., box
607, Taft papers, Library of Congress.

was packed with Administration partisans and had blocked similar measures in the past. The Judiciary Committee, more favorable to anti-strike legislation, by an almost unanimous vote recommended passage of the Connally Bill. That measure provided for government seizure of strike-bound plants and mines, and contained strong penalties for interference with war production. The Connally Bill was not entirely suited to the situation in the coal fields, but the Labor Committee seemed unlikely to report out a more appropriate substitute.[82]

On April 29, the Senate began debate on the proposed legislation. Senator Robert A. Taft (R., O.), speaking for those who wanted a stronger bill, introduced amendments for that purpose. Senator Connally cautioned that his proposal deliberately avoided "covering all the ground of labor unions and strikes. . . . We could never succeed in passing it." Disregarding Connally's admonition, Taft attempted to amend the bill so that court injunctions could be used against strikes.[83] The Senate, though angry at organized labor, was not ready to go that far and defeated the Taft amendment, 34-45.[84] Majority leader Alben Barkley (D., Ky.) thought the bill was still too severe even without the Taft amendment. The Connally Bill was "rigid anti-strike legislation," he told the Senate and asked his colleagues not to act "in anger."[85]

The crucial test came on Senator Burton K. Wheeler's motion to recommit the Connally Bill. The motion failed, 27-52. Seventeen non-Southern Democrats, 9 Republicans, and 1 Progressive voted to kill the Connally Bill, while 25 Republicans (74 percent of those voting), 17 Southern Democrats (100 percent of those voting) and 10 non-Southern Democrats (37 percent of those voting) favored passage. The strongest support for the bill came from the southern, plains and midwestern states, the predominantly agricultural areas of the country. Senators from those states cast 33 votes in favor of anti-strike legislation and only 5 votes for recommital. Even southern New Dealers like Senators Claude Pepper (D., Fla.),

---

[82]Congressional Record, 78th Congress, 1st Session, pp. 3767, 3903; Millis and Brown, From the Wagner Act to Taft-Hartley, pp. 298, 354; Young, Congressional Politics, p. 63.

[83]Congressional Record, 78th Congress, 1st Session, pp. 3768, 3886, 3983-3984; Millis and Brown, From the Wagner Act to Taft-Hartley, p. 354.

[84]For Senate roll call vote on Taft amendment, see Congressional Record, 78th Congress, 1st Session, p. 3984.

[85]Congressional Record, 78th Congress, 1st Session, p. 3889.

Lister Hill (D., Ala.) and Allen Ellender (D., La.) voted for the bill. Most of the resistance to the measure came from the urban industrial Northeast. Senators from New England and mid-Atlantic states cast 10 votes for recommital and 8 for passage.[86]

On May 5, the Senate, by a vote of 63-16, gave final approval to the Connally Bill. That outcome elated anti-labor members in the House, who realized that punitive legislation could at last be enacted. The House had passed anti-union bills in June 1940 and December 1941, but the Senate had refused to consider them. Now the Senate had acted. Opposition leaders in the House moved quickly to pass their own bill. They made sure that the "friends of labor" were given no opportunity to obstruct the legislative process.[87] Speaker Sam Rayburn (D., Tex.) obligingly referred the Connally Bill to the House Military Affairs Committee instead of the Labor Committee. Spurred by Representative Howard W. Smith (D., Va.), anti-labor members wrote a much more drastic bill than the original Connally plant-seizure measure. The House bill contained legal restrictions on the economic and political activities of organized labor, including a prohibition against political contributions by unions that was intended to weaken the influence of labor within the Democratic Party.[88]

Union leaders understood the implications of the pending legislation. Calling for "an end to this war against labor," CIO President Philip Murray asked Congress to reject the Smith-Connally Bill. Such lobbying by union spokesmen enraged Representative Smith, who complained "that the same old labor-leader goon squads who have appeared here so frequently in the past have invaded the Capitol again." The "main features of this bill," he continued, "are the same as the bill that passed this House in December 1941 by a vote of nearly two to one. There were only 136 votes against that bill," he reminded the House, "and of that 136 an even 50 were not reelected to this Seventy-eighth Congress."[89]

---

[86] For Senate roll call vote on the Connally Bill, see Congressional Record, 78th Congress, 1st Session, p. 3983; and Appendix VII, Guttman scaling table 6, item 5. See also Garson, Democratic Party and Politics of Sectionalism, p. 39; and Curry, "Southern Senators and Their Roll-Call Votes in Congress," pp. 254-255.

[87] Congressional Record, 78th Congress, 1st Session, p. 3993; Young, Congressional Politics, p. 64; Riddick, "First Session of the Seventy-Eighth Congress," pp. 308-309.

[88] Congressional Record, 78th Congress, 1st Session, pp. 4076, 4245, 5222-5225; Millis and Brown, From the Wagner Act to Taft Hartley, p. 355; Polenberg, War and Society, p. 167; Young, Congressional Politics, pp. 64-65.

[89] Quotations from Congressional Record, 78th Congress, 1st Session, pp. 3969, 5225.

On June 4, the House passed the Smith Bill, 233-141. One hundred thirty-three Republicans (73 percent of those voting), 80 Southern Democrats (94 percent of those voting), and 20 non-Southern Democrats (19 percent of those voting) favored the measure, while 83 non-Southern Democrats, 49 Republicans, 5 Southern Democrats, and 4 minor party members opposed it. The sectional alignment paralleled that in the Senate. Representatives from agricultural districts in southern, plains, mountain, and midwestern states voted in overwhelming numbers for the Smith Bill. A majority of those from the urban industrial Northeast voted against it.[90]

House and Senate conferees agreed to a compromise version of the Smith-Connally Bill that contained three major provisions: a thirty-day strike notice in private plants, coupled with a strike referendum conducted by the National Labor Relations Board; prohibition of strikes in government-seized plants or mines; and prohibition of political contributions by unions.[91] The bill then went to the President. On June 25, he vetoed it. Roosevelt assured Congress that he was "unalterably opposed to strikes in wartime" and would have signed the Smith-Connally Bill if it did not contain "other provisions which have no place in legislation to prevent strikes in wartime and which in fact would foment slow-downs and strikes." He predicted, accurately, that strike votes would stimulate labor unrest, not curtail it. The President also questioned the propriety of the ban on political contributions by labor organizations. "This provision," he declared, "obviously has no relevancy to a bill prohibiting strikes during the war in the plants operated by the government."[92]

On the same day that Roosevelt returned the Smith-Connally Bill without his signature, the House and Senate overrode his veto. Like the initial passage of the Smith-Connally Act, the motion to override carried because members from southern, plains, and midwestern states favored the bill by an overwhelming margin. The votes of those members reflected the feelings of their rural and small town constituents whose patriotic sensibilities had been offended by the coal strikes and who believed

---

[90] For House roll call vote on the Smith Bill, see Congressional Record, 78th Congress, 1st Session, pp. 5391-5392; and Appendix VI, Guttman scaling table 3, item 14. See also Young, Congressional Politics, p. 65.

[91] Millis and Brown, From the Wagner Act to Taft-Hartley, p. 355; Young, Congressional Politics, p. 65.

[92] Rosenman, Public Papers and Addresses of FDR 12: 1943, pp. 268-272; Polenberg, War and Society, pp. 167-168; Garson, Democratic Party and Politics of Sectionalism, p. 40.

that labor had received preferential treatment while farmers
had been slighted by the Roosevelt Administration. In part, at
least, the Smith-Connally Act was agriculture's revenge for
labor's insistence on farm price control and for the resort to the
strike in wartime.[93]

The act of revenge yielded mixed results. It was based on
the mistaken premise that irresponsible union leaders foisted
strikes on reluctant workers. In reality, labor leaders during
World War II strove to restrain union members who frequently
wanted to strike. If the Smith-Connally Act had any effect on
wartime labor disputes, it probably invited more strikes than
it prevented. The Smith-Connally Act was significant, however,
as a way-station on the road from the Wagner Act toward a national labor policy less favorable to unions. That road ended
in 1947 with the passage by a Republican Congress of the Taft-
Hartley Act, which embodied most of the proposals offered since
1939 to "equalize" labor policy in favor of business.[94]

Non-War Spending: NYA and FSA

As the campaign against reformers and labor crested, so too
did the effort to curtail non-war spending. Reduction of such
spending had proved an effective method of terminating New Deal
programs that members of the opposition wanted "dropped, not
only for the duration of the war, but forever after."[95] In
1942, the President's adversaries had drawn first blood by
abolishing the Civilian Conservation Corps. In 1943, they aimed
at the National Youth Administration and the Farm Security Administration. The debate over those agencies involved more than
the issue of non-war spending. The larger question was whether
NYA and FSA would survive to play a part in the Administration's
postwar program.[96]

[93]For House and Senate roll call votes to override the
President's veto, see Congressional Record, 78th Congress, 1st
Session, pp. 6489, 6548-6549; Appendix VI, Guttman scaling table
3, item 11; Appendix VII, Guttman scaling table 6, item 4; and
Curry, "Southern Senators and Their Roll-Call Votes in Congress,"
pp. 254-255.

[94]Millis and Brown, From the Wagner Act to Taft-Hartley,
pp. 298-299, 353, 356; Polenberg, War and Society, pp. 168-170.

[95]John Taber to Ray P. Chase, January 15, 1942, box 87,
Taber papers, Cornell University Library.

[96]Congressional Record, 77th Congress, 2nd Session, p. A4291;
New York Times, December 12, 1942, p. 34; Washington Post, Decem-
ber 12, 1942, p. 4; Garson, Democratic Party and Politics of
Sectionalism, pp. 35-36; Young, Congressional Politics, p. 24.

At Roosevelt's direction, the Bureau of the Budget had already made significant reductions in non-war spending. Though
the Byrd Committee insisted that "the possibilities for economies have been no more than scratched," a Budget Bureau report
showed that controllable spending had declined from approximately $5 billion in fiscal 1939 to about $2.5 billion in fiscal 1943. According to the Bureau's figures, 95 cents of every
dollar expended by the Federal government in fiscal 1943 went
toward the war effort. Only 5 cents of each dollar was spent
on non-war items.[97]

The President, describing the report to the press, said
that it demonstrated "the important reductions that have been
made."[98] Not everyone was convinced. Republicans accused the
Bureau of the Budget of classifying "nonessential" items as war
expenditures in order to make reductions appear larger than they
were. The report, concluded Representative George Bender (R.,
O.), was a "whitewash" intended to mislead Congress and the
country about the true extent of non-war spending.[99] The Citizens Emergency Committee on Nondefense Expenditures, which
lobbied for drastic retrenchment during the war years, voiced
similar criticisms.[100]

Roosevelt's budget message of January 6, 1943, kept the
debate alive. The President offered "to cooperate with the
Congress in effecting further reductions" in non-war expenditures.

---

[97] Quotation from U.S., Congress, Joint Committee on Reduc-
tion of Nonessential Federal Expenditures, Supplement Report,
S. Doc. 152, 77th Congress, 2nd Session, 1942, p. 5. See also
Bureau of the Budget, "Trends in Nonwar Federal Expenditures,"
October 15, 1942, General Records of the Director, series 39.27,
box 37, Records of the Bureau of the Budget, Record Group 51,
National Archives; and Harold D. Smith to President, October 15,
1942, General Records of the Director, series 39.27, box 37,
Records of the Bureau of the Budget, Record Group 51, National
Archives.

[98] Roosevelt, Complete Presidential Press Conferences
19-20: 1942, p. 20: 148.

[99] Congressional Record, 78th Congress, 1st Session, p. 618.

[100] Harold D. Smith to President, November 17, 1942, Presi-
dent's Official File 79, FDR papers, FDR Library; Harold D.
Smith to President, December 9, 1942, General Records of the
Director, series 39.27, box 37, Records of the Bureau of the
Budget, Record Group 51, National Archives; Harold D. Smith to
Henry M. Wriston, December 17, 1942, General Records of the Di-
rector, series 39.27, box 37, Records of Bureau of the Budget,
Record Group 51, National Archives.

He cautioned, however, "that we are fast approaching the subsistence level of government--the minimum for sustaining orderly social and economic progress. . . ."[101] Again the President's adversaries expressed doubt that non-war expenditures had been reduced to a minimum. Many of those opponents, interpreting the recent election results as a call for cessation "of New Deal social reform," argued that non-war spending should be further curtailed to carry out that mandate. "We all know," Representative John Taber (R., N.Y.) told the House on February 4, 1943, "that non-defense appropriations have run absolutely wild."[102]

Representative Taber, Senator Byrd, Senator McKellar and other proponents of retrenchment had repeatedly urged abolition of the National Youth Administration. Established by executive order on June 26, 1935, NYA had furnished financial aid that enabled thousands of indigent young people to continue their secondary and college educations. The Youth Administration also provided vocational training and work experience to assist young persons who had dropped out of school and could not find employment. The advent of the defense program forced NYA, like other relief agencies, to reorient its program. Roosevelt and his advisors decided to utilize NYA facilities to train young workers for jobs in armament plants.[103] As defense training expanded, the President and the Budget Director agreed that regular NYA activities, like the school aid and the out-of-school programs, should be phased out. That decision dismayed the friends of NYA in Congress. Despite their protests, Roosevelt declined to continue regular NYA programs at previous levels of funding. He argued that the draft and increased employment in defense industries would reduce the need for NYA assistance,

---

[101] Rosenman, Public Papers and Addresses of FDR 12: 1943, pp. 16-17.

[102] Quotations from Wayne Coy to Charles H. Crandon, November 30, 1942, General Records of the Director, series 39.27, box 37, Records of the Bureau of the Budget, Record Group 51, National Archives; and Congressional Record, 78th Congress, 1st Session, p. 618. See also Harold D. Smith to President, February 15, 1943, President's Official File 79, FDR papers, FDR Library.

[103] Franklin D. Roosevelt, Complete Presidential Press Conferences of Franklin D. Roosevelt, vols. 15-16: 1940 (New York, 1972), pp. 15: 402-403; Owen D. Young to Sidney Hillman, July 10, 1940, President's Personal File 61, FDR papers, FDR Library; U.S., Congress, Senate, Committee on Appropriations, Hearings Before the Subcommittee of the Committee on Appropriations on Department of Labor-Federal Security Agency Appropriation Act of 1944, 78th Congress, 1st Session, 1943, p. 218.

a prediction borne out by subsequent events.[104]

The demise of regular NYA activities caused supporters of the agency to worry that it might be completely dismantled.[105] The President tried to allay their fears. On January 3, 1942, he wrote that NYA had "made contributions to the development of American youth of such magnitude that we must conserve for use in the post-war period the experience and wisdom" accumulated by that agency.[106] Roosevelt intended to preserve NYA for a postwar youth program, but he realized the agency was "touchy with those who were advocating the clipping of so-called non-war agencies." In a discussion with Budget Director Smith on May 1, 1942, the President rejected the training of "persons not directly concerned with the war effort." Integration of NYA into the war program offered the best chance to retain the agency for it would answer the objections of Congressional econo-mizers while maintaining the administrative structure of the agency.[107]

Confining NYA to defense training deflected efforts to abolish the agency in 1942. The future of the Youth Adminis-tration, however, remained in doubt. Some Congressional critics complained that the President had merely reclassified the agency's relief program as war work. Others charged that NYA had moved into a new field, manpower training, without regard for legal authority.[108] The agency had other troubles as well.

---

[104]Ross A. Collins to President, March 7, 1941, President to Ross A. Collins, April 16, 1941, and John W. McCormack and others to President, October 24, 1941, President's Official File 444-d, FDR papers, FDR Library.

[105]Owen D. Young to President, December 23, 1941, Presi-dent's Official File 444-d, FDR papers, FDR Library.

[106]President to Owen D. Young, January 3, 1942, Presi-dent's Official File 444-d, FDR papers, FDR Library.

[107]Harold D. Smith, Memorandum of Conference with the President, May 1, 1942, Smith papers, FDR Library.

[108]Congressional Record, 77th Congress, 2nd Session, p. 4914; U.S., Congress, Senate, Committee on Appropriations, Hearings Before the Subcommittee of the Committee on Appropria-tions on Department of Labor-Federal Security Agency Appropria-tion Act of 1944, 78th Congress, 1st Session, 1943, p. 221; Henry Morgenthau, Jr., to Elbert D. Thomas, March 21, 1942, President's Official File 444-d, FDR papers, FDR Library; Polen-berg, War and Society, pp. 81-82; Sullivan, Bureaucracy Runs Amuck, p. 18.

In its struggle to survive, the Youth Administration encountered the persistent hostility of the education lobby in Washington. Educators had generally welcomed the NYA school aid program, but they condemned the agency's vocational training activities as competitive with the public schools' "established vocational program."[109] When the Byrd Committee urged abolition of NYA in its initial report of December 24, 1941, the education establishment eagerly endorsed that recommendation. Professional educators did not want funding of vocational training reduced but wanted money earmarked for NYA funneled instead through the Federal Office of Education into local school districts.[110]

The educators' "campaign against NYA" caused Aubrey Williams, head of the Youth Administration, to complain in April 1942 that "the most sinister thing we face is that the school crowd is determined to either get control of our whole development or to destroy it." Williams believed that the public schools were insensitive to the special problems of impoverished young blacks and women. Those groups, traditionally the last to be hired by private industry, now constituted the clientele of NYA and Williams was sure they would once again be ignored if the Youth Administration were eliminated. In his view, NYA served two equally vital purposes. It provided war production training and assistance to the disadvantaged. Both functions, he argued, justified continuation of the agency.[111]

Toward the end of 1942, a rapidly changing manpower situation forced the Roosevelt Administration to reassess the role of NYA. The draft, combined with the burgeoning demand for workers, had depleted the reservoir of young unemployed. Enrollment in the war training program had stabilized and seemed likely to decline in 1943. Bureau of the Budget officials

---

[109] Quotation from New York Times, September 22, 1940, p. 11. See also Owen D. Young to President, July 10, 1940, President's Personal File 61, FDR papers, FDR Library; and Harold D. Smith to C. A. Towle, October 17, 1940, General Records of the Director, series 39.27, box 43, Records of the Bureau of the Budget, Record Group 51, National Archives.

[110] New York Times, October 9, 1941, p. 25, December 26, 1941, p. 1, March 25, 1942, p. 18.

[111] Williams to President, April 15, 1942, President's Official File 444-d, FDR papers, FDR Library. See also Aubrey Williams, "Comment of Mr. Aubrey Williams, NYA Administrator, on the Report of the Joint Committee on Reduction of Nonessential Expenditures Relating to the National Youth Administration," n.d., entry 17, "Campaign Against NYA," Records of the National Youth Administration, Record Group 119, National Archives.

became increasingly skeptical about the agency's usefulness.[112]
On March 17, 1943, Budget Director Smith advised the President
to seek no appropriation for NYA. Industry was "hiring people
without background and was training them in specific operations
in the plants," Smith said. "The pressure on production had
changed the whole aspect of pre-employment training." But
Roosevelt overruled Smith and directed that a sum be included
in the fiscal 1944 budget for continued operation of the National Youth Administration.[113]

As the President expected, that request caused "a lot of
trouble on the Hill."[114] Roosevelt's adversaries voiced their
standard charges about profligate non-war spending. To no one's
surprise, the Byrd Committee and the National Education Association reiterated their earlier recommendation that NYA be terminated immediately. Influenced by Representative Taber and
Senator McKellar, the House and Senate Appropriations Committees voted to delete funds for NYA from the Labor-Federal
Security Appropriation Bill.[115]

The agency's friends still hoped to salvage the appropriation on the Senate floor. Senator Harry S Truman (D., Mo.)
introduced an amendment providing approximately $45,000,000 for
NYA war production training in fiscal 1944.[116] On June 28, the
Senate took up the Truman amendment. Adopting a strategy suggested earlier by the President, Administration supporters
avoided any discussion of the role of the Youth Administration

---

[112]Aubrey Williams to Eleanor Roosevelt, October 13, 1942,
and W. J. Rogers to Wayne Coy, October 30, 1942, General Records of the Director, series 39.27, box 43, Records of the
Bureau of the Budget, Record Group 51, National Archives;
Aubrey Williams to President, December 28, 1942, and Paul
McNutt to President, March 26, 1943, President's Official File
444-d, FDR papers, FDR Library.

[113]Harold D. Smith, Memorandum of Conference with the
President, March 17, 1943, Smith papers, FDR Library.

[114]Harold D. Smith, Memorandum of Conference with the President, March 17, 1943, Smith papers, FDR Library.

[115]Washington Post, December 11, 1942, p. 14; U.S., Con-
gress, Joint Committee on Reduction of Nonessential Federal
Expenditures, Additional Report, S. Doc. 54, 78th Congress, 1st
Session, 1943, pp. 1-12; Willard E. Givens to State Education
Associations, May 27, 1943, entry 17, "Campaign Against NYA,"
Records of the National Youth Administration, Record Group 119,
National Archives.

[116]Congressional Record, 78th Congress, 1st Session, pp.
6578-6580.

after the war. Instead they concentrated on the agency's contribution to war production.[117] Senator Scott Lucas (D., Ill.)
assured his colleagues that NYA may have "started out as a relief organization, it is true; but it has developed into a real
war effort organization." Opponents retorted that NYA had outlived its usefulness and unless abolished by Congress "would be
with us forever." Some critics complained that NYA recruited
youths needed in rural areas as farm laborers. Other members
opposed the agency because they distrusted its chief, Aubrey
Williams, characterized by Senator Bennett C. Clark (D., Mo.)
as "the same communist who was head of N.Y.A. when it started."
As Senator Robert M. La Follette observed, most enemies of the
Youth Administration could not "dissociate themselves from any
prejudices which they may have had against the past program."[118]
By a close vote, the Senate approved the Truman amendment,
41-37.[119]

The Senate had given NYA a reprieve, but it was only momen-
tary, for opposition to the Youth Administration was much stronger
in the House. A few border state Democrats, like Representatives
Mike Monroney (D., Okla.) and Jennings Randolph (D., W.Va.),
accused the agency of enticing "from the farm and rural districts
the boys who are so vitally needed to produce the food we need
to win this war." The large number of young blacks and women
enrolled in the NYA training program offended some members. Others
thought the agency, even if it were contributing to the war effort,
should not be continued into the postwar period. As Representative Charles A. Eaton (R., N.J.) said, he did not want to preserve social reform under "starry-eyed nincompoops" like Aubrey
Williams.[120] A majority of House members agreed, for on July 1
they rejected the Truman amendment, 176-197. NYA supporters included 82 non-Southern Democrats, 66 Southern Democrats, 24
Republicans, and 4 minor party members, while 161 Republicans
(87 percent of those voting), 26 Southern Democrats (28 percent
of those voting), and 10 non-Southern Democrats (11 percent of
those voting) opposed the agency. That roll call killed the
Youth Administration. House-Senate conferees dropped the item

---

[117] Harold D. Smith, Memorandum of Conference with the
President, March 17, 1943, Smith papers, FDR Library.

[118] Quotations from Congressional Record, 78th Congress,
1st Session, pp. 6597-6598, 6605, 6608, 6613, 6617.

[119] For Senate roll call vote on Truman amendment, see Congressional Record, 78th Congress, 1st Session, p. 6637; and
Appendix VIII, Guttman scaling table 6, item 2.

[120] Quotations from Congressional Record, 78th Congress,
1st Session, pp. 6956-6957, 6963. See also Polenberg, War
and Society, pp. 82-83.

from the appropriation bill.[121]

To some extent, the debate over NYA involved shadowboxing by those on both sides of the issue. The agency's friends wanted to retain the Youth Administration because it might be needed to deal with unemployment among youth at the end of the war. Fearing that the Congressional opposition would automatically reject a postwar youth program, the Administration and its supporters tried to justify continuation of the agency because of its real, though not crucial, contribution to war production.

In the same fashion, the enemies of NYA argued that the agency should be abolished to economize on government expenditures. Yet the liquidation of the agency saved no money. The funds that would have gone to the Youth Administration were subsequently appropriated for the Federal Office of Education.[122] Apparently, pressure exerted by the education lobby and Congressional unwillingness to continue a reform agency were the real reasons for termination of the National Youth Administration, not the wish to economize. As Representative Estes Kefauver explained, the vote on NYA was "a portent of the future," a test of Congressional attitudes toward postwar public policy.[123] Republicans and anti-Administration Democrats were determined to prevent any postwar revival of New Deal reforms.[124]

NYA was not the only agency either wholly or partially destroyed by the Congressional opposition in 1943. The Farm Security Administration, already crippled by its enemies, underwent similar treatment. In July, the opposition successfully inflicted disabling reductions in the agency's funds and forced the resignation of Administrator C. B. "Beanie" Baldwin. New Dealers warned the President that the destruction of Farm Security would allow corporate and large scale commercial farmers to dominate postwar American agriculture. They pleaded with

---

[121]For House roll call vote on the Truman amendment, see Congressional Record, 78th Congress, 1st Session, p. 6969; and Appendix VI, Guttman scaling table 1, item 22. See also Riddick, "First Session of the Seventy-Eighth Congress," p. 315.

[122]Morgenthau Diary, vol. 716, p. 137, FDR Library.

[123]Congressional Record, 78th Congress, 1st Session, p. 6948.

[124]Thomas L. Stokes, "The Congress," in Jack Goodman, ed., While You Were Gone: A Report on Wartime Life in the United States (New York, 1946), p. 147; Harvey, "The Politics of Politics," pp. 315-316; Polenberg, War and Society, pp. 83-84; Curry, "Southern Senators and Their Roll-Call Votes in Congress," p. 235.

him to fight for a continuation of the New Deal for small farmers. But Roosevelt would not expend his dwindling influence
with Congress in a major battle over FSA. Even if he had done
so, he probably would have been defeated by the intransigent
opposition that he now faced on domestic issues.[125]

To all the Congressional attacks on domestic agencies, the
President offered little more than token resistance. Undoubtedly he would have been pleased if the National Youth Administration had survived to become part of a postwar program for
disadvantaged youth. So, too, he favored continuation of the
Farm Security Administration. But his attention was riveted on
the problems of global war and he was reluctant to push hard
for preservation of NYA and FSA lest he stir up "a hornet's
nest in the Congress." Yet Roosevelt had not "turned his back
on all that the New Deal represented."[126] At the end of the
war, he intended reformist voices to speak again. Already he
was planning to rescue Aubrey Williams from his wartime exile by
appointing him head of the Rural Electrification Administration.
For the time being, however, his primary concern still remained
winning the war as speedily as possible.[127]

The Struggle Over Postwar Planning

"The ground-swell which has been notable up to date has now
developed into a fairly heavy sea," wrote one government official about the Congressional onslaught against the Roosevelt Administration. He predicted that "we may soon have a storm on

[125]Gardner Jackson to President, December 16, 1942, Presi-
dent's Official File 899, FDR papers, FDR Library; Jonathan
Daniels to President, June 14, 1943, and James M. Barnes to
President, June 19, 1943, President's Secretary's File 147, FDR
papers, FDR Library; Sidney Baldwin, Poverty and Politics: The
Rise and Decline of the Farm Security Administration (Chapel
Hill, N.C., 1968), pp. 383-394; Alfred D. Stedman, "The Poli-
tics of the Farmers in Wartime," in Ray F. Harvey and others,
The Politics of This War (New York, 1943), p. 163; Polenberg,
War and Society, pp. 85-86; Perrett, Days of Sadness, p. 406.

[126]Quotations from Harold D. Smith, Memorandum of Conference with the President, March 17, 1943, Smith papers, FDR
Library; and Baldwin, Poverty and Politics, p. 366.

[127]Jonathan Daniels to President, September 6, 1943, Presi-
dent's Official File 444-d, FDR papers, FDR Library; Joseph P.
Lash, Eleanor and Franklin (New York, 1973), p. 896; Garson,
Democratic Party and Politics of Sectionalism, p. 31; Perrett,
Days of Sadness, p. 287.

our hands of gale or even hurricane proportions."[128] Even some
Republicans feared that the Congressional opposition had gone
too far in its "zeal toward economy and disrupting New Deal agencies." Such actions "may be excessive and in the end injurious,"
observed one GOP Congressman.[129] In 1943, the Congressional
"hurricane" struck one more agency, the National Resources Planning Board. The struggle over the Board revealed, better than
did any other episode, the true nature of the conflict between
the Roosevelt Administration and its domestic opposition.

The National Resources Planning Board had become part of
the Executive Office of the President on July 1, 1939. The
agency, like its predecessor, the National Resources Committee,
performed long-range research on development of natural and
human resources. Under the general supervision of three Board
members, Frederic A. Delano, Charles E. Merriam, and George F.
Yantis, the technical divisions of NRPB carried on engineering
planning for water, land and energy development, housing,
transportation, and public works construction.[130]

Equally important, the Board served as a clearing house for
compensatory spenders who advocated expansionary fiscal policy
designed to achieve both full recovery and a greater share of
national income for the lower third of society. With NRPB as
their chief vehicle, Keynesian reformers exerted a telling influence on Federal fiscal policy even after defeat of their
offspring, the Self-Liquidating Projects Bill of 1939.[131]

[128]Ganson Purcell to President, June 5, 1943, President's
Personal File 1820, FDR papers, FDR Library.

[129]Polenberg, War and Society, p. 84.

[130]Frederic A. Delano to President, September 5, 1939,
General Records of the Director, series 39.27, box 35, Records
of the Bureau of the Budget, Record Group 51, National Archives;
Morgenthau Diary, vol. 485, pp. 413-417, FDR Library; Philip W.
Warken, "A History of the National Resources Planning Board,
1933-1943" (Ph.D. dissertation, Ohio State University, 1969),
pp. 106-134; Charles E. Merriam, "The National Resources Planning Board; A Chapter in American Planning Experience," American
Political Science Review XXXVIII (1944), pp. 1075-1078.

[131]Harold D. Smith, Daily Memoranda, July 6, 1939, September 8, 1939, November 24, 1939, October 23, 1940, Smith
papers, FDR Library; Charles W. Eliot to Harold D. Smith, May
17, 1941, General Records of the Director, series 39.27, box
35, Records of the Bureau of the Budget, Record Group 51, National Archives; Harold D. Smith, Memoranda of Conferences with
the President, March 4, 1941, March 4, 1942, Smith papers,
FDR Library; Warken, "History of NRPB," pp. 188-190; Byrd L.
Jones, "The Role of Keynesians in Wartime Policy and Postwar
Planning," American Economic Review LXII (May 1972), p. 127;
Mary H. Hinchey, "The Frustration of the New Deal Revival, 1944-
1946" (Ph.D. dissertation, University of Missouri, 1965), pp. 2-3.

With the outbreak of war in Europe, the National Resources Planning Board undertook research projects related to defense and war needs. The President, however, did not want the Board bogged down in wartime decision-making on prices, production, priorities, and the like. Instead, he instructed the NRPB, as the planning arm of the Executive Office of the President, to prepare plans and programs for the post-defense and postwar periods. Beginning in late 1939, the Board responded with postwar plans for full employment, social security, and "upbuilding America," which included conservation of resources, construction of needed public works, and the provision of public services for the welfare of the American people.[132]

The Board imbued its postwar planning with the philosophy of reform derived from the New Deal. Roosevelt's domestic policies, the officials of the Board believed, pointed to a new bill of social and economic rights for the American people. On August 19, 1939, the Board listed "some of the new rights of a socially-minded democracy,"

1. The Right to Educational Opportunity
2. The Right to Health and Medical Care
3. The Right to Decent Shelter--minimum housing standards for the "ill-housed"
4. The Right to Work--opportunity for employment and for profit
5. The Right to Security--particularly a long-range relief policy[133]

---

[132]Harold D. Smith, Daily Memoranda, August 18, 1939, September 5, 1939, Smith papers, FDR Library; Frederic A. Delano to President, August 25, 1939, and September 5, 1939, minutes of meeting of September 4, 1939, 103.71, box 218, Records of NRPB, Record Group 187, National Archives; George F. Yantis, "Notes on Conference with the President at the White House, Wednesday, September 6, 1939, at Noon," minutes of meeting of September 4, 1939, 103.71, box 218, Records of NRPB, Record Group 187, National Archives; "Report of Conference of National Resources Planning Board with the President at the White House," October 17, 1939, General Records of the Director, series 39.27, Records of the Bureau of the Budget, Record Group 51, National Archives; Frederic A. Delano to President, June 15, 1940, minutes of meeting of June 12-14, 1940, 103.71, box 222, Records of NRPB, Record Group 187, National Archives; Warken, "History of NRPB," p. 185.

[133]Frederic A. Delano to President, August 19, 1939, minutes of meeting of August 19, 1939, 103.71, box 218, Records of NRPB, Record Group 187, National Archives. See also Merriam, "National Resources Planning Board," pp. 1079-1080.

In its various formulations, the economic bill of rights embodied the commitment of NRPB to a more equitable distribution
of wealth. Like Roosevelt's "freedom from want," and Vice
President Wallace's "economic democracy," the objectives established by the Board constituted the unfinished agenda of reform.[134]

Meanwhile, the enormous Federal deficits required by defense, lend-lease, and war had produced the recovery that eluded
the New Deal. Indeed, after the fall of France in June 1940,
Keynesian economists associated with NRPB had urged all-out preparedness precisely because Federal expenditures would drive
the economy toward full capacity production. The booming prosperity of the war years substantiated their theories. They became more convinced than ever that properly managed Federal
fiscal policy could sustain full employment in the postwar
years. NRPB planning for the period after the war combined
faith in compensatory fiscal policy with a resolve to provide a
wider share in prosperity for the one-third of a nation ill-
housed, ill-clad and ill-nourished.[135]

Postwar planning by the National Resources Planning Board
proceeded slowly because of internal friction and external pressures. Frederic A. Delano, the chairman, had an impressive
background as a city and regional planner. But Delano, 72 years
of age in 1939, lacked the energy to exercise strong leadership.
Charles E. Merriam, political scientist at the University of
Chicago, emerged as the dominant figure on the Board. Merriam
favored long-term "pre-planning." In his view, NRPB should
serve as a "think-tank" for the Federal government. That position brought him into conflict with Charles W. Eliot, the executive director, who favored practical planning that would shape

---

[134]Charles W. Eliot, "Planning the Use of Our Resources,"
July 9, 1940, minutes of meeting of July 9, 1940, 103.71, box
222, Records of NRPB, Record Group 187, National Archives; Frederic A. Delano to President, July 31, 1940, and Charles E. Merriam, "Memorandum on Democracy and Planning in Crisis," July 31,
1940, minutes of meeting of July 29-31, 1940, 103.71, box 222,
Records of NRPB, Record Group 187, National Archives.

[135]See Mordecai Ezekiel, "Statement before the Temporary
National Economic Committee," Correspondence, 1935-1942, AD-071,
box 55, Records of the Farm Security Administration, Record Group
96, National Archives; Alvin H. Hansen, "Post-Defense Full Employment," May 14, 1941, General Records of the Director, series
39.27, box 35, Records of the Bureau of the Budget, Record Group
51, National Archives; Charles W. Eliot to Harold D. Smith, May
17, 1941, and Frederic A. Delano to President, December 4, 1941,
General Records of the Director, series 39.27, box 35, Records
of the Bureau of the Budget, Record Group 51, National Archives. See also Jones, "Role of Keynesians," pp. 125-126.

current policies and programs. Their disagreements limited
the Board's effectiveness as the central planning agency of
the executive branch.[136]

External pressures also hindered NRPB. Many of the executive departments conducted their own planning projects and resented the intrusion of the Board into their domains. NRPB
tried to overcome that resistance by closely coordinating its
research activities with those of the operating agencies. But
jealousy of the Board persisted.[137]

The most serious difficulty faced by the Board was opposition on Capitol Hill, especially from the pork-barrel bloc in
Congress. Traditionally, Congressmen selected public works
projects for their political value. Members voted for each
other's projects and then campaigned for reelection on their
ability to bring Federal money into their home states and districts. The Army Corps of Engineers, which supervised the construction of most river and harbor improvements, became a powerful ally and beneficiary of the pork-barrel bloc.[138]

The National Resources Planning Board considered the pork-
barrel method of public works construction wasteful and hap-
hazard. Concurring in that view, the President attempted to
curb the activities of the Army Corps of Engineers. He directed
NRPB to review proposed public works projects and to allocate
construction on the basis of utility and long-term value, instead of politics. The pork-barrel bloc resented the Board's
veto over Corps' projects and worked unceasingly to destroy
NRPB.[139]

---

[136]Harold D. Smith, Daily Memoranda, May 21, 1940, May 29,
1940, Smith papers, FDR Library; Harold D. Smith, Memorandum of
Conference with the President, June 3, 1943, Smith papers, FDR
Library; Barry D. Karl, Executive Reorganization and Reform in
the New Deal (Cambridge, Mass., 1963), pp. 50, 74; Arthur M.
Schlesinger, Jr., The Coming of the New Deal (Cambridge, Mass.,
1965), pp. 351-352; Warken, "History of NRPB," pp. 45-46.

[137]Schlesinger, Coming of the New Deal, p. 352; Warken,
"History of NRPB," pp. 66, 68-70, 106-107, 126-129; Merriam,
"National Resources Planning Board," pp. 1077, 1081.

[138]Warken, "History of NRPB," pp. 98-100.

[139]Congressional Record, 76th Congress, 3rd Session, pp.
4456-4457; John J. Cochran to President, February 8, 1939, President's Official File 1092, FDR papers, FDR Library; Harold D.
Smith, Daily Memoranda, January 29, 1940, February 29, 1940,
Smith papers, FDR Library; Charles W. Eliot to Frederic A. Delano
and others, February 27, 1940, minutes of meeting of March 2-3,
1940, 103.71, box 221, Records of NRPB, Record Group 187,

Congressional hostility toward the Board also arose from a general distrust of planning. The business community and its spokesmen in Congress believed that public planning was incompatible with private enterprise. Moreover, they correctly perceived the NRPB as an engine of reform and the chief locus of the new economics. For those reasons, they misconstrued the program of the Board as either socialism or communism. Because NRPB advocated a hybrid economy, a mixture of private capitalism and public planning, the members of the Congressional opposition made its dissolution one of their primary objectives during the war years.[140]

With such implacable adversaries on Capitol Hill, the Board had to fight constantly for survival. As was true of other agencies established during the New Deal, Congress had never approved a statute specifically authorizing the existence of NRPB. The Board traced its legislative authority back to the Federal Employment Stabilization Act of 1931, which had created a Federal Employment Stabilization Board to carry out advance planning of public works. The FESB experienced several reorganizations and eventually emerged as the National Resources Committee, the immediate ancestor of the National Resources Planning Board. Congress seemed to recognize the legitimacy of the planning agency when on June 7, 1939, it approved the President's Reorganization Plan One transferring the functions of the National Resources Committee and the old Federal Employment Stabilization Board to NRPB. The lack of a basic statute establishing a Federal planning agency had not proved a handicap while the New Deal was at its zenith, but as the Roosevelt Administration gradually lost control of Congress, NRPB became increasingly exposed to the thrusts of its enemies.[141]

At first, officials of the Board believed their new status as a division of the Executive Office of the President would protect NRPB from Congressional harassment. But in December 1939 the House subcommittee in charge of the Independent Offices Appropriations Bill claimed there was no "basic law authorizing

---

National Archives; Executive Order 8455, June 26, 1940, General Records of the Director, series 39.27, box 35, Records of the Bureau of the Budget, Record Group 51, National Archives; Warken, "History of NRPB," pp. 119-121.

[140]Congressional Record, 78th Congress, 1st Session, pp. 717-721; New York Times, May 3, 1940, p. 14; Warken, "History of NRPB," pp. 231, 240.

[141]U.S., Congress, Senate, Committee on Education and Labor, Hearings Before a Subcommittee of the Committee on Education and Labor on Post-Defense Planning, 77th Congress, 1st Session, 1941, pp. 15-16; George F. Yantis to Louis Brownlow, November 14, 1939, minutes of meeting of November 20-21, 1939,

its existence" and eliminated funds for the agency.[142] That action annoyed Budget Director Smith who told Roosevelt that Congress "should not be permitted to kick the Executive Office
around . . . when Congress sets its budget without any Executive interference."[143] A few days later, the President learned
that the real opposition to NRPB came from the Army Corps of
Engineers, which had been actively lobbying against the Board.
Roosevelt ordered the Army Engineers to cease their meddling
and urged Representative Clifton Woodrum (D., Va.) and Senator
James F. Byrnes (D., S.C.) to restore the NRPB appropriation.
Early in February 1940, the Senate approved $710,000 for the
Board, but the President had to intercede further to gain House
acceptance of the disputed appropriation.[144]

After that contest, the Board realized that the appropriations fight would become an annual event unless Roosevelt could
secure passage of a bill explicitly authorizing the existence

103.71, box 218, Records of NRPB, Record Group 187, National
Archives; Warken, "History of NRPB," pp. 41, 43, 104.

[142]Charles W. Eliot, "Status of Work," January 29, 1940,
minutes of meeting of February 12-13, 1940, 103.71, box 220,
Records of NRPB, Record Group 187, National Archives.

[143]Harold D. Smith to President, January 19, 1940, General
Records of the Director, series 39.27, box 35, Records of the
Bureau of the Budget, Record Group 51, National Archives; Harold
D. Smith, Memoranda of Conferences with the President, January
6, 1940, January 9, 1940, January 16, 1940, January 19, 1940,
January 22, 1940, Smith papers, FDR Library.

[144]Harold D. Smith to President, January 19, 1940, January
26, 1940, General Records of the Director, series 39.27, box 35,
Records of the Bureau of the Budget, Record Group 51, National
Archives; Lauchlin Currie to President, January 22, 1940, President's Secretary's File 95, FDR papers, FDR Library; Harold D.
Smith, Memoranda of Conferences with the President, January 24,
1940, January 25, 1940, January 27, 1940, Smith papers, FDR
Library; Harold D. Smith to President, January 26, 1940, President's Official File 79, FDR papers, FDR Library; Frederic A.
Delano to President, February 8, 1940, February 12, 1940, General Records of the Director, series 39.27, box 35, Records of
the Bureau of the Budget, Record Group 51, National Archives;
"Memorandum of a Conference with the President," February 12,
1940, minutes of meeting of February 12-13, 1940, 103.71, box
220, Records of NRPB, Record Group 187, National Archives; Frederic A. Delano to President, March 4, 1940, and Charles W. Eliot
to Frederic A. Delano, March 4, 1940, minutes of meeting of
March 2-3, 1940, 103.71, box 221, Records of NRPB, Record Group
187, National Archives; E. M. Watson to President, March 14,
1940, President's Secretary's File 187, FDR papers, FDR Library.

of a Federal planning agency.[145]   Assisted by the Bureau of the
Budget, NRPB officials drafted the necessary legislation and
asked the President to seek Congressional approval. Roosevelt
agreed to do so and in 1941 began to press for passage of the
NRPB bill. Both Senate and House Education and Labor Committees, those bastions of New Dealism, recommended passage of
the measure, and on February 19, 1942, the House took up the
NRPB bill.[146]   Its sponsor, Representative Alfred F. Beiter (D.,
N.Y.), explained that the proposed legislation would authorize
yearly appropriations "for the preparation now of plans for public works and related activities to be undertaken in the postwar period." Beiter immediately encountered a fusillade of
criticism from Republicans and renegade Democrats who contended
that the bill "gave the freedom of the seas to any board or
boards of visionary, impractical, star-gazing planners to work
any or all of their rattle-brained ideas in regard to post-war
planning." Members of the rivers and harbors group argued that
the Army Corps of Engineers, not NRPB, should conduct advance
planning for public works construction. Congress had previously
"refused to make this National Resources Planning Board a permanent body," observed Representative William Whittington (D.,
Miss.), and he saw no reason to do so now.[147]   By a vote of
104-252, the House rejected the NRPB bill. Favoring the measure
were 83 non-Southern Democrats, 13 Southern Democrats, 7 Republicans, and 1 minor party member, while 131 Republicans (95
percent of those voting), 74 Southern Democrats (85 percent of
those voting), 45 non-Southern Democrats (35 percent of those
voting) and 2 minor party members opposed it.[148]   The Board

---

[145]Harold D. Smith, Daily Memoranda, November 20, 1939,
Smith papers, FDR Library; Frederic A. Delano to President,
January 20, 1940, minutes of meeting of January 20, 1940, 103.71,
box 220, Records of NRPB, Record Group 187, National Archives;
Frederic A. Delano to President, February 12, 1940, minutes of
meeting of February 12-13, 1940, 103.71, box 220, Records of
NRPB, Record Group 187, National Archives; Frederic A. Delano
to President, December 4, 1941, General Records of the Di-
rector, series 39.27, box 35, Records of the Bureau of the
Budget, Record Group 51, National Archives.

[146]U.S., Congress, Senate, Committee on Education and
Labor, Hearings Before a Subcommittee of the Committee on Edu-
cation and Labor on Post-Defense Planning, 77th Congress, 1st
Session, 1941, pp. 13-46, 103-112; Congressional Record, 77th
Congress, 1st Session, pp. 4924, 7417.

[147]Quotations from Congressional Record, 77th Congress,
2nd Session, pp. 1487, 1491, 1494.

[148]For House roll call vote on the NRPB bill, see Congressional Record, 77th Congress, 2nd Session, pp. 1493-1494; and
Appendix III, Guttman scaling table 4, item 3.

remained a temporary agency totally dependent on the Congressional appropriations committees for authority as well as funds.

The existence of NRPB became more precarious as members of
the Congressional opposition learned about the work being done
by the agency. The Board had established a Post-War Agenda Section that sponsored a series of pamphlets dealing with long-
range social and economic problems. The first of those tracts,
After Defense--What?, published in August 1941, warned that
reconversion to peacetime production might result in another
depression. To avert such a collapse, the pamphlet called for
guaranteed full employment through investment in public works,
redistributive taxation, an expanded social security program,
and other measures designed to enlarge aggregate demand for
goods and services. The volume of private investment, NRPB
planners argued, would not be sufficient to sustain prosperity
after the war, just as it had not been sufficient to produce
recovery in the 1930s. Government "must take a leading part"
in assuring full capacity production.[149]

Ideas outlined in After Defense--What? received fuller
exposition in other publications sponsored by the Board. Among
those was After the War--Full Employment, written by Alvin H.
Hansen, the most prominent American disciple of John Maynard
Keynes and chief economic consultant to NRPB. Demobilization
of the armed forces and cessation of war production, Hansen
predicted, would force 18 to 23 million people to seek peacetime
employment. Unless government stabilized the reconversion process, Hansen feared a reversion to mass unemployment. He urged
a postwar program of sharply progressive corporate and individual taxation, reduced taxes on consumption, public works construction, and public welfare expenditures. Federal deficits
necessary to carry out such a program, said Hansen, would under-
write a high rate of national income and employment.[150]

Though intended to educate the public about the new economics, the Board's publicity may have backfired, for it

---

[149]National Resources Planning Board, After Defense--What?
(Washington, 1941), pp. 1-18, Records of NRPB, Record Group 187,
National Archives. See also Charles W. Eliot to L. C. Martin,
July 30, 1941, General Records of the Director, series 39.27,
box 5, Records of the Bureau of the Budget, Record Group 51,
National Archives; Frederic A. Delano to President, December 4,
1941, General Records of the Director, series 39.27, box 35,
Records of the Bureau of the Budget, Record Group 51, National
Archives; and Warken, "History of NRPB," p. 183.

[150]National Resources Planning Board, After the War--Full
Employment (Washington, 1942), pp. 1-19, Records of NRPB, Record Group 187, National Archives; Warken, "History of NRPB,"
pp. 191-192.

attracted intemperate attacks from critics who distorted the
ideas put forward by NRPB. Orthodox academic economists castigated the Board for proposing a constantly expanding national
debt. They claimed that "very heroic measures in governmental
economic planning and a very heroic spending program" during
the New Deal had failed to cure unemployment. According to
conventional economic theory, Keynesian policies would debauch
the currency, place a crushing tax burden on individual and
corporate wealth, discourage private investment, subject enterprise to excessive state control, and lead ultimately to a collapse of the entire economic system. Instead of relying on
"the philosophy of public debt" to sustain full employment, the
Federal government should balance the budget and reestablish an
institutional and legal framework in which private enterprise
could flourish.[151]

Many businessmen shared that view. In his wartime addresses to the Congress of American Industry, Alfred P. Sloan,
Jr., Chairman of the General Motors Corporation, warned repeatedly that a postwar revival of the New Deal would be cata-
strophic for business interests. Sloan blamed the failure of
recovery during the 1930s on the Roosevelt Administration. The
New Deal's "indiscriminate attacks" on business and its use of
taxing, spending and labor policies to redistribute wealth had
destroyed business confidence and the willingness to invest.
Fortunately, Sloan went on, wartime prosperity had weakened the
New Deal. After the war, private enterprise would have a
second chance to prove that it could provide jobs within a
purely capitalist framework.[152] The success of that effort
would depend on maintenance of government policies that would
benefit business and encourage private investment. Keynesian
policies, Sloan declared, "would mark the beginning of the
end--the end of the American competitive system as we have
known it, the beginning of the socialization of enterprise."[153] That doctrine was preached not only by Sloan,

[151] Quotations from Benjamin M. Anderson, statement on postwar economic planning, n.d., box 663, Taft papers, Library of
Congress; and U.S., Congress, Joint Committee on Reduction of
Nonessential Federal Expenditures, Additional Report, S. Doc. 140,
78th Congress, 1st Session, 1943, p. 7. See also William F. Hau-
hart, "Individual Freedom and Economic Planning," November 11,
1943, box 663, Taft papers, Library of Congress; Myron W. Watkins,
"Post-War Plan and Program," Journal of Political Economy LI
(1943), pp. 397-414; and Warken, "History of NRPB," pp. 192-193.

[152] Alfred P. Sloan, Jr., "Industry's Post-War Responsibilities," Vital Speeches 8 (January 1, 1942), pp. 174-176.

[153] Alfred P. Sloan, Jr., "The Challenge," December 10, 1943,
box 663, Taft papers, Library of Congress. See also Richard M.
Bissel, "The Anatomy of Public Spending," Fortune XXV (May 1942),
pp. 94-95, 114.

but by the National Association of Manufacturers, the National
Industrial Conference Board, and other business organizations
and corporate leaders.[154] Keynesian reform, they insisted,
would lead to "the accomplishment of socialism through the
spending by the government of all of the savings of all of the
people." The alternative they preferred was "the American system of free enterprise," the political economy of the 1920s.[155]

Other businessmen, like Beardsley Ruml of R. H. Macy Co.
and Eric A. Johnston, President of the United States Chamber of
Commerce, doubted that a return to the political economy of the
Harding-Coolidge-Hoover years was either possible or desirable.
Those corporate leaders, represented by the Department of Commerce and such private organizations as the newly-established
Committee for Economic Development, accepted the need for government deficits to maintain a high level of economic activity
after the war.[156] The business Keynesians welcomed Federal
expenditures and particularly tax reductions that would subsidize private enterprise and guarantee profits. In their view,
Keynesian policy could be adapted to preserve a healthy capitalist system. In fact, a constantly growing economy, by providing all levels of society with more wealth, would make
changes in the division of that wealth unnecessary and avert a
revival of reform that might jeopardize private management of
the economy.[157] The business Keynesian viewpoint was, in some

---

[154] Walter D. Fuller, "The Spirit of '42," Vital Speeches 8
(July 1, 1942), pp. 551-554; Virgil Gordon, "The Frame of the
Future," October 14, 1943, box 28, Taft papers, Library of Con-
gress. See also John T. Flynn, "National Resources Planning
Board," n.d., box 568, Taft papers, Library of Congress.

[155] Quotations from James S. Kemper, "On the Home Front,"
Vital Speeches 8 (December 15, 1941), p. 144; and Sloan, "Industry's Post-War Responsibilities," p. 175. See also John M. Blum,
ed., The Price of Vision: The Diary of Henry A. Wallace, 1942-
1946 (Boston, 1973), pp. 34-35; and Norman D. Markowitz, The
Rise and Fall of the People's Century: Henry A. Wallace and
American Liberalism, 1941-1948 (New York, 1973), pp. 62-63.

[156] Harold D. Smith, Daily Memoranda, November 24, 1939,
October 23, 1940, Smith papers, FDR Library; George F. Milton
to Pendleton Herring, September 2, 1942, November 4, 1942, series 41.3, box 22, Records of Bureau of the Budget, Record Group
51, National Archives; Congressional Record, 78th Congress, 1st
Session, pp. A2001-A2002; Perrett, Days of Sadness, p. 329.

[157] On the business Keynesian viewpoint, see David W. Eakins,
"Business Planners and America's Postwar Expansion," in David
Horowitz, ed., Corporations and the Cold War (New York, 1970),
pp. 143-169. See also Richard M. Bissell, "The Anatomy of
Public Spending," Fortune XXV (May 1942), p. 116, (June 1942),

measure, a compromise between extremes represented by Keynesian reformers on the left and anti-Keynesians on the right.

In Congress, the anti-Keynesian position dominated. Before the war, the Temporary National Economic Committee had endorsed "public investment" in housing, schools and transportation as the means to attain full employment.[158] During the war, however, the philosophy that commanded allegiance on Capitol Hill was not that of the defunct TNEC, but the fiscal orthodoxy promoted by the Joint Committee on Reduction of Nonessential Federal Expenditures. Referring to the "new philosophy of public debt," the committee denounced the theory that "a gradually expanding public debt is healthful to a country with a 'mature economy.'"[159] Senator Harry F. Byrd (D., Va.), the committee's chairman, was the leading Congressional exponent of "sound finance." Joined by other fiscal conservatives like Senator Walter F. George, Senator Robert A. Taft, and Representative John Taber, Byrd attacked what one critic called the "infernal resources board" for its alleged advocacy of endless deficits and a constantly rising national debt.[160]

Three reports issued by the Board--National Resources Development, Report for 1942, Post-War Plan and Program, and Security, Work, and Relief Policies--particularly enraged members of the Congressional opposition.[161] The first of those documents, transmitted to Congress on January 14, 1942, advised against a return to the status-quo and projected a new social and economic order after the war. If "political equality is to have any significance," the Board declared, "it must be translated into the life of the individual citizen." To that

---

p. 144; Rhoda D. Edwards, "The Seventy-Eighth Congress on the Home Front: Domestic Economic Legislation, 1943-1944" (Ph.D. dissertation, Rutgers University, 1967), pp. 379-381; and Markowitz, Rise and Fall of the People's Century, pp. 63-64.

[158]Calvin Crumbaker, "Note on Concentration of Economic Power," Journal of Political Economy L (1942), pp. 937-939.

[159]U.S., Congress, Joint Committee on Reduction of Nonessential Federal Expenditures, Additional Report, S. Doc. 140, 78th Congress, 1st Session, 1943, p. 7.

[160]Samuel Crowther to Robert A. Taft, August 9, 1943, box 663, Taft papers, Library of Congress. See also Robert A. Taft, transcripts of speeches, September 20, 1941, box 1257, November 21, 1941, box 1258, May 7, 1943, box 1261, Taft papers, Library of Congress.

[161]Robert A. Taft, speech notes, n.d., box 1260, Taft papers, Library of Congress; Warken, "History of NRPB," p. 214.

end, the Board unveiled its "new bill of rights," now more
fully developed than in its earlier formulations. "Any . . .
translation of freedom into modern terms," said the NRPB report,
should include the right to work; the right to fair pay; the
right to adequate food, clothing, shelter and medical care; the
right to security, with freedom from fear of old age, want, de-
pendency, sickness, unemployment, and accident; the right to
equality before the law; and the right to education.[162]

According to the NRPB Report for 1942, attainment of those
objectives depended on a carefully planned transition from "full
employment for war to a system of full employment for peace,
without going through a low-employment slump." The Board recommended government policies designed to expand mass purchasing
power and maintain a high level of consumer demand. More important than avoidance of underconsumption was prevention of
underinvestment. NRPB planners recognized that accumulated
shortages would "give us a vigorous private investment boom"
after the war. Sooner or later, though, "such a boom will end
in a depression." To supplement private investment, the Board
urged public expenditures for soil conservation, flood control,
irrigation, forest and park development, rivers and harbors improvements, airports, highways, pipelines, urban transit,
housing, power generation and distribution, public health, education, and recreation.[163]

That comprehensive list shocked members of the Congressional opposition. The Board had included "about everything to
usher in the fully perfect millenium," Representative Frederick
C. Smith (R., O.) commented sarcastically. He accused NRPB of
plotting "nothing less than the absorption by the state of all
economic functions and the complete demolition of all free
enterprise." The Board, he concluded, was "a grave menace to
our Nation and must be abolished, root and branch."[164]

Release of the Board's Post-War Plan and Program and Security, Work, and Relief Policies aggravated the adverse reaction
in Congress. The President had delayed transmitting the report
on social security for over a year, evidently because he

---

[162]National Resources Planning Board, National Resources
Development, Report for 1942, H. Doc. 560, 77th Congress, 2nd
Session, 1942, pp. 1-3, 9-10, 109.

[163]National Resources Planning Board, National Resources
Development, Report for 1942, H. Doc. 560, 77th Congress, 2nd
Session, 1942, pp. 10, 17, 20-130.

[164]Congressional Record, 78th Congress, 1st Session,
pp. 718, 721.

anticipated a fierce Congressional response.[165] Finally, on
March 10, 1943, he sent both documents to Capitol Hill. The
Post-War Plan and Program restated recommendations offered by
NRPB in earlier reports and pamphlets. The Board presented
policies for demobilization of the armed forces, urban renewal,
river valley development, energy resources development, public
works construction, equal access to education, health care, and
economic security. For all returning veterans, NRPB urged
generous government benefits, especially educational benefits,
to ease the transition from military to civilian life. Under
the heading of river valley development, NRPB suggested that
the Tennessee Valley Authority be used as a model for regional
development of the Arkansas river valley, Missouri river valley,
and Columbia river valley. The Board also proposed that the
Federal government assist in financing decent housing for lower
income groups. To assure equal access to education, NRPB recommended that "adequate funds be made available by the local,
State, and Federal governments" to guarantee a quality elemen-
tary and high school education for all children and to further
the education of college-age youth "according to their abilities
and the needs of society."[166]

Security, Work, and Relief Policies spelled out a program
to ensure equal access to health care and economic security.
If "private industry cannot provide jobs for those who are
willing and able to work," the report said, "it is the duty of
the government to do so." The Board therefore recommended a
public service jobs program for the unemployed. For those
people unable to work, for those who earned insufficient incomes, and for those only temporarily unemployed, NRPB suggested an expanded social insurance system, including unemployment compensation, old age pensions, and survivors benefits, as
well as public assistance for the destitute, for dependent
children and the handicapped. The report also invited consideration of a national health insurance system to protect

---

[165]Arthur J. Altmeyer, The Formative Years of Social Security (Madison, Wis., 1966), pp. 143-144; Warken, "History of
NRPB," pp. 224-226.

[166]National Resources Planning Board, National Resources
Development, Report for 1943, Part I: Post War Plan and Program, H. Doc. 128, part 1, 78th Congress, 1st Session, 1943,
pp. 2-3, 9-17, 20-81. See also Frank W. Herring and Robert W.
Hartley, "Public Works Planning for the Post-War Period," July
24, 1942, General Records of the Director, series 39.27, box
70, Records of the Bureau of the Budget, Record Group 51, National Archives; Charles E. Merriam to President, March 11,
1943, General Records of the Director, series 39.27, box 35,
Records of the Bureau of the Budget, Record Group 51, National
Archives; and Rosenman, Public Papers and Addresses of FDR 12:
1943, pp. 122-124.

citizens from illness and accident.[167]

Taken together, the Post-War Plan and Program and Security, Work, and Relief Policies provided a blueprint for full capacity production after the war and for creation of a genuine welfare state. The social security report resembled the famous Beveridge report, published by the British government on December 1, 1942. Both plans proposed a comprehensive social security program. The Beveridge plan was a carefully drawn contributory social insurance scheme while the NRPB report contained only general recommendations.[168]

Initially, public response to the NRPB reports was surprisingly favorable. AFL President William Green, CIO President Philip Murray, and National Farmers Union President James Patton called for speedy enactment of the Board's proposals. The press, however, generally condemned the postwar plan as a blueprint for socialism. Newspaper editorials objected to the "enormous cost" of the program, to the prospect of a larger Federal bureaucracy, and to the principles of compensatory finance on which the NRPB plans rested.[169] In Congress, a majority of legislators

---

[167]National Resources Planning Board, Security, Work, and Relief Policies, H. Doc. 128, part 2, 78th Congress, 1st Session, 1943, pp. 502-549. For the genesis of Security, Work and Relief Policies, see National Resources Planning Board, "Facts About the Report on Security, Work, and Relief Policies of the National Resources Planning Board," n.d., pp. 1-7, Records of NRPB, Record Group 187, National Archives; National Resources Planning Board, minutes of meeting of July 26-27, 1939, 103.71, box 218, Records of NRPB, Record Group 187, National Archives; Frederic A. Delano to President, August 25, 1939, minutes of meeting of August 19, 1939, 103.71, box 218, Records of NRPB, Record Group 187, National Archives; George F. Yantis, "Report of Conference of National Resources Planning Board with the President at the White House," October 17, 1939, minutes of meeting of October 16-18, 1939, 103.71, box 218, Records of NRPB, Record Group 187, National Archives; Harold D. Smith, Daily Memoranda, October 4, 1939, October 16, 1939, Smith papers, FDR Library; Ernest K. Lindley, "How the Postwar Reports Came to Be," Newsweek, March 22, 1943, p. 27; and Altmeyer, Formative Years of Social Security, pp. 114-115.

[168]National Resources Planning Board, "Major Similarities and Differences in NRPB Report and the Beveridge Report," n.d., pp. 1-3, Records of NRPB, Record Group 187, National Archives; Newsweek, March 22, 1943, p. 28; Perrett, Days of Sadness, p. 329.

[169]Roma K. McNickle, "Editorial Reaction to NRPB Security Report," n.d., pp. 1-9, Records of NRPB, Record Group 187, National Archives.

seemed stunned by the magnitude of the program. Although loyal New Dealers like Senators Claude Pepper (D., Fla.) and Robert Wagner (D., N.Y.) labeled the NRPB reports "nothing short of magnificent," they were distinctly in the minority. Representative John Rankin (D., Miss.) dismissed the plans as "the most fantastic conglomeration of bureaucratic stupidity ever sent to Congress." Senator Taft claimed that enactment of the reports would substitute government paternalism for the rugged individualism that had made America great. Other Republicans contended that the reports were propaganda for Roosevelt's upcoming reelection campaign. The NRPB postwar plan, observed Representative Harold Knutson (R., Minn.), was "the opening gun for a fourth term."[170]

Yet the President, having tossed the reports into the lap of Congress, did little to focus public attention on them. Moving with his usual caution, Roosevelt probably submitted the NRPB program to test Congressional and public responses, but he was not prepared to press for its adoption. With the exception of Vice President Henry Wallace, who thought "the people are now ready and eager for definite action looking toward the assurance of postwar jobs," Administration officials made almost no effort to sustain popular interest in the NRPB reports.[171] Within two weeks, they had ceased to be a subject of public discussion.[172]

On Capitol Hill, the reports remained a lively issue. Republicans and renegade Democrats referred to them sarcastically as "the womb-to-tomb" security plan and cited them as compelling justification for immediate destruction of the National Resources Planning Board. Otherwise, declared Representative Noah Mason (R., Ill.), the Board would continue scheming to create "a paternalistic, socialistic dictatorship."[173]

The Congressional opposition had already taken steps to liquidate the Board.[174] In February 1943, a House appropriations

---

[170] Newsweek, March 22, 1943, p. 28; Warken, "History of NRPB," pp. 226-236.

[171] Blum, Price of Vision, p. 181.

[172] Jerome S. Bruner, Mandate from the People (New York, 1944), p. 159.

[173] Congressional Record, 78th Congress, 1st Session, pp. 4380, 4382. See also Sullivan, Bureaucracy Runs Amuck, pp. 86-87.

[174] For additional background to the struggle over the NRPB, see Charles W. Eliot to President, May 4, 1942, President to Clifton A. Woodrum, May 5, 1942, and Charles W. Eliot to Frederic A. Delano and others, May 8, 1942, General Records of the

subcommittee deleted a budget request of $1,400,000 for con-
tinuation of NRPB. As in 1940, the President interceded per-
sonally on behalf of the Board. He asked the Senate Appropriations Committee to restore funds to the agency. He even appealed for assistance to the committee's chairman, Senator
Kenneth D. McKellar (D., Tenn.), who agreed to lead the fight
for restoration of the appropriation. But as a fiscal conservative and a churlish critic of the Administration since the
start of the war, McKellar conducted a halfhearted campaign
for NRPB.[175]

At first, though, it seemed that McKellar's influence and
Presidential pressure might save the Board. Then Senator Taft
delivered a devastating indictment of NRPB. Taft insisted that
he was not opposed to planning for postwar reconversion, but
he wanted that planning to be done by an instrumentality of the
Congress, not the executive branch. "I cannot understand," he
told the Senate, "why a Congress which believes . . . in one
philosophy of government . . . should provide hundreds of thousands of dollars promiscuously for the making of plans by an
agency which believes in an entirely different philosophy,
which appears to be partly socialist and partly the product of
a dangerous financial imagination." Taft condemned "the theory
of unlimited public spending" and "unlimited Government interference in and regulation of all business activity." As for a
new economic bill of rights, Taft dismissed that as "a combination of 'hooey' and false promises." The Board's prescription
for full employment, he said, would require either a staggering
tax burden on private wealth or huge deficits leading to un-
controlled inflation. Taft preferred a postwar program that
"encouraged private enterprise" by eliminating Federal regulation
and reducing taxation. NRPB menaced those policies and "ought
to be abolished now."[176]

Director, series 39.27, box 35, Records of the Bureau of the
Budget, Record Group 51, National Archives.

[175] George F. Milton to Harold D. Smith, February 15, 1943,
series 41.3, box 22, Records of the Bureau of the Budget, Record Group 51, National Archives; Morgenthau Diary, vol. 612,
p. 75, FDR Library; Harold D. Smith, Memorandum of Conference
with the President, April 9, 1943, Smith papers, FDR Library;
Rosenman, Public Papers and Addresses of FDR 12: 1943, pp. 98-
100; Newsweek, February 22, 1943, p. 29; Garson, Democratic
Party and Politics of Sectionalism, p. 33; Warken, "History of
NRPB," pp. 244-245; Hinchey, "Frustration of New Deal Revival,"
pp. 6-8.

[176] Congressional Record, 78th Congress, 1st Session,
pp. 4294, 4297, 4930. See also Morgenthau Diary, vol. 612,
p. 188, FDR Library.

After Taft's vigorous denunciation, the Senate voted, 31-43, to reject an amendment offered by McKellar that provided $534,000 for the Board. Favoring the appropriation were 16 non-Southern Democrats, 10 Southern Democrats, 4 Republicans, and 1 Progressive, while 26 Republicans (87 percent of those voting), 10 non-Southern Democrats (38 percent of those voting), and 7 Southern Democrats (41 percent of those voting) opposed funds for NRPB.[177] The Senate then approved $200,000 for the Board. That amount was so small that some Senators felt it would be better to abolish NRPB altogether.[178]

The President still hoped to save the planning agency, but Budget Director Smith advised him that "very little" should be done in the Board's behalf. Smith thought NRPB wanted "to do too much economic research" and that Board officials lacked political discretion in issuing their controversial reports. The "Resources Planning Board was dead," said Smith, "no matter what happened." He suggested that his own Bureau of the Budget take over the central planning functions previously exercised by the Board. Roosevelt agreed that NRPB had drafted "grandiose schemes" that Congress would never swallow in one gulp. Nevertheless, he asked Smith to "try to get the appropriation through."[179]

That task proved impossible. House conferees vehemently opposed the Board, while Senate conferees only tepidly supported the agency. On June 16, the House voted to insist that the Board be abolished effective August 31, 1943. The House specified that none of the functions of NRPB should be transferred to any other agency and that its records should be sent to the National Archives. Senate conferees bowed to House intransigence and agreed to abolish the agency.[180]

The struggle over the National Resources Planning Board was a test of political possibilities for postwar policy. The Board, said Senator Taft on July 28, had written the "New Deal

---

[177] For Senate roll call vote on NRPB appropriation, see Congressional Record, 78th Congress, 1st Session, p. 4965; and Appendix VII, Guttman scaling table 3, item 3.

[178] Congressional Record, 78th Congress, 1st Session, pp. 4965-4966.

[179] Quotations from Harold D. Smith, Memoranda of Conferences with the President, April 9, 1943, June 3, 1943, August 31, 1943, Smith papers, FDR Library.

[180] Congressional Record, 78th Congress, 1st Session, pp. 5937-5939; Warken, "History of NRPB," p. 245; Crider, Bureaucrat, p. 310; Young, Congressional Politics, p. 24.

program for 1944." In "the field of domestic policy," Taft went
on, "Congress realizes today that we are at the crossroads in
determining our future course." The Congressional opposition
attempted to block one road to the postwar era by abolishing the
National Resources Planning Board. Yet the opposition was "not
opposed to planning," as Taft pointed out.[181] Having destroyed
NRPB, the opposition established its own instruments--the special Senate and House Committees on Post-War Economic Policy and
Planning, chaired by Senator Walter F. George (D., Ga.) and
Representative William M. Colmer (D., Miss.)--to formulate reconversion policies.[182] The planning sponsored by those committees was short-term in character and founded on orthodox economic assumptions. According to the dominant Congressional
view, reconversion to peacetime production should be accomplished through rapid removal of wartime economic controls and
provision of incentives to private investment. Tax reduction
was the preferred method of stimulating business and employment.
A public works program should be used only as a last resort.
That prescription diverged widely from the program drafted by
the National Resources Planning Board.[183]

The demise of NRPB exemplified the fate of social and economic reform at the hands of the Congressional opposition.
Some of the social security measures proposed in Security, Work,
and Relief Policies were embodied in the Wagner-Murray-Dingell
Bill, introduced in 1943. That legislation would have extended
social security coverage, increased unemployment compensation,

---

[181]Robert A. Taft, transcripts of speeches, February 24,
1943, July 28, 1943, box 1261, Taft papers, Library of Congress.

[182]Congressional Record, 78th Congress, 1st Session, pp.
899-900, 1461, 1922-1923; Congressional Record, 78th Congress,
2nd Session, pp. 695, 701, 753-762.

[183]U.S., Congress, Senate, Special Committee on Post-War
Economic Policy and Planning, Preliminary Report, S. Rept. 539,
part 1, 78th Congress, 1st Session, pp. 1-3, Report, S. Rept.
539, part 2, 78th Congress, 2nd Session, 1944, pp. 1-13, Problem of Post-War Employment and Role of Congress in Solving It,
S. Rept. 539, part 4, 78th Congress, 2nd Session, 1944, pp.
1-11, Changes in Unemployment Compensation System, S. Rept. 539,
part 5, 78th Congress, 2nd Session, 1944, pp. 1-8. See also
"Problems Suggested for Consideration by the Senate Committee
on Post-War Economic Policy and Planning," n.d., box 568, Taft
papers, Library of Congress; "Comments on the Baruch Report,"
n.d., box 569, Taft papers, Library of Congress; James G.
Patton to President, March 1, 1944, President's Official File
899, FDR papers, FDR Library; V. O. Key, Jr., "The Reconversion
Phase of Demobilization," American Political Science Review
XXXVIII (1944), pp. 1152-1153; and Hinchey, "Frustration of
the New Deal Revival," pp. 10-11.

and most important, established a national health insurance
system to furnish medical care. The Wagner-Murray-Dingell plan
met determined resistance from members of the opposition, who
considered it the opening wedge of socialized medicine. It
had no chance in the 78th Congress.[184]

Only in the area of servicemen's readjustment did Congressional ideas coincide with those of NRPB. On October 27, 1943,
Roosevelt sent Congress a message calling for liberal unemployment, social security, and educational benefits for returning
war veterans. In January 1944, the American Legion sponsored a
comprehensive servicemen's readjustment plan that became popu-
larly known as the G.I. Bill of Rights. After prompt passage
by the Senate, the House scaled down the benefits, but then
passed the measure substantially intact in June 1944. The
Servicemen's Readjustment Act provided educational assistance,
readjustment allowances, and guarantees of low interest loans
for housing. A generous demobilization plan, the G.I. Bill of
Rights passed because it applied only to servicemen. It was a
veterans' bill that offended no major interest group while
winning the support of a grateful nation. But the Congressional opposition clearly did not intend the G.I. Bill of
Rights to become a model for broader social reform, though the
President had that possibility much in mind.[185]

The Conservative War

"The present Congress is not so friendly to the New Deal,"
Senator Taft had written with casual understatement on March 3,
1943, "and so it seems that we may be able to accomplish something."[186] Three months later he reviewed the record of the
78th Congress. Last year, he began, "we abolished the Civilian
Conservation Corps." This year Congress "has brought to an
end the W.P.A." and "after a bitter fight, we abolished N.Y.A."
Furthermore, Congress "cut off that part of the O.W.I. [Office
of War Information] which maintained offices throughout the
United States, and scattered leaflets and propaganda ostensibly
to assist the war, but actually to assist a fourth term."
Congress had cooperated "with the President on every war question,

---

[184] Polenberg, War and Society, p. 87; Blum, Price of Vision, p. 34.

[185] Rosenman, Public Papers and Addresses of FDR 12: 1943,
pp. 449-455; Warken, "History of NRPB," pp. 194-198; Burns,
Soldier of Freedom, pp. 362, 509; Polenberg, War and Society,
pp. 96-97.

[186] Taft to Mrs. Lloyd W. Bowers, March 3, 1943, box 28,
Taft papers, Library of Congress.

but it has differed with him on almost every domestic policy,"
including "his $25,000 limit on salaries." The "duty of Repub-
licans," the "duty of the anti-administration Democrats," Taft
said, was "to bring forward both outside of Congress and inside
of Congress a sound plan of dealing with the post-war difficulties in the United States." To that end, the Senate "has created the George Post-War Planning Committee," which "will present a very different and sounder plan than that of the National Resources Planning Board." This Congress, Taft concluded
with satisfaction, "is no rubber-stamp Congress."[187]

Administration officials regretfully agreed that the 78th
Congress was "no rubber stamp." They had expected the opposition to thwart the President on domestic issues but were
shocked by the size of hostile majorities and the intensity of
feeling in Congress. Reviewing the deplorable state of Execu-
tive-Congressional relations at the end of 1943, Budget Director Smith noted that "There is terrific tension on the Hill.
People who have been friends for years are doing the most er-
ratic things. We are just getting the backlash of all
this. . . ."[188] Roosevelt dealt with that backlash by appointing officials acceptable to the opposition as buffers between
Congress and the Administration. On May 27, 1943, he established the Office of War Mobilization, with former Senator
James F. Byrnes as Director. Fred Vinson, another former
Congressman, replaced Byrnes as head of the Office of Economic
Stabilization. Late in June, Roosevelt appointed Marvin Jones,
former Chairman of the House Committee on Agriculture, as War
Food Administrator. Byrnes, Vinson, and Jones were orthodox
Democrats who maintained friendly relations with the "Lords
of the Hill." If they could not get along with Congress, no
one could. In effect, Roosevelt divested himself of detailed
involvement in domestic political and economic concerns and
allowed Byrnes and his lieutenants to run the home front.[189]

---

[187]Robert A. Taft, transcript of speech, July 10, 1943,
box 1261, Taft papers, Library of Congress.

[188]Harold D. Smith, Daily Record, December 11, 1943, Smith
papers, FDR Library. See also Allen Drury, A Senate Journal,
1943-1945 (New York, 1963), p. 4.

[189]George F. Milton, "A War Cabinet for America," n.d.,
series 41.3, box 12, Records of the Bureau of the Budget, Record Group 51, National Archives; James F. Byrnes to President,
January 26, 1944, and President to James F. Byrnes, June 10,
1944, President's Secretary's File 145, FDR papers, FDR Library; Rosenman, Public Papers and Addresses of FDR 12: 1943,
pp. 232-238; Congressional Record, 78th Congress, 1st Session,
pp. 2424-2425, 6526; New Republic 107 (October 12, 1942),
p. 464.

Anxious that hostile Congressional factions support his military and foreign policies, the President tried to avoid further conflict over domestic policy. Even when he did fight, Roosevelt had little success. In February 1944, Congress passed a tax bill that fell far short of Treasury Department recommendations. Instead of raising $10.5 billion, as the Treasury and the President had requested, the bill provided only $2 billion of additional revenue. Increases in Federal taxation enacted since 1939 had amplified Congressional reluctance to adopt still heavier taxes, especially in an election year. Moreover, the bill permitted depletion allowances for minerals, exempted natural gas pipelines from the excess profits tax, and provided other loopholes for special interests. According to the Treasury, the measure was a serious defeat for the principles of anti-inflationary taxation and tax reform. Roosevelt's advisors and New Dealers in Congress urged him to veto the bill and on February 22 he did so. The revenue measure, he told Congress, did not meet the financial needs of a nation at war. Further, it granted "indefensible special privileges to favored groups." It was not a tax bill at all, "but a tax relief bill providing relief not for the needy but for the greedy."[190]

Infuriated by that harsh language, Congress speedily overrode the President's veto.[191] The Revenue Act was, nominally, at least, a Democratic bill, and when Roosevelt rejected it, Alben Barkley, a loyal lieutenant for many years, resigned his position as Senate majority leader in protest. Barkley condemned the veto message as a "calculated and deliberate assault upon the legislative integrity of every member of Congress."[192]

---

[190] Samuel I. Rosenman, ed., The Public Papers and Addresses of Franklin D. Roosevelt, vol. 13: 1944-45 Victory and the Threshold of Peace (New York, 1950), pp. 80-81. See also Harold D. Smith, Memoranda of Conferences with the President, January 7, 1944, February 16, 1944, Smith papers, FDR Library; Ed V. Izac to President, February 11, 1944, President's Official File 137, FDR papers, FDR Library; Edwards, "Seventy-Eighth Congress on the Home Front," pp. 337-361; Paul, Taxation, pp. 349-371.

[191] For House and Senate roll call votes to override the President's veto, see Congressional Record, 78th Congress, 2nd Session, pp. 2013, 2050; Appendix VI, Guttman scaling table 3, item 6; and Appendix VII, Guttman scaling table 2, item 2. See also Roy G. and Gladys C. Blakey, "Federal Revenue Legislation, 1943-1944," American Political Science Review XXXVIII (1944), pp. 325-327; Floyd M. Riddick, "The Second Session of the Seventy-Eighth Congress," American Political Science Review XXXIX (1945), pp. 318, 321-323, 330-331.

[192] Congressional Record, 78th Congress, 2nd Session, p. 1966.

The Democratic caucus immediately reelected Barkley to the
leadership post, but his resignation symbolized the gulf that
now divided most Congressional Democrats from the Administration.[193]

The strong anti-Administration tide in Congress alarmed the
reformist wing of the Democratic Party. Disheartened New Dealers thought the war had dealt their cause a mortal blow. Labor
leaders were equally disturbed because the adverse political
trend threatened "social and economic gains" won for workers
during the 1930s. Furthermore, destruction of the National
Resources Planning Board and rejection of its reports made it
appear that orthodox economic assumptions would dominate postwar planning. Labor leaders and reformers were certain that
8 to 10 million workers would be permanently unemployed unless
the government undertook an aggressive full-employment program.[194] Those considerations prompted Philip Murray and
Sidney Hillman to establish the CIO's Political Action Committee in July 1943. Initially a response to the Smith-Connally Act, which forbade direct financial contributions to political parties by labor unions, PAC became the chief vehicle
for a counterattack against the President's domestic opposition.
As Hillman informed Roosevelt on July 27, 1943, the Political
Action Committee would attempt "to unite the forces of labor
and mobilize them" in behalf of candidates who backed the
President.[195]

Both labor leaders and reformers realized that only the
election of a new, more liberal Congress could smash the

---

[193]Harold D. Smith, Daily Memoranda, February 23, 1944,
Smith papers, FDR Library; Congressional Record, 78th Congress
2nd Session, pp. 2049-2050; Paul, Taxation, pp. 371-375;
Garson, Democratic Party and Politics of Sectionalism, p. 53;
Blum, Years of War, p. 76; Crider, Bureaucrat, p. 398; Floyd
M. Riddick, "Congress Versus the President in 1944," South
Atlantic Quarterly XLIV (July 1945), pp. 309-311; Edwards,
"Seventy-Eighth Congress on the Home Front," pp. 362-368.

[194]Louis H. Bean to J. Weldon Jones, January 21, 1944,
General Records of the Director, series 39.27, box 70, Records
of the Bureau of the Budget, Record Group 51, National Archives.
See also James G. Patton to President, August 5, 1944, Presi-
dent's Official File 5404, FDR papers, FDR Library; James G.
Patton, "The Federal Government's Role in the Postwar Economy,"
American Political Science Review XXXVIII (1944), pp. 1124-
1125.

[195]Polenberg, War and Society, pp. 203-205. See also William H. Riker, "The CIO in Politics, 1936-1946" (Ph.D. dissertation, Harvard University, 1948), p. 111; Perrett, Days of
Sadness, p. 292; Burns, Soldier of Freedom, p. 525.

coalition of Republicans and renegades and give unreliable Democrats a compelling reason to follow Roosevelt's leadership.
Speaking to a conference of trade unionists, reformers, Keynesian economists, and friendly government officials in January
1944, CIO President Philip Murray asserted that protection of
labor's rights, a full employment economy, and a wider share
in prosperity for low income groups depended on the outcome of
the elections of 1944. A low turnout by workers in 1942 had
strengthened labor's foes. Therefore, organized labor should
"begin a great registration drive immediately." And, Murray
added, "we should see to it that all our boys and girls in the
armed forces are enabled to vote."[196]

No less than the leadership of the CIO, the President and
his political advisors understood that the outcome of the election might hinge on the soldier vote. Public opinion polls
suggested that a majority of the nine million servicemen would
vote Democratic, and the Administration naturally wanted as
many soldiers as possible to cast ballots. Republicans, on the
other hand, feared that a large soldier vote would jeopardize
their chances of defeating Roosevelt and his fourth term program. They formed an alliance with Southern Democrats who
opposed an absentee voting plan that might enfranchise black
soldiers. After a protracted struggle lasting from December
1943 to March 1944, that "unholy alliance" of Southern Democrats
and Republicans defeated the Administration's absentee voting
bill, which provided a Federal ballot intended to maximize
voting by soldiers.[197] Instead, Southern Democrats led by

---

[196]Louis H. Bean to J. Weldon Jones, January 21, 1944,
General Records of the Director, series 39.27, box 70, Records
of the Bureau of the Budget, Record Group 51, National Archives.
See also Sidney Hillman to Wayne Coy, January 8, 1944, General
Records of the Director, series 39.27, box 70, Records of the
Bureau of the Budget, Record Group 51, National Archives; and
Garson, Democratic Party and Politics of Sectionalism, pp.
58-60.

[197]Charles W. Vursell to Robert A. Taft, January 25, 1944,
box 771, Taft papers, Library of Congress; Congressional Record,
78th Congress, 1st Session, pp. 9790-9800, 9812-9818, 10057-
10083, 10109-10133, 10165-10175, 10177-10187, 10197-10201,
10204-10206, 10220-10228, 10268-10290, 10688-10695; Congressional Record, 78th Congress, 2nd Session, pp. 1014-1034, 1082-
1125, 1168-1228, 1291-1299, 1383-1404, 1517-1522, 2494-2516,2562,
2564-2573, 2610-2639; Rosenman, Public Papers and Addresses of
FDR 13: 1944-45, pp. 53-60; Drury, Senate Journal, pp. 15-19,
45, 48-49, 56-72; Burns, Soldier of Freedom, pp. 429-431;
Garson, Democratic Party and the Politics of Sectionalism,
pp. 44-45; Polenberg, War and Society, pp. 195-196; Riddick,
"Congress Versus President," pp. 311-313.

Senator James O. Eastland of Mississippi sponsored a state-controlled absentee voting plan that would keep most southern blacks from casting ballots. Republicans eagerly backed that bill because it was more cumbersome than a Federal ballot and would lessen participation in the election by soldiers. In December 1943, the "states-rights" soldier vote bill passed the Senate 42-37 with the backing of every southern Senator except Claude Pepper (D., Fla.). Southern Democrats were less united in the House than in the Senate, but enough of them collaborated with Republicans to kill the Administration bill and approve a measure providing for state control of absentee voting. Roosevelt considered the "states rights" bill unacceptable, but in March 1944, let it become law without his signature.[198]

The tussle over the soldier-vote bill brought to a culmination the tendency of Southern Democrats to coalesce with Republicans on controversial domestic issues. Since 1939, Southerners had, on occasion, voted as a bloc with GOP members, but it was not until the 78th Congress that the coalition solidified. The soldier vote issue revealed the bargain that had been struck. White southern politicians were increasingly disturbed by Federal policies that might undermine racial segregation. During the 1930s, the Roosevelt Administration had intermittently paid lip service to equality of opportunity for blacks, but had rarely ventured beyond rhetoric. During the war, the importance of the black vote in northern cities and the growing militace of black leaders forced the Administration to institute new policies designed to assist blacks in overcoming discrimination. The President's Committee on Fair Employment Practice, which Roosevelt reluctantly established in 1941, endeavored, most of the time with only token results, to prevent discriminatory hiring practices in war industries. Southern Democrats resented the existence of FEPC, as they did efforts to prohibit payment of poll taxes in southern states. Roosevelt, of course, never backed anti-poll tax legislation or took a strong stand against discrimination, but New Dealers in his Administration, especially Vice President Henry Wallace, had become outspoken advocates of equality of opportunity for blacks. Southerners sensed that support for black civil rights

---

[198]President to Patrick H. Drewry, March 7, 1944, President's Secretary's File 138, FDR papers, FDR Library; Rosenman, Public Papers and Addresses of FDR 13: 1944-45, pp. 111-116; Drury, Senate Journal, pp. 73-112; Garson, Democratic Party and Politics of Sectionalism, pp. 46-52; Perrett, Days of Sadness, p. 288; Riddick, "Second Session of the Seventy-Eighth Congress," pp. 324-325. For Senate and House roll call votes on the soldier vote bill, see Congressional Record, 78th Congress, 1st Session, p. 10290; Congressional Record, 78th Congress, 2nd Session, pp. 1228-1230; Appendix VI, Guttman scaling table 1, items 2, 8, 12; Appendix VII, Guttman scaling table 7, items 3-11; and Curry, "Southern Senators and Their Roll-Call Votes in Congress," pp. 262-268.

was gradually becoming a part of the agenda of reform.[199]

During the war, Southerners discovered that they had a community of interest with Republicans, who opposed a postwar revival of economic reform just as strongly as Southern Democrats opposed any tampering with white supremacy. The fourth term program appeared to threaten the interests of both groups. In the case of the soldier vote bill, Republicans assisted Southern Democrats in defeating a Federal ballot that might enable blacks to vote, and Southern Democrats assisted Republicans in making it more difficult for soldiers to cast ballots, in all probability, for Democratic candidates. More than any other episode during the war, the controversy over the soldier vote cemented a Southern Democratic-Republican coalition. As Roosevelt had long foreseen, the irruption of racial issues drove most southern Congressmen into the arms of the GOP.[200]

After defeats on taxation and absentee voting, Roosevelt concluded that it was "impossible to get along with the present Congress." For all practical purposes, he told Harold Smith, "we have a Republican Congress now."[201] In the "battle of Washington," the opposition had routed the Administration all along the line. Senator Taft claimed victory for the President's adversaries when he announced, "this is a conservative war."[202]

---

[199] George W. Norris to Henry A. Wallace, August 19, 1944, box 27, Norris papers, Library of Congress; Garson, Democratic Party and Politics of Sectionalism, pp. 18, 23, 47-48, 52; Polenberg, War and Society, pp. 97-98.

[200] Garson, Democratic Party and Politics of Sectionalism, pp. 48, 52, 94-104; Polenberg, War and Society, pp. 184, 192-193. For the President's fear that support for black civil and economic rights would drive Southerners into opposition, see Walter White, A Man Called White: The Autobiography of Walter White (New York, 1948), pp. 179-180. On the voting behavior of Southern Democrats, see John Robert Moore, "The Conservative Coalition in the United States Senate, 1942-1945," Journal of Southern History XXXIII (1967), pp. 368-376; Curry, "Southern Senators and Their Roll-Call Votes in Congress," pp. iii-iv, 241, 243-244; Appendix VI, Guttman scaling table 3, items 1, 2, 5-8, 10, 11, 13, 14; and Appendix VIII, Guttman scaling table 3, items 2-15.

[201] Harold D. Smith, Memorandum of Conference with the President, February 16, 1944, Smith papers, FDR Library. See also Harold D. Smith to President, January 9, 1944, Miscellaneous White House Memoranda, Smith papers, FDR Library.

[202] Robert A. Taft and others, "Is This A Conservative War?," March 14, 1943, box 1261, Taft papers, Library of Congress.

Reformers agreed with that judgment, though unlike Taft, they took no pleasure in it. Roosevelt had abandoned the New Deal, lamented left-wing columnist Malcolm Cowley. The President had thrown one New Deal agency after another to the Congressional wolves, "but the pack never stopped," Cowley wrote.[203] In late December 1943, Roosevelt himself seemed to proclaim the end of reform. "Dr. Win-the-War" had replaced "Dr. New Deal," the President said.[204] By early 1944, discouraged reformers were discussing "the tragic outlook for all liberal proposals, the collapse of all liberal leadership and the defeat of all liberal aims." As Archibald MacLeish noted, "It is no longer feared, it is assumed, that the country is headed back to normalcy, that Harding is just around the corner, that the twenties will repeat themselves."[205] Secretary of the Treasury Henry Morgenthau, Jr. had the same thought in mind when he commented sadly that he could fit all the remaining New Dealers in a bathtub.[206] Another Administration official labeled the events of the war years the "great liquidation" of the New Deal.[207]

Those pessimistic assessments contained a mixture of truth and exaggeration. In some ways, the war had protected and furthered reformist objectives. In the summer of 1939, the Congressional opposition had blocked any further extension of Roosevelt's domestic program. The following year, Administration loyalists were fighting a rear guard action in defense of social and economic reforms enacted during the 1930s. By assuring a third term for Roosevelt, the national emergency aided reformers, at least temporarily, in their defensive struggle. Though the President clearly had subordinated the New Deal to preparedness and foreign policy, he remained more sympathetic to reformist purposes than did the national leadership of the GOP.

If the war initially helped protect reform by keeping Roosevelt in office, it also solved some of the problems that had perplexed New Dealers during the 1930s. Production of the implements of war ended unemployment and raised living standards. The heavy taxation that Congress reluctantly enacted, coupled with a full employment economy, resulted in a significant

---

[203] Malcolm Cowley, "The End of the New Deal," New Republic 108 (May 31, 1943), p. 730.

[204] Rosenman, Public Papers and Addresses of FDR 12: 1943, pp. 570-571.

[205] Polenberg, War and Society, p. 73.

[206] Blum, Years of War, p. 35.

[207] Alan Johnstone to John Carmody, October 29, 1955, box 101, Carmody papers, FDR Library.

redistribution of income from the upper levels to the middle and lower levels of American society.[208] Public support for a generous veterans' readjustment program permitted passage of the G.I. Bill of Rights, which embodied some of the social security provisions that reformers hoped to apply to the entire population. The manpower shortage that developed in 1942 and 1943 enabled blacks and other minorities to gain access to job opportunities that had heretofore been denied them by discriminatory hiring practices. In all those respects, the war had not been a conservative experience.[209]

In other ways, however, the war had bolstered right-of-center forces and dealt severe blows to reformist institutions and leadership. The war forced the President to put a high priority on national unity and bipartisanship. To gain the necessary cooperation from the business community, Roosevelt replaced New Deal economists, lawyers and social workers with corporate executives and lawyers. Leon Henderson observed that "a whole stratum of young New Dealers felt they were barred" from policy-making positions during the war "because they have worked for the Administration."[210] After "a year of vain appeal to the patriotism of big business leadership," said one Senator, the President was forced to turn management of the war effort over to anti-Administration businessmen. That surrender placed the country "in the grip of a reactionary change."[211]

So it was also in the President's relationship with Congress. Roosevelt would not jeopardize his wartime objectives by defending or promoting domestic programs. That posture invited attacks by the Congressional opposition, especially since the war gave Republicans and their Democratic allies an excuse to reduce domestic expenditures and abolish New Deal agencies. Frequently, though, they were less interested in retrenchment than in revenge against the New Deal and preventing the survival of its programs into the postwar period.

The war also impaired reform by weakening and disrupting the Democratic Party. The prosperity of the war years made the electorate complacent and lessened popular enthusiasm for reform. That development, in conjunction with the low turnout in 1942, resulted in heavy Democratic losses in the elections of that year. Democrats who survived concluded that there was

---

[208]See Polenberg, War and Society, p. 94.

[209]See Perrett, Days of Sadness, pp. 330-356.

[210]Leon Henderson to Morris Ernst, October 13, 1943, President's Secretary's File 150, FDR papers, FDR Library.

[211]Morgenthau Diary, vol. 611, pp. 205-206, FDR Library.

little to be gained and much to be lost by supporting the Administration. With many New Dealers going down to defeat, the ideological center of the Congressional Democratic Party shifted to the right.[212]

Furthermore, the war raised issues that divided the party's membership in Congress. The Administration strove to maintain peace on the labor front by holding down the cost of living. That policy collided head on with attempts by agricultural organizations and their spokesmen to achieve higher farm prices. Democrats who represented rural districts, particularly in the South, joined Republicans in fighting agricultural price regulation and in attacking organized labor, now perceived as the main enemy of the farm bloc. The racial issues that surfaced during the war gave Southerners another powerful motive for voting with the opposition.

After 1943, the Roosevelt Administration faced hostile majorities in Congress. The political conflict between the President and his adversaries became entangled with an institutional clash between the executive and legislative branches. The members of the Congressional opposition exploited the widespread resentment of executive power by using it as a pretext to attack administrative agencies whose policies they disapproved and distrusted. Suspecting the existence of a conspiracy to make the country over under the cover of war, Republicans and anti-Administration Democrats made a determined effort to expel New Dealers from the Federal service. That effort had few concrete results, but it underscored the opposition's resolve to preserve the status-quo during the war.

Indeed, the overriding purpose of the Congressional opposition during the war years was to keep the "war effort along lines which will not after the war require any permanent change in the fundamentals of the American system," in Senator Taft's words.[213] The war should be fought to restore "the American system," not change it. That purpose clashed with hopes for a new social and economic order after the war. Unless the elections of 1944 swept away the alliance of Republicans and anti-Administration Democrats that had matured during the war, the road to that new social and economic order would be closed. In the realm of Congressional politics and public policy, the war had truly become a conservative war.

---

[212]Gary M. Fink and James W. Hilty, "Prologue: The Senate Voting Record of Harry S. Truman," Journal of Interdisciplinary History IV (Autumn 1973), pp. 211-212.

[213]Robert A. Taft, transcript of speech, January 15, 1942, box 1259, Taft papers, Library of Congress.

EPILOGUE

Throughout World War II, Roosevelt had accepted defeats on
domestic policy with little more than symbolic protest. Privately, he was planning to turn the tables on his adversaries.
The New Deal, he realized, had been partially undone, but there
would be "another program," he promised the press on December
28, 1943, "when the time comes. When the time comes."[1] In
1944, the President interrupted his almost exclusive concentration on the war to consider the more mundane, yet no less pressing concerns of election-year politics. When the Democratic
Party held its convention in July, Roosevelt's renomination was
assured. But there were still decisions to be made. Because of
the belief that the ill and weary President might not survive
another term, the various factions of the party quarreled over
the Vice Presidential nomination.

The reformist wing of the Democratic Party, including the
CIO unions, left-of-center journalists, National Farmers Union,
independent liberal groups, and many New Dealers, favored the
incumbent Vice President, Henry A. Wallace.[2] But the party pro-
fessionals, led by Democratic National Committee Chairman Robert
Hannegan, argued vehemently that Wallace would weaken the ticket.
Southern politicians, distressed by the Vice President's stand
on racial issues, joined the party bosses in demanding that
Roosevelt dump the incumbent.[3] The President, though he liked

---

[1]Samuel I. Rosenman, ed., The Public Papers and Addresses
of Franklin D. Roosevelt, vol. 12: 1943: The Tide Turns (New
York, 1950), pp. 574-575.

[2]Edward L. and Frederick H. Schapsmeier, Prophet in Politics: Henry A. Wallace and the War Years, 1940-1965 (Ames, Ia.,
1970), pp. 24-37, 72-74, 77-78, 100-101; Alonzo L. Hamby, Beyond
the New Deal: Harry S. Truman and American Liberalism (New York,
1973), p. 31; Norman D. Markowitz, The Rise and Fall of the
People's Century: Henry A. Wallace and American Liberalism,
1941-1948 (New York, 1973), pp. 36-74; John M. Blum, ed., The
Price of Vision: The Diary of Henry A. Wallace, 1942-1946
(Boston, 1973), p. 33.

[3]For accounts of the efforts to oust Wallace from the Democratic ticket, see Edward J. Flynn, You're The Boss (New York,
1947), pp. 178-182; James F. Byrnes, All In One Lifetime (New
York, 1958), pp. 216-217, 219-226; George E. Allen, Presidents
Who Have Known Me (New York, 1960), pp. 118-125; Blum, Price of

and respected Wallace, refused to insist on his renomination because he thought the Vice President had moved too far ahead of
public opinion. Wallace's visionary pronouncements on international collaboration after the war, on economic democracy for
the common man, and on equality of opportunity for blacks and
other minorities went beyond the consensus not only of a reactionary Congress but of the American people as well.[4] Moreover,
Roosevelt wanted a Vice President who could help win Congressional approval of the Administration's postwar international
and domestic objectives. Wallace had never ingratiated himself
on Capitol Hill and so failed on that count as he did on others.[5]

Instead of Wallace, most Southern Democrats wanted James F.
Byrnes, the "assistant President" for the home front during the
latter stages of the war. But the leadership of the CIO, along
with most New Dealers and reformers, opposed Byrnes. Furthermore, his presence on the ticket, it was feared, would jeopardize crucial black support in northern cities. Reformers and
labor leaders vetoed Byrnes' candidacy just as the city bosses
and Southerners had blackballed Wallace. As a compromise, the
President settled on Senator Harry S Truman of Missouri, a
border state politician who was enough of a New Dealer to satisfy
the reformist wing of the party without offending the Southerners or the bosses. When it finally became known that Roosevelt
preferred Truman, the Democratic convention nominated him over
Wallace on the second ballot.[6]

Vision, pp. 360-367; James M. Burns, Roosevelt: The Soldier of
Freedom (New York, 1970), pp. 503-504; Schapsmeier and Schapsmeier, Prophet in Politics, pp. 101-102; and Markowitz, Rise
and Fall of the People's Century, pp. 91-100.

[4]See the description of American public opinion in Jerome
S. Bruner, Mandate from the People (New York, 1944), pp. 153-
209. See also Blum, Price of Vision, p. 382; Samuel I. Rosenman, Working With Roosevelt (New York, 1952), p. 439; and
Eleanor Roosevelt, This I Remember (New York, 1949), p. 220.

[5]See Robert E. Sherwood, Roosevelt and Hopkins: An Intimate History (New York, 1948), pp. 881-882. See also Elliott
Roosevelt, ed., F.D.R.--His Personal Letters, 1928-1945, vol.
2: 1938-1945 (New York, 1950), p. 1233; and Mary H. Hinchey,
"The Frustration of the New Deal Revival, 1944-1946" (Ph.D.
dissertation, University of Missouri, 1965), pp. 19-21.

[6]Burns, Soldier of Freedom, pp. 504-506; John M. Blum,
From the Morgenthau Diaries, vol. III: Years of War, 1941-
1945 (Boston, 1967), pp. 280-281; Schapsmeier and Schapsmeier,
Prophet in Politics, pp. 103-108; Markowitz, Rise and Fall of
the People's Century, pp. 100-114; Blum, Price of Vision,
pp. 367-370.

Reformers understood that the defeat of their favorite was
a disappointing omen for the future. In their view, the President had betrayed Wallace and could no longer be trusted because
he had sold out to the most reactionary elements of the Democratic Party. Wallace shared those feelings of betrayal, but a
Dewey victory seemed such a desolate prospect that the Vice
President swallowed his injured pride and campaigned strenuously
for the Democratic ticket. As in 1940 and 1942, reformers were
again dissatisfied with Roosevelt but had nowhere else to go.[7]

In a series of speeches late in the campaign, the President
assuaged some of the anxiety reformers felt over his future
course. He called for fulfillment of the economic bill of rights,
the centerpiece of his new domestic program. He assailed the
selfishness of big business leadership, urged a permanent Fair
Employment Practices Committee, and pledged his Administration
to the goal of postwar full employment, which he defined as sixty
million productive jobs.[8] By emphasizing economic issues,
Roosevelt hoped to stimulate a heavy turnout by organized labor.
In that endeavor, he received indispensable support from the
CIO's Political Action Committee, which mobilized rank and file
union members behind the Democratic ticket.[9]

With the help of PAC, Roosevelt crushed Dewey by winning 36
states and 432 electoral votes, but the election was much closer
than those figures indicated. The President received 53.4 percent of the popular vote, the narrowest of his four victories
and the tightest Presidential election since Wilson edged Hughes
in 1916. The Democrats lost one Senate seat but increased their
margin in the House to 51 seats. The election hinged on the
urban vote, which went heavily Democratic. In a sense, one observer remarked, "the victory of the Democrats was a victory of
the city over the country."[10]

An exultant Henry Wallace wired Roosevelt, "You will now
have sufficient majority [in Congress] to put through full

[7]Markowitz, Rise and Fall of the People's Century, pp. 115-
117; Blum, Price of Vision, pp. 370-381; Schapsmeier and Schapsmeier, Prophet in Politics, pp. 108-116; Hamby, Beyond the New
Deal, pp. 32-33, 48.

[8]See, for example, Samuel I. Rosenman, ed., The Public
Papers and Addresses of Franklin D. Roosevelt, vol. 13: 1944-45
Victory and the Threshold of Peace (New York, 1950), pp. 369-378.

[9]Burns, Soldier of Freedom, pp. 524-525; Richard Polenberg,
War and Society: The United States, 1941-45 (Philadelphia,
1972), pp. 203-208.

[10]Polenberg, War and Society, p. 213.

employment legislation."[11] Like many other reformers, Wallace
hoped that the President would now boldly demand a program to
guarantee full capacity production and a wider share in prosperity for the common man. With a new, supposedly more liberal
Congress, and the war all but won, reformers expected Roosevelt
to lead a postwar revival of the New Deal.

Some signs ran counter to that expectation. In late November, the new Secretary of State, Edward R. Stettinius, Jr., sent
the President a list of those to be appointed Assistant Secretaries in the Department. Among the nominees were James Dunn,
Will Clayton, and Nelson Rockefeller, all of whom New Dealers
considered too closely associated with big business. Roosevelt,
however, endorsed the appointments.[12] Reformers experienced
another wave of disappointment. Mystified by the nominations,
a reporter asked the President "whether you are going right or
left politically." "I am going down the whole line a little
left of center," he replied.[13] His State Department nominations
revealed no such trend, but then in January 1945, Roosevelt
fired Secretary of Commerce Jesse H. Jones and announced that
former Vice President Wallace would replace him in the cabinet.

Wallace had asked for Commerce the previous August. In
that position, he was sure he could make a significant contribution to full employment after the war. Further, Wallace thought
it would be "poetic justice" if he succeeded Jesse Jones, with
whom he had tangled repeatedly during the war. Jones had become a symbol of reaction and Wallace wanted him out of the government. The President, too, was angry at Jones because of his
long record of disloyalty and his encouragement of anti-Roose-
velt forces in Texas. He agreed to get rid of Jones as soon as
the election was over. On November 30, Wallace reminded Roosevelt of that pledge: "my interest in poetic justice is stronger
now than ever," he wrote.[14] On Inauguration Day, 1945, the
President redeemed his promise.

The nomination of Wallace to be Secretary of Commerce
touched off a furious debate in the Senate. Reformers considered the appointment tangible evidence of Roosevelt's commitment

---

[11]Blum, Price of Vision, p. 389.

[12]Burns, Soldier of Freedom, pp. 552-553; Blum, Price of
Vision, pp. 400-401, 403-404, 405-409.

[13]Rosenman, Public Papers and Addresses of FDR 13: 1944-
45, p. 436.

[14]Blum, Price of Vision, pp. 382, 397. See also President
to Wallace, July 21, 1944, President's Personal File 41, FDR
papers, FDR Library; and President to Adelbert M. Scriber,
August 28, 1944, President's Personal File 2848, FDR papers,
FDR Library.

to a liberal postwar program. Senators Claude Pepper (D., Fla.), Joseph Guffey (D., Pa.) and James Murray (D., Mont.) organized Administration supporters in behalf of the former Vice President. On the other hand, Republicans and anti-Administration Democrats adamantly opposed Wallace because of the policies he espoused. Led by Senators Harry F. Byrd (D., Va.) and Robert A. Taft (R., O.), they fought to prevent his confirmation.[15]

The Commerce Department seemed a strategic post to both reformers and their adversaries because it controlled the Federal lending agencies, including the Reconstruction Finance Corporation. The Congressional opposition had permitted that accumulation of power to take place under Jones because he maintained close relations with Capitol Hill and his orthodox views constituted no threat to the status quo. The prospect of Wallace in charge of the lending agencies, however, frightened members of the opposition. They wanted to defeat the nomination, but they also wanted to separate the RFC and its subsidiaries from the Commerce Department in case Wallace might be confirmed.[16]

To that end, Senator Walter F. George (D., Ga.) offered a bill that would divest the RFC and subsidiary corporations from the Commerce Department. Not surprisingly, Jones strongly recommended passage of the George Bill. "Certainly the RFC," Jones told the Senate Commerce Committee on January 24, 1945, "should not be placed under the supervision of any man willing to jeopardize the country's future with untried ideas and idealistic schemes." The lending agencies, he insisted, should be run by businessmen, "by men who haven't any ideas about remaking the world."[17] Wallace, in contrast, asked Congress to leave the RFC intact. "There are some who have suggested," he told the committee "that this separation of the lending functions is desirable because of my alleged 'lack of experience.'" That argument, he charged, was a cloak for reactionary opposition to the ideas he advocated. It "is not a question of my lack of experience," said Wallace, rather "it is a case of not liking the experience I have." He went on to propose a broad Keynesian reform program based on the economic bill of rights. Wallace wanted to use the lending authority of RFC in a compensatory

---

[15] Congressional Record, 79th Congress, 1st Session, pp. 365-366, 370, 415-417, 434, 437-442.

[16] Markowitz, Rise and Fall of the People's Century, pp. 130-132; Schapsmeier and Schapsmeier, Prophet in Politics, pp. 121-124.

[17] U.S., Congress, Senate, Committee on Commerce, Hearings Before the Committee on Commerce on S. 375, A Bill to Provide for the Effective Administration of Certain Lending Agencies of the Federal Government, 79th Congress, 1st Session, 1945, pp. 24-25.

manner "to help carry out the President's commitment of 60,000,000 jobs." Projects that RFC could help finance, he said, included public housing, road construction, more TVA's, health insurance, social security expansion, and aid to education. With the Federal lending agencies as his instrument, he proposed to make a start on the unfinished agenda of reform.[18]

Wallace's forthright advocacy of compensatory lending for postwar prosperity reinforced the opposition's belief that he was a dangerous man. By a vote of 14 to 5, the Senate Commerce Committee, dominated by Republicans and renegade Democrats, recommended that the nomination not be confirmed. At the same time, the committee urged passage of the George Bill in order to strip the Commerce Department of its lending powers.[19]

In early February, Wallace's supporters in the Senate concluded that he could not be confirmed as Secretary of Commerce with the lending agencies intact. Too many orthodox Democrats would join Republicans and Democratic intractables in voting against the appointment. But if Congress first approved the George Bill and removed the lending agencies as a bone of contention, then most orthodox Democrats would back the nomination on the grounds that the President should be allowed to choose his cabinet officers without Congressional interference. Roosevelt assured the House and Senate leadership that he would not veto the George Bill and Wallace indicated his willingness to take the Commerce post even though its authority was diminished. After the George Bill passed both House and Senate, Wallace was confirmed as Secretary of Commerce on March 1, 1945, by a vote of 56 to 32.[20]

Both sides claimed victory. Reformers were encouraged because Wallace had replaced Jones in the cabinet. But the

---

[18]U.S., Congress, Senate, Committee on Commerce, Hearings Before the Committee on Commerce on S. 375, A Bill to Provide for the Effective Administration of Certain Lending Agencies of the Federal Government, 79th Congress, 1st Session, 1945, pp. 72, 73-84.

[19]Congressional Record, 79th Congress, 1st Session, pp. 674, 680, 694.

[20]Congressional Record, 79th Congress, 1st Session, pp. 680-693, 1143-1167, 1174-1197, 1231-1242, 1244-1252, 1600-1616; Hinchey, "Frustration of the New Deal Revival," pp. 26-28, 45-47; Markowitz, Rise and Fall of the People's Century, pp. 133-135; Schapsmeier and Schapsmeier, Prophet in Politics, p. 124. See also Wallace to President, February 28, 1945, President's Personal File 41, FDR papers, FDR Library. For Senate roll call vote on confirmation of Wallace, see Congressional Record, 79th Congress, 1st Session, p. 1616; and Appendix IX, Guttman scaling table 1, item 6.

Congressional opposition had denied Wallace the powers he
thought necessary to attain his goals. The fight over Wallace's
confirmation made it clear that in spite of Roosevelt's electoral triumph in 1944, anti-Administration factions still controlled Congressional decision-making.

That fact became even more apparent when the Senate consid-
ered Roosevelt's other major nomination of early 1945, that of
Aubrey Williams as chief of the Rural Electrification Administration. Frustrated by the confirmation of Wallace, Republicans
and renegade Democrats worked even harder to defeat Williams.
Senator Kenneth D. McKellar (D., Tenn.) launched a campaign of
vilification during which he denounced Williams as a communist.
Even more damaging were the attacks of Senator Theodore G.
Bilbo (D., Miss.), the most unabashed racist in the Senate.
Williams had gone on record as favoring equality of opportunity
for blacks, a position that Bilbo exploited mercilessly to
alienate crucial southern support. On March 23, the Senate rejected the nomination by a vote of 36 to 52. Nineteen Democrats voted against Williams and all but two of those were
Southerners.[21]

Taken together, the Wallace and Williams confirmation
fights constituted a defeat for the Administration's postwar intentions. The "new order of democracy" that reformers hoped
would emerge from the war depended on Congressional support for
a liberal postwar program. That support, as the response to
the Wallace and Williams appointments illustrated, was lacking.
Instead of initiating a revival of reform, the Wallace and
Williams nominations were only a postlude to the New Deal. The
contention that the war intervened before the President' adversaries "had really routed the New Deal" and that "it was not
until after the war that the anti-New Deal forces were able to
organize concerted resistance to the tide of political and economic changes" ignores the evidence.[22] The President faced the
same kind of intransigence on domestic issues in the new Congress
that had characterized the earlier war years.

---

[21] Congressional Record, 79th Congress, 1st Session, pp.
2017, 2104-2107, 2390-2410, 2463-2485, 2520-2545, 2599-2622,
2635-2652; John A. Salmond, "Postscript to the New Deal: The
Defeat of the Nomination of Aubrey W. Williams as Rural Electrification Administrator in 1945," Journal of American History,
LXI (September 1974), pp. 417-436. For Senate roll call vote
on confirmation of Williams, see Congressional Record, 79th
Congress, 1st Session, p. 2652; and Appendix IX, Guttman scaling
table 2, item 17.

[22] Joseph Boskin, ed., Opposition Politics: The Anti-New
Deal Tradition (Beverly Hills, Calif., 1968), p. 36.

Roosevelt did not have to deal with that intransigence for long, for he died on April 12, 1945, with his plans for the post-war era only half formed. Samuel Grafton of the <u>New York Post</u> wrote,

> One remembers him as a kind of smiling bus driver, with that cigarette holder pointed upward, listening to the uproar from behind as he took the sharp turns. They used to tell him that he had not loaded his vehicle for all eternity. But he knew he had it stacked well enough to round the next corner, and he knew when the yells were false and when they were real. . . . He is dead now, and the bus is stalled, far from the gates of heaven, while the riders hold each other in deadlock over how to make the next curve.[23]

The deadlock, of course, preceded Roosevelt's death. Overcoming the Congressional opposition might have been a task too great even for him. The politics of the postwar had arrived before the war itself was won.

---

[23]Grafton's eulogy quoted in William Manchester, <u>The Glory and The Dream: A Narrative History of America, 1932-1972</u> (Boston, 1974), pp. 355-356.

BIBLIOGRAPHICAL ESSAY

The study of Congressional politics and public policy during World War II must begin with the Congressional Record and other pertinent public documents of the time. Use of those voluminous sources was facilitated by the excellent coverage of Congress in the New York Times, Washington Post, Time, Newsweek, New Republic, Nation, and Congressional Digest. The essays of Floyd M. Riddick, appearing in the American Political Science Review, vols. XXXV-XXXIX (1941-1945), provided a helpful guide to each session of the 76th through the 79th Congresses. Summaries of "The Year in Congress" contained in The American Year Book, 1939-1945, edited by William M. Schuyler (New York, 1940-1946), served a similar purpose.

The public record was supplemented with research in manuscript and archival sources. Among the most useful of those consulted were the papers of Franklin D. Roosevelt and the papers of Harold D. Smith at the Franklin D. Roosevelt Library. Both collections furnished vital information about Administration policy and relations with Congress. The Diary of Henry Morgenthau, Jr., an assortment of letters, memoranda, transcripts and working papers also located at the Franklin D. Roosevelt Library, was especially illuminating on questions of fiscal policy and on the activities of the Joint Committee on Reduction of Nonessential Federal Expenditures. Other collections at the Franklin D. Roosevelt Library were of more limited utility. Among the manuscripts of Congressmen consulted, the most valuable were the papers of Robert A. Taft at the Library of Congress. The papers of Jesse H. Jones, also at the Library of Congress, provided important information about executive-legislative relations, fiscal policy, and disagreements within the Roosevelt Administration. Of the archival sources consulted, three proved exceptionally helpful. Most important were the records of the Bureau of the Budget at the National Archives Building. Because the Bureau dealt with both programmatic and budgetary concerns, its records contained a wealth of information about taxation, spending, efforts to continue New Deal policies, and postwar planning. The records of the National Resources Planning Board revealed the growing influence of Keynesian thought within that agency and the continuous pressure from Congress that NRPB encountered between 1939 and 1943. The records of the National Youth Administration furnished valuable material on the Congressional campaign against that New Deal agency.

Published memoirs, diaries, and public papers were indispensable. Preeminent among those were The Public Papers and

Addresses of Franklin D. Roosevelt, edited by Samuel I. Rosenman (vols. 7-13, New York, 1941 and 1950), and Franklin D. Roosevelt, Complete Presidential Press Conferences of Franklin D.
Roosevelt (vols. 11-22, New York, 1972). The following were
also useful: Alben Barkley, That Reminds Me (Garden City, N.Y.,
1954); John M. Blum, ed., The Price of Vision: The Diary of
Henry A. Wallace, 1942-1946 (Boston, 1973); Chester Bowles,
Promises to Keep: My Years in Public Life (New York, 1971);
James F. Byrnes, All In One Lifetime (New York, 1958); Tom Con-
nally, My Name Is Tom Connally (New York, 1954); Allen Drury,
A Senate Journal, 1943-1945 (New York, 1963); Marriner S. Eccles,
Beckoning Frontiers: Public and Personal Recollections (New
York, 1951); James A. Farley, Jim Farley's Story (New York,
1948); Harold Ickes, The Secret Diary of Harold Ickes (vols. II-
III, New York, 1954); Jesse H. Jones, Fifty Billion Dollars: My
Thirteen Years with the RFC (New York, 1951); David E. Lilien-
thal, The Journals of David E. Lilienthal, vol. I: The TVA
Years, 1939-1945 (New York, 1964); and Eleanor Roosevelt, This
I Remember (New York, 1949).

A few biographies of figures treated in this study provided
key insights. James M. Burns, Roosevelt: The Soldier of Freedom
(New York, 1970) interprets the wartime purposes of the President. Pertinent chapters of Joseph P. Lash, Eleanor and Franklin
(New York, 1973) touch on many of the subjects covered in this
dissertation. James T. Patterson, Mr. Republican: A Biography
of Robert A. Taft (Boston, 1972) offers a terse account of
Taft's activities during the war. John Robert Moore, Senator
Josiah William Bailey of North Carolina (Durham, N.C., 1968) is
revealing on the motives and strategy of conservative Southern
Democrats. Bascom N. Timmons, Garner of Texas (New York, 1948)
and Jesse H. Jones: The Man and the Statesman (New York, 1956)
furnish information on the widening fissures within the Democratic Party. J. Joseph Huthmacher, Senator Robert F. Wagner
and the Rise of Urban Liberalism (New York, 1968) describes the
fate of reform legislation during the war. In Prophet in Politics: Henry A. Wallace and the War Years, 1940-1965 (Ames, Ia.,
1970), Edward L. and Frederick H. Schapsmeier recount the career
of the leading wartime spokesman for reform, but their biography
should be supplemented by Norman D. Markowitz, The Rise and Fall
of the People's Century: Henry A. Wallace and American Liberalism, 1941-1948 (New York, 1973) and especially John M. Blum's
"Portrait of the Diarist" in The Price of Vision: The Diary of
Henry A. Wallace, 1942-1946 (Boston, 1973).

The secondary literature on domestic affairs during World
War II is sparse. The outstanding general treatment of the
subject is Richard Polenberg, War and Society: The United States
1941-1945 (Philadelphia, 1972), though Geoffrey Perrett, Days of
Sadness, Years of Triumph (New York, 1973) was also occasionally
helpful. Ray F. Harvey and others, The Politics of This War
(New York, 1943) contains essays that deal with many of the

subjects treated in this dissertation. James T. Patterson has chronicled the rise of Congressional opposition to the Roosevelt Administration in Congressional Conservatism and the New Deal (Lexington, Ky., 1967). Wartime disputes in Congress are covered topically in Roland A. Young, Congressional Politics in the Second World War (New York, 1956). Robert A. Garson, The Democratic Party and the Politics of Sectionalism, 1941-1948 (Baton Rouge, La., 1974) contains chapters on the growing estrangement between Southern Democrats and the national Democratic Party. Two dissertations shed additional light on Congress during the war. The most helpful is Lawrence H. Curry, Jr., "Southern Senators and Their Roll-Call Votes in Congress, 1941-1944" (Ph.D. dissertation, Duke University, 1971), which indicates that the Southern Democratic-Republican coalition did not fully emerge until the 78th Congress (1943-1944). The first chapter of Mary H. Hinchey, "The Frustration of the New Deal Revival, 1944-1946" (Ph.D. dissertation, University of Missouri, 1965) discusses briefly events during the last year of Roosevelt's Presidency. Another dissertation, Rhoda D. Edwards, "The Seventy-Eighth Congress on the Home Front: Domestic Economic Legislation, 1943-1944" (Ph.D. dissertation, Rutgers University, 1967) proved less useful than its title suggested.

Several articles treat particular aspects of Congressional politics between 1939 and 1945. James T. Patterson, "Eating Humble Pie: A Note on Roosevelt, Congress, and Neutrality Revision in 1939," Historian 31 (May 1969), pp. 407-414, describes Roosevelt's efforts to conciliate domestic critics in order to gain support for his foreign policy. Irving Richter, "Four Years of the Fair Labor Standards Act of 1938," Journal of Political Economy LI (1943), pp. 95-111, reviews Congressional attempts to emasculate that New Deal reform. Ferrel Heady and Eleanor Tabor Linenthal, "Congress and Administrative Regulation," Law and Contemporary Problems XXVI (1961), pp. 238-260, analyzes the Walter-Logan Bill of 1940. Arthur W. Macmahon, "Congressional Oversight of Administration: The Power of the Purse--I," Political Science Quarterly LVIII (1943), pp. 161-190, and "Congressional Oversight of Administration: The Power of the Purse--II," Political Science Quarterly LVIII (1943), pp. 380-414, summarize Congressional moves to circumscribe executive power. In "The 1942 Elections: A Case Study in Political Psychology," Public Opinion Quarterly VII (Summer 1943), pp. 221-241, Hadley Cantril and John Harding present a helpful explanation of Democratic reversals in the mid-term elections. Frederick L. Schuman, "Bill of Attainder in the 78th Congress," American Political Science Review XXXVII (1943), pp. 819-829, is a useful account of that episode. John Robert Moore, "The Conservative Coalition in the United States Senate, 1942-1945," Journal of Southern History XXXIII (1967), pp. 368-376, discusses briefly the maturation of the opposition in the Senate. John A. Salmond, "Postscript to the New Deal: The Defeat of the Nomination of Aubrey W. Williams as Rural Electrification

Administrator in 1945," Journal of American History LXI (September 1974), pp. 417-436, is the best account of the Williams confirmation fight.

A number of articles and books furnished valuable background on issues of public policy. Herbert Stein, The Fiscal Revolution in America (Chicago, 1969) is an important study of the impact of compensatory fiscal policy. It should be supplemented with Robert LeKachman, The Age of Keynes (New York, 1966), Alan Sweezy, "The Keynesians and Government Policy, 1933-1939," American Economic Review LXII (May 1972), pp. 116-124, and Byrd Jones, "The Role of Keynesians in Wartime Policy and Postwar Planning," American Economic Review LXII (May 1972), pp. 125-133. Randolph E. Paul, Taxation in the United States (Boston, 1954) is indispensable on its topic. Also helpful were Roy G. and Gladys C. Blakey, "The Two Federal Revenue Acts of 1940," American Economic Review XXX (1940), pp. 724-735, "The Revenue Act of 1941," American Economic Review XXXI (1941), pp. 809-822, and "Federal Revenue Legislation, 1943-1944," American Political Science Review XXXVIII (1944), pp. 325-330. John M. Blum, From the Morgenthau Diaries (vols. I-III, Boston, 1959, 1965, and 1967) is a rich resource for any scholar interested in public policy between 1939 and 1945. The uneasy relationship between organized agriculture and the Roosevelt Administration receives attention in Christiana McF. Campbell, The Farm Bureau and the New Deal (Urbana, Ill., 1962). Wesley McCune, The Farm Bloc (New York, 1943) is a knowledgeable account of the politics of agriculture during the early years of World War II. Sidney Baldwin, Poverty and Politics: The Rise and Decline of the Farm Security Administration (Chapel Hill, N.C., 1968) is a model study of the New Deal for the small farmer. Harry A. Millis and Emily Clark Brown, From the Wagner Act to Taft-Hartley (Chicago, 1950) traces Congressional efforts to repeal the National Labor Relations Act. John A. Salmond, The Civilian Conservation Corps, 1933-1942: A New Deal Case Study (Durham, N.C., 1967) contains a useful chapter on the demise of that New Deal agency. Charles E. Merriam, "The National Resources Planning Board: A Chapter in American Planning Experience," American Political Science Review XXXVIII (1944), pp. 1075-1088, reviews the activities of the NRPB but is silent on the Board's destruction at the hands of the Congressional opposition. Philip W. Warken, "A History of the National Resources Planning Board, 1933-1943" (Ph.D. dissertation, Ohio State University, 1969) gives a much fuller account of the NRPB's controversial reports and the reaction to them that resulted in the Board's abolition.

SELECTED BIBLIOGRAPHY

Manuscripts and Archival Records

Bean, Louis H. Papers, Franklin D. Roosevelt Library, Hyde Park, New York.

Berle, Adolf A., Jr. Papers, Franklin D. Roosevelt Library, Hyde Park, New York.

Carmody, John. Papers, Franklin D. Roosevelt Library, Hyde Park, New York.

Cox, Oscar. Papers, Franklin D. Roosevelt Library, Hyde Park, New York.

Gannett, Frank E. Papers, Cornell University Library, Ithaca, New York.

Green, Theodore F. Papers, Library of Congress, Washington, D.C.

Henderson, Leon. Papers, Franklin D. Roosevelt Library, Hyde Park, New York.

Jones, Jesse H. Papers, Library of Congress, Washington, D.C.

Lubin, Isador. Papers, Franklin D. Roosevelt Library, Hyde Park, New York.

McNary, Charles L. Papers, Library of Congress, Washington, D.C.

Morgenthau, Henry, Jr. Diary, Franklin D. Roosevelt Library, Hyde Park, New York.

Norris, George. Papers, Library of Congress, Washington, D.C.

Roosevelt, Franklin D. Papers, Franklin D. Roosevelt Library, Hyde Park, New York.

Rosenman, Samuel I. Papers, Franklin D. Roosevelt Library, Hyde Park, New York.

Smith, Harold D. Papers, Franklin D. Roosevelt Library, Hyde Park, New York.

Taber, John. Papers, Cornell University Library, Ithaca, New York.

Taft, Robert A. Papers, Library of Congress, Washington, D.C.

United States Bureau of the Budget. Records, Record Group 51, National Archives Building, Washington, D.C.

United States Civilian Conservation Corps. Records, Record Group 35, National Archives Building, Washington, D.C.

United States Department of the Treasury. Records, Record Group 56, National Archives Building, Washington, D.C.

United States Farm Security Administration. Records, Record Group 96, National Archives Building, Washington, D.C.

United States Federal Works Agency. Records, Record Group 162, National Archives Building, Washington, D.C.

United States National Resources Planning Board. Records, Record Group 187, National Archives Building, Washington, D.C.

United States National Youth Administration. Records, Record Group 119, National Archives Building, Washington, D.C.

United States Office of Government Reports. Records, Record Group 44, Federal Records Center, Suitland, Maryland.

United States Reconstruction Finance Corporation and Federal Loan Agency. Records, Record Group 234, National Archives Building, Washington, D.C.

United States Work Projects Administration. Records, Record Group 69, National Archives Building, Washington, D.C.

Wagner, Robert F. Papers, Georgetown University Library, Washington, D.C.

Williams, Aubrey. Papers, Franklin D. Roosevelt Library, Hyde Park, New York.

Public Documents

U.S. Congress. Congressional Directory. 76th Congress, 1st Session-79th Congress, 1st Session, Washington, D.C., 1939-1945.

U.S. Congress. Congressional Record. 76th Congress, 1st Session-79th Congress, 2nd Session.

U.S. Congress. House. Committee on Appropriations. Hearings Before a Subcommittee of the House Committee on Appropriations on the Independent Offices Appropriations Bill. 77th Congress, 1st Session, 1941.

U.S. Congress. House. Committee on Ways and Means. Hearings Before the Committee on Ways and Means on Revenue Revision of 1941. 77th Congress, 1st Session, 1941.

U.S. Congress. House. Committee on Ways and Means. The Revenue Bill of 1941. H. Rept. 1040 to accompany H.R. 5417. 77th Congress, 1st Session, 1941.

U.S. Congress. House. Select Committee to Investigate Acts of Executive Agencies Beyond the Scope of Their Authority. Report. H. Rept. 862, 78th Congress, 1st Session, 1943.

U.S. Congress. House. Special Committee to Investigate the National Labor Relations Board. Intermediate Report. H. Rept. 1902, 76th Congress, 3rd Session, 1940.

U.S. Congress. House. Special Committee to Investigate the National Labor Relations Board. Report. H. Rept. 3109, 76th Congress, 3rd Session, 1940.

U.S. Congress. Joint Committee on Reduction of Nonessential Federal Expenditures. Additional Report. S. Doc. 54, 78th Congress, 1st Session, 1943.

U.S. Congress. Joint Committee on Reduction of Nonessential Federal Expenditures. Additional Report. S. Doc. 140, 78th Congress, 1st Session, 1943.

U.S. Congress. Joint Committee on Reduction of Nonessential Federal Expenditures. Hearings. 77th Congress, 1st Session, 1941.

U.S. Congress. Joint Committee on Reduction of Nonessential Federal Expenditures. Hearings. 77th Congress, 2nd Session, 1942.

U.S. Congress. Joint Committee on Reduction of Nonessential Federal Expenditures. Preliminary Report. S. Doc. 152, 77th Congress, 1st Session, 1941.

U.S. Congress. Joint Committee on Reduction of Nonessential Federal Expenditures. Supplemental Report. S. Doc. 152, 77th Congress, 2nd Session, 1942.

U.S. Congress. National Resources Planning Board. National Resources Development, Report for 1942. H. Doc. 560, 77th Congress, 2nd Session, 1942.

U.S. Congress. National Resources Planning Board. National Resources Development, Report for 1943, Part I: Post War Plan and Program. H. Doc. 128, part 1, 78th Congress, 1st Session, 1943.

U.S. Congress. National Resources Planning Board. Security, Work, and Relief Policies. H. Doc. 128, part 2, 78th Congress, 1st Session, 1943.

U.S. Congress. Senate. Committee on Appropriations. Hearings Before a Subcommittee on Appropriations on H.R. 7181. 77th Congress, 2nd Session, 1942.

U.S. Congress. Senate. Committee on Appropriations. Hearings Before the Subcommittee of the Committee on Appropriations on Department of Labor-Federal Security Agency Appropriation Act of 1944. 78th Congress, 1st Session, 1943.

U.S. Congress. Senate. Committee on Appropriations. Transfer of Employees Conserving Office Space, Relief in Housing Conditions and Promotion of Economy and Efficiency. S. Rept. 1554, 77th Congress, 2nd Session, 1942.

U.S. Congress. Senate. Committee on Banking and Currency. Works Financing Act of 1939, Hearings Before the Committee on Banking and Currency. 76th Congress, 1st Session, 1939.

U.S. Congress. Senate. Committee on Education and Labor. Hearings Before a Subcommittee of the Committee on Education and Labor on Post-Defense Planning. 77th Congress, 1st Session, 1941.

U.S. Congress. Senate. Committee on Education and Labor. Hearings on S. 2295. 77th Congress, 2nd Session, 1942.

U.S. Congress. Senate. Committee on Finance. Hearings Before the Committee on Finance on H.R. 5417. 77th Congress, 1st Session, 1941.

U.S. Congress. Senate. Committee on Naval Affairs. Hearings Before the Committee on Naval Affairs on H.R. 9822. 76th Congress, 3rd Session, 1940.

U.S. Congress. Senate. Special Committee on Investigation of the Munitions Industry. Preliminary Report on Wartime Taxation and Price Control. S. Rept. 944, part 2, 74th Congress, 1st Session, 1935.

U.S. Congress. Senate. Special Committee on Investigation of the Munitions Industry. Report on War Department Bills S. 1716-S. 1722 Relating to Industrial Mobilization in Wartime. S. Rept. 944, part 4, 74th Congress, 2nd Session, 1936.

U.S. Congress. Senate. Special Committee on Post-War Economic Policy and Planning. Changes in Unemployment Compensation System. S. Rept. 539, part 5, 78th Congress, 2nd Session, 1944.

U.S. Congress. Senate. Special Committee on Post-War Economic Policy and Planning. Preliminary Report. S. Rept. 539, part 1, 78th Congress, 1st Session, 1943.

U.S. Congress. Senate. Special Committee on Post-War Economic Policy and Planning. Problem of Post-War Employment and Role of Congress in Solving It. S. Rept. 539, part 4, 78th Congress, 2nd Session, 1944.

U.S. Congress. Senate. Special Committee on Post-War Economic Policy and Planning. Report. S. Rept. 539, part 2, 78th Congress, 2nd Session, 1944.

U.S. Congress. Temporary National Economic Committee. Final Report and Recommendations. 77th Congress, 1st Session, 1941.

U.S. Congress. Temporary National Economic Committee. Investigation of Concentration of Economic Power, Hearings Before the Temporary National Economic Committee, part 9, Savings and Investment. 76th Congress, 1st Session, 1939.

U.S. National Resources Planning Board. After Defense--What? Washington, 1941.

U.S. National Resources Planning Board. After the War--Full Employment. Washington, 1942.

Newspapers and Magazines Cited

Congressional Digest

Nation

New Republic

Newsweek

New York Times

Time

Washington Post

Unpublished Studies and Histories

Bourneuf, Jesse C. "The Office of Civilian Defense." Manuscript prepared under the auspices of the Bureau of the Budget. Series 41.3, no. 227, Records of the Bureau of the Budget, Record Group 51, National Archives Building, Washington, D.C.

Curry, Lawrence H., Jr. "Southern Senators and Their Roll-Call Votes in Congress, 1941-1944." Ph.D. dissertation, Duke University, 1971.

Edwards, Rhoda D.   "The Seventy-Eighth Congress on the Home Front: Domestic Economic Legislation, 1943-1944." Ph.D. dissertation, Rutgers University, 1967.

Hinchey, Mary H.   "The Frustration of the New Deal Revival, 1944-1946." Ph.D. dissertation, University of Missouri, 1965.

Manley, John F.   "The Conservative Coalition in Congress." Manuscript furnished author by John F. Manley.

Margolis, Joel.   "The Conservative Coalition in the United States Senate, 1933-1968." Paper prepared for delivery at the 1972 annual meeting of the American Political Science Association, Washington, D.C., September 5-9, 1972. Copy of manuscript in author's possession.

Riker, William H.   "The CIO in Politics, 1936-1946." Ph.D. dissertation, Harvard University, 1948.

Tilman, Lee R.   "The American Business Community and the Death of the New Deal." Ph.D. dissertation, University of Arizona, 1966.

Warken, Philip W.   "A History of the National Resources Planning Board, 1933-1943." Ph.D. dissertation, Ohio State University, 1969.

Books

Allen, George E.   Presidents Who Have Known Me. New York, 1960.

Allswang, John M.   The New Deal and American Politics. New York, 1978.

Altmeyer, Arthur J.   The Formative Years of Social Security. Madison, Wis., 1966.

Anderson, Lee F., Meredith W. Watts, Jr., and Allen R. Wilcox. Legislative Roll-Call Analysis. Evanston, Ill., 1966.

Appleby, Paul H.   Big Democracy. New York, 1945.

Arnold, Thurman.   Fair Fights and Foul. New York, 1965.

Ashurst, Henry F.   A Many Colored Toga: The Diary of Henry Fountain Ashurst. Tucson, Ariz., 1962.

Baldwin, Sidney.   Poverty and Politics: The Rise and Decline of the Farm Security Administration. Chapel Hill, N.C., 1968.

288

Bargeron, Carlisle. *Confusion on the Potomac*. New York, 1941.

Barkley, Alben. *That Reminds Me*. Garden City, N.Y., 1954.

Barnes, Joseph. *Willkie*. New York, 1952.

Baruch, Bernard M. *The Public Years*. New York, 1960.

Berle, Beatrice B. and Travis B. Jacobs. *Navigating the Rapids*. New York, 1973.

Binkley, Wilfred E. *President and Congress*. New York, 1947.

Blachly, Frederick F. and Miriam E. Oatman. *Federal Regulatory Action and Control*. Washington, 1940.

Bloom, Sol. *The Autobiography of Sol Bloom*. New York, 1948.

Blough, Roy. *The Federal Taxing Process*. New York, 1952.

Blum, John M. *From the Morgenthau Diaries*, vol. I: *Years of Crisis, 1928-1938*. Boston, 1959.

_____. *From the Morgenthau Diaries*, vol. II: *Years of Urgency, 1938-1941*. Boston, 1965.

_____. *From the Morgenthau Diaries*, vol. III: *Years of War, 1941-1945*. Boston, 1967.

_____., ed. *The Price of Vision: The Diary of Henry A. Wallace, 1942-1946*. Boston, 1973.

Boskin, Joseph, ed. *Opposition Politics: The Anti-New Deal Tradition*. Beverly Hills, Calif., 1968.

Bowles, Chester. *Promises to Keep: My Years in Public Life*. New York, 1971.

Bruner, Jerome S. *Mandate from the People*. New York, 1944.

Burns, James M. *The Legislative Process and the Administrative State*. New York, 1949.

_____. *The Lion and the Fox*. New York, 1956.

_____. *Roosevelt: The Soldier of Freedom*. New York, 1970.

Byrnes, James F. *All In One Lifetime*. New York, 1958.

Calder, Angus. *The People's War: Britain, 1939-1945*. New York, 1972.

Campbell, Christiana McF. *The Farm Bureau and the New Deal*. Urbana, Ill., 1962.

Cantril, Hadley, ed. Public Opinion, 1935-1946. Princeton, 1951.

Catton, Bruce. The War Lords of Washington. New York, 1948.

Chamberlain, Lawrence H. The President, Congress, and Legislation. New York, 1946.

Chase, Stuart. Idle Money, Idle Men. New York, 1940.

Childs, Marquis. I Write from Washington. New York, 1942.

Clark, Wesley C. Economic Aspects of a President's Popularity. Philadelphia, 1943.

Cole, Taylor and John H. Hallowell, eds. The Southern Political Scene, 1938-1948. Gainesville, Fla., 1948.

Conkin, Paul K. The New Deal. New York, 1967.

Connally, Tom. My Name Is Tom Connally. New York, 1954.

Corey, Lewis. The Unfinished Task: Economic Reconstruction for Democracy. New York, 1942.

Coyle, David Cushman. Roads to a New America. Boston, 1938.

Crider, John H. The Bureaucrat. Philadelphia, 1944.

Daniels, Jonathan. Frontier on the Potomac. New York, 1946.

_____. White House Witness, 1942-1945. Garden City, N.Y. 1975.

Dewey, Thomas E. The Case Against the New Deal. New York, 1940.

Divine, Robert A. The Illusion of Neutrality. Chicago, 1962.

Donahoe, Bernard F. Private Plans and Public Dangers: The Story of FDR's Third Nomination. Notre Dame, Ind., 1965.

Drury, Allen. A Senate Journal, 1943-1945. New York, 1963.

Eccles, Marriner S. Beckoning Frontiers: Public and Personal Recollections. New York, 1951.

Farley, James A. Jim Farley's Story. New York, 1948.

Finney, Burnham. Arsenal of Democracy: How Industry Builds Our Defense. New York, 1941.

Flynn, Edward J. You're The Boss. New York, 1947.

Fungiello, Philip J. _Toward A National Power Policy_. Pittsburgh, 1973.

Gaer, Joseph. _The First Round: The Story of the CIO Political
Action Committee_. New York, 1944.

Galloway, George B. _Congress at the Crossroads_. New York, 1946.

Garson, Robert A. _The Democratic Party and the Politics of Sectionalism, 1941-1948_. Baton Rouge, La., 1974.

Gilbert, Richard V. and others. _An Economic Program for American Democracy_. New York, 1938.

Goldman, Eric F. _Rendezvous with Destiny_. New York, 1952.

Goodman, Jack, ed. _While You Were Gone: A Report on Wartime
Life in the United States_. New York, 1946.

Gordon, Robert A. _Economic Instability and Growth: The American Record_. New York, 1974.

Grafton, Samuel. _An American Diary_. Garden City, N.Y., 1943.

Graham, Otis L., Jr. _Toward A Planned Society: From Roosevelt
to Nixon_. New York, 1976.

Griffith, Ernest S. _Congress: Its Contemporary Role_. New York, 195

Halasz, Nicholas. _Roosevelt Through Foreign Eyes_. Princeton,
1961.

Hamby, Alonzo L. _Beyond the New Deal: Harry S. Truman and
American Liberalism_. New York, 1973.

Hansen, Alvin H. _Full Recovery or Stagnation?_ New York, 1938.

Harris, Herbert. _American Labor_. New Haven, 1939.

Harris, Joseph P. _The Advise and Consent of the Senate_. Berkeley, Calif., 1953.

Harris, Seymour E. _The Economics of American Defense_. New York,
1941.

Harvey, Ray F. and others. _The Politics of This War_. New York,
1943.

Hassett, William D. _Off the Record with F.D.R., 1942-1945_.
New Brunswick, N.J., 1958.

Henderson, Richard B. _Maury Maverick: A Political Biography_.
Austin, Tex., 1970.

Huthmacher, J. Joseph. Senator Robert F. Wagner and the Rise of Urban Liberalism. New York, 1968.

Ickes, Harold. The Secret Diary of Harold Ickes, vol. II: The Inside Struggle, 1936-1939. New York, 1954.

_____. The Secret Diary of Harold Ickes, vol. III: The Lowering Clouds, 1939-1941. New York, 1954.

Jackson, Carlton. Presidential Vetoes, 1792-1945. Athens, Ga., 1967.

Jones, Charles O. The Minority Party in Congress. Boston, 1970.

Jones, Jesse H. Fifty Billion Dollars: My Thirteen Years with the RFC. New York, 1951.

Karl, Barry D. Charles E. Merriam and the Study of Politics. Chicago, 1974.

_____. Executive Reorganization and Reform in the New Deal. Cambridge, Mass., 1963.

Key, V. O., Jr. Southern Politics in State and Nation. New York, 1949.

Kilpatrick, Carroll, ed. Roosevelt and Daniels. Chapel Hill, N.C., 1952.

Kimmel, Louis H. Federal Budget and Fiscal Policy, 1798-1958. Washington, 1959.

Krock, Arthur. Memoirs: Sixty Years on the Firing Line. New York, 1968.

Lash, Joseph P. Eleanor and Franklin. New York, 1973.

LeKachman, Robert. The Age of Keynes. New York, 1966.

Leuchtenburg, William E. Franklin D. Roosevelt and the New Deal. New York, 1963.

Lilienthal, David E. The Journals of David E. Lilienthal, vol. I: The TVA Years, 1939-1945. New York, 1964.

Lipset, Seymour M. Political Man. Garden City, N.Y., 1960.

McCune, Wesley. The Farm Bloc. New York, 1943.

McGuire, O. R. Americans on Guard. Washington, 1942.

Markowitz, Norman D. The Rise and Fall of the People's Century: Henry A. Wallace and American Liberalism, 1941-1948. New York, 1973.

Martin, Joseph W., Jr. My First Fifty Years in Politics. New York, 1960.

Millis, Harry A. and Emily Clark Brown. From the Wagner Act to Taft-Hartley. Chicago, 1950.

Milton, George Fort. The Use of Presidential Power, 1789-1943. Boston, 1944.

Milward, Alan S. War, Economy and Society, 1939-1945. London, 1977.

Mooney, Booth. Roosevelt and Rayburn. Philadelphia, 1971.

Moore, John Robert. Senator Josiah William Bailey of North Carolina. Durham, N.C., 1968.

Morison, Elting E. Turmoil and Tradition: A Study of the Life and Times of Henry L. Stimson. Boston, 1960.

Patterson, James T. Congressional Conservatism and the New Deal. Lexington, Ky., 1967.

_____. Mr. Republican: A Biography of Robert A. Taft. Boston, 1972.

Paul, Randolph E. Taxation in the United States. Boston, 1954.

Perkins, Frances. The Roosevelt I Knew. New York, 1946.

Perrett, Geoffrey. Days of Sadness, Years of Triumph. New York, 1973.

Polenberg, Richard. Reorganizing Roosevelt's Government: The Controversy Over Executive Reorganization, 1936-1939. Cambridge, Mass., 1966.

_____. War and Society: The United States, 1941-1945. Philadelphia, 1972.

Robinson, James A. The House Rules Committee. Indianapolis, 1963.

Rosenman, Samuel I., ed. The Public Papers and Addresses of Franklin D. Roosevelt, vol. 7: 1938 The Continuing Struggle for Liberalism. New York, 1941.

_____. The Public Papers and Addresses of Franklin D. Roosevelt, vol. 8: 1939 War and Neutrality. New York, 1941.

_____. The Public Papers and Addresses of Franklin D. Roose-velt, vol. 9: 1940 War and Aid to Democracies. New York, 1941.

_____. The Public Papers and Addresses of Franklin D. Roose-velt, vol. 10: 1941 The Call to Battle Stations. New York, 1950.

_____. The Public Papers and Addresses of Franklin D. Roose-velt, vol. 11: 1942 Humanity on the Defensive. New York, 1950.

_____. The Public Papers and Addresses of Franklin D. Roose-velt, vol. 12: 1943 The Tide Turns. New York, 1950.

_____. The Public Papers and Addresses of Franklin D. Roose-velt, vol. 13: 1944-45 Victory and the Threshold of Peace. New York, 1950.

_____. Working with Roosevelt. New York, 1952.

Roosevelt, Eleanor. This I Remember. New York, 1949.

Roosevelt, Elliott, ed. F.D.R.--His Personal Letters, 1928-1945. New York, 1950.

Roosevelt, Franklin D. Complete Presidential Press Conferences of Franklin D. Roosevelt, vols. 11-22. New York, 1972.

Salmond, John A. The Civilian Conservation Corps, 1933-1942: A New Deal Case Study. Durham, N.C., 1967.

Schapsmeier, Edward L. and Frederick H. Prophet in Politics: Henry A. Wallace and the War Years, 1940-1965. Ames, Ia., 1970.

Schlesinger, Arthur M., Jr. The Coming of the New Deal. Cam-bridge, Mass., 1965.

Schuyler, William M., ed. The American Year Book, 1939. New York, 1940.

_____. The American Year Book, 1940. New York, 1941.

_____. The American Year Book, 1941. New York, 1942.

_____. The American Year Book, 1942. New York, 1943.

_____. The American Year Book, 1943. New York, 1944.

_____. The American Year Book, 1944. New York, 1945.

_____. The American Year Book, 1945. New York, 1946.

Seidman, Joel. American Labor from Defense to Reconversion. Chicago, 1953.

Sherwood, Robert E. Roosevelt and Hopkins: An Intimate History. New York, 1948.

Stein, Herbert. The Fiscal Revolution in America. Chicago, 1969.

Stimson, Henry L. and McGeorge Bundy. On Active Service in Peace and War. New York, 1947.

Stone, I. F. Business As Usual: The First Year of Defense. New York, 1941.

Sullivan, Lawrence. Bureaucracy Runs Amuck. Indianapolis, 1944.

Summers, Harrison Boyd and Robert E. Summers, eds. Planned Economy. New York, 1940.

Terkel, Studs. Hard Times: An Oral History of the Great Depression. New York, 1971.

Timmons, Bascom N. Garner of Texas. New York, 1948.

_____. Jesse H. Jones: The Man and the Statesman. New York, 1956.

Tolley, Howard R. The Farmer Citizen At War. New York, 1943.

Tugwell, Rexford G. The Enlargement of the Presidency. Garden City, N.Y., 1960.

United States Bureau of the Budget, War Records Section. The United States at War: Development and Administration of the War Program by the Federal Government. Washington, 1946.

White, Walter. A Man Called White: The Autobiography of Walter White. New York, 1948.

Wright, Gordon. The Ordeal of Total War, 1939-1945. New York, 1968.

Young, Roland A. The American Congress. New York, 1958.

_____. Congressional Politics in the Second World War. New York, 1956.

Articles

Benjamin, Robert M. "A Lawyer's View of Administrative Proce-
    dure." Law and Contemporary Problems XXVI (1961), pp.
    203-237.

Berdahl, Clarence A. "Political Parties and Elections." Ameri-
    can Political Science Review XXXVII (1943), pp. 63-80.

Bernstein, Barton J. "The New Deal: The Conservative Achieve-
    ments of Liberal Reform." In Towards A New Past, edited by
    Barton J. Bernstein. New York, 1969.

Bissell, Richard M. "The Anatomy of Public Spending." Fortune
    XXV (May 1942), pp. 94-95, 111-112, 114, 116 (June 1942),
    pp. 105, 128, 130, 132, 134, 136, 138, 141-142, 144.

Blakey, Roy G. and Gladys C. "Federal Revenue Legislation,
    1943-1944." American Political Science Review XXXVIII
    (1944), pp. 325-330.

_____. "The Revenue Act of 1941." American Economic Re-
    view XXXI (1941), pp. 809-822.

_____. "The Two Federal Revenue Acts of 1940." American
    Economic Review XXX (1940), pp. 724-735.

Blum, John M. "'That Kind Of A Liberal': Franklin D. Roosevelt
    After Twenty-Five Years." Yale Review LX (Autumn 1970),
    pp. 14-23.

Cantril, Hadley and John Harding. "The 1942 Elections: A Case
    Study in Political Psychology." Public Opinion Quarterly
    VII (Summer 1943), pp. 221-241.

Cohen, Jerome B. "The Forgotten T.N.E.C." Current History I
    (September 1941), pp. 45-50.

Cowley, Malcolm. "The End of the New Deal." New Republic 108
    (May 31, 1943), pp. 729-732.

Crawford, Kenneth G. "Assault on the NLRB." Nation 149 (De-
    cember 30, 1939), pp. 726-727.

_____. "War and the Election." Nation 150 (February 10,
    1940), pp. 162-164.

Crumbaker, Calvin. "Note on Concentration of Economic Power."
    Journal of Political Economy L (1942), pp. 934-944.

Eakins, David W. "Business Planners and America's Postwar Ex-
    pansion." In Corporations and the Cold War, edited by
    David Horowitz. New York, 1970.

Fenno, Richard F. "President-Cabinet Relations: A Pattern and a Case Study." American Political Science Review LII (1958), pp. 388-405.

Finer, Herman. "Critics of 'Bureaucracy'." Political Science Quarterly LX (1945), pp. 100-112.

Fink, Gary M. and James W. Hilty. "Prologue: The Senate Voting Record of Harry S. Truman." Journal of Interdisciplinary History IV (Autumn 1973), pp. 207-235.

Fuller, Walter D. "The Spirit of '42." Vital Speeches 8 (July 1, 1942), pp. 551-554.

Gilbert, Donald W. "Taxation and Economic Stability." Quarterly Journal of Economics LVI (May 1942), pp. 406-429.

Griffith, Ernest S. "The Changing Pattern of Public Policy Formation." American Political Science Review XXXVIII (1944), pp. 455-459.

Hamby, Alonzo L. "Sixty Million Jobs and the People's Revolution: The Liberals, the New Deal, and World War II." Historian XXX (August 1968), pp. 578-598.

Harding, John. "The 1942 Congressional Elections." American Political Science Review XXXVIII (1944), pp. 41-58.

Heady, Ferrel and Eleanor Tabor Linenthal. "Congress and Administrative Regulation." Law and Contemporary Problems XXVI (1961), pp. 238-260.

Janeway, Eliot. "Trials and Errors." Fortune XXVI (December 1942), pp. 26, 30, 32.

Jones, Byrd L. "The Role of Keynesians in Wartime Policy and Postwar Planning." American Economic Review LXII (May 1972), pp. 125-133.

Kemper, James S. "On the Home Front." Vital Speeches 8 (December 15, 1941), pp. 143-146.

Key, V. O., Jr. "The Reconversion Phase of Demobilization." American Political Science Review XXXVIII (1944), pp. 1137-1153.

Kingsley, J. Donald. "Congress and the New Deal." Current History IV (March 1943), pp. 25-31.

Lindley, Ernest K. "How the Postwar Reports Came to Be." Newsweek, March 22, 1943, p. 27.

McCoy, Donald R. "Republican Opposition During Wartime, 1941-1945." Mid-America 49 (July 1967), pp. 174-189.

Macmahon, Arthur W. "Congressional Oversight of Administration: The Power of the Purse--I." Political Science Quarterly LVIII (1943), pp. 161-190.

_____. "Congressional Oversight of Administration: The Power of the Purse--II." Political Science Quarterly LVIII (1943), pp. 380-414.

Merriam, Charles E. "The National Resources Planning Board: A Chapter in American Planning Experience." American Political Science Review XXXVIII (1944), pp. 1075-1088.

Moley, Raymond, Rexford G. Tugwell, and Ernest K. Lindley. "Symposium: Early Days of the New Deal." In The Thirties: A Reconsideration in the Light of the American Political Tradition, edited by Morton J. Frisch and Martin Diamond. De Kalb, Ill., 1968.

Moore, John Robert. "The Conservative Coalition in the United States Senate, 1942-1945." Journal of Southern History XXXIII (1967), pp. 368-376.

Overacker, Louise. "Should The New Deal Be Dropped?" Current History VI (February 1944), pp. 110-115.

Patterson, James T. "Eating Humble Pie: A Note on Roosevelt, Congress, and Neutrality Revision in 1939." Historian 31 (May 1969), pp. 407-414.

Patton, James G. "The Federal Government's Role in the Postwar Economy." American Political Science Review XXXVIII (1944), pp. 1124-1136.

Price, Charles M. and Joseph Boskin. "The Roosevelt 'Purge': A Reappraisal." Journal of Politics 28 (1966), pp. 660-670.

Richter, Irving. "Four Years of the Fair Labor Standards Act of 1938." Journal of Political Economy LI (1943), pp. 95-111.

Riddick, Floyd M. "Congress Versus the President in 1944." South Atlantic Quarterly XLIV (July 1945), pp. 308-315.

_____. "The First Session of the Seventy-Eighth Congress." American Political Science Review XXXVIII (1944), pp. 301-317.

_____. "The First Session of the Seventy-seventh Congress." American Political Science Review XXXVI (1942), pp. 290-301.

_____. "The Second Session of the Seventy-Eighth Congress." American Political Science Review XXXIX (1945), pp. 317-326.

_____. "The Second Session of the Seventy-seventh Congress."
American Political Science Review XXXVII (1943), pp. 290-
305.

_____. "The Third Session of the Seventy-sixth Congress."
American Political Science Review XXXV (1941), pp. 284-
303.

Robey, Ralph. "The Defense Program and Business." Newsweek,
May 27, 1940, p. 62.

Roose, Kenneth D. "The Recession of 1937-38." Journal of
Political Economy LVI (1948), pp. 239-248.

Salmond, John A. "Postscript to the New Deal: The Defeat of
the Nomination of Aubrey W. Williams as Rural Electrification Administrator in 1945." Journal of American History
LXI (September 1974), pp. 417-436.

Schuman, Frederick L. "Bill of Attainder in the 78th Congress."
American Political Science Review XXXVII (1943), pp. 819-
829.

Sloan, Alfred P., Jr. "Industry's Post-War Responsibilities."
Vital Speeches 8 (January 1, 1942), pp. 174-176.

Sweezy, Alan. "The Keynesians and Government Policy, 1933-
1939." American Economic Review LXII (May 1972), pp. 116-
124.

Villard, Oswald G. "The Collapse of the War Liberals." Christian Century LXI (October 25, 1944), pp. 1227-1228.

Wallace, Henry A. "Foundations of the Peace." Atlantic Monthly
169 (January 1942), pp. 34-41.

Watkins, Myron W. "Post-War Plan and Program." Journal of
Political Economy LI (1943), pp. 397-414.

Wilcox, Francis O. "The Neutrality Fight in Congress." American
Political Science Review XXXIII (1939), pp. 811-825.

Index